FORFÁS

PERSPECTIVES ON IRISH PRODUCTIVITY

FORFÁS

PERSPECTIVES ON IRISH PRODUCTIVITY

EDITED BY

CIARÁN AYLWARD

AND

RONNIE O'TOOLE

First published in 2007 by
Forfás
Wilton Park House
Wilton Place
Dublin 2

ISBN: 978-0-9530379-1-9

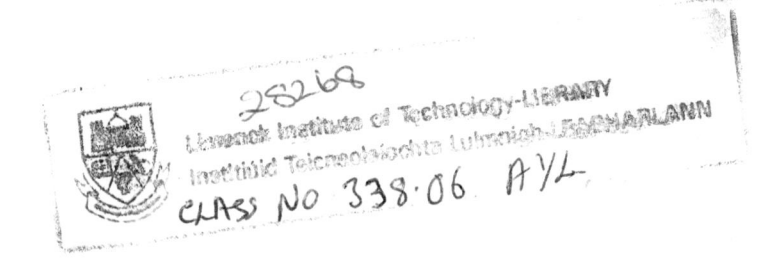

FOREWORD

Over the last decade Ireland has addressed the generational challenge of ensuring that there is enough paid employment for all those who want it, thereby ending the unemployment and emigration crises of the 1980s. Indeed, it has mostly been our employment performance - the greatly increased proportion of our population at work - that lies behind the improvement in Ireland's living standards in recent years relative to other countries.

With employment rates in Ireland now above the EU average, due to demographic change and the limits to migration, Ireland's ability to sustain our competitiveness will depend less on increasing employment, and more on increasing the productivity of those already at work. Accelerating Ireland's productivity growth will be the most important long term driver of Ireland's competitiveness and improvements in national living standards.

Yet despite the importance of productivity in raising living standards in Ireland, there has been only a limited amount of research on Ireland's productivity performance, and many questions remain unanswered. Why is it that productivity growth was so strong in the 1990s, but has slowed in more recent years? How is it that output per employee in Ireland, relative to other countries, appears so high in many manufacturing industries, and yet so low in some of our services sectors? Can the productivity performance of our large urban centres be replicated in the regions? How can we develop accurate and meaningful measures of productivity in those industries that are largely locally traded? How can we improve productivity in the delivery of public services, such as education and health?

The purpose of this publication is to examine whether existing productivity research has answered some of the questions and what questions remain to be answered. The volume also provides some new and interesting insights on the direction that future policy might take to promote future productivity growth.

I would like, on my behalf and on behalf of my colleagues in Government, to thank the contributors for their papers and Forfás for compiling and editing the publication and I am pleased to introduce the 'Perspectives on Irish Productivity'.

Micheál Martin T.D.
Minister for Enterprise, Trade and Employment

PREFACE

In 2005, the Minister for Enterprise, Trade and Employment, Micheál Martin T.D., asked Forfás to prioritise research into productivity growth. As an initial response to this request, we set out to compile a volume that can inform the debate in Ireland on how we can optimise our future productivity growth. To this end, we asked some of the leading economic and management thinkers in Ireland and overseas to prepare short, accessible papers on various aspects of Ireland's productivity challenge.

The result is 'Perspectives on Irish Productivity'. This publication contains 25 contributions, each focusing on a specific aspect of productivity. Each individual paper is categorised into one of six themed sections, with an introduction to each of these sections providing a brief summary of the major lessons of the papers.

Part I gives an overview of Ireland's productivity performance in recent years, both at a national and regional level, and asks where Ireland's future productivity challenge lies. Part II reviews the state of our knowledge of productivity performance at the sectoral level, while Part III reviews the role that competition policy and the more general institutional and regulatory setting have on Irish productivity. Part IV discusses the economic evidence regarding the role that agglomeration effects have played in developing particular regions and sectors in the economy. Part V discusses various aspects of the 'Knowledge Economy', in particular human capital, R&D and ICT, and discusses some evidence of the importance of each of these. Finally, Part VI examines firm level evidence regarding various aspects of firm performance.

While the individual contributions represent the views of the authors themselves, the volume also contains an introductory essay that reflects on some of the recurring themes and apparent contradictions in the papers, and provides some new policy insights that Forfás considers that policymakers should be aware of when formulating future policy.

On behalf of Forfás, I would like to thank each of the authors for their contributions. I hope the messages in these papers will inform the debate and discussion in this important area.

Martin Cronin
Forfás Chief Executive

ACKNOWLEDGEMENTS

The editors would like to thank a number of people. First and foremost, we would like to thank each of the contributors, without whose help this publication would not have been possible. We would also like to thank Andrew McDowell who is to be credited with the original idea for this volume, and to Declan Hughes and Eoin Gahan for helping guide the publication through its final stages.

Mairin Delaney and Nicola Faulkner in the Communications Department in Forfás played a critical role in seeing the initial rough concept for this book through to ultimate publication, and at all stages were very pro-active in developing ideas for the form and look of the book. During the final phases of preparing the manuscript for publication a number of Forfás employees, in particular Enda Carolan, provided invaluable assistance in editing, proof reading and preparing chapters. Finally, we would like to thank the staff at the printing company Power Design, who were professional and patient partners at all times.

Ciarán Aylward and Ronnie O'Toole
Editors

CONTENTS

List of Figures *12*

List of Tables *14*

List of Contributors *16*

Introduction and Overview 18

PART I: Assessing Ireland's Productivity Performance

Introduction 26

1. Trends in Output, Employment and Productivity in Ireland, 1995-2005
J.J Sexton, Economic Consultant 27

2. Service Sector Productivity: The Tigers Next Challenge?
Diana Farrell, Janna Remes and Conor Kehoe, McKinsey 52

3. Trends in the Regional Economic Activity of Ireland: The Role of Productivity
Edgar Morgenroth, ESRI 66

4. Perspectives on Northern Ireland's Productivity Performance
José Luis Iparraguirre D'Elia, Economic Research Institute of Northern Ireland 84

PART II: Sectoral Productivity Performance

Introduction 99

5. Public Sector Productivity Measurement: An Impossible Task?
Richard Boyle, IPA 100

6. Productivity in Irish Agriculture
Alan Matthews, Carol Newman and Fiona Thorne, TCD and Teagasc 116

7. Productivity in the Irish Residential Construction Industry
Ciarán Aylward and Ronnie O'Toole, Forfás 130

8. Productivity in the Irish Road Freight Industry
Ciarán Aylward and Ronnie O'Toole, Forfás 144

PART III: Institutions and Regulation

Introduction . . . 160

9. The Influence of Institutions
Rory O'Donnell and Noel Cahill, NESC . . . 161

10. Competition and Productivity
David Boyle and John Evans, Competition Authority . . . 179

11. Privatisation and Productivity Performance in Ireland
Donal Palcic and Eoin Reeves, University of Limerick . . . 193

12. Privatisation and Productivity: Lessons from the UK
David Parker, Cranfield University . . . 209

13. The Impact of Regulations in Ireland
Robert Watt and Derek Scully, INDECON . . . 223

PART IV: Agglomeration Economies

Introduction . . . 239

14. Productivity Spillovers from Multinational Companies
Holger Görg, University of Nottingham . . . 240

15. Regional Policy and Agglomeration Economies in Ireland
Eoin O'Leary, UCC . . . 253

16. The Role for Clusters in Irish Economic Development Policy
Eleanor Doyle and Connell Fanning, UCC . . . 267

17. Aggregate Productivity Effects of Road Investment: A Reassessment for Western Europe
Andreas Kopp, OECD . . . 282

PART V: Productivity and the Knowledge Economy

Introduction 296

18. Human Capital and Productivity in the Irish Context
Catherine Kavanagh and Eleanor Doyle, UCC 297

19. The Impact of R&D on Productivity
Dirk Czarnitzki and Niall O'Byrnes, KU Leuven 315

20. Public Investment in R&D in Ireland
Maurice Dagg, Forfás 330

21. ICT and Competitiveness: What Prospects for the Lisbon Strategy?
Susanne Mundschenk, Eurointelligence.com 342

22. Information Technology Performance and Process: Four Case Studies
Daniel Maddox, Waterford Institute of Technology and Gerry Boyle, NUI Maynooth . . 350

PART VI: Productivity and Firm Behaviour

Introduction 365

23. Exports and Productivity
Richard Kneller, University of Nottingham 366

24. Outward Direct Investment and Productivity
Ronnie O'Toole, Forfás 385

25. The Distribution of Productivity in Irish Manufacturing, 1995-2003
Stefanie Haller, ESRI 402

LIST OF FIGURES

LIST OF TABLES

LIST OF CONTRIBUTORS

Ciarán Aylward, Economist, Competitiveness Division, Forfás, Ireland

David Boyle, Case Officer, The Competition Authority, Ireland

Gerry Boyle, Professor, Department of Economics, NUI Maynooth, Ireland

Richard Boyle, Ph.D., Senior Research Officer, Institute of Public Administration, Ireland

Noel Cahill, Economist, National Economic Social Council, Ireland

Dirk Czarnitzki, Associate Professor, Department for Managerial Economics, Strategy and Innovation, and Steunpunt O&O Statistieken, KU Leuven, Belgium and ZEW Mannheim, Germany

Maurice Dagg, Policy Analyst, Science and Technology Division, Forfás, Ireland

José Luis Iparraguirre D'Elia, Senior Research Economist, Economic Research Institute of Northern Ireland, Northern Ireland

Eleanor Doyle, Ph.D., Department of Economics, University College Cork, Ireland

John Evans, Divisional Manager, The Competition Authority, Ireland

Connell Fanning, Professor, Department of Economics, University College Cork, Ireland

Diana Farrell, Director, McKinsey Global Institute, US

Holger Görg, Associate Professor, Leverhulme Centre for Research on Globalisation and Economic Policy, University of Nottingham, UK

Stefanie Haller, Ph.D., Macroeconomic & Resource Economics Department, The Economic and Social Research Institute, Ireland

Catherine Kavanagh, Ph.D., Department of Economics, University College Cork, Ireland

Conor Kehoe, Director, McKinsey & Co., UK

Richard Kneller, Ph.D., Leverhulme Centre for Research on Globalisation and Economic Policy, University of Nottingham, UK.

Andreas Kopp, Ph.D., Chief Economist, OECD/ECMT Transport Research Centre, France

Daniel Maddox, Waterford Institute of Technology, Ireland

Alan Matthews, Professor, Department of Economics, Trinity College Dublin, Ireland

Edgar Morgenroth, Ph.D., Senior Research Officer, The Economic and Social Research Institute, Ireland.

Susanne Mundschenk, Director, Eurointelligence.com.

Carol Newman, Ph.D., Department of Economics, Trinity College Dublin, Ireland

Niall O'Byrnes, Researcher, Department for Managerial Economics, Strategy and Innovation, KU Leuven, Belgium

Rory O'Donnell, Professor, Director, National Economic and Social Council, Ireland

Eoin O'Leary, Ph.D., Department of Economics, University College Cork, Ireland

Ronnie O'Toole, Ph.D., Senior Economist, Forfás, Ireland

Donal Palcic, Department of Economics, University of Limerick, Ireland

David Parker, Professor, School of Management, Cranfield University, UK

Jaana Remes, Ph.D., Senior Research Fellow, McKinsey Global Institute, US

Eoin Reeves, Ph.D., Department of Economics, University of Limerick, Ireland

Derek Scully, Economist, Indecon International Economic Consultants, Ireland

J.J. Sexton, Professor, Economic Consultant, Ireland

Fiona Thorne, Ph.D., Research Officer, Teagasc Rural Economy Research Centre, Ireland

Robert Watt, Economist, Indecon International Economic Consultants, Ireland

Introduction and Overview

1 Introduction

Ireland's recent economic growth has been characterised by increases in numbers employed and by growth in productivity. As the potential for employment growth wanes due to demographic change and the limits to migration, productivity growth will be the most important long term driver of Ireland's improvements in national living standards. However the requirements for success in promoting productivity growth can vary across markets, and can be subject to rapid change. The ability to work flexibly, and to redesign and change institutions as required, will be critical in driving Irish productivity growth in the future. In Chapter 1 of this volume, Sexton provides a comprehensive overview of Ireland's productivity performance since 1995, while in Chapter 4 Iparraguirre D'Elia reviews the productivity performance of Northern Ireland.

Ireland faces two productivity challenges going forward:

- How do we drive productivity growth in the non-exporting sectors of the economy? The measurement and promotion of productivity growth of these sectors has received relatively little attention, and will require a lot more policy action in the coming years.
- How do we maintain an attractive business environment for high-productivity exporting firms (both Irish owned and otherwise)? While the economic growth of the last two decades has been built on the success of the internationally traded sectors, continued productivity growth in these areas cannot be taken for granted. Increasingly, Ireland is facing significant competition in international markets, and Irish firms are competing on the basis of a higher cost environment.

This volume aims to provide insights that can help policymakers frame solutions for both of these challenges. Section 2 below outlines how competition has helped energise the exporting sector, and asks whether competition can play the same role in the non-exporting sector. In Section 3, we argue that ICT usage can play a vital role in transforming productivity, though to benefit from ICT, organisations need to have the flexibility and management expertise to initiate complementary organisational change. In Section 4 we discuss how industry networks can assist in further developing productivity. In Section 5 we discuss the role that industrial policy must play in the coming years, while the problem of lack of data is discussed in Section 6.

2 Competition is Key

Ireland's economic development strategy over the last number of decades has been multifaceted, characterised by the attraction of green-field investment, the investment in physical and human capital, the adoption of a competitive taxation regime and the creation of an attractive business environment. While these policies will continue to be critical going forward, a dominant theme that emerges from a number of the contributions in this volume is the importance of competition in boosting future productivity.

Boyle and Evans (Chapter 10) show that the strong link between competition and productivity is driven by a number of distinct effects. First, competition stimulates innovation as firms invest in the development of new products or production methods. Second, competition encourages efficiency improvements. As firms face competition they must reduce costs in order to compete for customers. This is achieved by finding quicker or more efficient methods of production. Third, competition promotes diffusion of technology as firms seek to improve productivity by adopting processes or products that may have been developed by market leaders. This diffusion process is prominent in markets that are open to international competition.

The importance of competition also emerges from an examination of those companies that transferred from public to private ownership. The evidence from Ireland (Palcic and Reeves, Chapter 11) and the UK (Parker, Chapter 12) is that the key success of 'privatisation' was not, as the name suggests, changing the ultimate ownership of the companies involved, but rather making the markets in which they operated contestable. In fact, much of the productivity growth achieved by these privatised companies accrued in the years prior to when they were formally divested. This can be seen in the cases of Greencore, B&I and British Airways, amongst others.

It is clear from a number of studies reported in this volume that the industries that work in a highly competitive global environment are constantly evolving in an effort to drive up productivity in response to this competition. For example Kneller (Chapter 23) shows the importance of dynamic entry and exit to an industry's overall productivity performance. While much of the productivity gain in the manufacturing sector of the economy is the result of highly successful firms increasing their productivity (the *within* effect), a very significant amount is due to new firms entering markets and taking share from less efficient incumbents (*net entry*, or the so called 'creative destruction' effect). Both sources of productivity growth may be limited in those industries where supply is 'co-ordinated' rather than subject to competition, for example in healthcare provision.

Unfortunately, there are many areas of the economy where competition is noticeably weak or absent. They are often the sectors where no good measures of productivity currently exist, so it is not possible to definitively conclude the extent of the productivity challenges facing these sectors. The one 'protected' sector where there is no shortage of data and where it is possible to develop robust measures of productivity is agriculture, and the costs of distorted competition can be readily seen. Matthews, Newman and Thorne (Chapter 6) show that with a very high share of farm income coming in the form of direct payments, farmers attention has switched from identifying on-farm technical improvements as a source of increasing income - a reward for meeting consumer demands - to ways of maximising premium income. This has resulted in a decline in total factor productivity in cattle production since 1980. This, however, will need to change. Productivity will increasingly become a focus for Irish farmers as they learn to compete in a much lower price environment in the future, even if the dismantling of the CAP's protective regime is still likely to take some time.

In conclusion, policymakers should recognise the potential of unleashing competition (with appropriate regulation) to deliver benefits to consumers. As discussed by Farrell, Remes and Kehoe in Chapter 2, future productivity growth nationally will require a better performance by a select number of non-exporting industries. The industries in question are among the most important and largest employers in the economy, and include financial services, utilities, health, education and legal services. The key role for the government in these markets should be to protect the wider public interest by setting quality standards, and to act as a purchaser of services for those who could not otherwise afford them for themselves. This does not require the government to act also as employer or direct provider. Competition in these industries can act as a catalyst for the delivery of great cost efficiencies and the discovery of innovative solutions to consumer needs, and it can guard these sectors from the demands of vested interests.

3 ICT Boosts Productivity, but is not a Silver Bullet

ICT is generally accepted as being one of the drivers of productivity growth in modern economies. What emerges from the contributions in this publication is that ICT can have a very positive effect on productivity growth, and indeed was the catalyst for the surge in productivity growth in the US over the last decade. However, there is also evidence that Europe has not been as successful as the US in optimising its use of ICT, despite the fact that the quality of the technology available to both economies is identical (Mundschenk, Chapter 21).

What is clear from the contribution of Maddox and Boyle (Chapter 22) is that the introduction of ICT per se might not necessarily have a large impact on productivity. They investigated the levels of ICT investment undertaken, and the subsequent performance benefits in four different Irish organisations, two of which were manufacturing firms (a high tech multi-national and a traditional indigenous firm), one was a medium sized bank while the last was a municipal authority. The research finds that ICT investment affected the high-technology firm in a most significant and positive way. At the other end of the performance scale, the municipal authority failed to put structures in place that would allow for the optimal use of their ICT investment.

ICT can have a role to play in boosting productivity, but policies that aim to transpose such technologies into a static regulatory or management environment, are unlikely to succeed in increasing productivity. Any efforts to promote ICT by public policy must recognise the importance of a corresponding reorganisation of an industry or company to take advantage of this technology. Public sector organisations in particular will have to become more open to such reorganisation and re-training to reap the full benefits of ICT.

4 Developing Industry Networks

The underdevelopment of business networks in Ireland appears to be preventing a number of industries from reaping the full productivity benefit of new technologies. As reported in this volume, both the residential construction sector (Chapter 7) and the road freight sector (Chapter 8) have failed of to take full advantage of ICT. There are examples, however, of Irish companies in both industries that are adopting world class management techniques.

In residential construction, the use of ICT could greatly facilitate more efficient site management where a large number of sub-contractors are involved in the completion of a single project. In road haulage, a centralised booking system could reduce the very high degree of empty loads, by more efficiently matching demand with potential supply. However, these two industries are typified by a large number of small firms. Clearly, these firms acting in isolation may not be able to optimise their use of ICT in the absence of a more widespread adoption across their respective industries. What is missing is an institution which can pull enough major players in an industry together to bring about such networks. In many countries, there exist business development institutions to fulfil this role. As O'Donnell and Cahill argue in Chapter 9, in Ireland there are few and comparatively weak associations in civil society devoted to technical, scientific or business development, and as such potential productivity enhancements are not realised.

5 Lessons for Industrial Policy

Ireland's industrial policy has played a central role in Ireland's phenomenal economic growth during the 'Celtic Tiger' period. Organisations such as the IDA and Enterprise Ireland, a pro-business policy environment and policy consistency on the part of a number of successive governments played a key role in attracting Foreign Direct Investment (FDI) into Ireland during the late 1980s and 1990s. This volume contains a number of lessons to inform Ireland's future industrial policy which are discussed under four headings, namely the impact of productivity spillovers, the regional distribution of economic growth, the role of R&D and the role of micro-policies aimed at supporting Irish enterprises.

Productivity Spillovers

Policymakers have long assumed that inward investment can bestow large economic benefits, not only in terms of new investment but also an inflow of new foreign knowledge and technology. This has led to greater importance being given to the notion of industrial clusters. This view of agglomeration economies based on industrial clusters derives largely from the work of Michael Porter, which is reviewed in detail by Doyle and Fanning in Chapter 16. The chapter concludes, however, that there is little evidence that such clusters have had a significant effect on productivity growth in Ireland. The review of the international evidence by Görg in Chapter 14 also finds that the evidence is at best mixed. O'Leary argues in Chapter 15 that agglomeration effects may be due to much broader considerations than suggested by a focus on clusters.

The arrival of multinationals probably did have very important spillover effects however, but they probably were felt much more broadly than the narrow industrial sectors which were analysed in these studies. In particular, the economic upturn from the beginning of the 1990s onwards resulted in a sea change in the way economic development was viewed in Ireland. It heralded a period of much greater cultural openness, and a greater understanding of the potential and limitations of competing in the global market. Policymakers, wary of losing multinational companies that had the potential to relocate, became more sensitive to the needs of the enterprise sector. This had a beneficial knock-on effect on Irish firms, who also benefited from this more enabling policy climate. Further, a generation of Irish workers experienced world-class management techniques and acquired specific market knowledge when working for particular industries, which are in turn increasingly being applied across a swathe of economic sectors. Not all of these benefits would be captured in a study examining only very narrow industry or geographic spillovers.

Regional Distribution of Growth

The vast majority of companies that have been attracted into Ireland have been attracted into one of our major cities. Morgenroth (Chapter 3) notes that the regional disparities in productivity growth are due to the fact that the Greater Dublin and South Western regions have been more successful in attracting highly sophisticated and productive foreign owned manufacturing firms. O'Leary (Chapter 15) argues that to the extent that agglomeration economies have influenced the location of many industries, these have been centred on the availability of labour supply with third level qualifications and the quality of life available in these population centres. Industrial development agencies and government policy have continually attempted to encourage more firms to set up outside of these regions, in an effort to promote more balanced regional growth. O'Leary recommends that in a country of Ireland's size, policy should focus on developing perhaps five or six highly urbanised centres in which the required concentration of factors such as skilled labour, educational institutions and infrastructural links could all be provided.

Kopp in Chapter 17 analyses the macroeconomic productivity effects of road investment in 13 western European countries and shows that the rate of return for many countries on past investment has been low. However, the quality of Irish infrastructure is thought to be inferior to these countries, so the rate of return for Ireland would be expected to be higher. That said, Ireland's dramatic economic takeoff at the start of the 1990s took place at a time when our infrastructure was deemed poor by international standards. Furthermore, the German economy has posted a below average performance over the last decade despite having an impressive existing transport network.

Building a Knowledge Economy

The concept of the 'knowledge economy' is based on the idea that science, research, technology and innovation play an important role in creating knowledge in modern economies. Kavanagh and Doyle in Chapter 18 review the compelling evidence in support of the view that increased human capital boosts growth, individual earnings, and firm level productivity. Turning to R&D, Czarnitzki and O'Byrnes (Chapter 19) conclude that R&D expenditure generates significant private and social returns. The social returns are substantially higher than the private returns due to the 'spillover' of research findings. They also find that countries which lag behind in R&D performance can benefit most from these spillovers, as long as they have sufficient absorptive capacity, though developing this capacity is in itself a significant undertaking. Dagg (Chapter 20) sets out the evolution of the R&D performance of Ireland.

Micro-Policies to Support Irish Firms

In Chapter 23 Kneller investigates whether the best firms become exporters or whether they somehow benefit as a result of being an exporter. While the chapter suggests that there is a learning effect once a firm starts exporting, the chapter notes that firm productivity would appear to be largely independent of the firm's export decision. In other words, the productivity growth in exporting firms generally occurs before rather than after the decision was made to export. While efforts to encourage exports are often useful in cases where firms do not recognise the benefits of exporting, where they cannot find customers, or where there are barriers to exporting, the research underpins a case for general support to firms, rather than targeted intervention.

Chapter 24 focuses on outward investment from Ireland, the pace and scale of which is likely to emerge as one of the most important features of Irish economic development over the next decade. The evidence shows that outward investment is associated with higher productivity, though the evidence is mixed regarding which firms/activities benefit most. In Chapter 25 Haller shows that at the root of productivity dynamics at the aggregate level are large differences in productivity between plants in even narrowly defined sectors. This chapter decomposes the changes in labour productivity in Irish manufacturing industries from 1995 to 2003. Finally, Watt and Scully in Chapter 13 discuss the regulatory burden in Ireland, and identify some potential areas for improving the Irish regulatory framework.

6. Building our Understanding of Productivity

"Real knowledge is to know the extent of one's ignorance."

Confucius, 551-479 BC

What is most striking about the volume is the extent of our lack of knowledge of productivity levels or growth in Ireland. While this volume contains many valid policy lessons in relation to productivity, many sectors are omitted, and many of the policy lessons are based on data from other countries.

It is very difficult to measure productivity properly. Traditionally economists have measured productivity by calculating the value added per worker. By this measure, the higher the value added in an industry, the higher is productivity. Economists like working in value added as these figures are easily collected by statistical agencies, and remove the requirement to measure the quality and quantity of outputs and inputs from an industry, data which is difficult to collect with any degree of accuracy.

For Ireland, this presents two challenges. First, the estimates of output and productivity for the exporting sector in Ireland can be affected by the treasury operations of some multinational firms. Second, this value added data is of limited value for measuring productivity for those goods and services which do not face international competition, but which are essential in a modern society. For example, the electricity generation and distribution sector in Ireland has a very high level of value added per worker, but suffers from a number of productivity shortcomings. The value-added in these sectors reflect domestic wage and profitability levels, and often have no correspondence to their productivity performance.

The greatest problems in understanding productivity are in the public sector. This is a serious constraint to understanding Ireland's overall productivity, as the productivity of the public sector is as important to the economic performance of a country as the productivity of the private sector. Productivity in the public service is currently measured based on the formula *Outputs = Inputs*. In other words, if inputs into healthcare increase by 15 per cent, it is assumed that output in that industry also increases by 15 per cent. Clearly, this assumption takes no account of changes in actual efficiency within the public sector.

Efforts have been made internationally to overcome these problems. As reported by Boyle (Chapter 5) in the UK, the Office for National Statistics (ONS) is developing measures of productivity. The ONS published a major review of health service productivity, with three different estimates of NHS productivity. Also in the UK, changes in local government performance are assessed using a sample of 63 indicators including 'Best Value' performance indicators, indicators from the Social Services Performance Assessment Framework, and indicators from the Department for Education and Skills. In Australia, a set of performance indicators for schools is being developed, incorporating equity indicators that measure how special needs groups compare in terms of participation and retention rates, and effectiveness indicators that measure learning outcomes with regard to reading, writing and numeracy.

Work in Ireland to deepen our understanding of productivity has also commenced. Two chapters in this volume report efforts to overcome research shortfalls in major non-exporting sectors of the economy, specifically in residential construction (Aylward and O'Toole, Chapter 7) and road freight (Aylward and O'Toole, Chapter 8). While these two chapters represent the first attempt to provide estimates of productivity based on direct output measures, both were hampered by insufficient data, despite the fact that these industries are two of the largest employers in the country.

We currently have very little information about the productivity of the vast majority of the Irish labour force and this is a major challenge for statisticians. Further, the focus of research to date of the economics community is unbalanced. There is already a large amount of productivity work on the exporting sectors of the economy. However, far fewer resources are aimed at studying non-exporting sectors, sectors where productivity underperformance is not necessarily self-correcting through competition, and which may in fact be more amenable to corrective policy action by the government. These sectors have a large impact on business costs, and therefore contribute crucially to the competitiveness of the economy as a whole and are worthy of further research.

PART I

ASSESSING IRELAND'S PRODUCTIVITY PERFORMANCE

INTRODUCTION

The chapters in this section survey our current knowledge of productivity performance in Ireland. In Chapter 1, Sexton reviews trends in real output, employment and labour productivity in Ireland between 1995 and 2005. Ireland's productivity performance in the second half of the 1990s was highly impressive, though Ireland's aggregate productivity growth appears to have slowed down in more recent years. This is mainly due to structural changes that have resulted in significant reductions in the share of employment in high value added manufacturing, while employment in service sectors with poor productivity performances continue to increase. In Chapter 2, Farrell, Remes and Kehoe also stress the importance of improving the productivity performance of Ireland's domestically traded service sectors. They show that service sectors, excluding IT, contributed just 14 percent to the productivity increase posted in Ireland between 1995 and 2002, but were responsible for the employment of 55 percent of the workforce. They cite retailing and banking as two industries where Irish productivity is poor. In Chapter 3, Morgenroth focuses on the influence that differential rates of productivity growth within the manufacturing industry have on determining regional divergence in Gross Value Added (GVA) per capita. Finally, in Chapter 4, Iparraguirre D'Elia reviews the productivity performance of Northern Ireland, which remains heavily dependent on the public sector.

CHAPTER 1

TRENDS IN OUTPUT, EMPLOYMENT AND PRODUCTIVITY IN IRELAND, 1995-2005

J.J. SEXTON[1]

ABSTRACT

This chapter reviews trends in real output, employment and labour productivity in Ireland between 1995 and 2005. The chapter concludes that productivity growth appears to have ceased, and may well turn negative, at least for a time. The analysis indicates that structural change in the economy has been the significant influence in reducing overall productivity growth, even though output per worker in some sectors has also made a contribution. With regards to structures, the rapid decrease in the relative importance of the manufacturing sector has been a major causative factor. The nature of these influences would suggest that any significant resumption of productivity growth is unlikely in the short-term unless substantial employment increases occur in high value added sectors.

1 The author would like to record his appreciation of the assistance provided by CSO staff, particularly Mr. Bill Keating, Mr. Michael Keating and Mr. Ciarán Counihan, in providing special tabulations from the National Accounts database. The author would also like to thank Dr. Jim Fitzpatrick, of Fitzpatrick Associates, Economic Consultants, for his assistance. The contents of this chapter remain, of course, the responsibility of the author.

1.1 Introduction

1.1.1 General Background

This chapter reviews trends in real output, employment and labour productivity in Ireland over the period since 1995. In order to facilitate an examination of such trends in the context of the overall performance of the economy, the analysis is set within the overall framework of the National Accounts estimates as published by the Central Statistics Office (CSO). It is, therefore, basically of a macro nature, even though it does contain a sectoral dimension, involving seven categories.

It should be borne in mind that the measurement of real output (and as a result productivity) is not a straightforward matter. There are different ways to approach this problem, and in some areas considerable difficulties arise in compiling volume measures. This is an issue that has been much discussed both nationally and internationally in bodies such as the UN, EU, and OECD etc. Generally it is possible to devise reasonable volume output indicators for sectors such as agriculture, industry and construction, and for services related to activities such as distribution and transport and communications, for which consistent and usable volume statistics are available. These are derived either from independent sources, or by deflating nominal or value series by means of appropriate price index series. However, the position is much more problematic in areas such as the public sector and for non-market services generally, where, for the most part, the services provided are not subject to commercial or sales transactions, or are made available in the form of collective services as a public good. Heretofore changes in real output for these spheres of activity have tended to be calculated from employment trends applied to base year value added, the latter usually proxied via labour costs. This effectively implies no change in productivity. Even though not discussed here, such methodological issues are important, and readers who are interested in a more detailed description of these aspects should refer to the study on which this chapter is based.[1]

1.1.2 Data Sources

Virtually all of the Irish data contained in this report has been obtained from CSO sources, either from the National Accounts database or (in the case of employment) from the Quarterly National Household Survey (QNHS). For the most part the output measures used in this chapter relate to Gross Value Added (GVA) at factor cost, as this allows one to simultaneously analyse overall and sectoral trends. Basically GVA is the sale of goods or services less the costs of production, apart from employee remuneration. The calculation is made before any allowance is made for depreciation. GDP, which is very similar to GVA in numerical terms, is obtained by adding product and non-product taxes (minus subsidies) to total GVA.[2] The employment figures relate to the totality of those at work compiled on an annual average basis, and include self employed and part-time workers.[3]

The analyses presented involve a sectoral classification with seven categories covering (1) agriculture; (2) modern manufacturing; (3) other (traditional) manufacturing; (4) building, (5) distribution, hotels, transport etc.; (6) finance and business services; and finally (7) other services. The 'modern manufacturing' category (which is now distinguished in the National Accounts publications) mainly covers high technology multinational enterprises engaged in manufacturing chemicals, computers (including software replication), instrumentation, electrical machinery and equipment and the reproduction of recorded media.[4] The remaining 'other manufacturing' category comprises more traditional areas such as food, beverages and textiles, and also includes mining and quarrying and utilities. The residual 'other services' group is, in fact, predominantly non-market (80 per cent in employment terms) and, in effect, broadly represents the wider public sector covering central and local administration, security, education and health/welfare services.[5]

1.1.3 Some Qualifications

Apart from the methodological qualifications as described earlier, analyses of the economy's overall performance are presented 'with' and 'without' what is termed the 'modern' manufacturing sector. While it is of interest, and indeed useful, to consider Irish performance in this way, this should not lead one to infer that the presence of the modern sector involved is in some sense questionable, or that the position should necessarily be otherwise. While it is true that Ireland is exceptional (indeed highly exceptional) in terms of the share of national output accounted for by high technology multinationals, this has been the position for quite a long time. Whatever views one might hold about the income losses due to profit repatriation etc., the reality is that the sector currently employs over 90,000 persons, significantly more than in 1995, even if the numbers have fallen in recent years.

While the omission of the modern industry sector from the calculation of the various measures may be mathematically correct, one should exercise caution in interpreting this approach in an economic context. The absence of the multinational high-tech sector from the Irish economy would have significant indirect effects (which are not captured by simple data exclusion). These industries generate knock-on activities in the rest of the economy through purchases of goods and services and the expenditure of wages etc. If these influences were accounted for in the exclusion exercise in question, the performance in the rest of the economy (as measured) would be set at a somewhat lower level.[6] Furthermore, in a human resource context, the expansion of the multinational sector in the period since the 1960s had substantial positive effects in enhancing skill levels and skill acquisition, and in widening attitudes and horizons, features that are now important in view of the imperative to compete in the global market. It is true, however, that the funds from the capital grants and other supports directed to the modern industrial sector would presumably have been available for investment elsewhere in the economy, although probably with less spectacular results. In summary, any comparisons between the two scenarios as described must be qualified, but are still useful and instructive, especially in view of the significant differences involved.

1.2 Output, Employment and Productivity

1.2.1 National Trends

Looking first at overall or national trends, Table 1.1 shows national annual figures for real GVA and average numbers at work for the period from 1995 to 2005. The real GVA figures are expressed in terms of constant 2004 prices. The table also shows the data in index number form, along with labour productivity indexes. The latter were derived by dividing the real output index values by the corresponding values of the employment index (i.e. they reflect GVA per person at work). Figure 1.1 gives a graphical representation of the three index number trends.

The data indicate that total GVA almost doubled in real terms between 1995 and 2005, or by seven per cent on an annual average basis. Output growth has been strong over the entire period, even though it displayed a tendency to moderate in recent years. The total number of persons at work in the Irish economy rose by nearly 670,000 over the ten-year span concerned, reaching a total of 1,952,100 in 2005. This represents a relative increase of more than 50 per cent, or 4.3 per cent annually on average. The increases were particularly rapid during the final years of the 1990s, peaking at well over 100,000 between 1997 and 1998. The increments moderated during the early years of this decade, but have recently accelerated.

Table 1.1: Real Output (GVA) Employment and Labour Productivity, 1995-2005

Year	GVA (2004 Prices) Euro Millions	Employment (000)	GVA	Employment Index 1995=100	Labour Productivity
1995	70034	1284.7	100.0	100.0	100.0
1996	76556	1330.7	109.3	103.6	105.5
1997	84221	1405.0	120.3	109.4	110.0
1998	89846	1525.8	128.3	118.8	108.0
1999	97412	1621.1	139.1	126.2	110.2
2000	106175	1696.4	151.6	132.1	114.8
2001	113481	1747.5	162.0	136.0	119.1
2002	119754	1778.6	171.0	138.5	123.5
2003	123869	1814.0	176.9	141.2	125.3
2004	130178	1865.0	185.9	145.2	128.0
2005	137293	1952.1	196.0	152.0	129.0
Annual Average Change (%)			**7.0%**	**4.3%**	**2.6%**

Figure 1.1: Indexes of GVA, Employment and Productivity (1995=100)

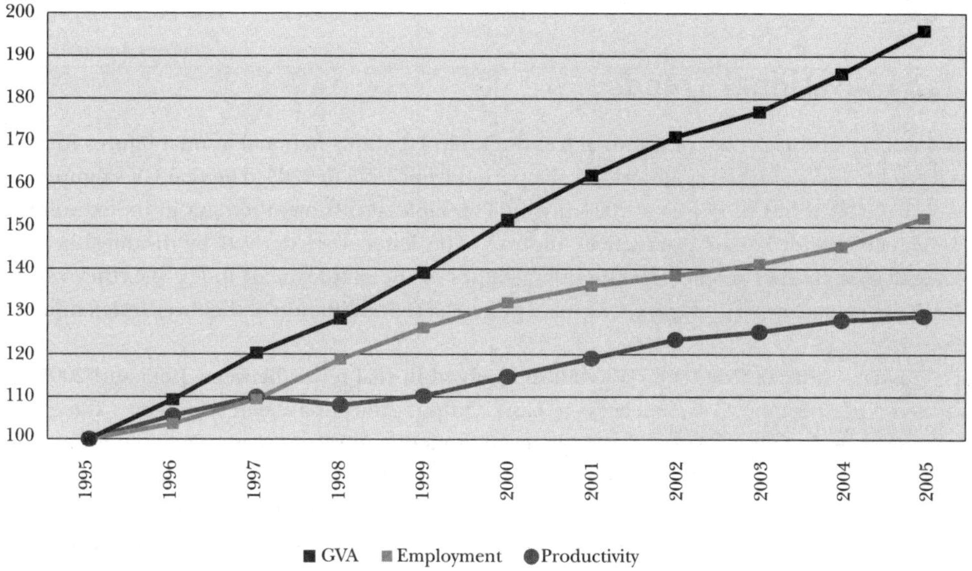

The productivity figures reveal some interesting features. Total labour productivity in the Irish economy rose by almost 30 per cent between 1995 and 2005, or annually by 2.6 per cent on average. However, while this measure recorded near continuous growth over most of the period, this began to slow noticeably after 2002, and the most recent data shows that the level of labour productivity remained virtually unchanged between 2004 and 2005. This recent trend, which differs from current experience in other developed economies, is examined further later in th s chapter.

1.2.2 Sectoral Shares of Output and Employment

Before proceeding to analyse trends for output and other data on a sectoral basis, it is useful to provide, in a cross-sectional context, some information on the relative size of the different sectors in order to indicate the scale of the contribution of each to economic activity. In this regard Table 1.2 shows the sectoral subdivision of employment and GVA for 2005, and figures for average GVA per person employed in different sectors (both calculated at 2004 prices).

With regard to GVA, manufacturing and finance and business services account for the greatest shares (over 25 per cent in each case). The modern sub-sector of manufacturing accounts for over 16 per cent of national output, but less than five per cent of employment. In fact both of the sectors referred to are in the high value added category, and between them are responsible for more than half of total GVA, but account for only 28 per cent of employment. In contrast the broad area covering other services (including distribution and transport) covers some 36 per cent of output, but over half of total employment. The building and construction industry accounts for less than ten per cent of national GVA and nearly 13 per cent of the jobs market.

Table 1.2: GVA and Employment Shares by Sector, 2005

Sector	GVA	Employment %	GVA/Person Employed (Euro Annual)
Agriculture	2.9	5.9	34,700
Manufacturing	26.8	15.0	125,600
Modern Manufacturing	16.3	4.7	241,800
Other Manufacturing	10.6	10.3	72,200
Construction	9.3	12.6	51,900
Distribution, Hotels, Transport etc.	17.5	26.1	47,200
Finance, Business Services, Insurance	25.2	13.3	133,500
Other Services	18.3	27.1	47,300
Total	**100.0**	**100.0**	**70,300**
Total excl Modern Manufacturing	-	-	**61,800**

Note: The financial data are at 2004 prices.

The figures for average GVA per head, shown in the final column of the table, essentially indicate why the output and employment shares vary so much across sectors. While the overall national average GVA per person employed is calculated at €70,000, this varies substantially across sectors. The figures that immediately stand out are those for manufacturing, with the average GVA per person for the modern sub-sector being as high as €242,000, compared with €72,000 for the 'other manufacturing' category. There are a number of reasons for this divergence. Value added for multinational chemical and high technology enterprises would incorporate research and development costs which, for the most part, are carried out externally, and would not necessarily feature in the cost structure for these companies in Ireland, especially in relation to aspects such as methodology and intellectual property. The much discussed and controversial issue of transfer pricing, which would serve to boost the profit component of total GVA, would be a further contributing factor. It should be noted (from the final row of this table) that the impact of the activities of these enterprises on GVA at a national level is substantial. If 'modern manufacturing' is excluded from the calculations the economy wide figure for GVA per person decreases to just under €62,000, a reduction of 12 per cent on the figure quoted previously.[7]

The GVA per person average is also relatively high for finance, insurance and business services activities (€133,500). This is not altogether surprising, as this sector involves sizeable numbers of employees with medium to high level skills and is essentially a high value added sector. The figures for construction, distribution and 'other services' lie within the €45,000 to €55,000 range. As for the last mentioned category, as this mainly consists of public service activities, output measurement is almost exclusively based on employee remuneration and must be viewed somewhat differently from other sectors. The lowest average GVA per person at work (under €35,000) is recorded for the agricultural sector.

1.2.3 Sectoral Trends in Economic Activity, 1995-2005

Sectoral trend changes in output, employment and productivity over time are best illustrated as index numbers, and in graphical form. In this regard the following commentary sets out annual average changes for a ten-year period for six sectors in Table 1.3, while Figures 1.2 to 1.4 chart sectoral movements in output, employment and productivity on an annual basis in index number form.

Table 1.3: Annual Average Change in Real GVA, Employment and Labour Productivity, 1995-2005

Sector	GVA	Employment	Productivity
Agriculture	2.6	-1.7	4.3
Manufacturing	8.4	0.9	7.4
Modern Manufacturing	11.7	2.1	9.4
Other Manufacturing	4.8	0.4	4.3
Construction	8.1	9.9	-1.7
Distribution, Hotels, Transport etc.	7.3	4.9	2.3
Finance, Business Services, Insurance	7.1	7.4	-0.3
Other Services	5.1	4.4	0.6
Total	**7.0**	**4.3**	**2.6**
Total Excl Modern Manufacturing	**6.3**	**4.4**	**1.8**

Trends in Real Output

Turning first to output, it has already been noted that total GVA almost doubled in real terms between 1995 and 2005, or by seven per cent on an annual average basis. The most notable changes are in the manufacturing area, with output in modern manufacturing showing a rise of some 200 per cent over the ten-year period in question (nearly 12 per cent annually). The more traditional 'other manufacturing' sector expanded by 60 per cent, or by 4.8 per cent annually. Figure 1.2 shows, however, that real output in modern industry has recorded virtually no growth since 2002. Throughout this more recent period, as indicated below, job losses in this sector were substantial. These trends are somewhat different to those for the more traditional manufacturing enterprises. In this area output continued to rise in recent years (albeit very slowly), and the employment level held up, at least until 2005 when it declined noticeably.

Real growth in the building industry was particularly strong and continuous over the entire period from 1995 to 2005, averaging more than eight per cent annually. As Figure 1.2 shows, expansion was particularly strong in 2004-05 (over nine per cent). Output performances in distribution, hotels, transport etc. and in financial and business services were also robust and sustained, recording annual increases of more than seven per cent on average.

Figure 1.2: Output Indexes (Real GVA) by Sector, 1995-2005 (1995=100)

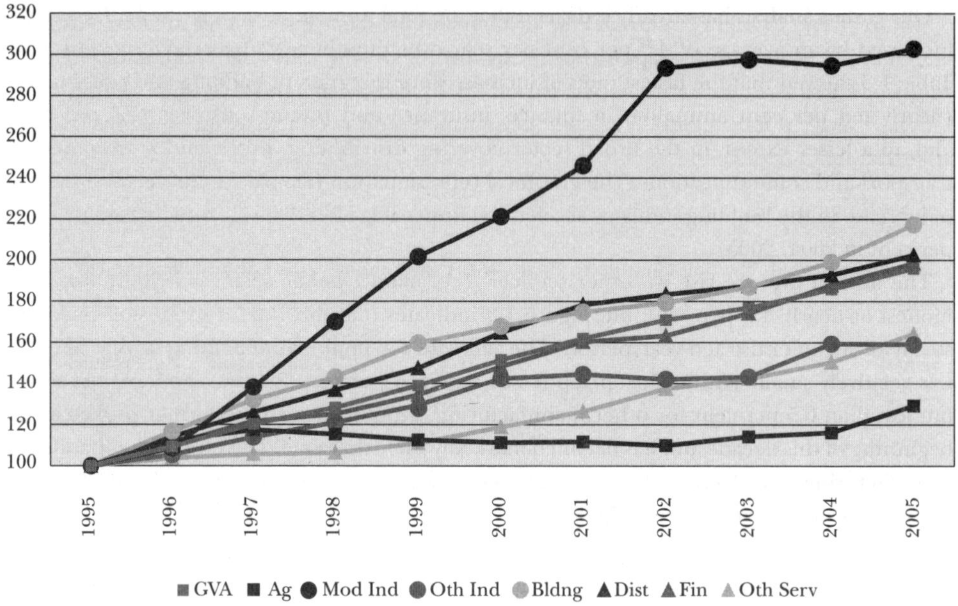

The volume rise in 'other services' activities, which mainly involves public or non-market services, was lower than in other areas (apart from agriculture), increasing by just over five per cent annually between 1995 and 2005. However, this divergence would be partly due to methodological differences in measuring real output. One would expect (or hope) that if a productivity element were included in the output calculations for this sector, the volume growth rates would be higher.

Real output growth in agriculture can only be described as minimal in the ten years up to 2005. It amounted to less than 30 per cent over the full ten-year period, averaging only 2.5 per cent per year. Some significant expansion was recorded in the early years of this period, but broadly speaking; in subsequent years output growth has been negative, apart from 2004 to 2005 when a significant gain was recorded. However, this was, in effect, a once-off phenomenon and more in the nature of a distortion, being due mainly to the change in the method of payment of farm supports from production based subsidies to fixed or flat payments.

Finally, it is of interest to observe the extent to which growth in modern or high technology manufacturing affects overall economic expansion. If this sub-sector is excluded from the total GVA real growth calculation, the annual average rate for the 1995-2005 period is reduced by 0.7 of a percentage point, from 7.0 to 6.3 per cent, not an unduly large amount, but significant nonetheless. However, as explained earlier, the exclusion of modern manufacturing from the growth calculation as illustrated here should, ideally, be done in a wider context that takes account of secondary effects.

Trends in Employment

Our earlier analysis has already indicated that the total number at work in the Irish economy increased by an average of 4.3 per cent per year over the ten years between 1995 and 2005. Table 1.3 showed that the fastest rates of increase were recorded in building and construction (nearly ten per cent annually), in finance, insurance and business services (7.5 per cent) and, to a lesser extent, in the broad sector covering distribution, hotels and restaurants and transport and communications. The graphical representation (Figure 1.3) reveals that the rate of increase in the building industry accelerated noticeably after 2003 (it rose by as much as 14 per cent in 2004/2005).

The annual average rise in 'other services' (i.e. mainly public sector activities) was more modest at nearly 4.5 per cent, but Figure 1.3 indicates that this rate of expansion remained steady over the entire ten-year period. The increase for total manufacturing at one per cent was relatively small. Within this group it was over two per cent for the 'modern' sub-sector, but less than 0.5 per cent for other manufacturing. Employment in the former peaked at the beginning of this decade and has declined markedly since that time. The numbers in traditional manufacturing also decreased in recent years, albeit more slowly, except in 2004-2005 when there was a sharp drop of nearly 7,000.

Figure 1.3: Employment Indexes (Real GVA) by Sector, 1995-2005 (1995=100)

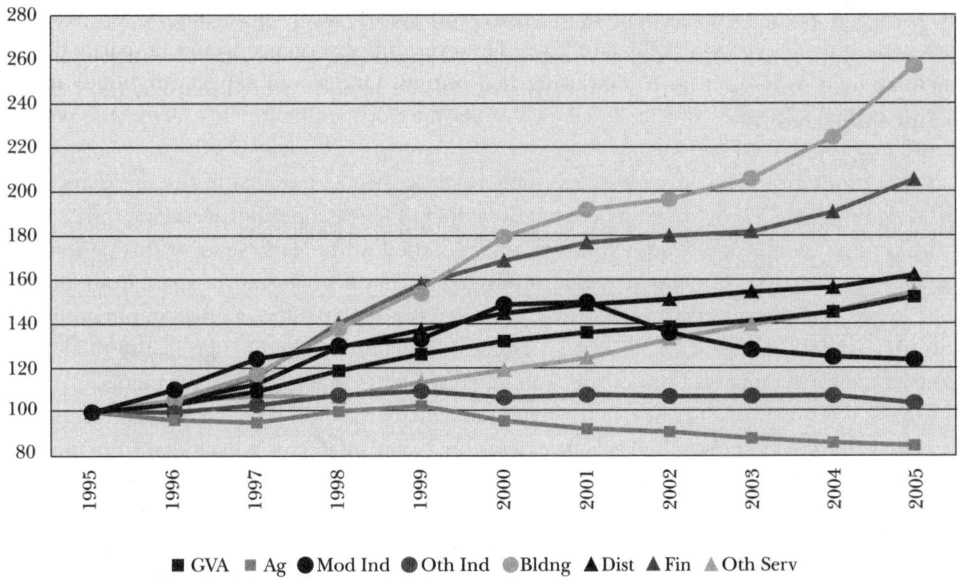

1.2.4 Labour Productivity

Let us now consider recent trends in labour productivity – perhaps the most interesting feature in this study. Table 1.3 showed that total labour productivity in the Irish economy rose by 2.6 per cent annually on average between 1995 and 2005, or by nearly 30 per cent over the full period. However, the growth in productivity has declined noticeably in the last few years and the level remained more or less static in 2004 and 2005. This has been mainly as a result of a number of parallel influences, involving structural changes in the economy, falling productivity in certain sectors (notably building and construction), as well as a tapering off in productivity growth in a number of other areas (e.g. financial and business services).

Turning first to sectoral trends for manufacturing as a whole. Productivity more than doubled in this period, but within this category productivity in modern manufacturing rose by 145 per cent (9.4 per cent annually) and by nearly 55 per cent in the more traditional area, or 4.3 per cent per year on average (see Figure 1.4). An interesting point to note in regard to the modern technology-based category is that since 2001 the rapid gain in productivity has derived more from declining employment rather than from rising output. A contributing factor was that many of the job losses related to the lower skill end of the sub-sector in question. This type of effect has now also begun to apply to labour productivity in traditional manufacturing; this sub-sector recorded a sizeable fall in employment in 2004-2005, but productivity continued to rise.

Outside of manufacturing, significant productivity gains were recorded in agriculture (4.3 per cent annually between 1995 and 2005) and in distribution, hotels, transport etc. which recorded an annual average rise of 2.3 per cent. In agriculture these gains were mainly achieved due to falling numbers at work in the sector. It should be noted, however, that for agriculture the average percentage increase has been significantly influenced by the large productivity growth recorded in 2005 (13 per cent), which is attributable mainly to the changes in the method of payment for farm subsidies. Productivity actually declined in building and construction – by 1.7 per cent per year on average over the full period covered – with the result that the level recorded in 2005 was over 15 per cent lower than in 1995. While this may appear somewhat surprising, it should be borne in mind that this sector has recorded extremely large employment increases during this time. A closer inspection of the results shows that productivity in this sector actually increased during the early years of the period covered, but has been falling continuously since 1997.

Figure 1.4: Labour Productivity Index by Sector, 1995-2005 (1995=100)

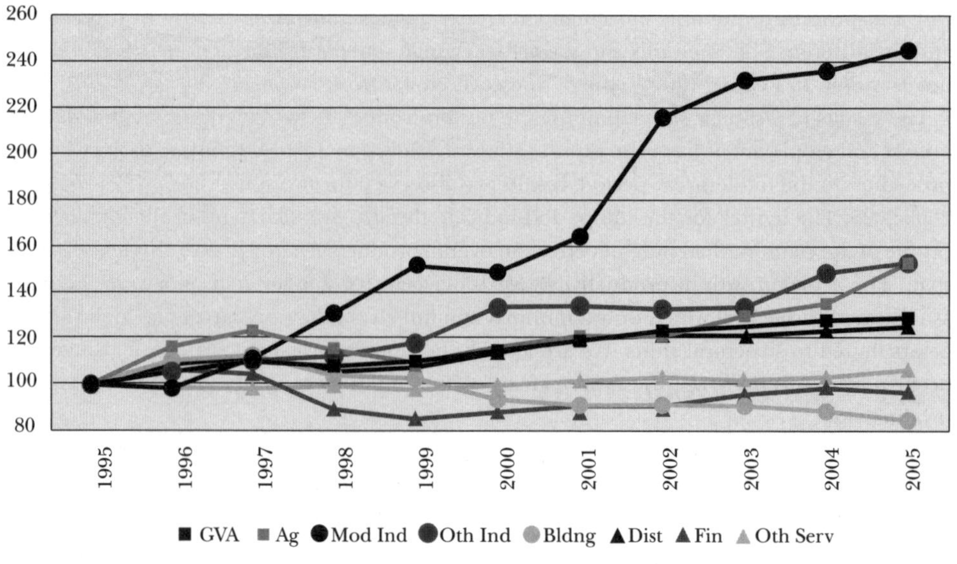

Labour productivity in the financial and business services sector also declined (albeit slightly) in the ten-year period between 1995 and 2005 – by just over three per cent (or 0.3 per cent annually). However, the trend within this period has been somewhat erratic. It rose initially between 1995 and 1997, but then fell sharply in the following two years when employment in the sector rose rapidly. However, it has been increasing steadily at a moderate pace since 1999, with the result that by 2005 the level was nearly 14 per cent above that for the 1999 valley point.

As indicated earlier, the 'other services' category consists predominantly of public service activities. As the methodological basis of the output calculations for this large component effectively implies a situation of zero productivity growth, one would expect that the productivity trend figures should reflect this. This is indeed evident from Figure 1.4, the values of which remain at or near the base-year axis (100) throughout the entire period involved. There is some evidence of a slight rise in productivity in the sector in recent years, which one presumes must derive from the small private sector component.

The Impact of Structural Changes on National Productivity Growth

While analyses of productivity for specific sectors are important and instructive, one must also bear in mind that overall productivity change at national level reflects the effect of structural variations in the economy over time. Such changes arise from the increasing importance in employment terms of certain sectors and corresponding relative declines elsewhere. The declining influence of the agricultural sector provides an example, a development that of itself resulted in an increase in the overall level of output per person employed due to the replacement of jobs giving low value added with higher output employment. Often such underlying causative factors tend to attract little attention, but they are, nonetheless, important.

This type of development was illustrated in Keating (2000). The method he employed was to estimate what output levels would have been in a current year if the distribution of the numbers employed in different sectors of the economy was as in the base-year of the period under discussion, and output per worker in each sector was expressed in current terms. In other words, with this procedure the only movements recorded relate to intrinsic changes in productivity, and the difference between this and the actual change reflect the impact of structural shifts in the economy. In Keating (2000), the period covered was from 1990 to 1999.

The results of a similar simulation for the period from 1995 to 2005 using sectoral data on output and employment from the present study are shown in Table 1.4. As well as applying the procedure to the full ten-year period, results are also given for two sub-periods, 1995-2000 and 2000-2005. The figures for the full period indicate the structural changes in the employment profile of the economy had little net effect on overall productivity growth over this ten-year time span. The actual growth in productivity was 29 per cent (or 2.6 per cent on average annually as indicated earlier), of which only a minimal amount (less than one percentage point) could be attributed to structural shifts. We are already aware that substantial structural changes did occur during this time, but these were clearly offsetting in terms of their impact on national productivity.

The results for the two sub-periods are quite different. Between 1995 and 2000 real national productivity growth was nearly 15 per cent, of which nine per cent related to intrinsic productivity growth within sectors, but this was augmented by a further six per cent arising from changes in the employment profile across sectors of the economy. The reasons for this are not difficult to identify.

Table 1.4: Relative Growth in Overall Real Productivity Between 1995 and 2005 Assuming No Change in the Sectoral Structure of Employment

	1995-2000	2000-2005 %	1995-2005
Productivity Growth with Base Year Employment Structure	9.0	17.2	28.1
Actual Productivity Growth	14.8	12.4	29.0

This was a time when employment in high productivity areas such as modern manufacturing and finance and business services was increasing rapidly. This, of itself, served to boost national productivity levels, irrespective of productivity movements within these sectors. However, the results for the period from 2000 to 2005 indicate trends which are, in effect, the opposite of those evident for the earlier sub-period. Actual real productivity growth was nearly 12.5 per cent, but the growth component involving the constant base year employment structure was actually higher, by almost five percentage points at 17.2 per cent. This indicates that the impact of structural trends in the economy were negative during this time, and in contrast to the earlier period, had the effect of reducing, not increasing, overall productivity. Again the underlying reasons are evident. This period saw a significant decline in the share of total employment accounted for by high value added manufacturing (both modern and traditional) and a rise in the share attributable to the low productivity in building and construction and 'other services' sectors. Furthermore, the employment share related to financial and business services, where productivity is high and stabilised after a period of increase.

Productivity Declines in Individual Sectors

In addition to the recent near disappearance of overall productivity growth, the sizeable decrease in output per worker in certain sectors has also become a source of debate (Keenan, 2006). It has been suggested, for example, that the absence of recording of black economy activity may have contributed to this phenomenon, or the recruitment of large numbers of foreign workers at relatively low rates of pay since the late 1990s. If the latter tends to depress real wages while simultaneously increasing employment, this can transmit into reductions in productivity. Not surprisingly, in view of the sectoral trends already indicated, the building industry has, in particular, been referred to as an area where these influences may apply, as has the catering sector. While one cannot offer any direct proof that events have materialised as suggested (or even if true whether they can be attributed to foreign workers), they are within the realm of possibility. If the cost of labour in a sector increases more slowly in real terms than that for other inputs, it allows the engagement of more workers while at the same time achieving real increases in what is termed the 'gross operating surplus' (i.e. GVA less wages). In these circumstances the additional increase in employment can result in a reduction in productivity in the sector as it is currently measured.

In summary, however, our analyses show that, in addition to declining productivity within some sectors, structural changes in the economy have been an even more significant influence in reducing overall national productivity growth in recent years. In view of this, since structural patterns tend to change slowly, any significant resumption of productivity growth is unlikely in the short-term, unless substantial employment increases occur in high value added sectors such as finance and business services.

Productivity Measured in Terms of Hours Worked

It is also relevant to consider the question of how different (or similar) the productivity outcomes would be if hours worked were used as a denominator instead of employment. Generally there have been indications for quite some time that the level of average weekly hours worked per person has been declining. This can be either due to a rising incidence of part-time work (at least in some sectors) and/or a tendency to work fewer hours anyway, irrespective of full-time or part-time status.

In dealing with this issue the basic data used relate to the information on usual weekly hours worked as obtained in the CSO QNHS. This, of course, ensures consistency with the employment data used earlier in this chapter and also allows the compilation of hours worked data for the same sectors. The time span covered extends from 1998 to 2005, and within this period data on hours worked for each quarter were used in order to derive a more representative picture on an annual basis.[8] In compiling the productivity series the output figures used as numerators were the same real GVA data as used in calculating the labour productivity indicators. Thus the essential difference between the two series derives solely from the use of hours worked figures instead of employment as denominator inputs. The results are summarised in Tables 1.5 and 1.6 and in Figures 1.5 and 1.6.

The aggregate index numbers for the two types of productivity measures given in Table 1.5 show that overall labour productivity rose by over 19 per cent between 1998 and 2005, while productivity based on hours worked increased by nearly 26 per cent. These represent annual average increases of 2.6 and 3.4 per cent respectively. The differences are significant, but not unduly large. The corresponding Figure 1.5 shows that the trend pattern for each indicator is very similar, with a noticeable tendency towards slower productivity growth in recent years. The divergence between the two measures widened progressively in the early years of the period covered, but seems to have stabilised somewhat over the last few years.

Table 1.6 shows annual average relative changes in labour and hours worked productivity by sector during the 1998 to 2005 period. The changes are also represented graphically in bar chart form in Figure 1.6. The pattern of change across sectors is much the same as shown by each measure, even though generally the increases in productivity indicated by the hours worked measure tend to be somewhat greater. However, in the case of agriculture, manufacturing and financial and business services these differences are minimal: in the building sector, where productivity fell, the relative changes are almost identical. However, for the distribution, transport etc. sector and for 'other services' the differences in question are more marked. In the case of the former category the annual average rise in labour productivity between 1998 and 2005 was 2.4 per cent, but 3.3 per cent when based on the hours worked related measure.

For 'other services' (which is predominantly public sector) the variation is relatively greater, the corresponding increases being one and 1.8 per cent respectively. It is of interest to note that these two sectors recorded the greatest reductions in average weekly hours worked between 1998 and 2005. Furthermore, as these sectoral categories are large in terms of their shares of total economic activity, the percentage increases in question have a significant effect on the overall economy wide difference between the two measures.

Table 1.5: Indexes of Overall Labour and Hours Worked Productivity (1998=100)

Year	Labour	Hours Worked
1998	100.0	100.0
1999	102.0	102.6
2000	106.3	108.9
2001	110.3	113.5
2002	114.3	118.4
2003	116.0	121.5
2004	118.5	124.4
2005	119.4	125.9
Ann. Average Change (%)	**2.6**	**3.4**

Table 1.6: Annual Average Changes in Labour and Hours Worked Productivity by Sector, 1998-2005

Sector	Labour Productivity %	Hours Worked Productivity %
Agriculture	4.2	4.5
Manufacturing	7.2	7.6
Building	-2.9	-2.8
Distribution, etc.	2.4	3.3
Finance, Business, Insurance	1.2	1.4
Other Services	1.0	1.8
Total	**2.6**	**3.4**

Figure 1.5: Indexes of Labour and Hours Worked Productivity (1998=100)

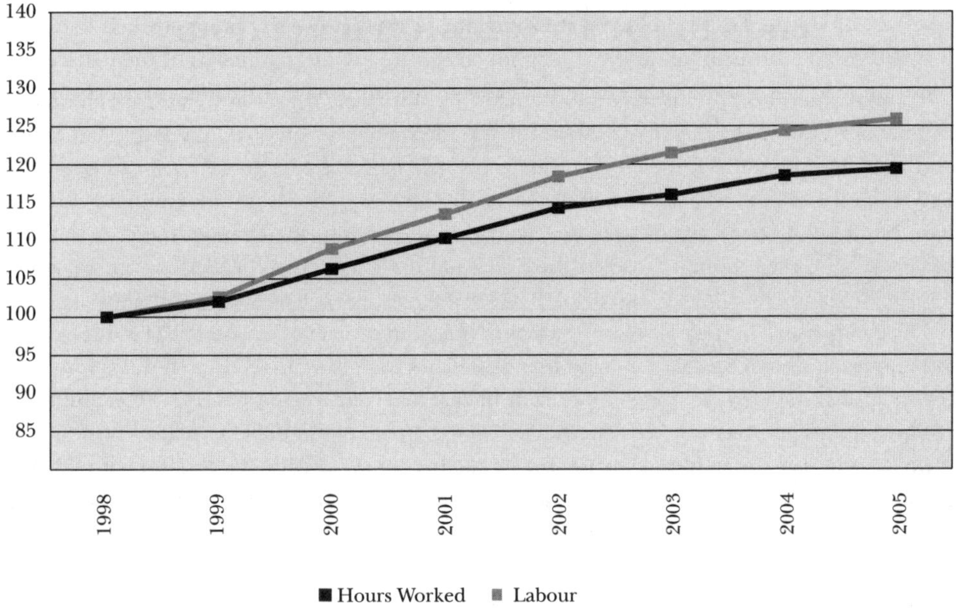

Figure 1.6: Annual Average Changes (%) in Labour and Hours Worked Productivity, 1998-2006

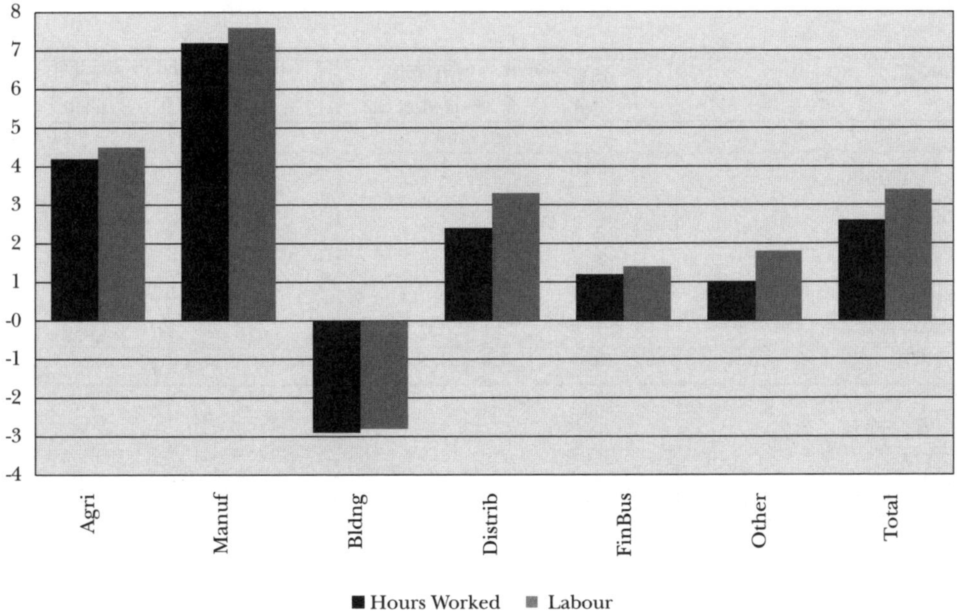

In summary, however, while the differences between the labour and hours worked productivity measures are significant and must be acknowledged, the message emerging from the analysis of each is much the same, and the variations are not of a sufficient order of magnitude so as to materially alter the conclusions of the earlier analyses based on labour productivity only.

1.3 Ireland's Performance Compared with Trends in the International Economy

In this section recent output, employment and productivity trends in Ireland are compared with those in two of the major regions of the international economy, i.e., the European Union and the United States.[9] The relevant data are given in Tables 1.7 to 1.9 and in Figures 1.7 to 1.9. All the trends are, as in most of the earlier analyses, shown in index number form to base 1995=100. For reasons of consistency with other tables in the chapter, the Irish data are based on GVA, even though those for the EU15 and the US relate to GDP. However, as already explained, the use of GVA instead of GDP makes little difference to the comparisons.

The comparative output data for the areas in question reveal considerable trend differences. Economic expansion has been much faster in Ireland than in both EU15 and the US. Annual real output growth averaged seven per cent in real terms in Ireland between 1995 and 2005, compared with just over two per cent in EU15 and 3.4 per cent in the US. As already indicated, if the 'modern manufacturing' sector is excluded from the Irish data, the annual real GVA increase for Ireland falls to 6.3 per cent. Leaving aside differences in growth levels, the graphical representation in Figure 1.7 shows that output in all regions rose steadily in the ten-year period concerned. It is noticeable however, that expansion faltered somewhat in the US at the beginning of the current decade, but began to increase again at a more rapid pace in recent years.

Table 1.7: Indexes of the Trend of Real Output in Ireland, EU15 and the US

Year	IRL GVA	IRL GVA Excl Mod Ind	EU15 GDP	US GDP
		1995=100		
1995	100.0	100.0	100.0	100.0
1996	109.3	109.4	101.6	103.7
1997	120.3	118.1	104.1	108.4
1998	128.3	123.3	107.2	112.9
1999	139.1	131.7	110.3	118.0
2000	151.6	143.4	114.2	122.4
2001	162.0	152.1	116.2	123.3
2002	171.0	156.6	117.5	125.7
2003	176.9	162.7	118.6	129.6
2004	185.9	173.1	121.4	135.4
2005	196.0	183.5	123.7	140.3
Ann Average Change (%)	**7.0**	**6.3**	**2.1**	**3.4**

Table 1.8: Indexes of Employment for Ireland, EU15 and the US

Year	IRL Total	IRL Excl Mod Ind	EU15	US
		1995=100		
1995	100.0	100.0	100.0	100.0
1996	103.6	103.2	100.5	101.7
1997	109.4	108.4	101.5	103.9
1998	118.8	118.1	103.3	106.3
1999	126.2	125.8	105.2	108.6
2000	132.1	131.0	107.3	111.1
2001	136.0	135.2	108.8	111.0
2002	138.5	138.6	109.5	110.1
2003	141.2	142.0	109.8	110.1
2004	145.2	146.4	110.6	111.3
2005	152.0	153.7	111.4	112.5
Ann Av. Change (%)	**4.3**	**4.4**	**1.1**	**1.2**

Table 1.9: Indexes of Labour Productivity for Ireland, EU15 and the US

Year	IRL Total	IRL Excl Mod Ind	EU15	US
		1995=100		
1995	100.0	100.0	100.0	100.0
1996	105.5	106.0	101.2	101.9
1997	110.0	108.9	102.8	104.1
1998	108.0	104.5	104.0	106.1
1999	110.2	104.7	105.3	108.7
2000	114.8	109.5	107.0	110.4
2001	119.1	112.6	107.5	111.0
2002	123.5	113.0	108.2	114.3
2003	125.3	114.5	108.9	117.9
2004	128.0	118.2	110.7	121.8
2005	129.0	119.4	112.5	124.9
Ann. Av. Change (%)	**2.6**	**1.8**	**1.2**	**2.2**

Note: The data for EU 15 and the US contained in Tables 1.7 to 1.9 are taken from the EU Commission publication 'Employment in Europe, 2005'

Figure 1.7: Indexes of Real Output in Ireland, EU15 and US (1995=100)

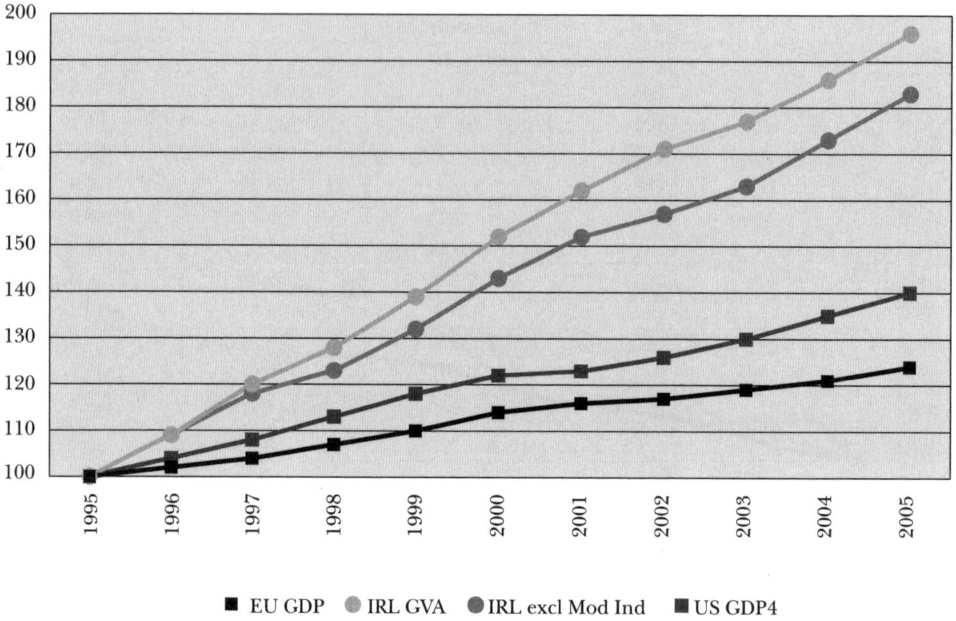

Figure 1.8: Employment Indexes for Ireland, EU15 and US (1995=100)

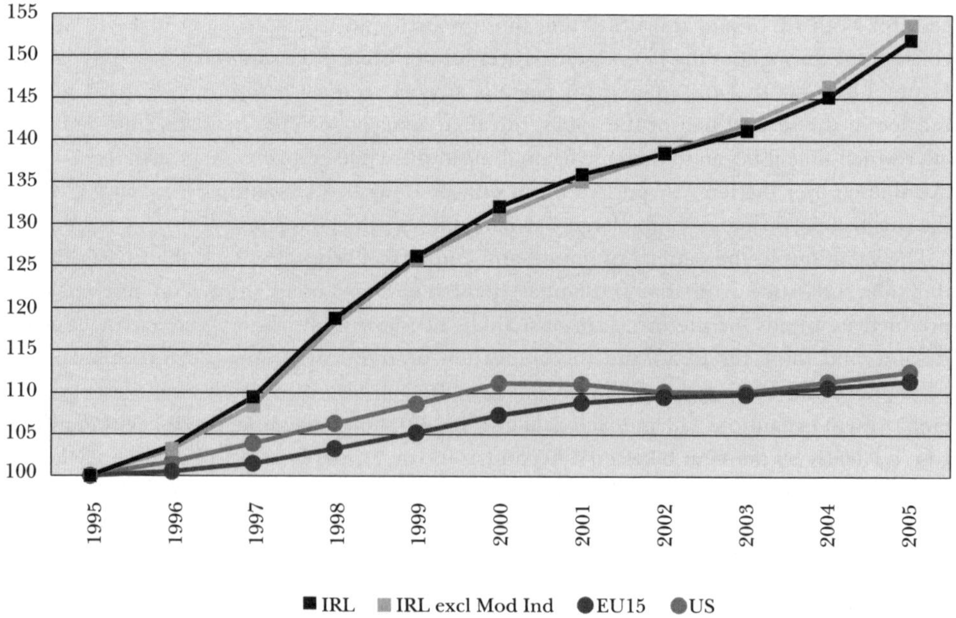

Figure 1.9: Indexes of Labour Productivity in Ireland, EU15 and US (1995=100)

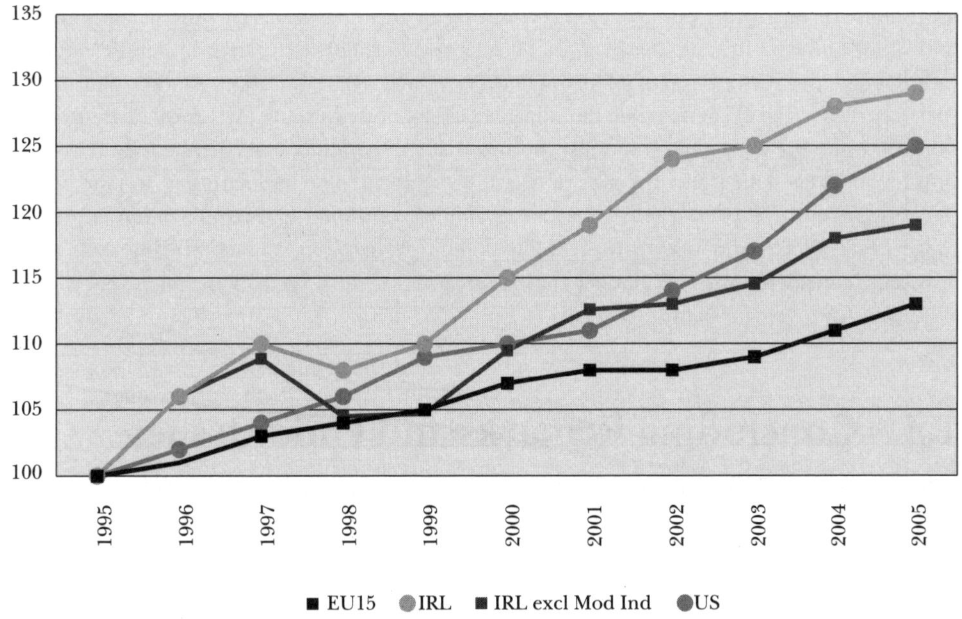

The comparative employment trends (Table 1.8 and Figure 1.8) show even greater divergence between Ireland and the other two regions. The annual average jobs gain in Ireland between 1995 and 2005 was 4.3 per cent, compared with corresponding increases of just over one per cent for both EU15 and the US. While the upward trend in employment in EU15 applied consistently throughout the period, the figures for the US reveal a somewhat different pattern. Figure 1.8 shows that the number of persons at work in the US rose more rapidly than in Europe in the second half of the 1990s, but then actually declined between 2000 and 2002, after which time it began to increase again, but slowly. While employment growth in EU15 was maintained over the ten-year period, it can only be described as painfully slow, largely due to the sluggish performance of the large German and French economies.

The variations in the pattern of output and employment trends as described (even though they may not appear all that substantial) have had a profound impact on differences in productivity trends for the three regions. Table 1.9 shows that labour productivity trends in Ireland, and those for EU15 and the US do not diverge to the same degree as for output or employment. During the period in question Ireland also achieved a much faster rate of employment expansion. The indexed data in Table 1.9 show that labour productivity in Ireland rose by nearly 30 per cent between 1995 and 2005, or 2.6 per cent on average annually. The corresponding increase in EU15 for the same period was nearly 13 per cent (1.2 per cent annually) and 25 per cent (2.2 per cent per year on average) in the US. However, if the high technology modern sector is excluded from the Irish data, it is interesting to note that the productivity increase for the period concerned is reduced to 1.8 per cent, which is somewhat below the US annual average figure.

The trends in Figure 1.9, from which one can more readily observe changes over time, provide a more revealing picture. While labour productivity growth has been substantial in Ireland over almost the entire period under study, as noted earlier, it began to decelerate after 2002. The productivity rise in EU15, as with output and employment, has been slow but consistent.

The data for the US is, perhaps, the most interesting. Productivity increased significantly throughout most of the 1995-2005 period, even though it lost its upward momentum and all but stabilised for a short period at the beginning of this decade (even though employment fell). It is of interest to note, however, that it increased strongly thereafter, in parallel with the (admittedly slow) resumption of jobs growth. This indicates that the labour market adjustments that occurred in the US at this time initially involved job losses among low productivity, low skill workers, while the increasing job opportunities that subsequently emerged benefited workers with higher skills. This is the opposite of what now appears to be happening in Ireland, where the disappearance of productivity growth at a time of continued high employment expansion suggest that the latter primarily involves low skill employees. On balance, leaving aside other economic considerations (US budget deficits etc.) the US productivity trends reveal a more solid basis for future growth.

1.4 Concluding Remarks and Policy Issues

1.4.1 Changing Growth Patterns

Arising from the results as presented, an important aspect which calls for comment is the extent to which the structure of economic growth in Ireland has altered over the ten year time span covered, especially in recent years. The widely varying growth rates for different sectors have created a situation where the current basis of output expansion is heavily dependent on building and construction and on the public services dominated 'other services' category. Table 1.10 shows that these two categories alone accounted for nearly 45 per cent of total growth in 2004-2005, with the distribution, hotels, transport etc., (which, apart from tourism related activities, is primarily driven by domestic consumption) adding a further 15 per cent. This means that 60 per cent of the overall growth increment in this twelve month period was generated by these three sectors, with about 40 per cent generated by the goods producing areas and business and financial services. It should be noted that, apart from tourism, the latter broad group encompasses almost all of the export-oriented activities in the economy. The position was virtually the opposite five years earlier in 2000/2001, when the two growth shares were just under 57 per cent for goods producing and business activities, and 44 per cent in aggregate for the other mainly non-traded sectors. The imbalances as described are even more extreme if economic expansion is viewed in terms of employment.

Table 1.10: Shares of Annual Real Output (GVA) Growth in 2001 and 2005

Sector	2000-01 %	2004-05 %
Agriculture	0.2	5.7
Manufacturing	27.7	8.0
Modern Manufacturing	25.1	8.4
Other Manufacturing	2.6	-0.4
Construction	5.6	15.1
Distribution, Catering, Transport etc.	21.9	15.9
Finance, Business Services	28.7	25.9
Other Services	16.0	29.3
Total	**100.0**	**100.0**

This is a situation which cannot be sustained for long and calls for steps to be taken to constrain output demand in building and construction and, possibly, some curbs on personal spending (or at least the discretionary parts thereof). While every effort should be made to promote expansion in export oriented goods producing sectors and in business services (see below), it is not realistic to expect that growth in these areas, where enterprises face strong competition in the global market, can be raised to the extent that an appropriate balance can be restored. In effect, what is being suggested implies slower but more sustainable growth. It is recognised that, when viewed in political terms, this is not an easy time to apply curbs, but it would be preferable to exercise a measure of control over corrective mechanisms, rather than allow them to be imposed in an uncontrolled manner by economic imperatives which may be much more painful.

1.4.2 Best Prospects for Future Growth

Another major issue of relevance to future economic performance is which sectors should be targeted, and if necessary supported, if reasonable growth rates are to be maintained. In addressing this issue it is, however, necessary to lower our sights overall, as one cannot expect to repeat the extraordinary overall growth rates achieved in recent years, at least not in the medium term.

While policy must strive to enhance growth in all areas of the economy, both traded and non-traded, our main concern must focus on those areas that have export potential and are not unduly dependant on domestic demand. The possibilities are not numerous. The main contributions to growth in the past have come from exports from agriculture and manufacturing industry and export tourism. In more recent years, international business services have become increasingly important, a feature which is discussed in more detail below.

Historically agriculture, or agriculture based industries, has been an important contributor to growth (prior to the 1960s they were virtually the only source). However, our analyses show that output in the primary sector has now become more or less static, as Ireland has been obliged to reduce trade barriers and dismantle internal supports as part of the wider application of WTO sponsored global trade agreements. This trend is unlikely to change, as trade liberalisation is likely to progress, even if slowly.[10] While agriculture will, of course, remain an important output component in the Irish economy, it cannot be expected to make a substantial or above average contribution to future economic expansion.

Manufacturing (especially the multinational high-technology sector) has effectively been the engine of growth in the Irish economy for many decades. This has been due not only to rapidly rising output in the sector, but also from knock-on effects in the rest of the economy. Furthermore, in a wider sense, the positive social or psychological impact on Irish society in having developed a sizeable high-tech sector, which provided numerous high-skill employment opportunities, has been substantial. However, things are obviously beginning to change. The data presented earlier in this chapter show that volume output in the modern sector has moderated and employment has declined substantially in the last few years. This cannot be attributed to cyclical influences, but is of a more fundamental nature as enterprises (particularly those at the lower skill end of the sector) transfer operations to low-cost countries. The ultimate vision here is a sector that has fewer but larger units engaged in a range of core activities (including research and development) which require significant investment and high-skill HR inputs. Because of its strategic value, high-technology manufacturing will continue to be an important, indeed crucial, element in fostering economic growth in Ireland, but is unlikely to occupy the dominant position it has held since the 1960s.

With regard to tourism, while this sector has also contributed substantially to growth over a prolonged period, this has not been the case in recent years. Total gross income from international tourism and travel (which amounted to €4.3 billion in 2005) rose by 11 per cent per year between 1995 and 2000, but this rate declined to 3.3 per cent in 2000-2005 (CSO, 2005). The latter figure in fact represents a slight decrease in real terms when the cost inflation is taken into account.[11] The output figures just quoted are broadly consistent with recent trends in employment in the tourism related sector covering hotels, restaurants etc. which has recorded a minimal net jobs increase since 2000, even though total employment in the economy rose by as much as 250,000 between 2000 and 2005.

The foregoing comments should not, of course, be taken to imply that the current situation in tourism will (or should be allowed to) continue indefinitely. Export tourism will continue to be an important component in achieving growth and every effort should be taken to ensure that it will continue to expand as rapidly as possible. Current trends do suggest, however, that in the year's ahead growth rates will be constrained and, thus, any contribution to overall expansion will be limited, at least in the medium term. All the signs are that many of the major difficulties affecting tourism (e.g. uncompetitive prices, environmental issues and attitudinal problems) are features that permeate throughout the economy generally, and corrective measures will take time to have effect.[12] While acknowledging the pressures of international competition, tourism is, nonetheless, an area where corrective measures are largely in our own hands, and thus offers real opportunities for contributing to growth.

On the basis of the above brief sectoral review, international business services would appear to be the most obvious export oriented area which offers the opportunity to generate rapid or above average growth and become the prime focus or centrepiece of overall economic advance. Expansion in this area (both in a domestic and international context) has the added advantage in that it involves high value added activities and thus can make an important contribution to raising overall productivity levels. It should be mentioned that 'services exports' as referred to in this context are intended to embrace more than what may be described as conventional commercial activities. It also covers professional expertise in areas such as professional and technical agricultural assistance, education, public administration etc.

This is, in fact, an area which has already been recommended for targeting by the State development agencies and, indeed, considerable progress has been made to date. [13] The value of services exports from Ireland increased nearly fourfold between 1998 and 2005 from €12.4 billion to €46.1 billion, representing an annual average rise of over 20 per cent.[14] While a volume series is not available, the scale of domestic and international price movements over this period makes it clear that this is a very substantial advance in real terms.[15] Within this broad services category business and financial services accounted for about €39 billion in 2005 (85 per cent), within which computer services comprised €15 billion, or nearly a third of the overall total. Nearly two thirds of Irish service exports went to EU25 countries, but a surprisingly small share (just over five per cent) went to the US and Canada. The latter feature does, perhaps, point to an area which offers opportunities for further expansion.

One notable setback in relation to fostering international trade in services (outside of the EU) is the failure of the recent WTO Trade Negotiations (in which services was an important element) to conclude a satisfactory agreement. While this may have caused some interests here to heave a sigh of relief, in the wider context of overall growth prospects for Ireland it is a setback, and is likely to result in a slower rate of expansion in world trade than would otherwise emerge. However, the threads of these negotiations are likely to be picked up again, and the general movement towards greater free trade is likely to continue, even if more slowly.

1.4.3 Productivity

Finally the trends in recent years which reveal a marked decline in labour productivity growth in the economy call for some comment.[16] At present productivity growth seems to have ceased, and may well turn negative, at least for a time. Our analysis indicates that changes in the sectoral profile of the economy has been a significant influence in reducing overall productivity growth in recent years, even though output per worker in some sectors (e.g. building) has also contributed to this. With regard to structures, the rapid decrease in the relative importance in the economy of the manufacturing sector (especially in the high-technology area) has been a major causative factor. Falling productivity in building and construction has tended to attract much attention in the current debate, but in fact changing sectoral structures have been a more important, if silent, influence. The nature of these influences would suggest that any significant resumption of productivity growth is unlikely in the short-term, unless substantial employment increases occur in high value added sectors such as finance and business services.

The imperative of having to compete in the high-skill/technically advanced end of the global market renders it essential that national productivity be enhanced, not only by targeting high value added sectors, but also through productivity across the wider spectrum of economic activities. In this context recent Government initiatives to aid and promote research and development and high-skill education/training are to be welcomed.

The achievement of higher productivity should not, however, be regarded solely as an end in itself. The average output per worker or per inhabitant may well increase, but it may conceal a less than equitable distribution of the additional wealth created, with some interests benefiting, and others being left behind. This is an issue on which the Celtic Tiger phenomenon has been criticised. Therefore redistributive options may have to be considered, bearing in mind the need to maintain growth rates and to remain globally competitive.

Notes

1 This chapter is a shortened version of Sexton (2006).
2 Typically, on the basis of recent data, this aggregate represents almost 90 per cent of GDP at market prices. Annual average real GVA growth between 1995 and 2005 was seven per cent, compared with 7.3 per cent for GDP.
3 The share of persons in part-time work remained reasonably constant over the period covered. It is unlikely, therefore that part-time work trends would have a major effect on productivity movements in the period under consideration. It should be noted that, in any event, the chapter contains a supplementary analysis in which productivity is based on hours worked rather than employment.
4 In terms of the EU NACE industrial classification the categories cover classes 223, 24, 30, 31, 32 and 33.
5 It should be noted that while most of the sectoral data shown was provided by the CSO, the separate trend volume indicators for financial and business services and the residual services category were estimated by the author as the CSO could only provide aggregate figures. The methodology used is described in Sexton (2006).
6 There is evidence to suggest that the secondary effects are significant (O'Malley, 1995).
7 Further insights into the issues raised here are given in O'Malley and McCarthy (2006).
8 Comparable data on hours worked are not available for the years prior to 1998.
9 The indexes for the European Union relate to EU15, as the relevant data for some of the ten new Member States were not available for the full period under consideration.
10 The recent WTO trade negotiations which took place in Geneva are of particular relevance in this regard. The outcome may not have been satisfactory, but the movement towards freer trade is likely to continue.
11 The annual average GDP deflator was 3.7 per cent over the same period.
12 Many of these problems were highlighted in the Tourism Policy Review Group Report (2003).
13 See also, Enterprise Strategy Group Report (2004).
14 CSO (a) Balance of International Payments Q1 2006. (b) Service Exports and Imports 2003 and 2004. (c) Website database on Services Exports and Imports.
15 Further evidence of the growth in business services in Ireland is indicated by the rapid increase in employment in this sector between 1995 and 2005 (see Table 1.3). This data covers both domestic and external service activities.
16 For a further analysis of national productivity issues see Tansey (2005).

References

CSO (2005), Annual Tourism and Travel Data 2005 (and earlier), *Central Statistics Office.*

Enterprise Strategy Group (2004), *Ahead of the Curve: Ireland's Place in the Global Economy*, Forfás, Dublin.

Keating, W. (2000), "Measuring the Economy – Problems and Prospects", read before the *Statistical and Social Inquiry Society of Ireland* on 26 October, Dublin.

Keenan, B. (2006), "All These Extra Jobs, But Where is the Output?", *Irish Independent,* 20 July.

O'Malley, E. (1995), "An Analysis of Secondary Employment Associated with the Manufacturing Industry", *ESRI General Research Series,* paper No.167, Dublin.

O'Malley, E. and McCarthy, Y. (2006), "New Drivers of Growth? Sectoral Contributions to the Irish Economy", *ESRI Quarterly Economic Commentary,* Dublin.

Sexton, J.J. (2006), "A Review of Recent Trends in Output, Employment and Productivity in Ireland", read before the *Statistical and Social Inquiry Society of Ireland* on 19 October, Dublin.

Tansey, P. (2005), *Productivity: Ireland's Economic Imperative. A Study of Ireland's Productivity Performance and the Implications for Ireland's Future Economic Success,* published by Microsoft.

Tourism Policy Review Group (2003), *New Horizons for Irish Tourism – An Agenda for Action,* report presented to the Minster for Arts, Sport and Tourism, Dublin.

CHAPTER 2

SERVICE SECTOR PRODUCTIVITY: THE TIGER'S NEXT CHALLENGE?

DIANA FARRELL, JAANA REMES AND CONOR KEHOE

ABSTRACT

By 2004, value added per person at work in manufacturing industries was twice that recorded in services sectors and the gap between the two widened considerably since 1995. The underperformance of the service sector is critical for the Irish economy since two out of three people in the workforce are now employed in services. This chapter dispels some myths surrounding service sector productivity, and based on McKinsey's research of domestic service sectors provides some key policy priorities relevant to Ireland if it is to improve its productivity performance in this area.

2.1 Introduction

Ireland posted productivity growth of 63 per cent between 1995 and 2002, making it the best performer in Europe. But Ireland's productivity record is not as impressive as this headline figure suggests, and further progress may prove difficult. Indeed, Ireland's productivity progress is now slipping, according to the latest statistical evidence.

Research by the McKinsey Global Institute (MGI) has found that 70 per cent of this productivity growth has come from foreign-owned companies in just a handful of sectors—high-tech components, chemicals, electrical machinery, food and drink, and IT services. Although these companies have proved dynamic, importing best practice into Ireland's economy, they still contribute just under a quarter of Ireland's total GDP and employ only 15 per cent of the country's workforce. Productivity growth outside these sectors has been patchy and, in some cases, weak. Productivity improvement in agriculture has proved elusive; but even more pertinently for a modern economy, service-sector productivity has been weak.

Figure 2.1: Index of Private Service Sector Productivity, 2003

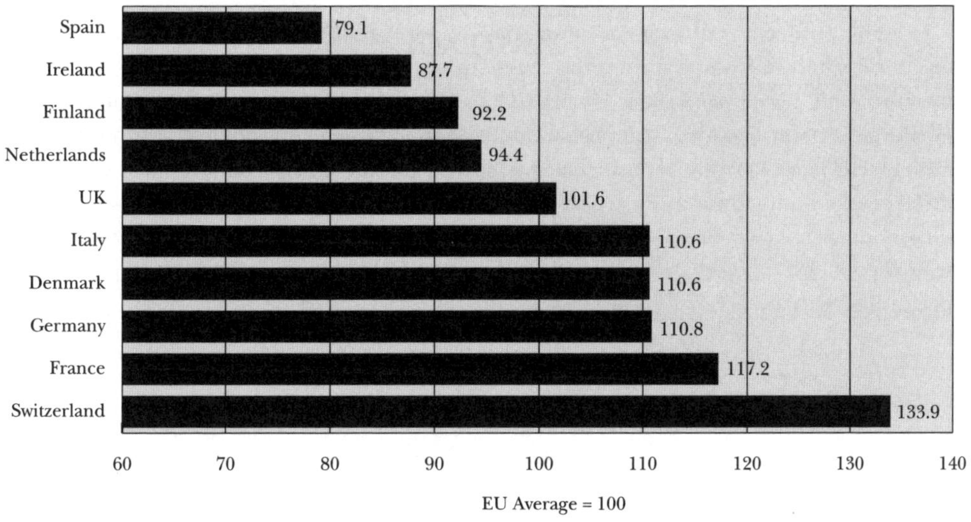

Source: European Competitiveness Index, 2004.

MGI research shows that service sectors, excluding IT, contributed just 14 per cent to the productivity increase posted in Ireland between 1995 and 2002, but was responsible for the employment of 55 per cent of the workforce. In retailing, for example, Irish productivity is clearly below the average of the 15 Member States of the European Union prior to the latest round of enlargement in 2004.[1] Measuring the performance of this sector in terms of value added per employee, Irish retail stood at 88 per cent of the EU-15 average. In retail banking, our research found that productivity in Ireland stood at roughly half the level recorded in Belgium and Sweden—the two countries with the highest productivity in this sector. Service providers may argue that they cannot exploit economies of scale in Ireland's relatively small economy. But Finland, with a comparable GDP, exceeds the EU-15's overall average service productivity by 26 per cent while Ireland exceeds it by just seven per cent. In terms of productivity growth in retail banking, Ireland posted a compound annual growth rate in productivity per employee in the period between 1995 and 2002 of three per cent. This compared with 9.9 per cent in Portugal, 5.6 per cent in Spain, 4.4 per cent in Germany, and 3.8 per cent in the Netherlands.

Ireland's productivity imperative has been accentuated by the fact that it has now become a relatively high-wage economy with a rising population. After years of net emigration, Ireland is now seeing the return of many of its citizens who had been living and working in the diaspora. In these circumstances, it is vital for Ireland to achieve broad gains in productivity.

Research by the MGI across a number of middle-income and developed economies has consistently shown a strong link between competitiveness, productivity, and economic growth, and has found surprisingly significant potential in creating this virtuous circle in domestic service industries (McKinsey Global Institute, 2005). It is clear that services are the best source of long-term employment and economic growth for developed economies. Domestic services have the potential to create more jobs in Ireland than service exports and raising the productivity of Ireland's domestic service sector is the key to the country's continuing economic renaissance.

2.2 Ireland's Productivity Record

Ireland's productivity growth was substantially above the European average during the 1980s, and the highest in Europe during the 1990s, using the Central Bank of Ireland's preferred measure, GNP per hour worked (Hurley, 2005). Using another measure—Gross Value Added (GVA) per person at work—Irish productivity rose by almost 36 per cent in real terms between 1995 and 2004, an increase of more than 3.5 per cent a year over a period of nine years (Tansey, 2005).

Figure 2.2: Sectoral Contribution to Productivity Growth and Employment Share by Sector.

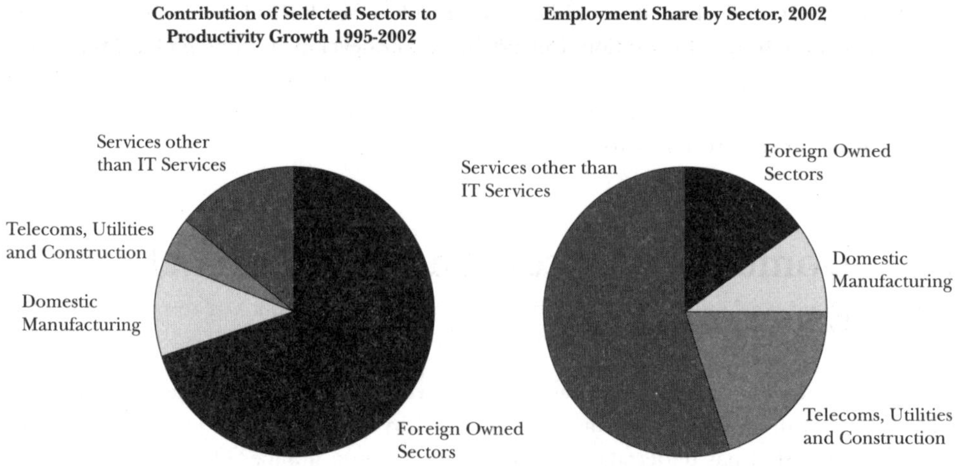

Source: Groningen Growth and Development Centre; McKinsey Global Institute analysis.

Note: Foreign Owned Sectors includes high-tech components, chemicals, electrical machinery, food and drink and IT services.

However, it is clear that most of that productivity increase has come from manufacturing and, within manufacturing, has been dominated by foreign-owned companies in a limited number of sectors. By 2004, value added per person at work in industry was twice that in services and the gap between the two widened considerably between 1995 and 2004. Productivity growth in services was relatively subdued between 1995 and 2004. Real GVA per person edged ahead by just 9.1 per cent, a compound growth rate of less than one per cent a year. This poor productivity performance is particularly critical for the Irish economy because two out of three people in the workforce are employed in services and 80 per cent of new jobs generated by the Irish economy between 1995 and 2004 were in the services sector.

Evidence of a particularly large gap between the productivity performance of Irish industry versus services comes from a 2003 study by the European Commission, which compared hourly labour productivity growth in the business sector from 1996 to 2000 (Cassidy, 2004). The results showed that Ireland saw total business productivity rise by 8.4 per cent during this period, 7.3 per cent of which came from manufacturing and only 1.8 per cent from private services. In comparison, the United Kingdom saw a total increase of 2.6 per cent, with 1.9 per cent coming from private services and only 0.8 per cent from manufacturing. In the United States, the total business productivity increase was 3.1 per cent with 2.0 per cent coming from private services and 1.2 per cent from manufacturing.

In recent years, the pace of overall productivity growth has decelerated with GNP-based measures of output per worker showing growth of less than one per cent from 2000 to 2004. According to the Governor of Ireland's Central Bank, productivity growth in Ireland's manufacturing sector has slowed significantly in the past two years from more than 14 per cent in 2002 to around 3.5 per cent in 2004 (Hurley, 2005). In the first half of 2005, the Bank said that, on a year-on-year basis, productivity growth in manufacturing was negative.

The Bank noted that this weakening reflected the overall slowdown in economic growth during this period, but judged that it is unlikely that labour productivity growth can recover to the high rates Ireland experienced in the late 1990s (Cassidy, 2004). There is concern that the stellar overall productivity-growth performance of Ireland in recent years could have been largely a one-off due to the significant influx of Foreign Direct Investment (FDI). If the rate of FDI flows were to decline, it would be very difficult to see Ireland being able to replicate these gains in the future. In addition, Ireland, like other developed economies, is likely to see a gradual, continuing shift from manufacturing to services and this, without action to boost productivity in service sectors, will mean that overall productivity growth will fail to keep pace with the experience of recent years.

2.3 Domestic Services -The International Experience

The experience of other economies around the world offers a strong argument to Irish policy makers to turn their attention to the weak productivity of its ever-more important domestic services sector. MGI has undertaken extensive research in a number of middle-income and developed economies, which shows that domestic services account for more than 60 per cent of all jobs and virtually all net new job creation (Figure 2.3). Since 1997, employment has declined in the goods-producing sectors of most developed and many developing economies and it is increasingly clear that, given the increasing share of services in consumption and labour-saving new technologies, manufacturing is unlikely to prove a sustainable source for employment growth in any economy in the future.

Figure 2.3: Service Sector as a Percentage of GDP, 1970-2001

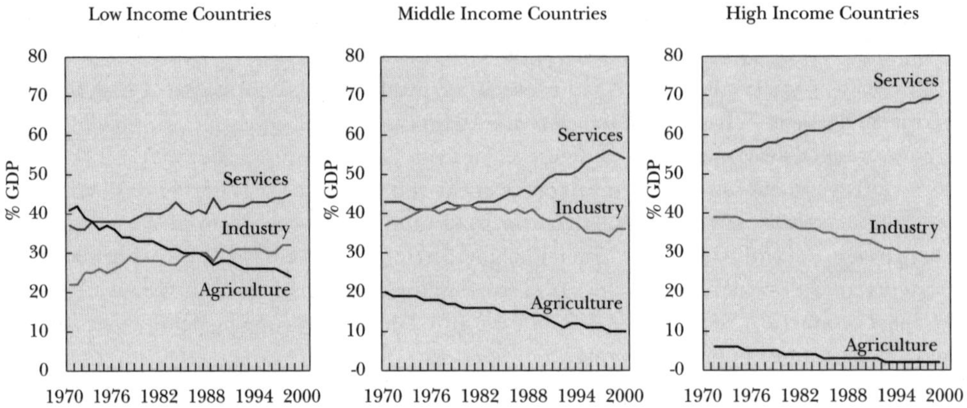

Source: World Bank; World Development Indicators.

Domestic services suffer from an economic image problem. Too often, they are regarded as a poor relation to high-tech sectors, manufacturing exports, and high value-added services that can be exported internationally. But domestic services are much more than fast-food vending or shoe repair. In Ireland, and around the world, they also comprise very significant sectors that are crucial to economic development, including power supply, transport, retail, construction and telecommunications, as well as a range of high-skill, high-wage occupations, from accountants, to advertisers, to rock stars.

As economies grow richer, business-to-business services represent an increasing share of total economic activity. These activities include professional services such as law, accountancy and consulting; technical services such as IT and software support; wholesale trade services and employment services. The recent rapid growth in business services in developed economies is an outcome of specialisation. As companies focus increasingly on their core competencies, they buy more non-core services from third parties.

Figure 2.4: The Share of Services, 2004

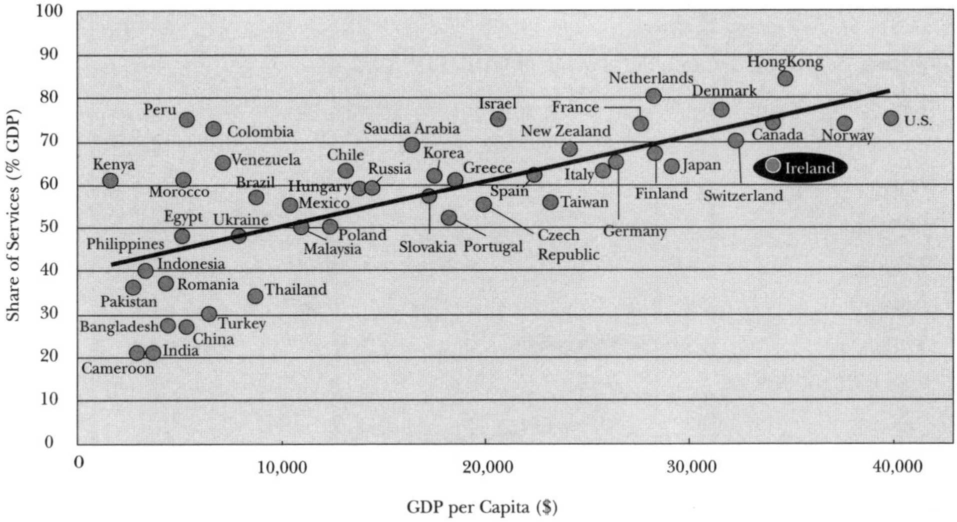

Source: World Development Indications, Global Insight.

The sheer size of domestic service sectors makes them powerful drivers of overall GDP growth, and their share of the economy rises as countries develop (Figure 2.4). Services account for roughly half of GDP in India and the Philippines, but 68 per cent in Japan and 75 per cent in the United States. The quality of those services affects growth rates in other sectors because every enterprise must use them. Efficient, good-value domestic services also help to attract FDI. India's offshoring sector, for example, did not take off until telecom reforms were adopted in the early 1990s.

As a result of more efficient use of labour, automation, and new IT, manufacturing employment is shrinking. Despite policy efforts to preserve them, roughly 22 million manufacturing jobs disappeared worldwide between 1995 and 2002. Even China, the so-called 'factory floor' of the world, has shed more than 15 million manufacturing jobs since 1995. So, as MGI research shows, services are now critical to sustain growth, to create jobs, and to boost productivity (Figure 2.5).

Figure 2.5: Contribution of Services to Job Growth

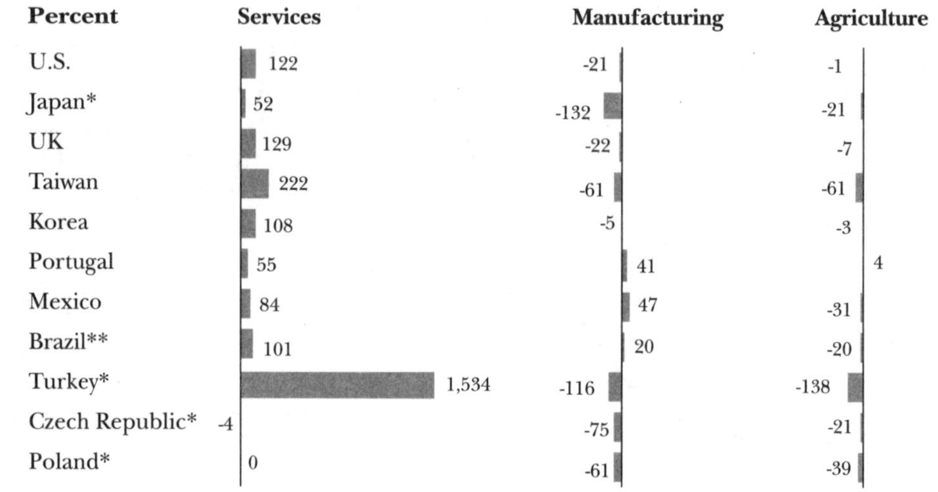

Source: OECD.

Notes: *Negative overall net job creation means that sector contributions sum up to -100 per cent.

**1997-2001.

Among middle and high-income economies today, services generate 62 per cent of all employment on average, and the higher a country's GDP per capita, the higher the share of service employment. Somewhat surprisingly, service industries actually create more high-skilled occupation than manufacturing. In the United States, more that 30 per cent of service jobs are in the highest-skill category of professional, technical, managerial, and administrative occupations. In contrast, only 12 per cent of all manufacturing jobs are in this category, and the same pattern holds in other developed nations (OECD, 2005). Services also provide many well-paid blue-collar jobs, such as electricians, plumbers and auto mechanics. In fact, the distribution of wages in the United States looks broadly similar in services and manufacturing (Figure 2.6).

Figure 2.6: The Distribution of Manufacturing and Service Earnings

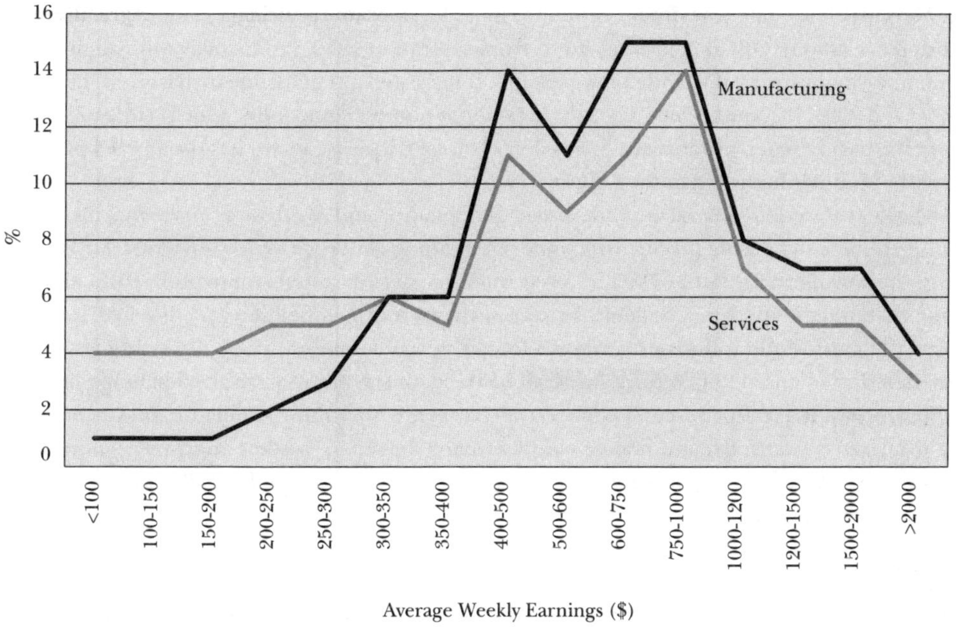

Source: US Census Bureau, Current Population Survey.

There are more low-wage jobs in services, but also many high-wage jobs. The variance within each sector is actually greater than the variance between them. Moreover the experience of some countries in Europe shows that trying to contain growth in low-skill jobs by imposing high minimum wages and other labour market restrictions results in higher overall unemployment, not more high-skill jobs.

The failure to promote productivity in services has been a significant factor holding back major economies. Take Japan. By the end of the last century Japan's world-class manufacturers of autos, steel, machine tools and consumer electronics were legendary for their performance. However, their manufacturing output made up only ten per cent of GDP, while productivity in the rest of the economy was very poor relative to US levels (Kondo et al., 2000).

Low productivity in local services goes a long way towards explaining why Japanese GDP growth tailed off in the 1990s, just as subsequent incremental reforms of service sectors helps to explain the recent improvement in Japan's economic performance. Japan's Cabinet Office calculates that deregulating telecoms, transport, energy, finance and retailing were responsible for 4.6 per cent of the country's GDP in 2002 (The Economist, 2005).

In Europe, service industries, from hairdressers to retailers to accountants, accounted for some 70 per cent of Europe's GDP and all of its net job creation over the past five years. But services continue to be crippled by a thicket of regulation. Germany, for instance, limits retailers' opening hours; Portuguese hotels must employ a set number of staff in each job category, depending on the hotel's size; and across the Continent, family-run corner shops with low productivity and relatively high prices are protected by tax and zoning laws.

MGI studied six major European countries and found that their low growth and high unemployment were not caused by a lack of technology (as many European policymakers believe) but rather from too little competition.

Sweden is an interesting case (McKinsey Global Institute, 2006). At the beginning of the 1990s, Sweden went through its own share of turbulence, which threatened to eat away at its generous welfare state and vibrant economy. By 1998, Sweden's per capita income had fallen to 16th place among OECD countries, down from seventh in 1980. Productivity was flagging and unemployment rising. But, with a few changes, it managed a remarkable turnaround. Between 1998 and 2004, income growth has outstripped that of most comparable OECD countries. And over the past 12 years, productivity in Sweden's private corporate sector has risen by 3.3 per cent a year - 1.5 times higher than the OECD average.

The key to Sweden's revival was widespread deregulation and regulatory reform that increased competition and boosted productivity while maintaining generous social provisions. First, entry into the European Union in 1995 lowered trade barriers, boosted competition from abroad, and encouraged efficiency. Second, stricter antitrust and competition laws levelled industry playing fields; whole industries could no longer adopt common prices, for example. Third, Sweden started micro-level reform. In retail banking, new entrants were given banking licenses which intensified competition. Sweden's retail banks are now more productive than their peers in the United States, Britain, France, and Germany. In retail, Sweden improved zoning laws, giving new entrants access to land. As a result, productivity improved rapidly and food prices fell by more than 25 per cent compared with other European countries.

Sweden has more to do in order to ensure that its productivity improvement continues, particularly in an era in which so many service jobs are offshored. For instance, Sweden continues to be hobbled by high employment taxes that make services such as restaurants and retailing prohibitively expensive. For instance, Swedish pay rates go up by about 70 per cent for overtime on weekday evenings and 100 per cent on weekends, raising the cost of opening stores at these times and limiting employment. Britain's retail sector, without such regulations, employs almost twice as many workers per capita as Sweden's does. Sweden's construction sector, too, continues to suffer from over-regulation, which have curtailed its annual productivity increases to only 0.7 per cent since 1990.

2.4 Four Myths About Service Sector Productivity

Despite the increasing importance of domestic services to growth and job creation evident in middle-income and developed economies, there has been little focus on how to improve productivity in services sectors. A number of myths about service industries have been demotivational:

Myth 1: Reforming Domestic Services will not Improve Productivity Significantly Because They Offer So Little Scope for Innovation;

Productivity improvements in service industries like electricity supply and telecommunications have been important drivers of overall productivity growth in developed economies. For example, in the United States, the late 1990s boom in productivity was due in large part to innovations in service industries such as retail, wholesale, and financial services—not just high-tech sectors. Indeed, MGI's studies of countries around the world show that gaps between productivity levels in their large, employment intensive local-service sectors, such as retail and construction, explain a substantial amount of the gaps between their respective GDP per head figures. In Turkey, labour productivity in manufacturing averaged 64 per cent of the US level but only 33 per cent in services.

Retail sector reforms are particularly important in triggering productivity growth, partly because these sectors employ so many people, and partly because improvements here stimulate productivity advances among upstream suppliers. For example, the liberalised retail sector in the US has been one of the top three contributors to aggregate productivity increases since 1995. Research has shown that removing restrictions on outlet size, opening hours, or product selection from retailers in other OECD countries would allow their retailers likewise to streamline distribution systems and grow both sales volumes and employment. Their consumers, too, would benefit from lower prices and a broader array of services (Nicoletti and Scarpetta, 2003).

Myth 2: Manufacturing Jobs are Higher Skilled and Better Paid than Services Work;

On the contrary, service industries create more high skilled occupations than manufacturing. In the United States, more than 30 per cent of service jobs are in the highest-skill category of occupations, which includes managers, researchers and engineers, in contrast to only 12 per cent of all manufacturing jobs. Further, as we have noted, the distribution of wages across the US service and manufacturing sectors is similar.

Myth 3: Manufacturing Jobs are More Stable than Jobs in Services;

This clearly cannot be true since manufacturing employment is shrinking worldwide. It is the case that job turnover in service industries tends to be higher than in manufacturing. However, service jobs provide a much more reliable source of overall employment than manufacturing. In any given year, on average roughly ten per cent of all jobs in an economy come to an end because workers quit or become redundant. More jobs end in services than manufacturing, particularly in service segments dominated by small-scale operations, with their relatively high failure rates.

Service industries as a whole, however, create more jobs than they lose, often through the activity of new entrants (Davis and Haltiwanger as cited in Ashenfelter and Card, 1991).[2] Creating a dynamic service sector, therefore, more reliably guarantees lifetime employment opportunities for everyone, if not the same job for life. For example, from 1977 to 1987, the US auto repair industry lost 49 per cent of its jobs, but at the same time took on new employees in jobs equivalent to 56 per cent of total employment in the industry. So although almost half of all auto repair jobs ended over the period, net employment in the sector grew by seven per cent (Foster, Haltiwanter and Kirzan, 1988). Data from middle-income economies, albeit limited, suggest that the prevailing dynamics of service job destruction and creation are similar (Davis and Haltiwanger, 1991).

Myth 4: Reforming Service Sectors will Lead to More Unemployment.

This fear centres on the retail sector, where big modern stores could drive out smaller, traditional ones. Policymakers rightly believe that more productive supermarket and discount formats will drive out traditional, less productive, small stores. But this is precisely how economies develop, resulting in a bigger national income for everyone to share and higher overall employment. This fear ignores the fact that larger stores offer lower prices and better service, which boosts demand and causes stores to hire more people. This is why the United States, with its highly productive retail sector, employs proportionally more people in this sector than countries where traditional stores prevail.

2.5 How To Develop A Dynamic Local Service Sector

Some key policy priorities emerged from MGI's research into the domestic services sectors of middle-income and developed economies and their key role in driving productivity improvement. Some - including the lack of level playing fields in terms of fiscal, financial, and development policies between services and manufacturing - are pertinent in many developing economies and do not particularly apply to Ireland. However, a number of policy areas are particularly relevant to Ireland if it is to improve service sector productivity:

1. **Remove Product Market Barriers Limiting Competition in Services;**
   MGI productivity studies have shown that the biggest barrier to increased competition is inappropriate product-market regulations governing service sectors, which hinder the diffusion of more productive processes. Product-market regulations govern company ownership, trade, FDI, land use, prices, and products. Misconceived regulations make competition less intense by limiting the entry of new players (particularly global ones), discouraging innovation among existing competitors, and restricting enterprise scale (Lewis, 2004).

   The Annual Competitiveness Report, 2005, issued by the National Competitiveness Council, concluded that taxation and regulation remains one of Ireland's strengths, noting that Ireland's corporation tax rate and personal tax rates were low by international comparison and that labour market regulations do not hinder business relative to other countries. However, it noted that the "intensity of local competition and the efficiency of competition legislation is perceived as being low" (National Competitiveness Council, 2005).

   A report on productivity by Forfás also called for market liberalisation to increase competition, make markets more responsive to change and increase the speed of diffusion of new productivity-enhancing innovation (Forfás, 2006). The report cited the OECD's survey of Ireland, which observed that there are many sectors in Ireland—including electricity, telecoms, law, pharmacies, and the pub trade—where producers are shielded from competition. It also noted a range of factors that inhibit service-sector innovation including market-related obstacles such as rigid industry-specific structures and a lack of competition or overcapacity in certain industry sectors.

2. **Reduce Public Sector Ownership;**
   Utilities, telecommunications, and banking remain in government hands in many emerging and even developed economies and lack of investment and low productivity in such businesses stunt not only their own, but also their customers' growth. Ireland's electricity sector, for instance, remains in state hands and a recent report by Deloitte concluded that labour costs in the Power Generation unit at ESB are 20 to 30 per cent higher than those of comparative electricity generators in Europe, and that Ireland ranks consistently in the top three most expensive countries for industrial consumers of electricity in Europe (Deloitte, 2005).

3. **Revise Unnecessary Barriers to Scale;**
   Scale can yield substantial productivity gains to enterprises. Yet many companies face limits to scale, like restrictions on store size and land use, which makes them less productive. Many governments also restrict store sizes, including the Irish government, which has recently made an exception to allow Swedish mass-retailer IKEA to open up a store in the country. This may protect small stores from large-scale retail outlets, but at the cost of higher retail productivity.

4. **Eliminate Red Tape;**
   Streamlining what businesses must do to comply will also encourage them to enter the formal sector. Lots of companies, for example, never register because the process is so long and complicated. In an unpublished working paper in 2003, the noted economist and author Hernando de Soto found that in Egypt it takes an average of 549 days to register a new bakery. Levying taxes on unregistered businesses is almost impossible, hence the importance of making registration simpler. Simplifying tax practices will compound the benefit. In Ireland, a 2003 survey, cited in a 2004 speech by Bertie Ahern the Irish Taoiseach, found that 72 per cent of companies found it difficult to keep track of regulations affecting their business, while 62 per cent said that they believed the regulatory burden was growing.[3] In January 2004, the Government launched a White Paper, Regulating Better, which included proposals for reviews of the regulatory regime for different economic sectors, more transparent and accessible legislation and reductions in red tape.

5. **Facilitate 'Creative Destruction' in Services.**
   Services are dynamic by nature. To maximise overall service employment, companies must be free to start up, grow and create more jobs or - if they can't compete - they shrink, lay off workers and close. To lubricate this process of creative destruction, governments need to make detailed policy changes to make it simpler to create and grow new firms, and close failing ones; and to enhance labour mobility. Forfás argues that, within services, there are many generic 'soft' skills that are transferable across sectors, including ICT literacy, communication, team-building, language, process, organisational and management skills. Wide availability of such skills - which Ireland needs to develop through the educational system, particularly at secondary and higher education levels - across the economy, it argues, will enhance labour market flexibility and enable increased mobility between services sectors according to market demands (Forfás, 2006).

2.6 Conclusion

Policymakers in different economies around the world have not placed nearly as much emphasis on domestic services as on, for instance, import substitution, export manufacturing, and more recently, services for export. But dynamic, competitive local services can unlock a huge contribution to overall GDP growth and employment. In fact, achieving higher productivity in local services is the only way for middle income - and developed - economies to ensure lifetime employment for all.

Given recent evidence that Ireland's productivity boom has not only been very narrowly based in the foreign-owned segments of manufacturing but has now markedly decelerated economy-wide, it is time for Irish policymakers to examine how to create the competitive environment in domestic services that have the potential to become a powerful source of wealth creation and jobs.

Notes

1 The pre-2004 expansion Member States were Austria, Belgium, Denmark, Finland, France, Germany, Greece, Ireland, Italy, Luxembourg, the Netherlands, Portugal, Spain, Sweden, and the United Kingdom.

2 Our turnover rates reported here reflect the share of jobs being destroyed and replaced by others - or half of the excess reallocation rate used in the economic literature (sum of creation and destruction rates minus the absolute value of net employment change).

3 Speech by the Taoiseach, Mr Bertie Ahern, T.D., at the IBEC Conference on EU-US Perspectives on Regulation, Dublin, April 2004.

References

Cassidy, M. (2004), "Productivity in Ireland: Trends and Issues", Central Bank of Ireland, *Quarterly Bulletin,* Spring.

Davis, J.S. and Haltiwanger, J. (1991), "Gross Job Flows", in Ashenfelter and Card (1991), "Handbook of Labour Economics", Vol. 3, 2711-2805.

Deloitte (2005), *Review of the Electricity Sector in Ireland, Final Report,* Deloitte, Dublin.

Forfás (2006), *The Changing Nature of Manufacturing and Services: Irish Trends and International Context,* Forfás, Dublin.

Foster, L., Haltiwanger, J. and Krizan, C.J. (1988), "Aggregate Productivity Growth: Lessons from Microeconomic Evidence", *NBER Working Paper,* 6803.

Hurley, J. (2005), "Innovation and Productivity in Ireland", speech by John Hurley, Governor, to *Leinster Society of Chartered Accountants,* 13th October, 2005.

Kondo, J., Lewis, W., Palmade, V. and Yokoyama, Y., (2000), "Reviving Japan's Economy", *The McKinsey Quarterly 2000 Special Edition,* Asia Revalued.

Lewis, B. (2004), *The Power of Productivity: Wealth, Poverty, and the Threat to Global Stability,* University of Chicago Press.

McKinsey Global Institute (2006), "Sweden's Growth Paradox", *The McKinsey Quarterly,* June.

McKinsey Global Institute (2005), "Domestic Services: The Hidden Key to Growth".

National Competitiveness Council (2005), *Annual Competitiveness Report 2005,* Forfás, Dublin.

Nicoletti, G. and Scarpetta, S. (2003), "Regulation, Productivity and Growth", OECD Economics Department, Working Paper No 347.

OECD (2006), "Economic Survey of Ireland".

OECD (2005), "Enhancing the Performance of Service Sectors".

Tansey, P. (2005), "Productivity: Ireland's Economic Imperative, A Study of Ireland's Productivity Performance and the Implications for Ireland's Future Economic Success", Available online: www.microsoft.com/ireland.

The Economist (2005), "Capitalism with Japanese Characteristics", 6th October.

CHAPTER 3

TRENDS IN THE REGIONAL ECONOMIC ACTIVITY OF IRELAND: THE ROLE OF PRODUCTIVITY

EDGAR MORGENROTH

ABSTRACT

The analysis in this chapter shows that the differential rate of growth in the manufacturing sector was the key driving force behind regional disparities in Ireland, and that this in turn has been driven by differential productivity growth. The degree to which the divergent pattern is due to the underlying industry characteristics was considered in detail. The analysis suggests that there are substantial differences between regions in terms of those characteristics and that these are significantly related to economic performance. These characteristics include the average scale, the degree of foreign ownership and the level of process sophistication, which in turn impact on the level of productivity and profitability.

3.1 Introduction

Perhaps the most pervasive feature about economic activity is that it is not spread evenly across space. Thus, regional disparities can be observed in all countries. Economists have extensively researched the underlying processes that lead to these disparities over the last decade and a half, following a long period over which economists largely ignored economic geography. This literature shows that while the uneven distribution of economic activity is an equilibrium phenomenon, this need not be the most efficient outcome as it results from externalities and path dependencies.[1] This justifies the political concerns about regionally balanced development. In Ireland, these political concerns appear to have grown over recent years with the Government seeking to bring about more balanced regional development through the National Development Plan and the National Spatial Strategy.[2]

The degree to which regional disparities can be observed depends crucially on the variable chosen. Thus, for example if one considers labour market indicators the differences between Irish regions are modest and declining. The difference between regions regarding the employment rate has declined from 7.7 per cent in 1998 down to 4.2 per cent in 2005. More strikingly, the unemployment rates across regions have converged almost continually between 1988 and 2005 with the gap between regions with the highest and lowest unemployment rates declining from 7.1 per cent to 2.9 per cent.[3] Another commonly used indicator is population growth. Again this shows that if anything, the more peripheral regions are performing better than those considered to be part of the core. Between 2002 and 2006 the slowest population growth was recorded in Dublin and the Mid-West while the fastest growth was recorded in the Mid-East and the Midlands. While the growth in these regions is likely to be related to the growth of the Greater Dublin metropolitan region, the growth in counties such as Leitrim, Cavan and Wexford also substantially exceeded the national average.

Turning to the variables more commonly considered by economists in relation to regional performance, a somewhat contradictory picture emerges. The overall gaps with regard to total per capita income and per capita output have declined between 1991 and 2003 from 33 per cent to 25 per cent and from 71 per cent to 66 per cent respectively. This suggests that there is convergence relating to these variables but a closer inspection through the calculation of the standard deviation reveals that while the level of income per capita has indeed converged, the level of per capita output has in fact diverged, which is a continuing trend (see Boyle et al., 1999 or O'Connor, 1999).

The fact that the labour market, demographic and income trends show convergence suggests that either the market is delivering a more even pattern of development or government policies aimed at generating more balanced regional development are effective. Of course there may well be a pay off between efficiency and spatial equity so this outcome is not necessarily the welfare maximising outcome.

While the regions are converging in terms of most variables, the divergence in output suggests that a closer analysis of output is warranted. This is clearly important for policy formation since the underlying driving forces that are behind the trends in output may well require policy intervention in order to safeguard the future economic performance at the regional level. In particular, the degree to which these differences are driven by productivity differences and their underlying factors is important and that is the subject of this chapter.

The analysis presented here updates previous work by Bradley and Morgenroth (1999) and to some extent the work of O'Leary (2001) which both covered the period to 1996 thus omitting a large part of the boom period of the late 1990s. In updating the analysis of Bradley and Morgenroth (1999), the focus is on the evolution of the key characteristics of the industrial sector at the regional level, rather than the analysis at the regional and county level at one point in time. Unfortunately, data limitations mean that a comprehensive analysis is only possible for manufacturing and thus the services sector, which is becoming increasingly important, has to be largely ignored.

This chapter is organised as follows. Section 3.2 considers the evolution of regional output and its structural change. Section 3.3 decomposes the growth in output per capita into its productivity and labour market components. Section 3.4 outlines in more detail the underlying industry characteristics at the regional level while Section 3.5 briefly reviews some other underlying factors. Section 3.6 summarises the findings and draws some conclusions.

3.2 Gross Value Added and Structural Change

As was outlined above, in terms of Gross Value Added (GVA) per capita, there appears to be a process of divergence across regions. This is apparent in Figure 3.1, which shows that apart from Dublin, only the South-West has a GVA per capita in excess of the national average. Thus, the highest level of output per capita is found in the two regions with the largest urban centres. While the relative position of Dublin has remained relatively stable the South-West has substantially improved its relative position over time. Indeed it is the region with the most substantial change in the index. Of course, Dublin and the South-West together account for 57 per cent of total GVA and so they substantially determine the national average. While the overall pattern is characterised by divergence, if one excludes Dublin and the South-West then no pattern of convergence or divergence is observed. Therefore the divergence is driven substantially by the change in the relative position of the South-West. The remainder of this section investigates the sources of the divergence in more detail. It is however important to note that, as was pointed out by O'Leary (1999; 2001) among others, the published GVA figures are distorted through transfer pricing and profit repatriation of foreign multinationals, which is more important in some regions than in others.

Figure 3.1: Index of per Capita GVA

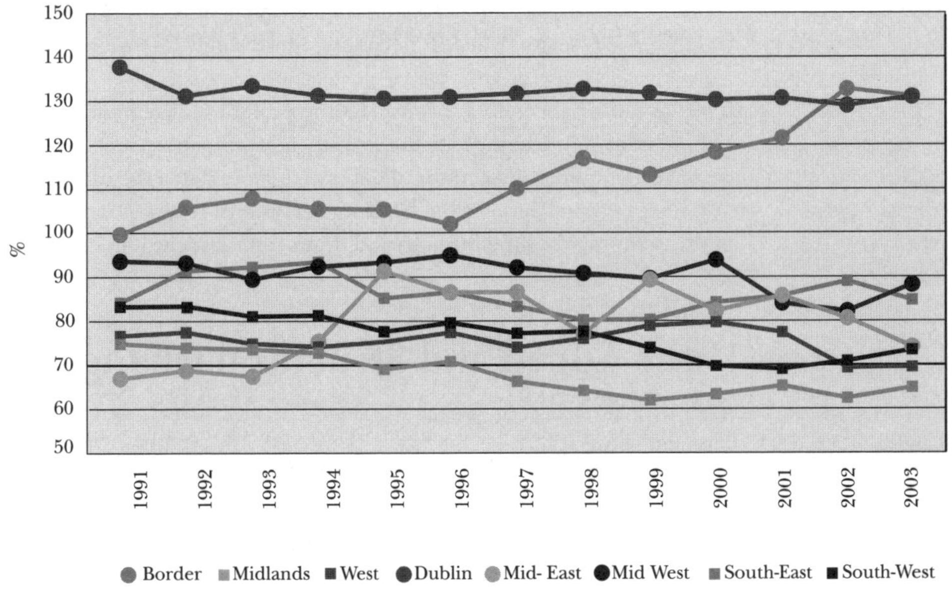

Source: CSO County Incomes and Regional GDP.

As a first step to analysing the sources of divergence, it is useful to consider the sectoral contributions to regional economic activity. A high share in more traditional activities and especially the primary sector has been shown to contribute to poor economic performance and consequently a shift towards more modern sectors contributes significantly to convergence (see Paci and Pigliaru, 1999).

Table 3.1 shows the sectoral shares to GVA in 1991 and 2003. The most striking feature is the substantial decline in the share of the primary sector (primarily agriculture) which now only accounts for 2.5 per cent of GVA. This trend is shared across all regions and indeed regions with a larger share in the primary sector in 1991 recorded a substantially faster decline than other regions (correlation coefficient –0.98). Industry recorded an overall increase in importance but this was not a trend shared across all regions, in that industry declined in importance in all regions except for the Mid-East, South-East and South-West. These regions also recorded a decline in the importance of market and non-market services, contrary to the overall trend of a growing importance of services. Unfortunately the data on the secondary sector cannot be disaggregated into building/construction and manufacturing, which would allow for an assessment of the role of the construction sector in driving the growth of the secondary sector.

Table 3.1: Sectoral Distribution of GVA by Branch, 1991 and 2003

Region	Agriculture, Forestry and Fishing		Manufacturing, Build. and Constr.		Market and Non Market Services		Total GVA
	1991	2003	1991	2003	1991	2003	
Border	13.1%	5.3%	42.4%	35.4%	44.5%	59.3%	100%
Midlands	15.5%	5.0%	35.6%	29.7%	48.9%	65.3%	100%
West	13.4%	4.6%	33.9%	30.2%	52.6%	65.2%	100%
Dublin	0.5%	0.2%	28.8%	27.0%	70.7%	72.7%	100%
Mid-East	12.2%	3.2%	36.9%	47.5%	50.9%	49.2%	100%
Greater Dublin	2.0%	0.8%	29.9%	30.6%	68.1%	68.6%	100%
Mid-West	11.3%	3.4%	41.3%	40.6%	47.4%	55.9%	100%
South-East	16.4%	4.9%	39.1%	4.0%	44.6%	51.1%	100%
South-West	12.7%	2.8%	42.0%	57.3%	45.3%	39.9%	100%
State	**8.2%**	**2.5%**	**35.2%**	**38.1%**	**56.6%**	**59.4%**	**100%**

Source: CSO County Incomes and Regional GDP.

It is possible to decompose the sectoral sources of regional growth and their contribution to overall growth relative to the national average (see Morgenroth and O'Malley, 2003), the results of which are shown in Table 3.2. As can be seen from the first set of rows in the table, in all regions except Dublin there was a negative growth rate for the primary sector. However, since the relative share of the primary sector is quite small its performance makes only a small contribution to the overall growth rate (see the second set of rows). The tertiary sector has on average the largest contribution to overall growth, but in the case of two regions, namely the Mid-East and the South-West, the secondary sector has grown particularly strongly.

Considering the performance of each sector in each region relative to the national performance of that sector (the third set of rows) reveals the source of the convergence trends. This analysis reveals that the performance of the secondary sector had the largest bearing on the convergence/divergence performance of the regions. Of course the data limitations do not allow for a disaggregating, which could reveal which sub-sector has contributed most to divergence. However, sectoral employment trends indicate that the regional differences in the building and construction sector may in fact be the source of the regional divergence. Furthermore, a more detailed sectoral breakdown, were it available, might indicate whether some of the divergence is simply driven by data distortions due to transfer pricing by foreign multinationals.

Table 3.2: Decomposition of Growth and Convergence

Region	Agriculture, Forestry and Fishing	Manufacturing, Build. and Constr.	Market and Non Market services	Total GVA
Sectoral Growth Rates				
Border	-1.7	6.0	15.0	9.0
Midlands	-3.1	6.3	15.6	9.4
West	-2.5	8.1	14.8	10.2
Dublin	0.5	9.5	11.2	10.7
Mid-East	-1.8	26.0	17.3	18.2
Greater Dublin	-1.3	12.2	11.8	11.7
Mid-West	-3.1	10.1	14.0	10.5
South-East	-2.8	15.0	15.4	12.3
South-West	-3.0	28.2	15.0	18.3
State	**-2.5**	**13.9**	**13.2**	**12.2**
Contributions to Total Growth Rate				
Border	-0.2	2.5	6.7	9.0
Midlands	-0.5	2.3	7.6	9.4
West	-0.3	2.8	7.8	10.2
Dublin	0.0	2.7	8.0	10.7
Mid-East	-0.2	9.6	8.8	18.2
Greater Dublin	0.0	3.6	8.1	11.7
Mid-West	-0.4	4.2	6.6	10.5
South-East	-0.5	5.8	6.9	12.3
South-West	-0.4	11.8	6.8	18.3
State	**-0.2**	**4.9**	**7.5**	**12.2**
Growth Relative to National Average				
Border	0.0	-2.4	-0.8	-3.2
Midlands	-0.3	-2.6	0.2	-2.8
West	-0.1	-2.1	0.3	-1.9
Dublin	0.2	-2.2	0.5	-1.5
Mid-East	0.0	4.7	1.3	6.0
Greater Dublin	0.2	-1.2	0.6	-0.5
Mid-West	-0.1	-0.7	-0.9	-1.7
South-East	-0.2	0.9	-0.6	0.1
South-West	-0.2	7.0	-0.7	6.1

Source: Own calculations using data from the CSO County Incomes and Regional GDP various issues (this data is also available from www.cso.ie).

3.3 The Role of Productivity Growth

Output growth is a function of productivity growth, employment growth and demographic factors and it is straightforward to decompose the total growth into these sources (see Bradley et al., 1997, and at the regional level O'Leary, 2001). More formally we can write the relationship as follows:

$$\frac{Y}{P} = \frac{Y}{L}\frac{L}{P}$$

where Y is the level of GVA, P is the population and L is the number of workers. Thus, GVA per capita is equal to GVA per worker times the employment rate. The latter term could be further decomposed into age dependency; labour force participation and the inverse of the unemployment rate (see Bradley et al., 1997). Since the focus of this paper is on productivity, the simple decomposition of the growth in output per capita is preferred here. Instead of decomposing GVA, O'Leary (2001) used this type of decomposition to analyse the sources of income growth where the effect of profit outflows is accounted for. He found that there was weak divergence between 1979 and 1996, which was largely due to a slowdown in productivity convergence. Here we focus our attention on the published data, which of course is distorted due to profit repatriation. However, since the published data is the data used for policymaking such as the determination of Structural Funds eligibility, it is nevertheless important to consider the official data.

Figure 3.2 shows the decomposition of output per capita growth into the two components, which together account for the total growth in output per capita. The figure shows that the growth of the employment rate was more evenly distributed across the regions than productivity growth, which was quite heterogeneous. Overall, the two contributed equally in the first two periods but in the more recent period productivity was the predominant source for growth. Particularly significant was the growth in productivity in the Mid-East for the second half of the 1990s and the strong growth in the South-West during all periods. The employment rate increased particularly strongly over the latter half of the 1990s but has not grown as strongly between 2000 and 2003.

Interestingly, the standard deviation of productivity growth has declined significantly from the early 1990s and the productivity growth in the more recent periods is negatively correlated with that in the early 1990s, which indicates that productivity growth differentials are decreasing. The decomposition suggests that over the more recent period productivity growth differentials were not responsible for the further widening in output disparities in the Border and Midlands regions while they actually helped the South-East in improving its relative position. However, in the West the decline in productivity has had a negative effect on the relative position in terms of output per capita.

A closer inspection of productivity at the sectoral level, which due to the lack of consistent sectoral employment data can only be conducted for the period 1994 to 2003, shows that the level of productivity in the primary sector has been steadily increasing and that productivity levels have been converging. This is consistent with positive structural change in the agricultural sector where the number of full time farmers has declined. On the other hand, productivity in industry, while recording strong growth on average, has not been evenly distributed and in fact has been subject to strongly divergent patterns. Finally, services productivity, while growing more modestly than that of industry, has not been subject to a divergent pattern. Thus, overall, the evidence suggests that the differential performance of industry is the significant driver of divergence in output per capita.

Figure 3.2: Average Productivity and Employment Growth Rate for Three Sub-Periods

(A)

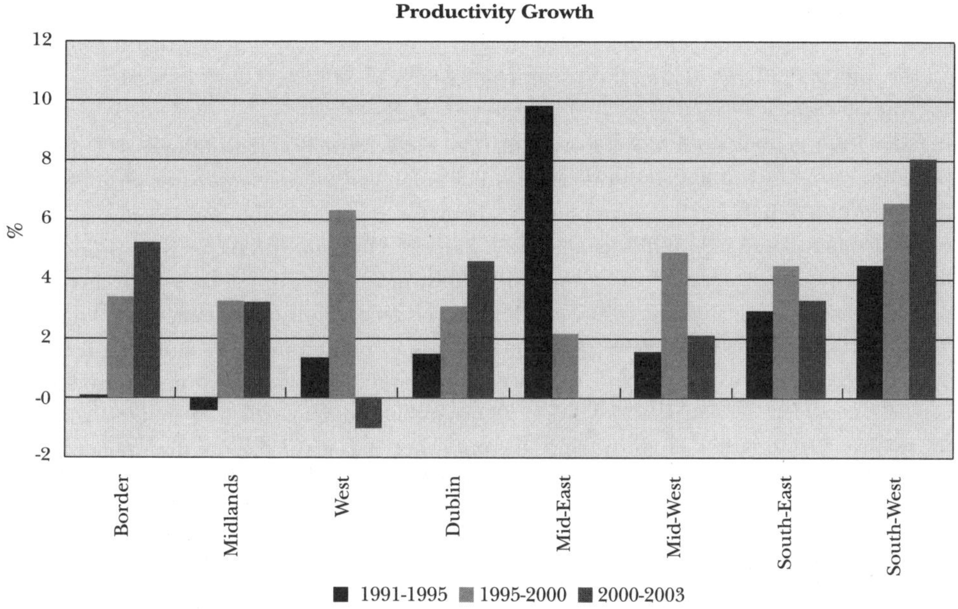

(B)

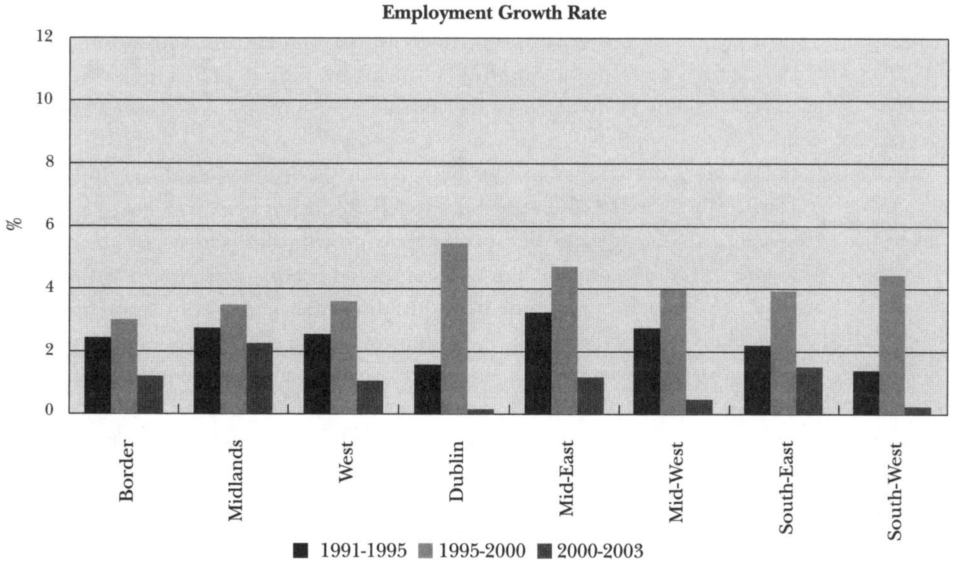

Source: Own Calculations using CSO County Incomes and Regional GDP, various issues, CSO Quarterly National Household Survey, CSO Labour Force Survey, CSO Census of Population, and CSO Population and Migration Estimates, various issues.

3.4 Regional Industrial Development

Following Bradley and Morgenroth (1999), it is useful to consider a small set of relevant indicators that capture the key characteristics of manufacturing at the regional level. Of particular interest will be to identify regions where the characteristics of the local manufacturing base are unfavourable (e.g., traditional activities, less skilled jobs, low pay, low technology, etc.). The variables considered here are:

1. Average plant size, which indicates the potential for plant level returns to scale;
2. The percentage of employment in foreign owned plants;
3. The ratio of industrial to administrative/technical workers is a proxy measure for the complexity of the regional industrial base (a high ratio indicates a more traditional type of manufacturing process);
4. Gross output and net output per local unit indicate average size of plants;
5. Net output per worker which measures the level of labour productivity; and
6. The wage bill expressed as a share of net output which gives a measure of the profitability of the regional manufacturing base.

Starting with the average size of these firms (Figure 3.3), this shows that during the 1980's the average size of manufacturing firms declined while it rose in the 1990's only to decline again in recent years. The largest average size is found in the Mid-West region while the lowest is found in the Border and Midlands regions. Overall this indicator is positively correlated with productivity suggesting that a greater scale does indeed result in significant economies.

Figure 3.3: Average Size of Firms

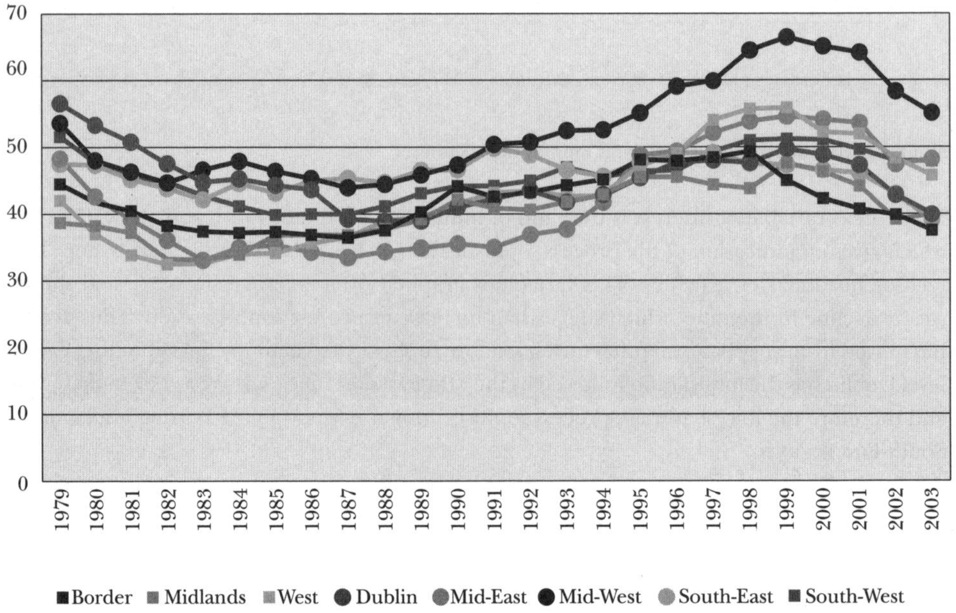

Source: Census of Industrial Production, various issues.

As was mentioned above, the importance of foreign owned firms differs between regions and this is an important source of data distortions especially with regard to output measures. It is therefore useful to consider the degree to which manufacturing employment is dominated by foreign firms at the regional level, which is shown in Figure 3.4. Overall the importance of foreign firms increased continuously in all regions until the early 1990s at which point a number of regions recorded a decline in the importance of foreign firms. This was particularly pronounced in the Midlands region where the foreign share declined from 51 per cent to 33 per cent. The Border region also recorded a declining share in foreign employment.

Figure 3.4: Percentage of Employment in Foreign Owned Firms

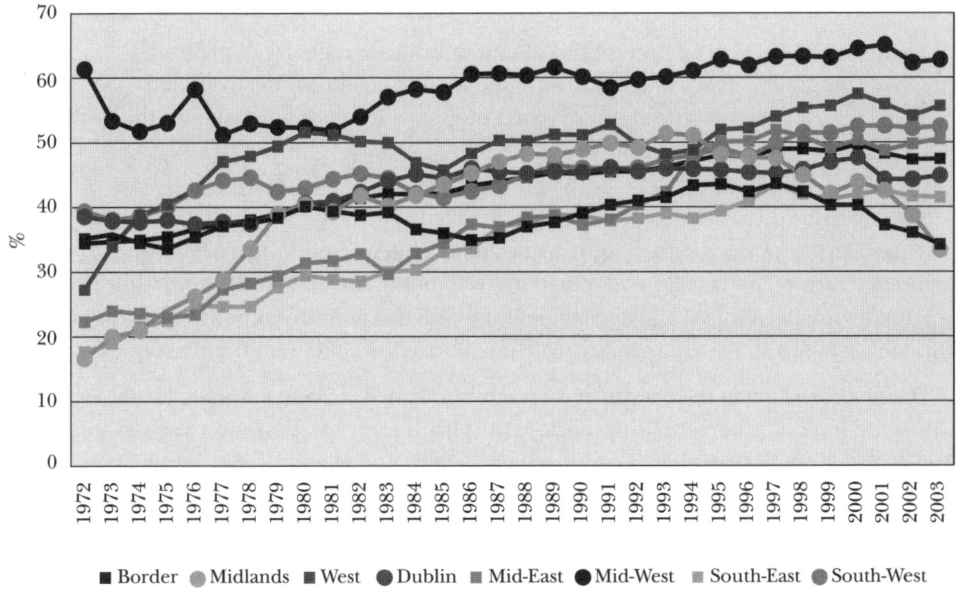

Source: Own Calculations using Forfás Employment Survey.

The next variable of interest is the ratio of industrial to administrative and clerical workers, which gives an indication of the process sophistication. A lower ratio is related with more high-tech or headquarter activities. This variable is graphed over time in Figure 3.5, and shows a steady decline in the ratio, which suggests an increase in process sophistication. Thus, Ireland has moved from very basic manufacturing to more sophisticated manufacturing. At the regional level Dublin has the lowest ratio followed by the Mid-East and the South-West. The highest ratios and therefore the lowest average process sophistication are found in the Border, Midlands and South-East regions.

Figure 3.5: Ratio of Industrial Workers to Administrative and Clerical Workers

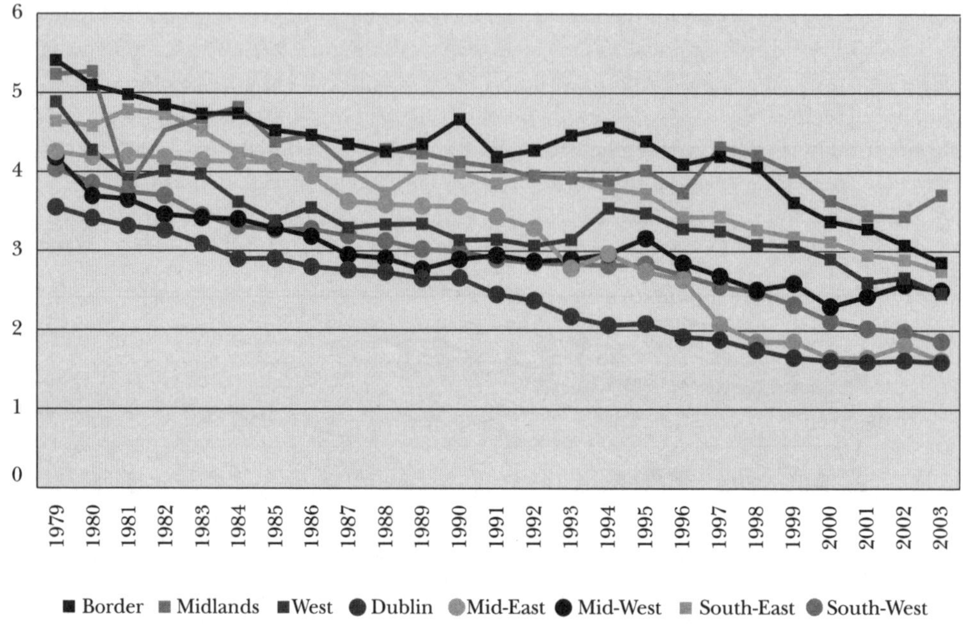

Source: Census of Industrial Production, various issues.

The next two figures refer to the level of output, scaled in different ways. Firstly, Figure 3.6 shows the level of gross output per local unit. This is increasing for most regions except the Midlands region. Noticeable is also a clear pattern of divergence with gross output being highest in the South-West and Mid-West. Once we take out the influence of intermediate inputs, the picture changes slightly (Figure 3.7), in the sense that the very high level of gross output per local unit for the Mid-West is not replicated with regard to net output. Thus, the manufacturing plants of the Mid-West region have a high level of intermediate input usage.

Figure 3.6: Real Gross Output per Local Unit

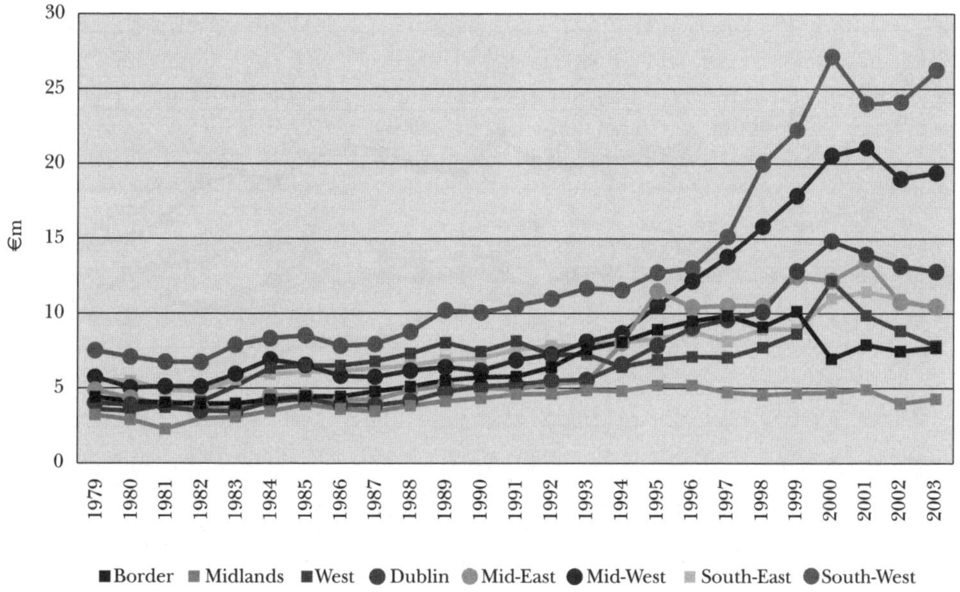

Source: Census of Industrial Production, various issues.

Figure 3.7: Real Net Output per Local Unit

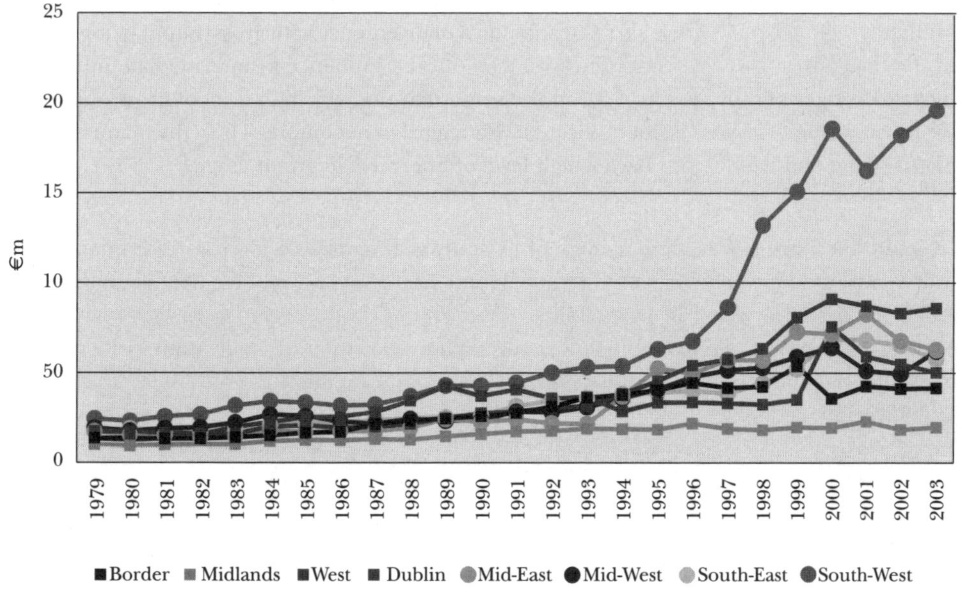

Source: Census of Industrial Production, various issues.

The same pattern of increasing differences between regions regarding output per local unit is also noticeable with regard to net output per worker (productivity), which is extremely high in the South-West region, reaching just over €400,000 per worker in 2003. Clearly this kind of productivity is not realistic and it points to the predominance of foreign multinationals, which report high profits in Ireland for tax purposes. This important distortion has been pointed out by O'Leary (1999; 2001) who shows that once one adjusts the GVA data for profit shifting then the South-West region appears considerably less prosperous.

Figure 3.8: Real Net Output per Worker

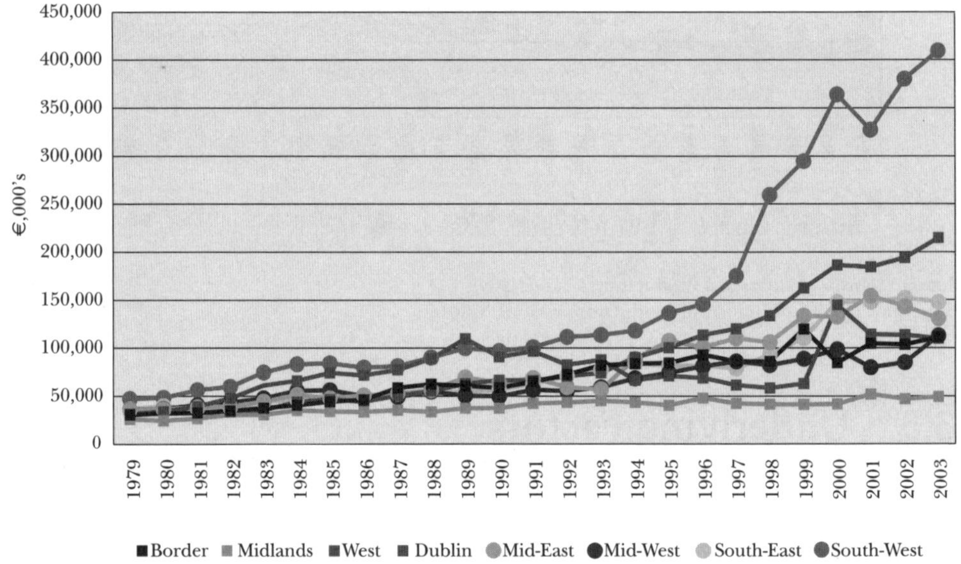

Source: Census of Industrial Production, various issues.

Finally, the wage bill as a percentage of net output (Figure 3.9) gives an indication of the profitability of manufacturing at the regional level. The general trend is a decline in the ratio, which implies an increase in profitability. Again, the Midlands region performs very poorly, while the South-West region has the lowest ratio. There is also a noticeable jump in the ratio for the Mid-West region over recent years, which might indicate that the profitability is declining in that region.

Figure 3.9: Wage Bill as a Percentage of Net Output

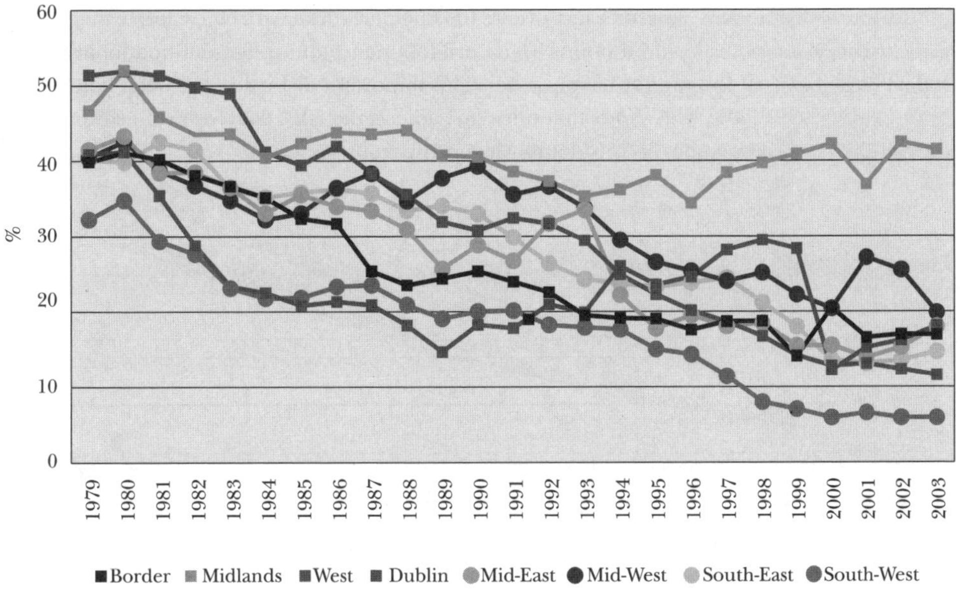

Source: Census of Industrial Production, various issues.

3.5 Underlying Factors

The basic characteristics outlined above are also related to the fundamental drivers of growth identified in the economic growth literature, namely education, R&D and infrastructure.[4] The level of human capital is particularly important if the regions are to attract high value added activities, and to stay competitive. In the literature a number of different measures of the level of human capital have been put forward including enrolment rates, expenditure, and average years of schooling. While these variables are not available for Irish regions, the Census of Population gives details of the highest educational attainment of the population. Figure 3.10 shows the percentage of those in the population that have completed their education that have attained a third level qualification. This includes non-degree qualifications (e.g. certificates and diplomas). The figure clearly shows a strong increase in the numbers that hold such a qualification. Unsurprisingly the more prosperous regions such as Dublin and the Mid-East have the highest shares while the poorer regions have the lower shares (e.g. Border). However, it is also evident that there is strong divergence between the regions regarding this variable. This may well be an important explanation for the divergence in output.

Figure 3.10: Percentage of the Population with Third Level Qualifications

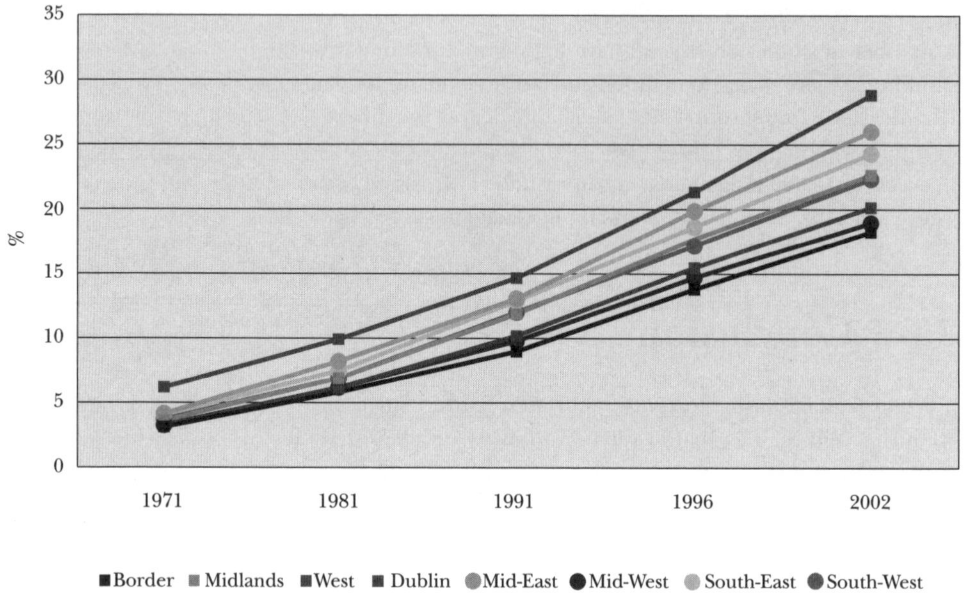

Source: Own calculations, using Census of Population, various issues.

Closely related to the divergence in educational attainment is the capacity of the regions to innovate. The recent gateways study (Fitzpatrick Associates, 2005) shows that third level based research capacity is heavily concentrated in Dublin and to a lesser extent in Cork, Limerick and Galway. Since the international literature on spillovers from university research suggests that such spillovers are quite limited in distance, the concentration of university-based research could impact negatively on region economic development. However, Jordan and O'Leary (2004) suggest that in Ireland firms utilise a wider network for innovative activities. This may well be related to the high level of FDI in Ireland where the Irish operation of a foreign multinational will have the closest connection with their headquarters rather than firms located in closer proximity. This might also hold for the relationship between firms and universities.

It is more difficult to get a good indication of the level of infrastructural endowment at the regional level. The most useful data is published by the Department of the Environment, Heritage and Local Government as part of their annual review of the construction sector, which includes a regional breakdown of public investment at the regional level. This data is available only from 1995 so it cannot be easily used to construct capital stock. However if one accumulates the real investment between 1995 and 2004 on a per capita basis, an assessment of the addition to the infrastructural stock can be made. Taking investments in roads, water services, education, health, social housing and public buildings this shows that there is relatively little difference on a per capita basis between most of the regions. The highest level of spending is recorded in the Mid-East and the lowest in the South-East, which is something of an outlier. Of course this does not account for differences between the regions in terms of the starting stock in 1995, but recent investment does not seem to systematically disadvantage the weaker regions in that the average per capita public investment in the Borders Midland and West (BMW) regions slightly exceeds the national average.

Apart from these conventional growth drivers, the economic geography literature has identified agglomeration economies and in particular the density of economic activity as an important factor in determining productivity (see Ciccone and Hall, 1996 and Ciccone, 2002). A number of studies on Ireland have highlighted the underdeveloped urban system and the resulting low level of agglomeration and density as an underlying source for regional disparities (Bradley and Morgenroth, 1999). To a large degree the differences arise out of the dominance of Dublin where in 2002, 94 per cent of the population resided in urban areas with a population in excess of 10,000 inhabitants. In contrast, the lowest level of urbanisation is found in the West where just 21 per cent of the population resided in such urban centres.

3.6 Conclusion

While regional disparities in Ireland are relatively small compared to those in most other countries, and the fact that in relation to many variables these disparities have declined, the regional focus of policy appears to have strengthened. The key indicator that has been subject to divergence is GVA per capita. This chapter first considered the components that are driving this divergence. In this respect the analysis showed that the differential rate of growth in the manufacturing sector was the key driving force, and that this in turn has been driven by differential productivity growth.

The degree to which the divergent pattern is due to the underlying industry characteristics was considered in detail. This analysis suggests that there are substantial differences between regions in terms of those characteristics and that these are significantly related to economic performance. These characteristics include the average scale, the degree of foreign ownership and the level of process sophistication, which in turn impact on the level of productivity and profitability. In most cases, the differences in underlying characteristics are persistent and divergent suggesting that they play an important role in driving divergence in growth or at least the lack of convergence.

Finally, the chapter briefly considered some of the key growth drivers, which given data availability is not an easy task. Particularly in relation to the educational attainment of the population there appears to be a strong divergent trend, which is likely to have a significant impact on the regional economic performance, especially since the more viable activities in the future will be high skilled knowledge based activities.

While the chapter could show the importance of the various factors in driving the regional performance, it could not assess whether the resulting outcome, with divergence in output levels and convergence in other variables constitutes an inefficient or inequitable outcome. If it is established that the outcome is sub-optimal, then the persistence of the underlying processes suggests that policy intervention is called for.

From a policy perspective, the divergence in output is significant if it signals more fundamental regional problems that might reduce the overall performance of the Irish economy. However, if the relatively poor performance in some regions does not have a negative impact overall, and if other variables such as income are converging, policymakers should not be overly concerned about the divergence in itself. Of course the mechanisms by which incomes are converging are important from an efficiency and equality perspective. Commuting is likely to be the key means by which incomes are converging while output levels are diverging since output is measured where it is produced and income is measured in terms of the residence of individuals. Of course long distance commuting is neither efficient nor environmentally friendly. Apart from commuting, state transfers also play an important role in reducing income differentials across regions. Unfortunately there has been no research on the magnitude of transfers and spatial equity.

Notes

1 A trade-off between equity and efficiency has also been the focus of some recent research. Williamson (1965) showed that promoting national growth may require concentration of economic activity in the core region at the expense of lagging periphery. At the earlier stages of integration, inter-regional linkages, factor movements and central government policies are selective in favour of the centres. This tendency is reversed as integration proceeds and the income levels converge. A number of new economic geography models directly address the trade-off between efficiency and income (see for example, Martin, 1999). Some empirical evidence has supported the existence of the trade-off between equity and efficiency (e.g. De la Fuente (1996) in a study of Spain or Barrios and Strobl (2005) in a recent study for European regions). For Ireland the correlation coefficient between the standard deviation of regional per capita GVA and national per capita GVA growth is –0.6, which is statistically significant, indicating that the strong national growth led to a relative concentration of activity (see Morgenroth and Fitz Gerald, 2006).

2 Regional policy measures and approaches have changed over the post war period. Specific policy measures included the designation of certain areas for preferential industrial grants rates, building of advance factories, the establishment of the Shannon Free Trade zone etc. A thorough review of these policies can be found in Bannon and Lombard (1996).

3 See Walsh (2006) for a detailed discussion.

4 See Morgenroth (2003) for a review of this literature.

References

Bannon, M. and Lombard, M. (1996), "Evolution of Regional Policy in Ireland", in Shannon Development, *Regional Policy: A Report by a Regional Policy Advisory Group to Forfas.*

Barrios, S. and Strobl, E. (2005), "The Dynamics of Regional Inequalities" *European Economy Economic Papers,* No. 229. Brussels: Directorate General for Economic and Financial Affairs.

Boyle, G., McCarthy, T. and Walsh, J. (1998-1999), "Regional Income Differentials and the Issue of Regional Equalisation in Ireland", *Journal of the Statistical and Social Inquiry Society of Ireland.* Vol. 28(1): 155-99.

Bradley, J., Fitz Gerald, J., Honohan, P. and Kearney, I. (1997), "Interpreting the Recent Irish Growth Experience" in Duffy, D., Fitz Gerald, J., Kearney, I. and Shortall, F. (eds.), *Medium-Term Review 1997-2003,* ESRI, Dublin.

Bradley, J. and Morgenroth, E. (1999), "Celtic Cubs? Regional Manufacturing in Ireland", in Duffy, D., Fitz Gerald, J., Kearney, I. and Smyth, D. (eds.), Medium-Term Review 1999-2005, *Medium Term Review Series No. 7,* ESRI, Dublin.

Ciccone, A. and Hall, R. (1996), "Productivity and the Density of Economic Activity", *American Economic Review*, Vol. 86(1), 54-70.

Ciccone, A. (2002), "Agglomeration Effects in Europe", *European Economic Review*, Vol. 46(2), 213-227.

De la Fuente, A. (1996), *Inversion Publica Y Redistribucion Regional: El Caso De Espana En La Decada de Los Ochenta,* (Papers de Treball 50.96), Barcelona.

Fitzpatrick Associates (2005), *Implementing the NSS: Gateways Investment Priorities Study,* Department of the Environment, Heritage and Local Government, Dublin.

Jordan, D. and O'Leary, E. (2005), "The Roles of Interaction and Proximity for Innovation by Irish High-Technology Businesses: Policy Implications" in D. McCoy (ed.), *ESRI Quarterly Economic Commentary* (Summer).

Martin, P. (1999), "Public Policies, Regional Inequalities and Growth", *Journal of Public Economics*, Vol. 73(1), 85-105.

Morgenroth, E. and O'Malley, E. (2003), "Regional Development and SMEs in Ireland" in Fingleton, B., Eraydin, A. and Paci, R. (eds.), *Regional Economic Growth, SMEs and the Wider Europe,* Ashgate, London.

Morgenroth, E. (2003), "What Should Policy Makers Learn From Recent Advances in Growth Theory and Economic Geography?" in O'Leary, E. (ed.), *A New Agenda for Irish Regional Development,* Liffey Press, Dublin.

Morgenroth, E. and FitzGerald, J. (eds.) (2006), *Ex-ante Evaluation of National Investment Priorities 2007-2013,* Policy Research Series Paper, ESRI, Dublin.

O'Connor, F. (1999), "Regional Variation in Economic Activity: Irish Regions," ESRI Seminar Paper presented at the Economic and Social Research Institute, Dublin, 4th of April.

O'Leary, E. (1999), "Regional Income Estimates for Ireland: 1995", *Regional Studies,* Vol. 33(9), 805-814.

O'Leary, E. (2001), "Convergence of Living Standards among Irish Regions: The Roles of Productivity, Profit Outflows and Demography, 1960-1996", *Regional Studies.* Vol. 35(3), 197-205.

Paci, R. and Pigliaru, F. (1999), "European Regional Growth: Do Sectors Matter" in Adams, J. and F. Pigliaru (eds.), *Economic Growth and Change,* Edward Elgar, Cheltenham.

Walsh, B. M. (2006), "Labour Market Adjustment in the Irish Regions, 188-2005" *Planning and Environmental Policy Research Series (PEP) Working Paper* 06/07, Department of Planning and Environmental Policy, University College Dublin.

Williamson, J.G. (1965), "Regional Inequality and the Process of National Development: A Description of the Patterns", *Economic Development and Cultural Change,* Vol. 13(4), 1-84.

CHAPTER 4

PERSPECTIVES ON NORTHERN IRELAND'S PRODUCTIVITY PERFORMANCE

JOSÉ LUIS IPARRAGUIRRE D'ELIA

ABSTRACT

In this chapter Iparraguirre D'Elia outlines the productivity performance of Northern Ireland between 1995 and 2002. The results indicate that while Northern Ireland returned the highest rate of economic growth of all UK regions between 1989 and 2004, its productivity performance has been poor, with most of the economic growth over this period being attributable to increasing employment levels. Northern Ireland's economy is dominated by high rates of employment in the public administration, health and education sectors, sectors that typically have less potential for future productivity growth.

4.1 Introduction

Northern Ireland returned the highest rate of economic growth (measured in terms of Gross Value Added (GVA) per capita) of all UK regions between 1989 and 2004, although most of this positive economic performance took place before 1997. Since 1995 Northern Ireland's economic performance has remained above the UK average, but it has been overtaken by four other regions within the UK. However, the productivity performance of the Northern Irish economy has been poor, with most of the economic growth over this period being attributable to increasing employment.

Investigating the role productivity growth plays in economic activity is of crucial importance for policymaking. What makes an economy more productive? Is it the skill of its workforce, the level of entrepreneurship, the level of fixed investments in machinery, equipment and infrastructure or expenditure on Research and Development (R&D) activities? This chapter discusses these questions for Northern Ireland within the context of other regions in the UK. It draws upon recent research carried out by the Economic Research Institute of Northern Ireland (ERINI).

4.2 Labour Productivity in Northern Ireland

Figure 4.1 shows the average growth in both GVA per head and labour productivity for the regions in the UK and for the Republic of Ireland between 1995 and 2002. Northern Ireland is the only UK region that exhibited a higher than average growth in GVA per capita along with a lower than average growth in labour productivity. Furthermore, Figure 4.1 illustrates that there was a significant disparity between the UK and Republic of Ireland's performance. The economy in the Republic has grown at more than twice the rate of even the fastest growing region within the UK over the period, and has substantially outperformed the most productive UK region.

Figure 4.1: Annual Changes in Labour Productivity and GVA, UK and ROI, 1995-2002

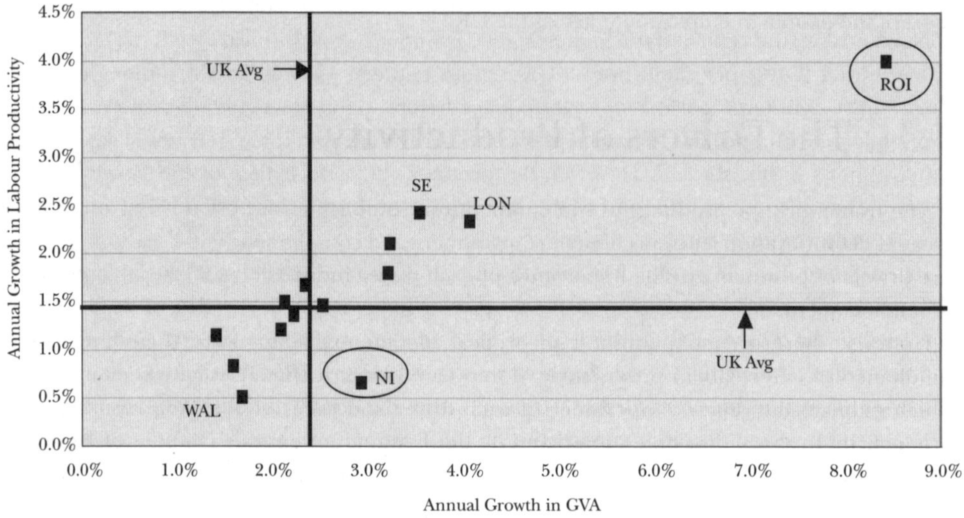

Source: For UK Regions, Iparraguirre D'Elia (2005); for Republic of Ireland, CSO.

Note: ROI = Republic of Ireland, SE = South-East, Lon = London, WAL = Wales, NI = Northern Ireland.

The Republic of Ireland's economy grew by 68 per cent between 1997 and 2005 while GDP per capita increased by 49 per cent. This impressive performance was facilitated by increasing employment levels, with total employment growing by 41 per cent. Hourly productivity (i.e. GDP per hour worked) has increased by 20 per cent since 1997, while stagnating in Northern Ireland. This is the most remarkable difference between the recent productivity performance in the Republic of Ireland and Northern Ireland.

In order to understand the elements that have contributed towards differing economic and productivity growth performances within the UK, we decomposed Northern Ireland's GVA per head gap vis-à-vis the UK average for the period 1989 to 2004. We have considered five elements:[1]

1. Hourly labour productivity (i.e. GVA per hour worked);
2. Hours worked per person in employment;
3. Employed people as a percentage of labour force;
4. Economic activity rate (i.e. the ratio of the labour force to the population of working age); and
5. The dependency rate (i.e. the ratio of the population of working age to total population).

Northern Ireland's economic growth between 1989 and 1997 (the most successful period in recent times in terms of economic growth), was not the result of growth in productivity. On the contrary, the region had the lowest levels of regional productivity per worker over the period. Furthermore, hourly labour productivity was the main negative contributor to economic performance in Northern Ireland vis-à-vis the other UK regions. Most of the economic growth Northern Ireland experienced over the period can be attributed to increasing employment. Northern Ireland also falls behind in terms of activity rates, and that the only positive contribution has come from the relatively high number of hours worked. In other words, Northern Ireland had the lowest percentage of the population who were economically active and these were the least productive workforce, although those who were in employment worked longer hours than most of the people in employment across the UK.

4.3 The Drivers of Productivity

The framework for productivity and competitiveness policy in the UK is based on five key areas: skills, innovation, entrepreneurship, investment and competition. These are known as the five drivers of productivity. The importance of each driver individually on labour productivity is well documented.

However, there are no published theoretical models explaining how these five drivers simultaneously affect labour productivity. Moreover, no empirical analyses have been published which estimate the relative importance of each driver and their interrelationships to labour productivity. In short, the contention that skills, innovation, entrepreneurship, investment and competition are the main drivers of productivity has neither been theoretically formulated in full nor empirically validated.

Many factors that have been omitted from this policy framework are also germane to labour productivity performance, such as social capital, organisational restructuring, innovation absorptive capacity, industrial structure, agglomeration, firm exit or churning, or distance to main economic hub.

Consequently, in a paper soon to be published, the ERINI set out a model to estimate the direct and indirect effects of each driver on labour productivity and their interrelationships, both in the UK and in a group of 83 countries.[2] The main finding is that there is no one single driver that can boost regional productivity on its own. Promoting entrepreneurship, spending more on R&D, increasing the capital to worker ratio and the percentage of the workforce with higher qualifications have a significant bearing on regional labour productivity. In contrast, competition and regulatory barriers do not seem to affect labour productivity at a regional level, although we obtained some positive effects of competition and negative effects of regulation upon labour productivity in our cross-country estimation.

Having a skilled workforce not only directly affects productivity, but it also impacts positively on the level of entrepreneurship and investment. Therefore, it contributes to productivity in an indirect way. Another relevant finding is that an increase in the number of start-ups impacts positively on levels of expenditure on R&D.

Northern Ireland labour productivity has clearly been affected by its performance for each of the five main drivers (see Figure 4.2). Northern Ireland stands out as the region with the fourth highest investment ratio (net capital expenditure/GVA). However, for all the other indicators, it ranks below average.

Figure 4.2: Regional Rankings by Productivity Driver, 2003

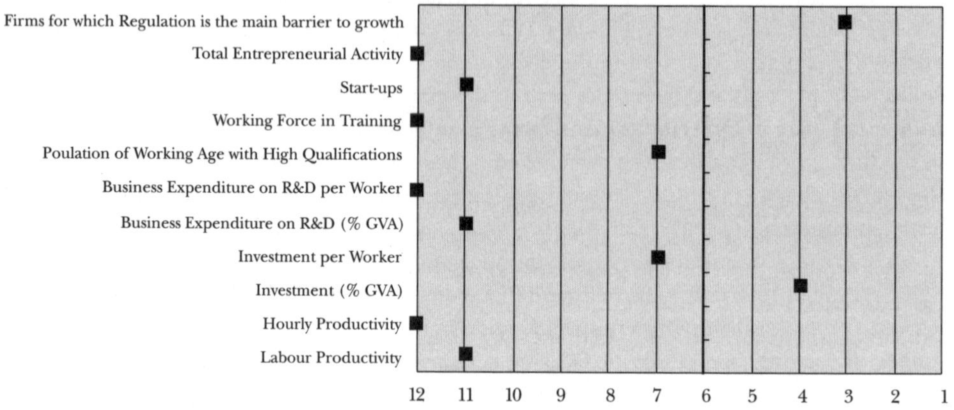

Source: Iparraguirre D'Elia (forthcoming).

Finally, we compared how both the Republic of Ireland and Northern Ireland fare in four of the five drivers of productivity. Table 4.1 provides some insight into the factors underlying the much higher labour and hourly productivity performance of the Republic of Ireland vis-à-vis Northern Ireland. The Republic of Ireland ranks better than Northern Ireland in total entrepreneurial activity, gross fixed capital formation and R&D expenditure as a percentage of GDP. Northern Ireland only ranks better than the Republic of Ireland for the skills indicator.

Table 4.1: Drivers of Labour Productivity[4]

Driver	Republic of Ireland	Northern Ireland
Entrepreneurship	9.8	4.8
Skills	20.9	26.5
Investment	23.5	12.8
Innovation	1.1	1.1

4.4 Productivity Across Industrial Sectors

Regional economic processes are rarely smoothly distributed across industries. For example, labour productivity in the manufacturing sector grew by five per cent between 1995 and 2002, whilst labour productivity in the extractive industries (i.e. agriculture, hunting, forestry, fishing, mining and quarrying) fell by eight per cent over the same period.[5]

Three sectors account for almost 66 per cent of total employment in Northern Ireland: the non-market sector (public administration, health and education), the distribution sector (which includes hotels and restaurants), and the manufacturing sector. Labour productivity increased by almost 47 per cent in the distribution sector but fell in the non-market sector by almost eight per cent and by two per cent in the manufacturing sector. Although weighted by the sectoral share in total employment, labour productivity in the distribution sector increased by almost 22 per cent, whereas it diminished by around six per cent in the two other sectors.[6] The average change in labour productivity for all other sectors amounts to 3.7 per cent for the period in question.

In a study of sectoral differences in output, employment and productivity across the UK regions between 1995 and 2002, we found that Northern Ireland presented the second highest degree of output and employment specialisation in the UK (after London).[7] However, whereas London has mostly specialised in banking, finance and insurance and manufacturing, the Northern Ireland economy is dominated by employment in public administration, health and education and manufacturing. An increase in the sectoral specialisation in employment or productive structure positively affects labour productivity in a region when it comes as a result of changes in innovation and skills rather than in price-related factors. A higher concentration of economic activity or employment in highly competitive industries would contribute more to labour productivity than a relative concentration in less competitive industries or declining sectors. The sector in which Northern Ireland exhibited the highest concentration in production was in agriculture, hunting, forestry and mining, while it exhibited the highest employment concentration in construction.

Another structural indicator is the speed of re-allocation of employment across industries, which reflects the adaptability of labour as a factor of production and the degree of mobility of the industrial structure in a region. The efficient re-allocation of employment across industries is a sign of a healthy economic structure seeking optimisation of its productive resources. Of all the regions in the UK, Northern Ireland exhibits the highest speed of sectoral re-allocation between 1995 and 2005. A high degree of re-allocation fosters employment growth; consequently it should come as no surprise that regional employment has grown faster in regions with a higher speed of labour re-allocation adjustment than in regions exhibiting a lower speed of adjustment.

We found that sectoral specialisation in production had a significant effect on labour productivity across regions in the UK, but we failed to find any statistically significant relationship between employment, sectoral specialisation and labour productivity at the regional level. With regards to concentration of GVA and employment, we found a significant positive association with regional labour productivity.

A different perspective on regional output, employment or productivity growth distinguishes whether the process is due to:

1. General increases at the national level;
2. Cross-regional increases; or
3. Factors specific to the region

We found that most of the labour productivity growth in Northern Ireland's market sector (i.e. excluding the public sector) between 1995 and 2002 was a result of positive changes at the national level, mainly via changes in GVA. Both the mix of slow and fast growing industries and in particular, variables specific to the region, had an adverse impact on the labour productivity growth, particularly in the market sectors. In other words, most of the change in the labour productivity gap between Northern Ireland and the UK average was explained by the negative incidence of sectoral shocks specific to the region and intra-sectoral differences vis-à-vis the UK as a whole. Furthermore, employment growth in the market sector in the region positively and substantially responded to domestic factors, with a negative impact on labour productivity.

It is also worth comparing productivity performance between both regions in different industrial sectors. Due to data limitations for Northern Ireland, we will cover the period 1997 to 2003. Figure 4.3 presents hourly productivity and employment growth rates by sector in both the Republic of Ireland and Northern Ireland between 1997 and 2003.

Figure 4.3: ROI and Northern Ireland's Hourly Productivity and Employment Growth Rates per Sector, 1997-2003[8]

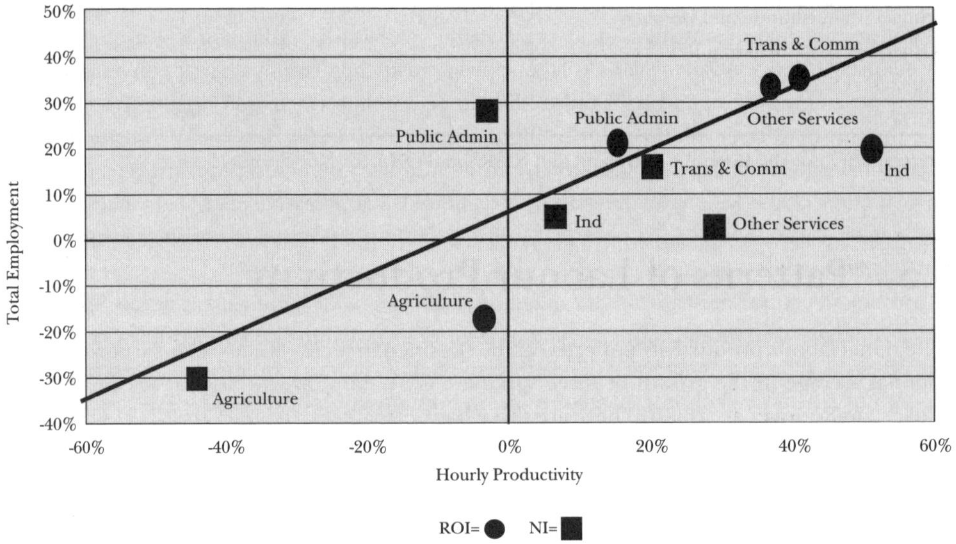

Sources: CSO, for the Republic of Ireland and NISRA and ONS, for Northern Ireland.

In the Republic of Ireland, hourly productivity has grown in all sectors except agriculture – and the same applies to employment. Furthermore, in all sectors, except public administration, hourly productivity has increased. The sector in which hourly productivity increased most was in industry.

In contrast, in Northern Ireland hourly productivity fell in agriculture and public administration, while growth rates for all other sectors were lower than those recorded in the Republic of Ireland. In addition, total employment levels also grew less in all sectors in Northern Ireland compared to the Republic of Ireland, except in public administration. Hourly productivity grew more in Northern Ireland in the 'other services' sector, mainly due to the strong performance of the banking, finance and insurance sector.

Table 4.2 summarises the relative labour productivity (as opposed to hourly productivity) performance by sector in the Republic of Ireland and Northern Ireland between 1997 and 2003. For the economy as a whole, labour productivity grew by 14 percentage points more in the Republic of Ireland than in Northern Ireland. Excluding public administration, the difference is still remarkable. Labour productivity in the market economy sectors grew by eight percentage points more in the Republic of Ireland. In particular, the labour productivity of the 'industry' sector in Republic of Ireland was almost 30 percentage points better than that in Northern Ireland.

Table 4.2: ROI and Northern Ireland Labour Productivity Growth 1997-2003 by Sector

Industrial Sector	**ROI**	**NI**	**Difference**
	%		**(percentage points)**
Agriculture Forestry and Fishing	13.9	-14.0	27.9
Industry	28.3	-1.4	29.7
Distribution Transport and Communication	4.1	2.5	1.7
Public Administration and Defence	-8.2	-33.6	25.4
Other Services (including Rent)	2.1	23.4	-21.3
All Market Sectors	17.1	8.7	8.4
All Sectors	17.2	2.9	14.3

Sources: CSO, for the Republic of Ireland and NISRA and ONS, for Northern Ireland.

4.5 Patterns of Labour Productivity

Regional labour productivity patterns can be classified in terms of the differences against the national average in the growth of three variables: GVA, employment and labour productivity (Cuadrado-Roura et al., 2000). There are three basic categories: virtuous growth, restructuring and vicious circle.

1. Virtuous growth is the process in which a region or sector presents higher labour productivity, GVA and employment growth rates than the nation as a whole;
2. Restructuring can happen via productivity or employment. Restructuring via productivity implies that labour productivity grows more, but employment less in a region or sector than at the national level. Restructuring via employment means that labour productivity grows less and employment more in a region or sector than at the national level; and
3. Finally, a vicious circle of economic decline occurs when the region or sector presents lower labour productivity, GVA and employment growth rates than the national average.

Two sectors in Northern Ireland, construction and manufacturing, underwent a process of virtuous growth in their labour productivity. In these sectors, output and employment levels grew more than the UK average. Given that production grew more than employment, labour productivity also grew more than the UK average.

The sectors 'wholesale, retail trade, hotels and restaurants' and 'transport and communication' underwent a process of relative restructuring via productivity. Labour productivity grew more in Northern Ireland than it did in the UK as a whole, while at the same time they experienced higher GVA growth rates and lower and negative growth rates in employment than the UK average. 'Energy and water' went through a process of absolute restructuring via productivity (i.e. labour productivity increased vis-à-vis the UK average), whilst both GVA and employment fell in comparison to the UK average. 'Banking, finance and insurance' went through an intensive restructuring process via employment, in that labour productivity fell behind the UK average whilst GVA and employment grew more than average.

Finally, the public sector and the extractive sectors went through a conservative restructuring process via employment. In these sectors, both labour productivity and GVA grew less in Northern Ireland than in the UK, but employment grew more in Northern Ireland than in the UK as a whole. Since 1995, no sector in Northern Ireland experienced a vicious circle of economic decline when compared against their UK counterparts.

Thus, the three largest sectors in terms of employment share – public administration (which includes education and health), wholesale and retail (which includes hotels and restaurants), and the manufacturing sector all present different patterns of productivity growth when compared against the UK. Figure 4.4 summarises the findings.

Figure 4.4: Changes in GVA and Employment by Sector – Differences between Northern Ireland and the UK Average, 1995-2002[9]

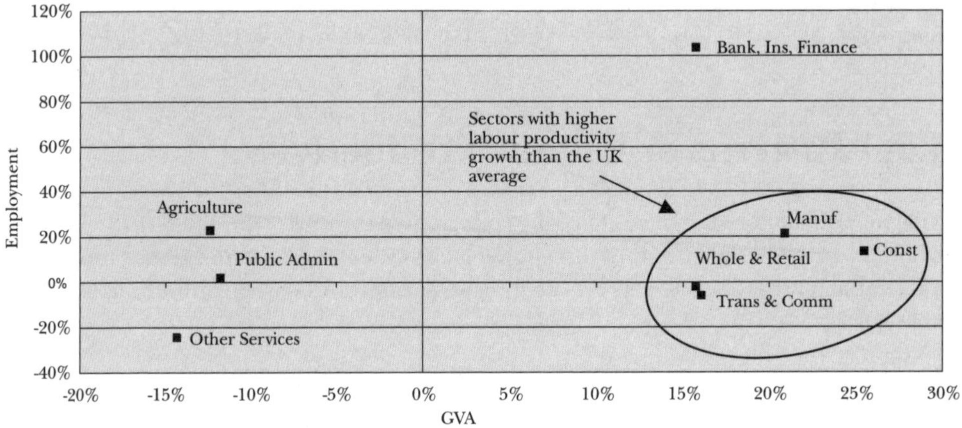

Source: Iparraguirre D'Elia, (2005).

4.6 Convergence and Divergence of Labour Productivity Across Regions and Sectors

Convergence in regional labour productivity over a given period of time means that regions with lower productivity at the beginning of the period have been catching up, in the sense that their labour productivity has grown faster (or decreased less) than that of the regions that initially had higher productivity levels.

We carried out estimates of convergence coefficients for labour productivity since 1995 and also for output per capita for the UK regions between 1989 and 2003. With respect to GVA per head, there has been a very slight convergence across the UK regions over the period 1989-2003 of around 0.3 per cent a year. However, labour productivity has been slightly diverging across regions in the UK since 1995. Labour productivity in regions with higher labour productivity in 1995 has grown faster on average, than in those that initially had lower productivity.

Divergence in regional labour productivity has not been homogeneous across sectors. For example, there has been some regional convergence in the manufacturing industries and construction sector. In contrast, divergence was very pronounced in the banking, finance and insurance sector, but less so in the public administration, education and health sectors.

Within Northern Ireland, labour productivity growth across industries since 1995 has not been uniform. Labour productivity fell by almost 0.5 per cent a year in the manufacturing sector, by over four per cent in the banking, finance and insurance sectors, by over eight per cent per year in the extracting industries and by over one per cent a year in the public sector. Productivity grew by over four per cent a year in the construction sector and by almost six per cent a year in the wholesale, retail trade and hotels and restaurant sector. Figure 4.5 presents the relationship between labour productivity and changes in employment share by sector between 1995 and 2000 in Northern Ireland. We can see that by and large, the bigger the change in employment share of a sector in 1995, the better its labour productivity changed over the period.

Figure 4.5: Changes in Productivity by Sector, Classified in Terms of Employment Share, 1995-2002[9]

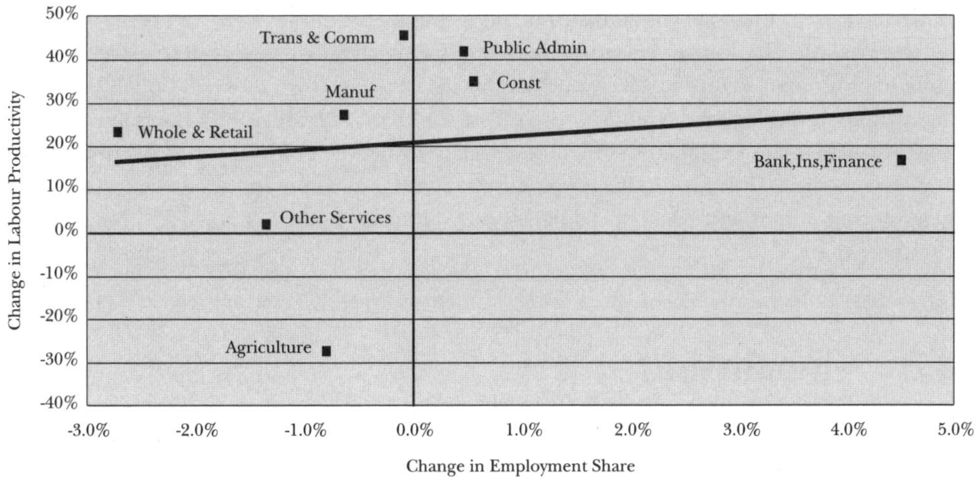

Source: Office for National Statistics.

4.7 The Cyclical Nature of Productivity

D. Parham (2002: 7), from Australia's Productivity Commission, states:

> Some, but not all, troughs and peaks in productivity cycles correspond to troughs and peaks in business cycles. The overlaps reflect the importance of the business cycle as a short-term influence on movements in productivity. But other influences on productivity... can operate independently from the business cycle. The productivity cycle can therefore capture more information relevant to changes in underlying productivity trends than can the business cycle.

A recent paper disentangled the cyclical components from the permanent components in GVA, labour productivity and employment for the UK regions between 1975 and 2003.[10] We failed to find any statistically significant breaks in the long-run trends in labour productivity in any UK region. Furthermore, we did not detect any significant structural differences between the productivity cycles across the regions.

On the other hand, the cyclical behaviour of productivity in the UK as a whole was found to be positively and significantly correlated with cycles of regional productivity. Northern Ireland in particular, was the region which presented the second weakest relationship between its cycle of productivity and that of the UK as a whole.

Iparraguirre D'Elia (2006b) looked on the influence of the regional industrial structure on the cyclical behaviour of productivity. The paper concluded that regional structure has some impact on the extent to which fluctuations in the productivity at the national level affect fluctuations at the regional level. The Great-East (the East, South-East and London regions in England) and Wales exhibited the highest associations between cyclical variations in GVA and employment levels. In contrast, the lowest correlation was obtained for Northern Ireland. This suggests that output and labour productivity were the least related in Northern Ireland than elsewhere in the UK.

4.8 Conclusion

Economic growth is not sustainable in the long run without increasing productivity. Northern Ireland was the best performing region in the UK between 1989 and 1997, but since then it has grown slightly above the national average and has been overtaken by four other regions. However, Northern Ireland exhibited the lowest levels of regional labour and hourly productivity in the UK. In fact, most of its economic achievement was due to a large increase in employment levels.

A combination of a highly skilled working force, high levels of capital formation, entrepreneurship, and innovation along with market regulations that do not hamper competition seems to be the main ingredients of a recipe for productivity success. Northern Ireland lags behind most of the UK regions in terms of entrepreneurship and innovation and also ranks poorly with regards to skills and investment per worker. This constitutes the reason for the region's poor productivity performance.

In contrast, the Republic of Ireland's remarkable recent economic growth has been achieved with significant improvements in productivity. When we compare both countries in terms of the drivers of productivity, the Republic of Ireland outshines Northern Ireland in all indicators but skills. Furthermore, in the manufacturing sector, a sector which is central to labour productivity performance and competitiveness, the Republic of Ireland outperforms Northern Ireland by almost 30 percentage points.

We estimated that productivity has been diverging across the UK regions since the mid-1990s. Labour productivity in regions with higher labour productivity in 1995 has grown faster, on average, than in those that initially had lower productivity. The Republic of Ireland depicts a trend similar to the best performing regions in the UK and, consequently, its labour productivity has been diverging from Northern Ireland's.

Lee Hamilton, former Chairman of the Joint Economic Committee of the United States House of Representatives once stated:

> One of the most useful roles an economist can perform is to remind policymakers that the economy is complex and that choices must be made among competing objectives. We politicians don't always want to hear these things, but it is important that we do (Dixit, 1997: 150).

With this caveat in mind, there are some important lessons from this paper that policymakers in the Republic of Ireland can take with on a general level.

Firstly, the five drivers is an accurate framework for thinking and designing growth and productivity policy. Provided the foundations are right, labour productivity growth depends on a highly entrepreneurial and skilled workforce, high levels of investment and R&D expenditure per worker, and a regulatory framework that does not stifle competition. An attractive financial climate in which to do business is also, of course, an essential ingredient.

Furthermore, some of these drivers reinforce each other. For example, the higher the proportion of highly skilled individuals in the workforce, the higher the entrepreneurial activity tends to be. Thus, productivity growth depends on all its drivers growing in harmony. Any one driver may become a bottleneck for labour productivity growth if it is not nurtured or promoted as much as the rest. A country may, for example, attempt to attract internationally mobile investment to bolster cutting-edge technological activities with high value added or an export bias by introducing financial incentives to potential foreign investors. However, if the existing skills base or the basic infrastructure is not satisfactory enough, the policy will only attract, at best, foreign investment with low value added.

Two recent papers that discuss specific policy measures in Northern Ireland (Harris et al., 2006 and ERINI, 2006b) favour this broad, holistic approach to policymaking. Harris et al. (2006) assess the case for a higher rate of R&D tax credit in Northern Ireland and also discuss the relative effectiveness of the alternative strategy of providing selective financial assistance to stimulate R&D expenditure.[11] The paper concludes that fiscal incentives are better than financial assistance, but that the long-run R&D stock resulting from a more generous tax scheme could be halted if "the supply-side provision of R&D facilities (especially personnel)" is not significantly increased at the same time. Furthermore, ERINI (2006a: 2) points out that "behind the apparently simple question of whether a different rate of R&D Tax Credit would be justified for Northern Ireland, there lies a great complexity of issues".

ERINI (2006b) examines the case for a differential rate of corporation tax in Northern Ireland. It concludes that although a reduced rate of corporation tax could yield significant benefits, these would not materialise if support mechanisms and institutional infrastructure are not refocused towards improving how Northern Ireland engages through trade and other means with the world. Thus, fostering R&D or reducing the corporation tax without, for example, also taking measures to improve the supply of specialised skills will not optimise the economic returns to Northern Ireland.

Notes

1 See Iparraguirre D'Elia (2006a).
2 Iparraguirre D'Elia (2006, forthcoming).
3 We could not find any comparable indicators for competition for both countries.
4 The measures for this table are as follows:
   1. Entrepreneurship = Total Entrepreneurial Activity 2005 (Source: Global Entrepreneurship Monitor)
   2. Skills = Percentage of Population of Working Age with University Degree or Equivalent Qualification 2003 (Sources: CSO and DTI)
   3. Investment = Gross Fixed Capital Formation as a percentage of Gross Domestic Product /Gross Value Added 2003 (Sources: CSO and DTI)
   4. Innovation = Gross Expenditure on R&D as a percentage of Gross Domestic Product / Gross Value Added 2003 (Sources: CSO and DTI)
5 See Iparraguirre D'Elia (2005).
6 See Esteban (2000) and Iparraguirre D'Elia (2005).
7 Iparraguirre D'Elia (2005).
8 Key: Agriculture = Agriculture, Fishing, Forestry and Mining; Industry = Manufacturing and Construction; Other Services = Financial Services, Health, Education and Other Services; Public Admin = Public Administration and Defence; Trans & Comm = Transport, Communication and Distribution; Other Services = Financial Services, Health, Education and Other Services.
9 Key: Agriculture = Agriculture, Hunting, Forestry, Fishing, Mining and Quarrying; Bank, Ins, Finance = Banking, Insurance and Finance; Const = Construction; Manuf = Manufacturing; Other Services = Other Services including Energy and Water; Public Admin = Public Administration, Education and Health; Trans & Comm = Transport and Communications; Whole & Retail = Wholesale and Retail Trade including Hotels and Restaurants.
10 Iparraguirre D'Elia (2006b).
11 See also ERINI (2006a).

References

Cuadrado-Roura, J., Mancha-Navarro, T. and Garrido-Yserte, R. (2000), "Regional Productivity Patterns in Europe: An Alternative Approach", *Annals of Regional Science*, 34(3), 365-384.

Dixit, A. (1997), *The Making of Economic Policy: A Transaction Cost Politics Perspective,* (Munich Lectures in Economics), M.I.T. Press.

ERINI (2006a), *Assessing the Case for a Higher Rate of R&D Tax Credit in Northern Ireland. A Statement by the ERINI Board,* ERINI Board Statements - No. 1.

ERINI (2006b), *Assessing the Case for a Differential Rate of Corporation Tax in Northern Ireland,* David Greenaway, Holger Görg, Frank Barry, and Regional Forecasts Limited. Economic Research Institute of Northern Ireland.

Esteban, J. (2000), "Regional Convergence in Europe and the Industry Mix: A Shift-Share Analysis", *Regional Science and Urban Economics,* Vol. 30: 353-364.

Harris, R., Cher Li, Q. and Trainor, M. (2006), *Assessing the Case for a Higher Rate of R&D Tax Credit in Northern Ireland,* ERINI Monographs No. 10.

Iparraguirre D'Elia, J. (2005), *Labour Productivity, Gross Value Added and Employment by Industry in Northern Ireland, A Structural and Shift-Share Analysis.* ERINI Monographs - No. 6 - December, Economic Research Institute of Northern Ireland, Belfast.

Iparraguirre D'Elia, J. (2006a), *Decomposition of Regional GVA per Capita Gap by UK Region,* ERINI Monographs - No. 7 - January, Economic Research Institute of Northern Ireland, Belfast.

Iparraguirre D'Elia, J. (2006b), *Cycles in Regional Labour Productivity in the UK,* ERINI Monographs - No. 9.

Iparraguirre D'Elia, J. (forthcoming), *The Five Drivers of Productivity. How Much Does Each One Contribute? Causal Analysis of Regional Labour Productivity in the UK,* Economic Research Institute of Northern Ireland, Belfast.

PART II

SECTORAL PRODUCTIVITY PERFORMANCE

INTRODUCTION

The contributions in this section outline some of the problems and solutions associated with measuring productivity at the sectoral level. Measuring sectoral productivity performance when the sectors concerned are locally traded, or where prices are distorted in some other way, is notoriously difficult and requires a quality and volume of data that is often not available. In Chapter 5, Boyle shows that public sector productivity is very difficult to measure, not only in Ireland but also internationally. He examines the efforts being made in the UK and other countries to overcome these problems, and argues that a similar effort must be initiated in Ireland. In Chapter 6, Matthews, Newman and Thorne analyse the productivity performance of the Irish agriculture sector, and find that its technical performance has lagged behind competing countries. The quality and volume of data on agricultural outputs and inputs is far superior than is available in other areas of the economy, and shows what type of analysis can be done with the right data. In Chapters 7 and 8, Aylward and O'Toole present novel approaches to examining the productivity of two sectors which are critical to the overall health of the economy, namely residential construction and road freight transport. They find that while productivity in both sectors has improved in recent years, both industries still lag behind international best practice.

CHAPTER 5

PUBLIC SECTOR PRODUCTIVITY MEASUREMENT: AN IMPOSSIBLE TASK?[1]

RICHARD BOYLE[2]

ABSTRACT

The productivity of the public sector is as important to the economic performance of a country as the productivity of the private sector. But public sector productivity is notoriously difficult to measure, not only in Ireland, but also internationally. Assessing the productivity of policy-oriented organisations has also proved particularly challenging. In this chapter, an examination of international experience in assessing public service productivity is presented. Lessons learned from this international experience that might be applied in Ireland are also discussed.

1. Much of this chapter is abstracted from the original research undertaken at the Institute of Public Administration for the Committee for Public Management Research (Boyle, 2006).
2. The views expressed in this paper are solely those of the author and do not necessarily reflect those of any other person or organisation.

5.1 Why Research Public Sector Productivity?

The pay awards recommended by the Public Service Benchmarking Body and implemented as part of the social partnership arrangements have generated significant public discussion about the productivity gains realised in return for pay increases in the public sector. Getting productivity increases in return for pay awards is vital for the long-term health of the economy. But many commentators are concerned that increases in public funding are not being matched by more efficient use of resources. Afonso, Schuknecht and Tanzi (2006) note the nature of the potential problem:

> Health, education and similar activities absorb a large share of the government payroll and the personnel who work for government... If mostly higher salaries absorb additional resources allocated to these activities and the higher salaries are not accompanied by higher productivity of the public employees, the higher public spending can be unproductive and produce little additional benefits to the students or patients.

The productivity of the public sector is as important to the economic performance of a country as the productivity of the private sector. Thornhill (2006) identifies three main reasons why public sector productivity is important. First, the public sector is a major employer. Second, the public sector is a major provider of services in the economy, particularly business services (affecting costs of inputs) and social services (affecting labour quality). Third, the public sector is a consumer of tax resources. Changes in public sector productivity can have significant implications for the economy.

But public sector productivity is notoriously difficult to measure, not only in Ireland, but also internationally. Much productivity data for the public sector is of questionable validity and/or reliability. Assessing the productivity of policy-oriented organisations has proved particularly challenging. In these circumstances, it is legitimate to ask if public sector productivity can ever be measured in a meaningful way, or will it always be subject to debate with opposing sides arguing their case in an environment devoid of meaningful evidence?

In recent years, a number of international studies have been carried out that address the issue of public sector productivity measurement. There are also initiatives underway at present that have the potential to further the examination of public sector productivity. In this chapter, an examination of international experience in assessing public service productivity is presented. Lessons learned from this international experience that might be applied in Ireland are drawn together at the end of the chapter.

5.2 Some Definitions and Challenges

Productivity is generally defined as a measure of the amount of output generated per unit of input. In many countries, including Ireland, public sector productivity has been assumed to be zero in the national accounts. The output of the government sector has been measured as of value equal to the total value of inputs. This output=input convention in the national accounts has increasingly come under scrutiny in recent years. The challenge is to make alternative estimates based on output measurement in a public sector context where there is the provision of collective services, and where there is no market transaction in services provided to individuals in most instances.

However, this definition of productivity as being concerned with the relationship between outputs and inputs does not cover issues that many people have in mind when they talk about public sector productivity. A more general interpretation of productivity encompasses broader concerns about the outcomes achieved by the public sector. In common parlance, when many people talk about public sector productivity, they have in mind the general question of what value they are receiving from public services in return for the application of public funds.

Putnam (1993) rejects the idea of including outcomes in productivity measurement. His argument is that to focus on outcomes (changes in health rather than patients treated; changes in educational status rather than numbers of lessons taught) includes changes over which the government has no control:

To include social outcomes in an assessment of government performance is to commit the "Massachusetts Miracle Fallacy": only a modest part of the praise for the affluence of New England in the 1980s (and a similarly modest portion of the blame for the subsequent recession) was realistically attributable to state government, despite 1988 presidential campaign rhetoric to the contrary.

Notwithstanding the problems with assessing productivity using an outcomes focus as indicated above, in this chapter, both the output/input measurement and broader assessments of public sector productivity including a focus on outcomes are included in the discussion on productivity. It is accepted that for national accounts purposes and when attributing changes in productivity to the public sector, strict definitions of an output/input nature are needed. But the broader interpretation of productivity as including a concern with outcomes, while having statistical and measurement limitations, nevertheless has resonance with the general public and may raise interesting questions even if it does not provide definitive answers.

A further challenge with regard to output measurement for productivity purposes is how to incorporate changes in the quality of outputs. The importance of this point is illustrated by Pritchard (2002a), of the Office of National Statistics in the UK, who states that: "...the measurement process must reflect the fact that 100 units of good quality this year represent more output than 100 units of a lesser quality last year".

Yet another challenge with regard to measurement relates to possible time lags between the inputs and outputs. Money spent on public sector inputs may not have an impact in terms of improved outputs for some time (in some cases years) after the initial expenditure.

In summary, there are considerable technical and other challenges associated with measuring public sector productivity, however defined. This makes comparability of trends, over time and across sectors and countries, particularly problematic. In any discussion on measuring public sector productivity, these challenges must be borne in mind and factored into interpretations of findings.

5.3 Lessons from Cross-National Comparisons

A small number of studies have been carried out that compare administrative efficiency and performance internationally at the aggregate level (Van de Walle, 2005). These studies aim to give some idea about the productivity and efficiency of the public sector in a comparative context. The studies are briefly summarised below, along with some of the main findings emerging and limitations of the studies outlined.

5.3.1 European Central Bank

Afonso, Schuknecht and Tanzi (2003) examine the performance and efficiency of the public sectors of 23 industrialised OECD countries. They develop measures of both public sector performance (which they define as the outcome of public sector activities) and efficiency (which they define as the outcome relative to the resources employed).

The study finds that the difference in public sector performance overall is moderate across the sample countries. Countries with small public sectors (public spending less than 40 per cent of GDP) on average report the highest scores, especially for administrative and economic performance. Countries with large public sectors (public spending over 50 per cent Of GDP) show more equal income distribution. Regarding public sector efficiency, countries with small public sectors display considerably higher indicators of efficiency than countries with medium-sized or big public sectors. However, the authors caution that the results must be seen as indicative and need to be interpreted with great care.

This latter point about caution is well made. Taking the indicator of administrative performance as an illustration, Van de Walle (2005) notes that contrasting this indicator with government goods and services expenditure to develop a measure of efficiency fails to recognise that the goods and services category in the national accounts is a crude approximation of what is spent on the public administration and judiciary. It is not possible to put too much weight on the European Central Bank findings.

5.3.2 Netherlands Social, Cultural and Planning Office

As part of the Dutch presidency of the European Union in the second half of 2004, the Dutch Ministry of the Interior and Kingdom Relations asked the Social and Cultural Planning Office of the Netherlands to investigate public performance in the EU member states and four major non-EU Anglo-Saxon countries (Social, Cultural and Planning Office, 2004). The report covers four main areas: education, health care, law and order, and public administration. It also assesses the overall performance of the public sector.

The scores on various government functions are combined in one overall index of public sector performance. The combined score represents four main dimensions of performance: stabilisation and growth of the economy, distribution of welfare, allocation of public services, and quality of public administration. Roughly speaking, the study finds little connection between public sector performance and the level of public and private spending. But using a global efficiency measure, Kuhry, Pommer and de Kam (2006) find:

> By this measure, Finland is the most efficient in producing public services of high quality at moderately high costs, while - in terms of efficient production – Ireland scores slightly above average at low costs. Just behind these leaders we find Sweden, Denmark, Austria, Luxembourg and the Netherlands; the first three countries post relatively high spending levels, while the last two have fairly average spending. Australia, Canada, Spain and the Czech Republic combine an average performance score with fairly low government spending, while others (particularly Germany, Belgium and France) occupy fairly average positions in both respects. The US and the United Kingdom perform fairly poorly at relatively low spending levels.

Like the European Central Bank study, the authors urge caution with regard to the interpretation of the results.

As part of ongoing work in the productivity area, an updating of some of this work of the Social, Cultural and Planning Office (SCP) has been carried out, highlighting Ireland's comparative ranking (Boyle, forthcoming) with regard to public administration. Figure 5.1, taken from this study, shows a quality of public administration composite indicator and contrasts this with expenditure per capita on general public services (this was the expenditure indicator used by the SCP). As with the SCP experience, a weak relationship between expenditure and business perception of quality of public administration is shown. Ireland comes relatively well out of this picture, achieving a relatively high score for quality of public administration with a relatively low level of expenditure.

5.3.3 World Bank Governance Indicators

Since 1996, the World Bank has been developing governance indicators as part of its work in promoting good governance. Governance indicators are produced for just over 200 countries every two years. Kaufmann, Kraay and Mastruzzi (2005) note that the governance indicators used measure six dimensions of governance: voice and accountability; political instability and violence; government effectiveness; regulatory quality; rule of law; and control of corruption.

Most relevant from the perspective of this study is the government effectiveness indicator. It aims to measure the competence of the bureaucracy and the quality of public service delivery. For 2004, the latest date for which the indicators are produced, Ireland ranked ninth of the EU25 countries against the government effectiveness indicator.

A significant concern with regard to the World Bank governance indicators is that a recent OECD study has questioned their statistical legitimacy for comparing country scores and lack of comparability over time (Arndt and Oman, 2006).

5.3.4 OECD Management in Government

The Public Governance Committee of the OECD has mandated the Public Governance and Territorial Development Directorate to assess the feasibility of developing comparable data and indicators of good government and efficient public services. This project, entitled *Management in Government: Comparative Country Data*, aims to provide good empirical data and indicators of good government. The intention is to move, on a phased basis, to the production of a publication provisionally entitled *Government at a Glance*, which will mirror the OECD's *Education at a Glance* publication and show comparative cross-national data on an annual basis.

An initial assessment of available data has been undertaken, alongside a detailed literature review (OECD, 2005). The focus is on several types of measures: inputs, processes, outputs, outcomes and antecedents or constraints that put government efficiency in context. The intention is to produce a first working paper towards the end of 2006, mostly concerned with inputs and processes, as these are the most readily available data. Data concerning outputs and outcomes are seen as more difficult to gather, but the intention is to gradually improve coverage in these areas.

5.3.5 Conclusions

There has been a growth in recent years in international comparative studies of public sector performance. Some of these explicitly include productivity measurements; others focus more generally on broad performance issues. These international studies provide scope for a comparative assessment of how Ireland is performing, particularly if studies are repeated over time, allowing trends to be established.

However, the studies themselves warn of the danger of putting too much faith in drawing comparisons, given qualifications about the type and reliability of data used to generate the indicators used in the studies. It is clear that findings are of a tentative nature, and that improvements are needed if such studies are to provide a sound evidence base.

Figure 5.1: Quality of Public Administration (2006) and Expenditure per Capita on General Public Services (2003)

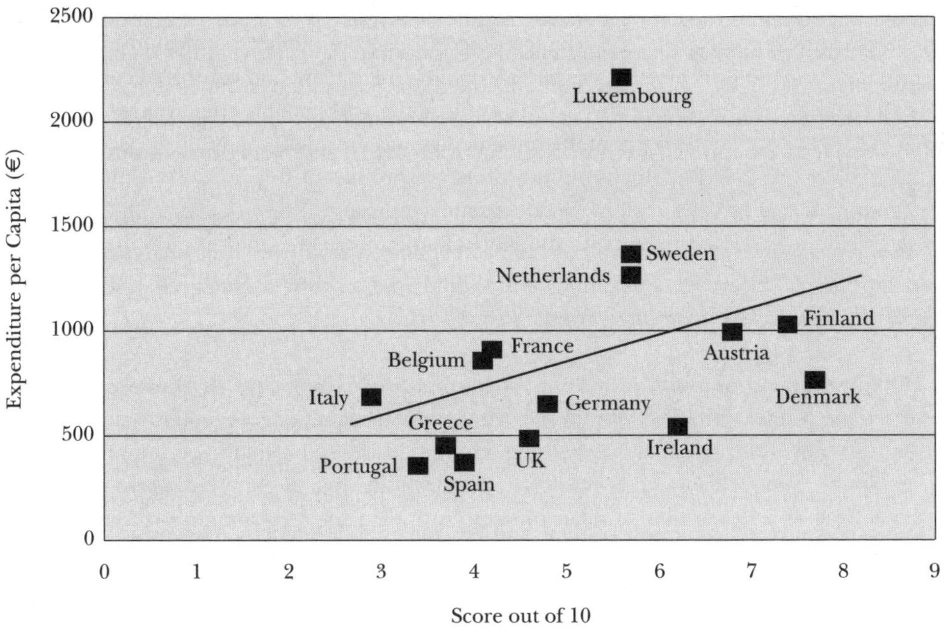

Source: Eurostat and IMD, 2006

Note: Excluding debt interest payments (classified as property income consolidated) and foreign transfers (classified as other current transfers consolidated).

5.4 Lessons from National and Sectoral Productivity Measurement Initiatives

In terms of getting a picture on public sector productivity, national level initiatives may offer more concrete evidence than international comparative studies. In recent years, various countries at both national and sectoral level have engaged in productivity measurement initiatives. In this section, steps taken by the UK are briefly reviewed, as the UK is seen as leading the work on public service productivity measurement internationally. This is followed by illustrative examples of productivity measurement in three sectors: health, education and local government.

5.4.1 Measuring Public Sector Productivity in the UK

Since 1988, the Office for National Statistics has been progressively moving away from the output=input approach to productivity, and incorporating direct measures of the volume of government output in the national accounts. By 2005, these direct output estimates accounted for two-thirds of general government final consumption. In the context of this focus on output measurement, the UK government commissioned Sir Tony Atkinson to undertake a review of the measurement of government output in the national accounts. This review (Atkinson, 2005) provides a comprehensive overview of developments and recommendations for future progress.

The Atkinson review outlines a number of principles covering the measurement of outputs, inputs and productivity. One particularly significant point is that the review strongly recommends that, in principle, measures of output growth should take account of quality change. Also, and specifically with regard to productivity, the review states:

> Outputs divided by inputs provides a measure of productivity change. However, the move from the (output=input) convention to direct measurement of government output should be carefully interpreted. It is a definite advance in the sense that government output is no longer simply assumed to equal measured inputs, but the move should not be seen as solving at a stroke the complex problem of measuring government productivity. The statistic obtained by dividing outputs by inputs may no longer be equal to 1 by definition, but no single number, however carefully constructed, can fully capture the performance of complex public services with multiple objectives. Productivity change should be interpreted in the light of a range of other information – the triangulation principle.

The UK government accepted the findings and recommendations of the Atkinson review, and the Office for National Statistics is taking the lead role in taking forward the recommendations.

5.4.2 Health Sector Productivity Measurement

The UK Office for National Statistics (2006) has published a major review of health service productivity. Using available data, the Office for National Statistics produced three different estimates of NHS productivity. The first estimate is based on current national accounts estimates of output. Using this measure, NHS productivity is estimated to have fallen during the period 1995 to 2004 by an average of between 0.6 and 1.3 per cent per year. The second estimate is based on the principle outlined in the Atkinson Review (Atkinson, 2005) that output should be adjusted to take into account quality change. On this basis, productivity is estimated to have either increased by an average of 0.2 per cent per year, or has fallen by an average of 0.5 per cent per year depending on how quality is measured. The third estimate is also based on a recommendation outlined in the Atkinson review, that the value of NHS output should be adjusted by rising real earnings in the economy to reflect the fact that health becomes increasingly valuable in a growing and increasingly productive economy. On this basis, NHS productivity is estimated to have increased by an average of between 0.9 and 1.6 per cent per year. These estimates of productivity are further tested against wider corroborative evidence:

> ...since 1991/92 the average length of stay in hospital has been falling steadily (apart from a small rise between 1999/00 and 2000/01); and there has been a steady increase in the rate for elective day case treatments. This suggests a shift towards more cost effective treatment and would be consistent with a productivity increase from NHS resources. At the same time, emergency re-admission rates have increased very slightly over the period. If this requires additional NHS resources, this could dampen down productivity (Office for National Statistics, 2006).

This process of checking productivity estimates against other corroborative evidence is known as triangulation. It is important in a context where "It is unlikely that a single number for productivity will ever capture all the costs and benefits of the NHS" (Office for National Statistics, 2006).

5.4.3 Education Sector Productivity Measurement

Education is one of the services measured by a review of government services in Australia. A framework model is used to develop a set of performance indicators for schools. Equity indicators measure how special needs groups compare in terms of participation and retention rates. Effectiveness is measured in terms of learning outcomes with regard to reading, writing and numeracy. Efficiency is measured in terms of government expenditure per student, staff expenditure per student, and student to staff ratios (Banks, 2005).

Different states are compared and contrasted in terms of performance against the agreed indicators. Comparing the unit costs of providing a particular service across jurisdictions is seen as a way of helping states to identify if they have scope for improvements in their efficiency.

5.4.4 Local Government Productivity Measurement

In the UK, changes in local government performance are assessed using a sample of 63 indicators including 'Best Value' performance indicators, indicators from the Social Services Performance Assessment Framework, and indicators from the Department for Education and Skills (Martin and Bovaird, 2005). This grouping of indicators is used by the Office of the Deputy Prime Minister as a 'basket' of indicators showing the cost-effectiveness of local authorities. The indicators are arranged by service area. The basket of indicators suggests that overall performance has improved by 12.5 per cent between 2000/01 and 2003/04. There are significant variations between authorities. There are also large variations between services, with particularly large improvements in waste management and culture.

When similar services are provided by entities such as local authorities, there is also scope for comparative productivity analysis. For example, Haubrich, Gutierrez and McLean (2006) are using an econometric analysis technique called panel data analysis to try to identify relatively efficient and inefficient authorities.

5.4.5 Conclusions

The evidence from national and sectoral studies of public sector productivity measurement is that productivity measurement is still in its early stages. Despite efforts going back to the 1980s, the productivity measures being produced need to be interpreted cautiously. The findings from the UK health sector productivity studies, which represent the state-of-the-art, yet still show widely varying estimates of productivity depending on which factors are included or excluded, illustrate some of the problems. There is also the danger that over simplistic use of the measures could lead to perverse consequences. For example, the number of vehicle kilometres is an output measure sometimes used for public roads. Using this measure, it is possible to increase productivity by increasing vehicle kilometres, but this is likely to run counter to transport policy aimed at moving people from cars to public transport and cutting down on unnecessary travel: the policy goal may be to reduce vehicle kilometres.

It is clear that no single productivity figure can be used for public sector activities, unless there is clear and widespread agreement that it is an appropriate measure. The Atkinson (2005) recommendation that a range of supporting information – the triangulation principle – should evidence productivity change is one that should be applied generally.

5.5 Lessons from 'Bottom Up' Productivity Measurement

So far, the productivity measures examined have been sectoral or national in nature, and often driven from a 'top down' perspective. It is important to note that, at a more micro level, productivity measurement in the public sector can also take place at the level of the organisation and from a 'bottom up' or service user perspective.

The World Bank has adopted this approach with regard to assessing some aspects of the effects of regulation with the development of their *Doing Business* database (www.doingbusiness.org). Three indicators from this *Doing Business* database are particularly relevant to the assessment of public administration quality and productivity:

1. **Paying Taxes:** This topic addresses the taxes that a medium-sized company must pay or withhold in a given year, and the administrative burden associated with paying taxes.
2. **Dealing with Licenses:** This topic records all procedures required for a business in the construction industry to build a standardised warehouse. These include obtaining all necessary licenses and permits, completing all required notifications and inspections and submitting the relevant documents to the authorities. Procedures for obtaining utility connections are also recorded. A survey divides the process of building a warehouse into distinct procedures and calculates the time and cost of completing each procedure under normal circumstances.
3. **Starting a Business:** This topic identifies the steps an entrepreneur must take to incorporate and register a new firm. It examines the procedures, time and cost involved in launching a commercial or industrial firm with up to 50 employees and start-up capital of ten times the economy's per capita gross national income.

Taking the last indicator, starting a business, the steps and costs associated with starting a business are assessed and the results compared over time and across countries. Local incorporation lawyers and government officials complete and verify the data. The key indicators used to assess performance are the number of procedures the applicant is required to go through, the number of days each procedure takes, and the cost of start up (The World Bank Group, 2006). The results for Ireland for 2005 are given in Table 5.1. This information can be compared with results achieved in other countries, and changes from year to year. Boyle (forthcoming) presents some initial findings for Ireland in a comparative context against these three indicators.

Table 5.1: Starting a Business in Ireland

Nature of Procedure (2005)	Procedure	Duration (days)	US$ Cost
The founder swears before a Commissioner for Oaths	1	1	5.63
File application with register	2	15	1,781.52
Make a company seal	3	1	22.82
Register for taxes and employment payments	4	7	0.00
Totals:	**4**	**24**	**$1,809.97**

Source: The World Bank Group (2006).

Another example of this bottom up approach to productivity measurement is a study of the institutional performance of regional governments in Italy undertaken by Putnam (1993). In this study, one of the indicators used to assess institutional performance, and the most relevant from the point of view of productivity, is bureaucratic responsiveness. Bureaucracies in each region were approached with mail requests for information about three specific (but fictitious) problems:

1. The health department was asked about reimbursement procedures for a medical bill incurred while the inquirer was on vacation abroad;
2. The vocational education department was asked about job training facilities for a 'brother' just finishing junior high school; and
3. The agriculture department was asked, on behalf of a 'farmer friend', for information about loans and subsidies for experimental crops.

Replies were evaluated for promptness, clarity and comprehensiveness. If no reply was received, follow up telephone calls and subsequent personal visits were made. Information was brought together in a composite index of the responsiveness of the three agencies examined, comparable across twenty regions.

Similarly, the Department of Enterprise, Trade and Employment, as part of its work on customer care research, has conducted mystery shopping surveys where queries on aspects of the department's work are put over the phone to the relevant division. Examples of the kind of question asked are 'what are the maximum hours that people under eighteen are permitted to work?' and 'how are annual holidays calculated?' Both the timeliness and quality of reply to these and other scenarios are assessed. It would be possible to repeat such surveys and track changes over time.

5.5.1 Conclusions

The bottom up/service user measurements examined here are not productivity measurements in the strict sense, as they are focused on the outputs and outcomes of public sector organisations rather than linking this data to inputs in a direct manner. However, such measures do help provide a picture of what value is being delivered by public services in return for the expenditure supports provided. As such, they have a potentially important role to play in productivity measurement in its broad sense. Bottom up measures can also be a helpful source of information to provide triangulation data for more conventional productivity studies. In many ways, such productivity measures relate more to people's perceptions about what public sector productivity is or should be about, and as such provide evidence that people can relate to in a realistic manner.

5.6 Implications for Policy in Ireland

So what are the implications of this review of public sector productivity measurement for policy makers in Ireland? What lessons can be learned and what steps might be taken to improve public sector productivity measurement? First, it should be noted that information on public sector productivity in Ireland is currently very limited. In order to improve the evidence base, Boyle (2006) provides a framework for the development of productivity measurement, outlined in Table 5.2. This framework proposes that action is taken at a number of levels – cross national, national and sectoral, and organisation-based and bottom up – and by a number of organisations to develop information on public sector productivity in Ireland. In this way, a diversity of approaches to productivity measurement can be used to provide a broad picture of productivity developments. The framework draws from lessons learned from international experience.

Table 5.2: A Framework for the Development of Public Sector Productivity Measurement in Ireland

Productivity Initiative	Action Required
Cross-National Comparative Studies	• Track Ireland's comparative performance in periodic studies of public sector performance and efficiency such as the World Bank and European Central Bank studies. • Actively participate in and encourage the OECD *Management in Government Comparative Country Data* initiative.
National and Sectoral Initiatives	• The Central Statistics Office should take a lead role in the development of the measurement of government output and subsequent productivity studies. • Annual output statements being developed by government departments should inform productivity studies. • The health and education sectors should be priorities for productivity studies. • Relevant state bodies and academic institutions should be encouraged to undertake research into public sector productivity measurement. • Benchmarking of comparable organisations should take place.
Organisation-Based and Bottom Up Initiatives	• Organisation-based measures of productivity should be developed, using annual output statements as a basis for this work. • Central agencies should sponsor a number of service user based studies of the efficiency of public service provision across a range of sectors, repeated periodically. • Benchmarking with comparable organisations should be encouraged.

5.6.1 Cross-National Comparative Studies

There are a small number of cross-national studies of public sector efficiency and performance. These studies have methodological limitations, but nevertheless provide some basis for discussion on productivity. Ireland is included in these studies, which provide an opportunity for contrasting Irish experience with that of other countries. It is suggested that:

1. Ireland's comparative performance is tracked in studies such as the World Bank, European Central Bank and Netherlands Social and Cultural Planning Office studies. Examination of common trends and differences across the studies may highlight issues for further attention. Boyle (forthcoming) begins to address this issue; and
2. The Irish government should actively participate in and encourage the OECD *Management in Government: Comparative Country Data* project. This project provides an opportunity to develop performance and productivity measures which can be tracked over time and across all OECD countries.

5.6.2 National and Sectoral Initiatives

Cross-national comparative studies, while of interest, are likely to be restricted in the amount of information they provide on productivity. High levels of aggregation, and differences in national practices and definitions mean that they are of limited value. National and sectoral trends over time provide a more robust foundation for productivity measurement. It is suggested that:

1. The Central Statistics Office takes a lead role in the measurement of government output and subsequent productivity studies. The Eurostat directive (Eurostat, 2001) suggests a key role for national statistics offices in public sector output measurement. Productivity studies are a natural follow on once output measures are in place;
2. Annual output statements being developed by government departments should inform productivity studies. In Budget 2006, the Minister for Finance announced that from 2007, individual ministers must produce an annual statement on the outputs and objectives of their departments, and from 2008 the actual outturns, for presentation to the relevant Oireachtas committee. In this context, the Taoiseach has indicated that he wishes to see aggregate indicators developed that show the impact of total public spending (Ahern, 2006);
3. The health and education sectors should be priorities for productivity studies. Health and education are major components of public expenditure. There are also several studies of productivity in the health and education sectors in other countries to draw on;
4. Relevant state bodies and academic institutions should be encouraged to undertake research into public sector productivity. In particular, adjusting output figures to reflect quality changes is an important topic for detailed consideration. Bodies such as the Economic and Social Research Institute and Forfás with a track record in productivity and performance issues are well placed to undertake or coordinate such work; and
5. Where institutions provide similar services (local government, hospitals etc.), benchmarking of performance should be encouraged. This is in line with a call to improve productivity in the public sector by de Buitléir (2006).

5.6.3 Organisation-Based and Bottom Up Initiatives

Sectoral, national and cross-national studies of productivity are important in providing a macro-level overview. But it is also important that public sector productivity is assessed at an organisational level. Moreover, getting a service user perspective of public sector efficiency at the micro level can further our understanding of productivity in its broader sense. It is suggested that:

1. Organisation-based measures of productivity should be developed. For government departments, such organisation level measures should link in with and make use of the output statements to be produced from 2007 as part of the reforms of the budgetary process outlined in *Budget 2006* (Department of Finance, 2005);
2. Central agencies should sponsor a number of service user-based studies of the efficiency of public service provision across a range of sectors. These studies should be repeated periodically to assess change over time; and
3. As at the national and sectoral level, benchmarking of performance with comparable organisations has a role to play. Organisations should be encouraged to identify appropriate benchmark organisations when assessing their efficiency. The Taoiseach (Ahern, 2006) has indicated that he wishes to examine how Irish public services perform relative to their international peers, identifying how we compare with those who are recognised as representing good practice.

5.7 Conclusion

Measuring public sector productivity presents major challenges. Until recently, the convention in national accounts was to assume that outputs equalled inputs, and that therefore, year-on-year there was no productivity change taking place in the public sector. Clearly this is not the case, and attempts are now being made in several countries to develop productivity measures based on government output data. This chapter has examined some of the main initiatives in public sector productivity measurement that are taking place internationally. On the basis of these developments, proposals are made to improve productivity measurement in the Irish public sector. There is a strong case for devoting more attention and resources to improving the measurement of public sector productivity.

References

Afonso, A., Schuknecht, L. and Tanzi, V. (2003), "Public Sector Efficiency: An International Comparison", Working Paper No. 242, *European Central Bank Working Paper Series,* Frankfurt, European Central Bank.

Ahern, B. (2006), Speech by the Taoiseach, Mr Bertie Ahern, T.D. at the *Inaugural IPA National Conference* on "Moving Towards the Public Sector of the Future" in the Grand Hotel Malahide, 8th June (www.taoiseach.gov.ie).

Arndt, C. and Oman, C. (2006), *Uses and Abuses of Governance Indicators,* Paris, OECD.

Atkinson (2005), *Atkinson Review: Final Report - Measurement of Government Output and Productivity for the National Accounts*, Final report, Basingstoke, Palgrave Macmillan.

Australian Productivity Commission (2006), *Report on Government Services 2006*, report of the Steering Committee for the Review of Government Service Provision, Canberra, Australian Productivity Commission.

Banks, G. (2005), "Comparing School Systems across Australia", address to *Australia and New Zealand School of Government* (ANZSOG) conference, 'Schooling in the 21st Century: Unlocking Human Potential', 28-29 September, Sydney.

Boyle, R. (2006), *Measuring Public Sector Productivity: Lessons from International Experience*, Committee for Public Management Research Discussion Paper No. 35, Dublin, Institute of Public Administration.

Boyle, R. (forthcoming), *How Good is Ireland's Public Administration?*, work in progress for the Committee for Public Management Research (www.cpmr.gov.ie).

de Buitléir, D. (2006), "Promoting Productivity in a Diverse Public Sector", presentation at *Institute of Public Administration* seminar on promoting productivity in a diverse public sector, Dublin, 21 April.

Department of Finance (2005), *Budget 2006*, Dublin, Stationery Office.

European Commission (2004), *European Competitiveness Report 2004*, Commission Staff Working Document SEC(2004)1397, Brussels, European Commission.

Eurostat (2001), *Handbook of Price and Volume Measures of National Accounts*, Brussels, European Commission.

Finance Ministry (2005), Budget Report 2005, Copenhagen: Ministry for Finance.

Haubrich, D., Gutierrez, R. and McLean, I. (2006), "Three Years of Assessing Local Authorities Through CPA – A Research Note on Deprivation and Productivity", paper presented at the *National Institute of Economic and Social Research* (NIESR) fourth Public Sector Performance Conference, London, 20 January.

IMD (2003), *World Competitiveness Yearbook 2003*, Lausanne, Institute for Management Development.

Kaufmann, D., Kraay, A. and Mastruzzi, M. (2005), *Governance Matters IV: Governance Indicators for 1996-2004*, World Bank Policy Research Working Paper 3630, Washington, DC, The World Bank.

Kuhry, B., Pommer, E. and De Kam, F. (2006), "Public Sector Performance, An International Comparison", paper presented at the *National Institute of Economic and Social Research* (NIESR) fourth Public Sector Performance Conference, London, 20 January.

Martin, S. and Bovaird, T. (2005), *Meta-evaluation of the Local Government Modernisation Agenda: Progress Report on Service Improvement in Local Government,* London, Office of the Deputy Prime Minister.

Ministry of Finance (1997), *Public Sector Productivity in Sweden,* Stockholm, Ministry of Finance.

Musgrave, R.A. (1959), *The Theory of Public Finance,* New York, McGraw Hill.

Niemi, M. (1998), "Measuring Government Sector Output and Productivity in Finland – Application of the Output Indicator Method", agenda item 1, OECD meeting of National Accounts Experts, Statistics Directorate, STD/NA(98)4, 22-25 September, Paris: OECD.

OECD (2005), *Management in Government: Feasibility Report on the Development of Comparative Data,* GOV/PGC (2005)10, 31st October, Paris, OECD.

Office for National Statistics (2006), *Public Service Productivity: Health,* February, London: Office for National Statistics.

Pollitt, C. and Bouckaert, G. (2004), *Public Management Reform: A Comparative Analysis,* Oxford: Oxford University Press.

Pritchard, A. (2002a), "Measuring Productivity Change in the Provision of Public Services", *Economic Trends,* No. 582, May, 20-32.

Pritchard, A. (2002b), "Measuring Productivity Change in the Provision of Public Services", paper presented at the *National Institute of Economic and Social Research* (NIESR) Conference on Productivity and Performance in the Provision of Public Services, London, 19 November.

Putnam, R. D. (1993), *Making Democracy Work: Civic Traditions in Modern Italy,* Princeton, NJ: Princeton University Press.

Social and Cultural Planning Office (2004), *Public Sector Performance: An International Comparison of Education, Health Care, Law and Order and Public Administration,* The Hague: Social and Cultural Planning Office.

The World Bank Group (2006), Doing Business: Methodology – Starting a Business, Washington, DC: The World Bank.

Thornhill, D. (2006), "Productivity Attainment in a Diverse Public Sector", presentation at *Institute of Public Administration* seminar on promoting productivity in a diverse public sector, Dublin, 21 April.

Van de Walle, S. (2005), "Measuring Bureaucratic Quality in Governance indicators", paper presented at *European Group of Public Administration* (EGPA) study group on productivity and quality in the public sector, Bern, 31 August-3 September.

CHAPTER 6

PRODUCTIVITY IN IRISH AGRICULTURE

ALAN MATTHEWS, CAROL NEWMAN AND FIONA THORNE

ABSTRACT

While detailed analysis of the productivity of many sectors of the Irish economy are not possible because of a lack of data, the quality and volume of data on agricultural outputs and inputs allows such an analysis. In this chapter, a picture of the productivity performance of the Irish agriculture sector based on various different measures is presented and compared with the performance of Ireland's key competitors in this area. The measures of partial productivity discussed in this chapter indicate that the technical performance has lagged behind competing countries. In absolute terms, the overall productivity performance of Irish agriculture between 1984 and 2004 was poor.

6.1 Introduction

Farm policy in Ireland has traditionally focused on improving farm incomes, both in absolute terms and relative to average incomes in the non-farm population, and on maintaining as many people as possible working in agriculture. Improving productivity as a policy goal, while not neglected, was not a priority objective. This was particularly the case during the 'MacSharry era' of the EU's Common Agricultural Policy (CAP), which lasted for the decade 1993-2004.[1] This era was characterised by the growing substitution of direct payments for market price support as a way of maintaining farm incomes. In Ireland, direct payments as a proportion of the value of gross agricultural output (including these payments) rose from seven per cent in 1992 to 24 per cent in 2004. As a share of the operating surplus in agriculture (used as a measure of aggregate income from farming), their importance was even higher, rising from 18 to 66 per cent over the same period.

With such a high share of farm income coming in the form of direct payments, it should not be surprising that attention switched from technical improvements in agriculture as a source of increasing income, to ways of maximising premium income. Direct payments were paid on a per hectare or per animal basis; if a farmer increased yield per hectare in cereals or yield per animal in livestock production, it made no difference to premium income which was now the largest contributor to income on the farm. Indeed, eligibility for premium income was conditional on measures to restrain productivity improvements. In cereal production, larger farms were required to set-aside a proportion of their land each year on a rotational basis; in dry stock production, payments were limited by stocking density restrictions and additional payments were made to encourage further extensification. In the milk sector, production quotas had been introduced in 1984. While this, in itself, did not prevent individual farmers from trying to increase their productivity in order to produce their quota entitlement at minimum cost, the accompanying rules restricting the transfer of quotas between farms. This was designed in part to maintain milk production in higher-cost areas of the country as part of a rural development policy and ensured that the total cost of producing the national milk quota remained higher than otherwise would have been the case.

The volume of Irish agricultural output, after increasing steadily since EU accession in 1972, levelled out during the 1990s. This was also the period when growth in the non-agricultural economy surged ahead, particularly after 1994. It is possible that agriculture would not have been able to compete for resources with the rapidly growing non-agricultural sector during this period under any policy scenario, but it is clear that the agricultural sector was engaging in this competition with a heavy weight penalty as a result of the policy environment in place.

This policy environment is now changing rapidly. The 2003 Luxembourg Agreement on CAP reform brought the MacSharry era to an end by decoupling the majority of direct payments from production. These payments are now made to farmers according to entitlements based primarily on the level of payments received in the past, and subject to compliance with good farming practice and various statutory regulations on the environment, food safety and animal welfare. Importantly, farmers are now encouraged to base their production decisions on actual market prices, rather than attempting to maximise premium income.

The level of market prices for the major agricultural commodities is also under downward pressure as a result of policy reform. Farm prices within the EU are heavily supported by a mix of import tariffs and export subsidies. These policy interventions maintain prices for commodities such as beef, butter, skim powder, sugar and so on well above world market levels. In the Doha Round of trade negotiations the EU is negotiating with its trade partners to lower barriers on market access. It has agreed conditionally, as part of an overall agreement, to abolish export subsidies by 2013 at the latest. While the Doha Round negotiations are currently suspended, the pressure for policy reform is unlikely to ease. Irish farmers will compete in a much lower price environment in the future, even if the dismantling of the CAP's protective regime is still likely to take some time.

Greater attention is now being given to the underlying competitiveness of agriculture in each Member State in an effort to learn how each might fare in the new policy environment. Evidence suggests that, in the past, Ireland has fared badly in terms of technology-based productivity growth, a key component of competitiveness, unlike the majority of other EU countries where productivity growth improved after joining the EU (Leetmaa et al., 2004). Recent work suggests that there has been a further erosion of Ireland's competitiveness in the late 1990s and early 2000s based on a variety of cost competitiveness indicators (Boyle, 2002). These trends have led to some concern about the future viability of farming in Ireland in the face of increasing costs and falling prices.

As a result, understanding the factors driving productivity growth in Irish agriculture is more important than ever as we try to ascertain how Irish farming will fare in a more liberal market environment. In this chapter, recent research analysing various aspects of the productivity performance of Irish agriculture is presented. A number of productivity indicators are considered. One set of indicators are accountancy measures, based on comparing detailed production costs and revenues for representative farms across a number of countries (Boyle, 2002; Thorne 2004; 2006). Production costs are normalised by expressing them as a percentage of the value of output, or per unit of output. The greatest difficulty in comparing production costs across countries lies in the treatment of family-owned resources in agriculture (family labour, family-owned land and capital). For these reasons, the distinction is made between cash costs (the cost of purchased intermediate inputs) and economic costs (which include, in addition, the imputed cost of family-owned resources). These indicators give a good summary of competitiveness outcomes or performance. Changes in these indicators can come about either because of changes in price ratios across countries or because of changes in input-output ratios (productivity). Thus it is important to dig behind these numbers to understand the factors responsible for changes over time.

Productivity change in agriculture is often measured using partial productivity indicators, such as output per unit of labour (labour productivity), output per unit of land (yields), milk yields per cow, or lambs per ewe. These are partial indicators because they compare output to a single input, such as land area or breeding herd. These indicators are easily available, and they are concrete and understandable. However, they can also be misleading because a high level of productivity on one indicator may be due to the generous use of another input. For example, farm labour productivity may be high in one country compared to another, but this may be because of greater use of capital and land. In calculating productivity change, it is desirable to take into account the relationship between the change in output and the change in the use of all inputs. Such a measure is called a Total Factor Productivity (TFP) Index. Such an index can be calculated using aggregate data based on the Economics Accounts for Agriculture (for an Irish example, see Matthews, 2000), or on the basis of farm-level data through statistical estimation of the farm technology and its change over time (O'Neill and Matthews, 2001; Newman and Matthews, 2004).

The Agri-Food 2010 Committee concluded in 2000 that there was insufficient work and data in the area of competitiveness (DAFRD, 2000). Following from this report, the Rural Economy Research Centre, Teagasc, responded to the recommendation from the committee for 'the collection and publication on a regular basis of key competitiveness indicators, with appropriate international comparisons" (DAFRD, 2000: 40). Appropriate indicators of competitiveness were identified and calculated for the years 1996 to 2003. These indicators provide a baseline upon which relative productivity and competitiveness of Irish agriculture can be examined on a regular basis (Thorne, 2004; 2006). A further study of productivity growth in Irish agriculture was supported by the Department of Agriculture and Food's Research Stimulus Fund (Newman and Matthews, 2004). This chapter summarises the findings of these studies in presenting an analysis of productivity growth in Irish agriculture.

6.2 Lessons From Accountancy and Partial Productivity Measures

Figure 6.1 shows the relative competitive performance of the main sectors of Irish agriculture for the period 1996-2003.[2] The European Commission's Farm Accountancy Data Network (FADN) was the primary source of data used in the analysis. Data analysis was confined to specialist dairy, sheep, beef finishing, beef fattening and cereal farms, as defined by FADN, on which the standard gross margin from each of the respective enterprises accounted for at least two-thirds of the farm total gross margin.[3]

Figure 6.1: Cash and Economic Costs as a Percentage of Average of Selected Countries, 1996-2003

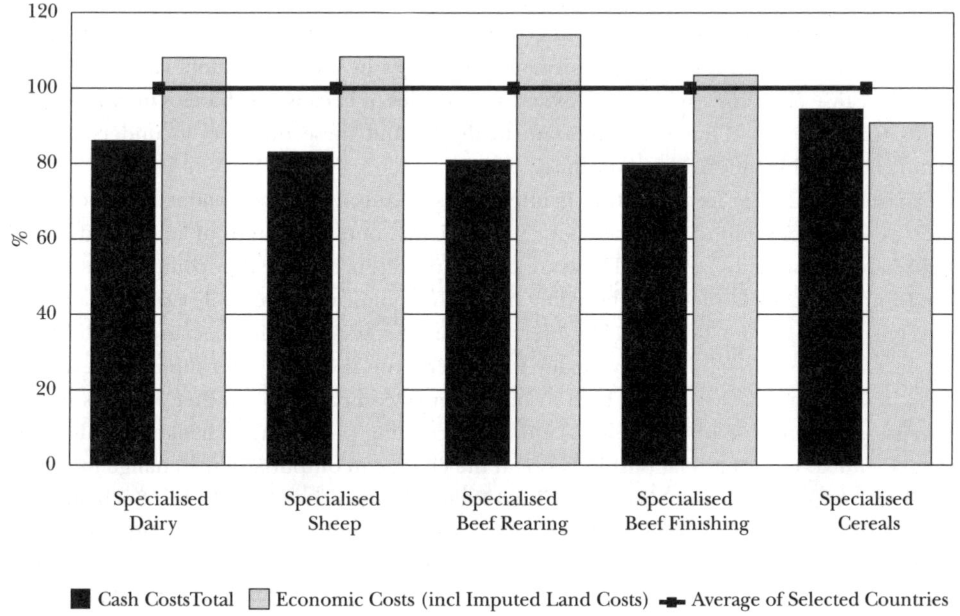

6.2.1 Milk Sector

Selected partial productivity measures (milk yield, labour productivity and stocking rate) for Irish dairy herds were generally lower over the period 1996 to 2003, compared to the other countries examined. Furthermore, land productivity measures for Irish farms declined over the period relative to the average of all countries in the analysis.

While partial productivity indicators were worrying for Irish dairy farms, the profitability indicator of competitive performance (costs as a per cent of dairy output value) was positive for Ireland over the period 1996 to 2003 compared to the other countries examined. Italy had the lowest cash costs as a percentage of output (at 60 per cent), but the cost structure in Ireland was only slightly higher (64 per cent). The highest cash costs as a percentage of output were experienced in Denmark where cash costs were 87 per cent of total output of the enterprise. Further analysis of specialist dairy farms that had between 50-99 dairy cows did not show substantial deviation from these results.

However, the competitive advantage displayed by Irish milk producers deteriorated when total economic costs were considered. Total economic costs as a percentage of output were highest in Ireland for the average size farm at 122 per cent of output. The competitive position of the larger size dairy farms in Ireland was more positive on a total economic cost basis, where total economic costs as a per cent of output value was on a par with the average of other countries. The most significant imputed cost that contributed to the relatively high total economic costs experienced in Ireland over the period was the charge for owned land. Thus, the opportunity cost of land has a major impact on the competitive position of Irish milk producers in the long term.

6.2.2 Beef Sector

Analysis was undertaken on two categories of specialist cattle holdings: (1) Specialist cattle – mainly rearing; and (2) Specialist cattle – mainly fattening. Ireland's productivity in these two beef systems was generally lower for the period 1996 to 2003 compared to competing beef producers in Europe.

Accountancy indicators for the beef rearing and fattening enterprises show that, over the period 1996 to 2003, Irish producers had a competitive advantage when cash costs were examined. However, the competitive position exhibited by Irish beef farms was much weaker when total economic costs were considered. The imputed charge for owned land and labour had a large negative influence on the relative competitive advantage of Irish beef farms.

The role of direct payments must be considered in evaluating the longer-term competitiveness of Irish beef production systems. To investigate this issue the accountancy based indicators of competitiveness were revisited to determine the ability of Irish cattle farmers to survive in a decoupled policy scenario. For the period 1996 to 2003, Irish beef rearing and fattening farms had on average a 15 per cent and four per cent lower cash cost to market based output ratio, respectively, compared to the average of all countries in the analysis. Again, however, Irelands' competitive position deteriorated when economic costs were considered as a percentage of market based output, relative to total output (excluding direct payments).

6.2.3 Cereals Sector

Selected partial productivity indicators on Irish cereal farms were generally more positive than for the other enterprises examined. Yields were well in excess of the average of all countries examined and labour productivity levels were similar to the average for all countries. Furthermore, there was no consistent relative productivity trend over time observed for Irish cereal farms.

Accountancy measures of competitiveness indicate that Irish cereal producers maintained a competitive advantage relative to the average of all countries in the analysis, when cash costs and economic costs were considered. For example, Irish cereal producers had the second lowest cash cost to output ratio at 73 per cent, compared to the other countries examined. Even when total economic costs were measured Irish cereal producers maintained a competitive advantage compared to the average of all countries. When direct payments were excluded from the analysis, Irish cereal producers remained competitive during the period 1996 to 2003.

6.2.4 Sheep Sector

Selected partial productivity indicators show that Ireland and the UK had relatively low stocking rates and land productivity compared to France over the period 1996 to 2003, but Irish sheep farms had higher technical performance based on these two measures compared to the UK. However, the UK and France both outperformed Ireland in terms of labour productivity.

Accountancy measures based solely on cash costs show that Irish sheep producers have a comparative advantage compared to France and the UK. Irish producers have the lowest cash costs as a percentage of output and the highest margin over cash costs per 100kg of product volume. However, French producers replaced Irish producers with the highest margin over cash costs per forage hectare. This advantage experienced by French producers in terms of margin over cash costs per hectare can be attributed to the high stocking rate per hectare on French sheep farms, which is associated with intensive indoor feeding of sheep for milk production.

Various measures of cost competitiveness show that Ireland's comparative advantage on a cash cost basis disappeared when economic costs were considered over the period 1996 to 2003. Furthermore, over the period Irish sheep producers relied more heavily on subsidies to supplement the revenue of the sheep enterprise, compared to the UK and France. Consequently, when costs were expressed as a percentage of market based output, Irish producers were surpassed by French producers, who had the lowest cash costs as a percentage of market based output. On an economic cost basis Ireland again emerged as the highest cost producer.

6.3 Lessons From Total Factor Productivity Measures

Newman and Matthews (2004) measured TFP growth in Irish agriculture over the period 1984 to 2000 by estimating econometric models of the production technology in use on Irish farms using data from the National Farm Survey. The study estimates productivity growth by farming system, where each of the four systems examined (dairy, tillage, sheep and cattle) is dominated by a specific enterprise. Total factor productivity growth is decomposed into three elements:

1. Technical change, or the movement in the production frontier over time as a result of research and innovation;
2. Technical efficiency change, or the change in the gap between the efficiency of the 'average' farm and the efficiency of best practice farms; and
3. Scale efficiency change, or the change in efficiency brought about by changes in the scale of operations on farms.

Figure 6.2 presents the overall trend in productivity growth for each farm system while Table 6.1 presents the productivity growth index by system and its decomposition for the 1984 to 2000 period.

Figure 6.2: System-by-System TFP Trend

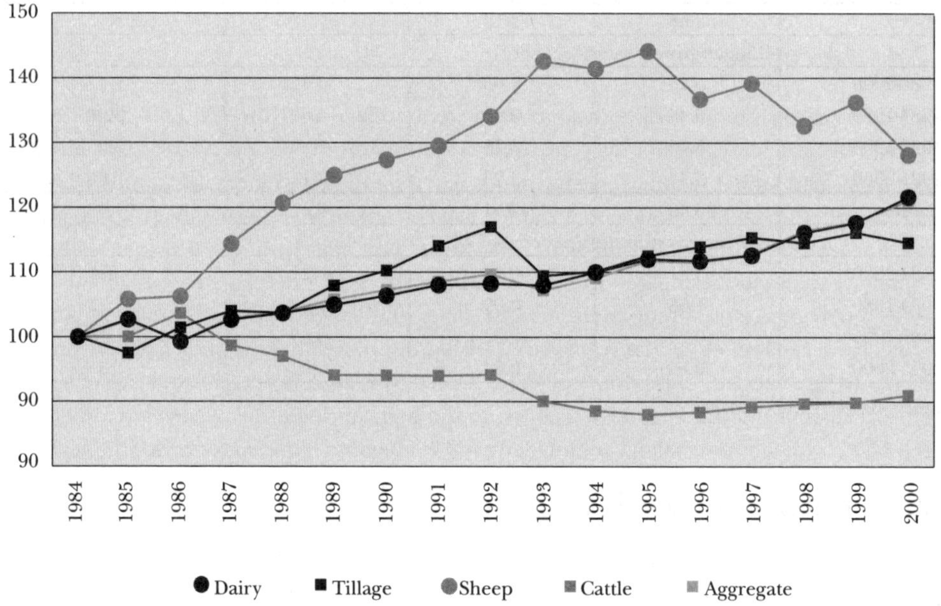

Table 6.1: Productivity Change and Decomposition on Irish Farms, 1984-2000

	Technical Change	Efficiency	Returns to Scale	TFP
Dairy	122.91	99.15	99.82	121.65
	Linear growth rates (per cent)			
1984-2000	1.42	-0.19	-0.01	1.20
1984-1989	0.65	0.24	-0.01	0.89
1989-1995	1.48	-0.49	-0.01	0.95
1995-2000	2.32	0.18	-0.01	2.48
Tillage	137.94	82.46	100.70	114.54
	Linear growth rates (per cent)			
1984-2000	2.40	-0.99	0.07	1.06
1984-1989	3.03	-1.20	0.12	1.74
1989-1995	2.51	-1.49	-0.09	0.31
1995-2000	1.54	-0.60	-0.04	0.45
Sheep	181.68	73.16	96.40	128.13
	Linear growth rates (per cent)			
1984-2000	5.25	-1.63	-0.10	2.14
1984-1989	6.44	-0.41	-0.63	5.08
1989-1995	5.46	-1.28	0.16	3.29
1995-2000	3.34	-3.23	-0.11	-3.00
Cattle	96.59	97.51	96.62	91.00
	Linear growth rates (per cent)			
1984-2000	-0.21	-0.46	-0.21	-0.84
1984-1989	-1.06	0.09	-0.28	-1.25
1989-1995	-0.21	-0.93	-0.13	-1.18
1995-2000	0.65	0.04	-0.09	0.57

Note: Base = 1984 (100.00).

6.3.1 Enterprise Level Analysis

Figure 6.2 shows that the trend in overall productivity growth differs markedly across farm systems. The sheep system exhibits the best performance due to an early burst in productivity growth rates. Total factor productivity grew by 28 per cent over the sample period at a linear rate of 2.1 per cent per annum. However, the decomposition of productivity growth rates into three different time periods illustrates that productivity gains have been exhausted since the mid-1990s. This is, in part, due to an apparent slowing down in the rate of technical change over time, but also due to an increasing gap between efficiency levels on the average sheep farm and best practice farms.

The cattle system, on the other hand, had the poorest performance of all systems.[4] In total, productivity fell by nine per cent over the sample period with negative linear growth of 0.8 per cent per annum. This was mainly due to technical regress between 1984 and 1995 accompanied by negative efficiency growth, particularly between 1989 and 1995. Positive productivity growth between 1995 and 2000 provides evidence of a recovery in the productivity performance of the system in the latter portion of the sample period.

Productivity grew slowly in the dairy farm system at the beginning of the period with productivity gains of 0.9 per cent per annum. However, in more recent years of the sample period productivity grew at a linear rate of almost 2.5 per cent per annum yielding an overall increase in total factor productivity of almost 22 per cent for the sample period as a whole. The overall growth in productivity in the dairy system was driven by technical progress at an average rate of 1.4 per cent per annum, increasing over the sample period. The efficiency gap between the average farm and the best practice farm on the whole remained stable despite a widening in the gap between 1990 and 1997. This may reflect the quickening pace of technical progress observed where leading-edge farmers are innovating more quickly than dairy farmers on average. A noticeable result is the improvement in average efficiency levels evident in the third period while the best practice frontier shifts outward at a linear rate of 2.3 per cent per annum. Not only are the 'best' dairy producers adopting more efficient technologies at an increasing rate, but also the average producers are increasingly managing to keep up. This may reflect structural change in the system, and the more rapid exit of less efficient producers from the industry in the more recent period.

The tillage system shows the reverse pattern with a gradual loss of momentum in productivity gains in the later years of the sample period. This can be attributed to a sharp fall in efficiency levels between 1992 and 1993 coinciding with the introduction of set-aside on tillage farms. Productivity growth recovered somewhat in the last 5 years of the sample with a linear growth rate of 0.5 per cent observed for the 1995 to 2000 period. Productivity growth is driven by technical progress over the sample period at a rapid rate of 2.4 per cent annually but is dampened by a poor average efficiency performance particularly in the middle years of the sample.

6.3.2 Total Productivity Growth in Irish Agriculture

Overall productivity in Irish agriculture grew by 21.1 per cent over the sample period at a linear rate of just over one per cent per annum. Boyle (1987) estimated a total productivity growth rate of just over one per cent for the 1960 to 1982 period suggesting that productivity growth between 1960 and 2000 has remained fairly steady. However, total factor productivity fell from an estimated growth rate of 1.5 per cent for the 1980s to 0.7 per cent for the 1990s. The former is consistent with Bureau et al.'s (1995) estimate of productivity growth of 1.35 per cent annually for the 1973 to 1989 period. The decline in productivity is consistent with Boyle's (2002) study, which identified a significant deterioration in the competitiveness of Irish agricultural production relative to the most efficient world producer of each commodity between 1988/89 and 1998/99. These results are also consistent with other estimates of slowing productivity growth derived using other methodologies. Matthews (2000) found an annual rate of total factor productivity growth in Irish agriculture of 2.3 per cent per annum in the 1980s falling to 0.8 per cent annually in the 1990s. O'Neill et al. (2002), using farm level data and an aggregate model of Irish agriculture, found that productivity growth slowed from an estimated 2.3 per cent annually between 1984 and 1989 to an annual average rate of 1.5 per cent between 1990 and 1998.

6.4 Relevance of Research Findings to Policymakers

6.4.1 Partial Productivity and Accountancy Indicators

The various measures reviewed each focus on different aspects of the productivity story in agriculture. Partial productivity measures are useful in comparing absolute productivity levels across countries, but may be biased because they ignore the use of complementary inputs. Comparative studies of agricultural TFP tend to measure the growth rates of TFP, not relative levels. From a competitiveness perspective, lower productivity levels can be offset by lower production costs or higher output prices, and the accountancy indicators take these factors into account. The cash costs indicator is best interpreted as a short-run indicator of a sector's ability to withstand a price-cost squeeze. The economic costs indicator takes into account, in addition, the opportunity cost of family-owned resources. These will be influenced by developments in the wider economy and thus provide a better basis for assessing the longer-run competitiveness of the sector in relation to its trading partners.

The research on partial productivity and accountancy indicators for Ireland indicates that, over the period 1996 to 2003, the competitive position in Ireland for all four enterprises was positive when cash costs were considered ignoring imputed charges for owned resources.

When the imputed charges for owned resources were considered, the competitive ranking for Irish agriculture deteriorated relative to other countries for all commodities examined. However, in most cases the exclusion of imputed charges for owned land from the analysis reinforced the competitive position of Irish farms. In addition, the larger sized Irish dairy farms were also more competitive on a total economic cost basis compared to the average sized dairy farm. Thus, part of the explanation of the deterioration of competitive ranking for the average Irish farm when total economic costs are considered relates to 'the relatively low scale of primary agricultural activity in Ireland' (Boyle, 2002: 177). This result is indicative of the small-scale farming that is predominant in the Irish dairy industry relative to competing industries. As Irish dairy farming transforms to larger scale production its competitive position would be strengthened and be better able to cope with a cost/price squeeze, given current projections for a decline in farm milk prices.

Another interesting result which could have implications for Irish agriculture in a decoupled policy environment is evident in the beef and sheep sectors, where Irish beef farms (both rearing and fattening) and sheep farms appeared to be less competitive relative to the average of all countries when costs were expressed as a percentage of market based output. This is important in the context of recent reforms to the CAP, where direct payments have become either fully or partially decoupled from production. As relative economic costs are considered as a relative guide to the longer-term competitive position of competing countries, these findings could be considered as warning signals for the future competitive performance of these sectors of Irish agriculture.

To understand the strengths and weakness which underpinned the relative performance of Irish agriculture over the period, the indicators of competitive potential were examined, namely, partial productivity and accountancy measures. Most of the indicators of partial productivity indicated that the technical performance of Irish agriculture was lagging behind competing countries. However, productivity levels on Irish cereal farms were on average more positive than the results for the other commodities. While these indicators of productivity were not very positive for Irish agriculture, it is important to remember that these indicators are only partial productivity measures, and indicators of total factor productivity provide a more informative picture of relative productivity performance.

6.4.2 Total Factor Productivity

Unfortunately, there is no recent data which would allow us to compare the absolute level of TFP in Irish agriculture with levels elsewhere. Data for the period 1973 to 1993 show Ireland lagging well behind the sample of other European countries and the US which were examined (Ball et al., 2001). In 1990, for example, Ireland's TFP was 88 per cent of the US figure, compared to a EU average of 93 per cent. In the past, this productivity disadvantage could be offset by lower factor input costs, but Ireland has now become a high-cost economy. In future, the relative change in TFP will determine the sustainability of Irish agricultural production in a more market-oriented environment.

The research reviewed earlier presents a rather sombre picture. In aggregate, the agricultural sector experienced productivity growth of 21.1 per cent for the 1984 to 2000 period, at a linear rate of just over 1 per cent per annum. There is evidence, furthermore, of a slowdown in growth in the 1990s. The study also shows that clear differences exist in the productivity performance of different farming systems in Ireland. Sheep farming exhibits the most impressive performance due to an early burst in productivity growth rates. However, productivity gains have been exhausted since the mid-1990s and there has been no further productivity growth since then. Dairy farming improved its productivity performance throughout the period, albeit from what might be considered a weak performance in the second half of the 1980s. Tillage also performed well at the beginning of the period but productivity performance has been relatively poor in recent years. Cattle farming performed poorly throughout.

A number of potential explanations are given for the trends observed with some implications for future policy developments presented. In relation to the dairy system, Newman and Matthews (2006) point out that productivity growth of 0.9 per cent annually in the 1984 to 1990 period is the lowest of the three periods examined, and may reflect the productivity cost of the dislocation and adjustments required on dairy farms immediately following the introduction of the quota regime. On this interpretation, the acceleration of productivity growth in subsequent sub-periods may reflect the re-establishment of more 'normal' growth rates as farmers learned to live with the quota regime and as the regime in recent years has become less restrictive.

Similarly, Newman and Matthews (2004) suggest that the relatively poor performance of the tillage system between 1989 and 1995 compared with 1984 and 1989 may reflect the adjustment problems associated with the introduction of the MacSharry reforms to the CAP. More recently, the system has recovered exhibiting faster growth rates between 1995 and 2000.

Explanations for the trend observed in the sheep system are also advanced. After a spectacular productivity performance in the early years, a slowdown in productivity growth was evidenced post-1992. While there was a steady growth in the lambing percentage throughout the whole period, productivity may have been adversely affected after 1992 by the growth of extensification payments and agri-environment payments. Both schemes would have encouraged farmers to make less efficient use of their resources. In the case of the extensification scheme, the incentive was to reduce sheep numbers per hectare in return for higher levels of direct payments. In the case of the Rural Environmental Protection Scheme, higher levels of on-farm costs would be associated with environmental improvements rather than higher levels of physical output, which are not captured in the output variable used in the analysis.

A similar attempt to maximise premium income rather than efficiency or productivity could also explain the cattle system findings. The poor productivity performance of the cattle system was associated with a strong premium-driven expansion in the suckler cow herd from 410,000 in 1981 (when the Suckler Cow Premium was introduced) to peak at just under 1,200,000 in 1998. Extensification payments and stocking rate restrictions required for eligibility for premium payments for male animals post-1992 would also have contributed to the distortion of incentives. If this were the case then the introduction of decoupling in 2005, which eliminates the incentive for farmers to manage their livestock enterprises with a view to maximising direct payment receipts, could lead to a rebound in productivity growth. Evidence from New Zealand suggests that TFP growth averaged only 1.5 per cent annually during its high subsidy period (1972-84) but since the elimination of subsidies has improved to 2.5 per cent per annum (Lattimore, 2006).

6.5 Concluding Remarks

In this chapter a picture of the productivity performance of the Irish agricultural sector based on various different measures has been presented. Of key interest is how well the sector performs relative to its key competitors. The measures of partial productivity discussed in this chapter indicate that the technical performance of Irish agriculture was lagging behind competing countries. Recent data is not available to compare productivity performance with other EU countries on the basis of total factor productivity measures. In absolute terms, however, the overall productivity performance of Irish agriculture between 1984 and 2000 was poor. Hadley (2006), for example, reports rates of technical change in England and Wales for arable farms in the range 3.7 to 5.2 per cent annually, and for livestock farms (excluding pigs and poultry) of between 2.0 and 3.3 per cent.

Eurostat has begun to provide harmonised long-term productivity series for all EU Member States (Eurostat, 2002). In addition to partial measures, it calculates a 'multi-factor' measure. This is defined as the relationship between the growth of output and the growth of a bundle of inputs comprising capital, raw materials and labour, but excluding land. Thus it is close to, but not identical with, a measure of total factor productivity. Results for this multifactor productivity measure can now be compared for most EU countries for the 1990s, although because of the problems of harmonisation, the Irish data refer only to the shorter time period 1995 to 2001. The Irish rate of growth of 1.3 per cent in multi-factor productivity for this shorter period falls below the average of 1.7 per cent over the 1990 to 2001 period achieved for all countries for which results are reported. This confirms the trend presented in this chapter of a below average performance of Irish agriculture. It is unlikely that productivity growth rates of this magnitude will be sufficient to maintain farm incomes in the face of a stagnant or declining price of output and inflationary increases in costs suggesting that more rapid structural change in the sector is inevitable.

Notes

1 The MacSharry CAP reform was implemented in 1993 and was followed in 1999 by the Agenda 2000 reform of the CAP. As this latter reform continued the reform strategy initiated by MacSharry, the entire period covered by these two reforms is called the 'MacSharry era'.
2 The results in this section are based on Thorne (2004 and 2006).
3 The competitive position of Irish (i) dairy farms was compared against Belgium, Denmark, France, Germany, Italy, the Netherlands and the UK; (ii) sheep farms was compared against the UK and France; (iii) beef farms was compared against France, Germany and the UK; and (iv) cereal farms was compared against Denmark, Germany, France, Italy and the UK.
4 Some caution must be exercised in interpreting all results from the model of the Irish cattle system due to data problems associated with measuring the 'volume' of cattle output on farms, which may lead to some bias in the reported results.

References

Ball, E., Bureau, J.C., Butault, J.P. and Nehring, R. (2001), "Levels of Farm Sector Productivity: An International Comparison", *Journal of Productivity Analysis*, 15, 5-29.

Boyle, G. (1987), *How Technically Efficient is Irish Agriculture? Methods of Measurement.* Socio-Economic Research Series No. 7, An Foras Taluntais, Dublin.

Boyle, G. (2002), *The Competitiveness of Irish Agriculture*, mimeo. Research Stimulus Fund Project Report, Department of Agriculture and Food.

Bureau, J.C., Färe, R. and Grosskopf, S. (1995), "A Comparison of Three Nonparametric Measures of Productivity Growth in European and United States Agriculture", *Journal of Agricultural Economics* 46, 3, 309-326.

Department of Agriculture and Food (2004), *"Report of the Agri Vision 2015 Committee"*.

Eurostat (2002), *Income from Agricultural Activity in 2001 – European Union and Candidate Countries*, Luxembourg, Eurostat.

Hadley, D. (2006), "Patterns in Technical Efficiency and Technical Change at Farm Level in England and Wales 1982-2002", *Journal of Agricultural Economics*, 57(2).

Lattimore, R. (2006), "Farm Subsidy Reform Dividends". Paper prepared for the North American Agrifood Market Integration Consortium Meetings, May 31-June 2, 2006, Calgary, Alberta.

Leetmaa, S., Arnade, C. and Kelch, D. (2004), "A Comparison of US and EU Agricultural Productivity with Implications for EU Enlargement". In Normile, M. and Leetmaa, S. (eds.) US-EU Food and *Agriculture Comparisons. Agriculture and Trade Report No. WRS04-04, 33-47.* Washington DC: Economic Research Service, United States Department of Agriculture.

Matthews, A. (2000), "Productivity Growth in Irish Agriculture", *Journal of the Statistical and Social Inquiry Society of Ireland,* XXIX, 315-358.

Newman, C. and Matthews, A. (2004), *Measuring and Understanding Productivity Growth in Irish Agriculture,* Wissenschaftsverlag Vauk, Kiel.

Newman, C. and Matthews, A. (2006), "The Productivity Performance of Irish Dairy Farms 1984-2000: A Multiple Output Distance function Approach", *Journal of Productivity Analysis,* 26(2).

O'Neill, S., Leavy, A. and Matthews, A. (2002), *Measuring Productivity Change and Efficiency on Irish Farms,* End of Project Report 4498, Rural Economy Centre, Teagasc, Dublin.

O'Neill, S. and Matthews, A. (2001), "Technical Change and Efficiency in Irish Agriculture", *Economic and Social Review,* 32(3): 263-284.

Thorne, F. (2004), "Measuring the Competitiveness of Irish Agriculture: 1996-2000". *Rural Economy Research Series, No. 9.* Dublin: Teagasc.

Thorne, F. (2006-forthcoming), "Measuring the Competitiveness of Irish Agriculture: 1996-2003". *Rural Economy Research Series,* Teagasc.

CHAPTER 7

PRODUCTIVITY IN THE IRISH RESIDENTIAL CONSTRUCTION INDUSTRY

CIARÁN AYLWARD AND RONNIE O'TOOLE[1]

ABSTRACT

Irish residential construction is currently undergoing a transformation in productivity terms. This was achieved through increased skills in the industry, increased mechanisation, the use of more modern site management techniques and increases in the average scheme size. This has occurred mostly in urban centres, with rural areas still typified by traditional, low-productivity methods. We estimate that while it took 33 workers a year to complete ten homes in 1993, by 2003 it took only 26 workers to build the same number of homes of a similar size.

1 The views expressed are solely those of the authors and do not necessarily reflect the views of Forfás.

7.1 Introduction

The purpose of this chapter is to provide an assessment of the productivity performance of the Irish residential construction sector and its drivers since 1993. We estimate that the productivity levels of the Irish residential construction sector grew by 27 per cent from 1993 to 2003. Section 7.2 of this chapter presents an outline of the key characteristics of the sector and its importance to the Irish economy. Section 7.3 describes the methodology used, which is based on a measure of physical outputs and inputs (number of houses produced divided by number of employees) rather than value added. This estimate is adjusted for factors such as changes in house quality etc. Section 7.4 decomposes the estimate of productivity into the role played by increased technical efficiency/mechanisation and changes in scheme size. Section 7.5 sets out the implications of this improvement in productivity on the wider economy, while Section 7.6 concludes with areas for further research.

7.2 The Irish Construction Sector

Some key characteristics of the Irish residential construction sector are summarised below.

- The construction sector in Ireland is a key driver of economic growth and employment. In 2005, the sector accounted for ten per cent of the value added in the Irish economy and 12 per cent of the Irish labour force. Further, of the total growth in employment in the economy of 530,000 from 1998 to 2006, over one-quarter is accounted for by the construction industry;
- The residential construction sector accounts for almost 62 per cent of the value of output from the construction sector.[1] Given that residential construction is relatively labour intensive compared to other areas of construction, its share of employment is even higher. The other key segments of the sector are commercial and infrastructure construction;
- In 2005, there were over 80,000 new house completions in Ireland, which per capita, is around four times the European average;
- The construction sector is characterised by a large number of small companies. Of the 200,000 people employed in the sector in 2003, less than 30 per cent worked for companies with more than 20 employees. This compares to a corresponding figure for manufacturing industries of 88 per cent;
- The construction sector works through a complex system of contractors and sub-contractors, which allows for a great deal of flexibility and specialisation. However, it also requires strong project management skills to coordinate the various contractors and sub-contractors that may be working on an individual project; and
- The labour market is very open, with free entry into the crafts. Education is provided by a number of bodies, including FÁS and the Construction Industry Federation (CIF) and Dublin City University (DCU). An important feature of the Irish construction labour market over the last number of years has been the increasing role of migrants, particularly from the ten new EU Member States.

7.3 Outline of Methodology

This chapter calculates productivity as the number of residential units completed in a particular year divided by the number of hours worked in the construction sector, with an adjustment for changes in average new home size and quality. As such, productivity would increase if output were maintained in the face of lower employment or a shorter working week, or if more or larger homes were built with the same amount of labour.[2]

Output in the residential construction sector is calculated as the sum of two components, namely increases in number of new homes completed, and increases in average home size. It is based on the assumption that productivity growth from 1993 to 2003 in residential construction was the same as in non-residential construction. It is calculated in five steps:

- **Step 1: Calculate Home Completions, 1993 – 2003;**
  This is calculated as the sum of houses and apartments. Data on the number of house and apartment completions is provided by the Department of Environment, Heritage and Local Government (DOEHLG). The DOEHLG data is based on the number of new dwellings connected by the Electricity Supply Board (ESB).

- **Step 2: Adjust Home Completions for Changes in Average Size of New Homes;**
  The increase in average new home size is not directly observable, so it is taken from the CSO planning permissions data. This figure is then adjusted to allow for the fact that increasing aggregate floor space by increasing average home size requires only half of the labour needed to achieve the same increase through an increase in house numbers.

- **Step 3: Adjust for Changes in Quality;**
  Interviews with industry experts suggest that there have been improvements in the quality of new homes over the period in question. These arise from improvements in the skill level of the industry, regulatory changes in terms of improved disabled access and significant improvements in the quality of social housing. It is not possible from existing data to measure the impact of these changes. For the purposes of this report, we assume that improvements in quality equivalent to a four per cent increase in output per house were achieved in the period 1993 to 2003.

- **Step 4: Adjust for Repair and Maintenance Employment;**
  While output in the construction industry is based on new housing, employment is based on both new housing and Repair and Maintenance (R&M) of existing housing. Figures for R&M output, which only go back as far as 1997, suggest that it did not grow as fast as new housing output in the period 1997 - 2003. Therefore, an adjustment must be made to remove R&M construction labour from the calculations. This is done by assuming that 50 per cent of all R&M is non-household labour – i.e. involves outside contractors. This estimate is based on a compromise between two opposing estimates of the importance of external labour in R&M. First, 68 per cent of all R&M expenditure involves significant projects (attic conversions, garden walls etc.), a lot of which are likely to be done by outside contractors. The remaining 32 per cent expenditure relates to small projects, which are likely to be dominated by own labour (DIY). Second, the Household Budget Survey shows that only ten per cent of all repairs and improvements expenditure is on external contractors.

- **Step 5: Change in Productivity in Construction**
  The adjusted total new home completions are then combined with changes in non-residential construction, with the weightings being based on the estimate employment shares of residential (75 per cent as of 2003) and non-residential (25 per cent) in total construction employment. This provides an index of output in the construction sector. This is then divided by total construction employment to arrive at a productivity estimate. No adjustment is made for possible changes in the ratio of black market employment as a percentage of total employment in construction. Industry feedback suggests that black market employment was a higher share of construction employment in 1993 compared to 2003, suggesting that the productivity estimate produced in this report is an underestimate of actual productivity improvements in the industry.

7.4 Analysis of Productivity Changes, 1993 – 2003

This chapter calculates productivity as the number of residential units completed in a particular year divided by employment in the construction sector, with an adjustment for changes in average new home size and quality. As such, productivity would increase if output were maintained in the face of lower employment or a shorter working week, or if more or larger homes were built with the same amount of labour.[3]

Based on the measure chosen, we estimate that productivity in the Irish residential construction sector grew by 27 per cent from 1993 to 2003. An initial estimate was calculated based on the number of dwellings completed per hour worked in the construction industry in Ireland (26 per cent). This figure was then adjusted for factors such as quality, repair and maintenance and change in average dwellings size, leading to a final central estimate of 27 per cent.

This estimate suggests that while it took on average 33 workers one year to complete ten homes in 1993, today it only takes 26 workers to build the same number of homes of a similar size and quality as in 1993.

The output of residential construction sector has increased substantially since 1993, most importantly due to increases in numbers employed, but also because of improvements in productivity. The sector is now producing more than three times as many houses than in 1993, with these units being on average almost 20 per cent larger than those completed in 1993.

Despite the significant growth in productivity in Irish residential construction, the sector may still lag behind European best practice. A recent study in 2006 for the European Commission compiled an index based on a composite of a number of physical and value added measures of productivity in the wider construction sector.[4] The results suggest that the overall efficiency of the Irish construction sector falls below that achieved in many European countries. This is based on a compilation of various indices of labour and input usage, which span a period from 2000 – 2005.

The sources of these productivity changes can be divided into two categories, namely improvements in technical efficiency and increases in the scale and type of building schemes. Changes in technical efficiency have made the greatest contribution to productivity growth (22 percentage points), though larger scheme sizes and greater housing density also helped (five percentage points). In terms of the former, many of the greatest efficiencies realised over the last number of years can only be fully taken advantage of by having building schemes of a sufficient size. This estimate of 22 percentage point productivity improvement should be interpreted as the improvement in productivity that would have been realised even if average scheme size in Ireland had remained unchanged. However, building houses in larger schemes has always been more productive than building isolated units - what has changed is that this productivity gap has widened. As such, the increase in average scheme size would have increased productivity regardless of whether efficiency had changed or not, and it is on this basis that the five percentage point increase is calculated.

This increase in residential construction productivity has been reflected in a greater number of dwelling completions, an increase in the average home size and improvements in building quality. Figure 7.1 illustrates the sources of productivity improvement. Section 7.4.1 analyses the sources of improvements in technical efficiency, Section 7.4.2 discusses the impact of an increase in the scale of building, while Section 7.4.3 analyses changes in the type of home output.

Figure 7.1: Decomposition of Productivity Changes, 1993 – 2003

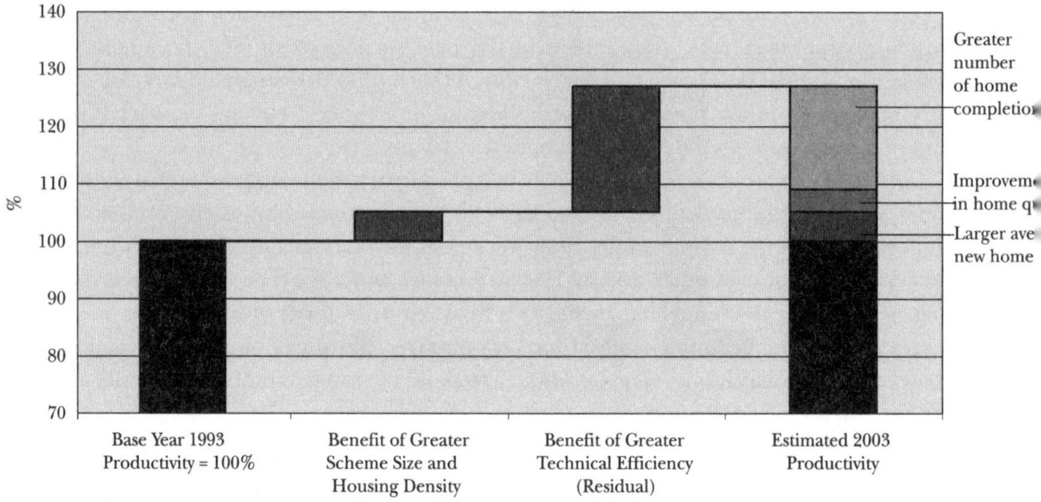

Source: Authors Calculations.

7.4.1 Improvements in Technical Efficiency

Our estimates suggest that improvements in technical efficiency account for much of the productivity gains in the sector from 1993 to 2003. Interviews with industry participants suggest that this performance has been driven by three key factors: improvements in construction labour skills, the increased use of mechanisation, and changes in management and organisational structure.

Labour Skills

Growing skills intensity in the residential construction sector has been an important source of productivity growth, through the formal development of core and specialist building skills using apprenticeships schemes. The number of National Craft Certificates awarded per annum to apprentices whose trades are oriented towards residential construction increased from 518 to 3,727 between 1999 and 2004. This represents an average annual increase of almost 57 per cent per annum compared to construction employment growth of eight per cent per annum during the same period. FÁS and the CIF also provide a number of non-apprentice courses in disciplines such as crane operation and site management.

Figure 7.2: Apprentices Awarded National Craft Certificate, 1999 and 2004

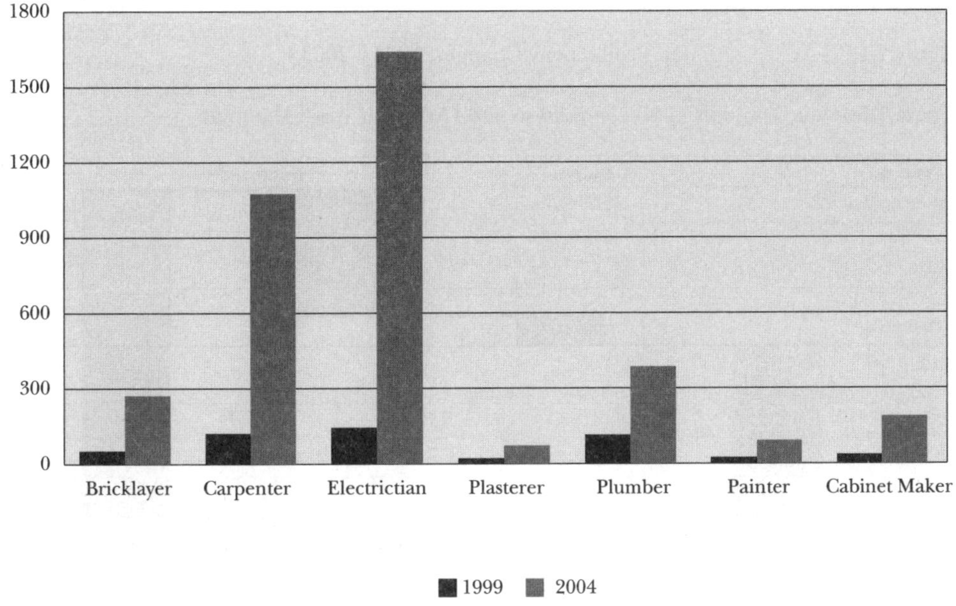

Source: FÁS, unpublished data.

Other factors have contributed towards increasing the skills base of the industry, such as the increase in the number of school leavers entering construction with Leaving Certificate qualifications and the influx of skilled immigrants. Further, buoyant demand is enabling construction companies to pay what it takes to attract skilled labour from other sectors of the economy to the construction sector.

One impediment to promoting training through apprenticeships is that the length of time required for an apprentice to be awarded a National Craft Certificate is the same regardless of the level of skill involved. Furthermore, the move to greater specialisation in the sector as a whole has not been reflected in the structure of apprenticeships, and as such skills are more general than is required. For example, while a National Craft Certificate is available for relatively generic skills such as carpenters/joiners, there is currently none available for apprentices wishing to specialise in roofing or crane operation.

Mechanisation and Quality of Work Materials

The construction industry in Ireland has seen an increased use of labour-saving machinery (mechanisation) over the last decade, as well as an increased use of work materials which improve efficiency. Both of these contribute towards reducing input costs and increasing labour productivity.

Some of the major changes include the gradual shift away from traditional bricklaying in favour of pre-cast concrete and steel or timber framed structures. This reduces the need for bricklayers, is more time efficient, and reduces the time needed to plaster, plumb and wire a residential unit. Other simple but effective changes in mechanisation include increased use of nail guns and telescopic handlers. Innovative working materials are also increasingly being used, such as the adoption of polyethylene piping as a substitute for traditional copper piping. Figure 7.3 reviews the key developments in mechanisation and material inputs that have occurred within the eight main building processes between 1993 and 2003, and assesses their impact on productivity.

Figure 7.3: Developments in Mechanisation and Quality of Work Materials

Process	Changes	Importance
Bricklaying	Pre-cast concrete Steel Frame Ready to Use Mortar Telescopic Handlers	High
Plastering	Ready to use plaster	High
Roofing	Pre-made Segments off-site Telescopic handlers Nail guns	Medium
Glazing	Pre-made in factory	Medium
Wiring	Little change	Medium
Plumbing	Polyethylene piping	Medium
Tiling	Bathroom pods	Medium
Painting	Little change	Low

Source: Industry Interviews.

Industry interviews suggests that many of these developments have contributed significantly to productivity improvements in large scale residential developments, but not in smaller scale developments or once off housing. This reflects both a lack of knowledge by purchasers/developer/architects of once off housing as to the possible advantages of some of these innovations, as well as the fact that many of the innovations are dependent on sufficient scale to make their introduction financially worthwhile. An example of the latter is pre-cast and steel frames. These are commonly used in industrial construction and have been incorporated into some large-scale residential developments, but may not be economical in smaller developments.

Better Management and Organisational Structure

In an effort to reduce cost, construction companies have been adopting site management techniques that aim to cut down on the time lost between the completion of sequential tasks. This requires a very tight sequencing and control of construction tasks. For example, it requires that a task such as bricklaying be completed on time so that subsequent tasks such as wiring can be planned for with a high degree of precision. Further, it requires that building materials arrive in sufficient time so as not to delay work, but not so early that they are lying around on a building site, where there is a greater chance of loss through theft, damage or degradation.

In an effort to improve the predictability of when each stage of a project will be completed, some firms have decided to reduce their use of on-site labour. This has been done in part by designing buildings so that labour intensive tasks such as bricklaying are minimised. Furthermore, many firms are increasingly opting for prefabrication. For example, in many of the larger apartment complexes currently under construction prefabricated pod bathrooms are being used, greatly reducing the need for a large number of different tradesmen (e.g. plumbers, tilers and plasterers) on site. Often, these options can cost more than traditional labour-intensive methods, but are favoured because of the greater predictability they offer. The efficiency savings enabled by greater predictability outweighs the additional cost involved.

Another important change in the way construction tasks are organised is a greater specialisation of tasks, particularly in urban areas, which has improved productivity. In Ireland, this has been achieved through the practice of sub-contracting to specialised smaller firms. However, evidence from Europe suggests that larger firms with greater in-house specialisation are generally more productive than those with extensive sub-contracting.[5] The increased use of lean construction and sub-contracting depends on better management skills. Feedback from industry interviews suggests that project management skills in Ireland are weak.

7.4.2 Increases in the Scale and Type of Building Schemes

Our estimates suggest that increases in building scheme scale coupled with a move to denser housing in Ireland have accounted for up to five percentage points of the total productivity gains of 27 per cent over the 1993 to 2003 period.

Figure 7.4: Productivity of House Construction Based on Scheme Size

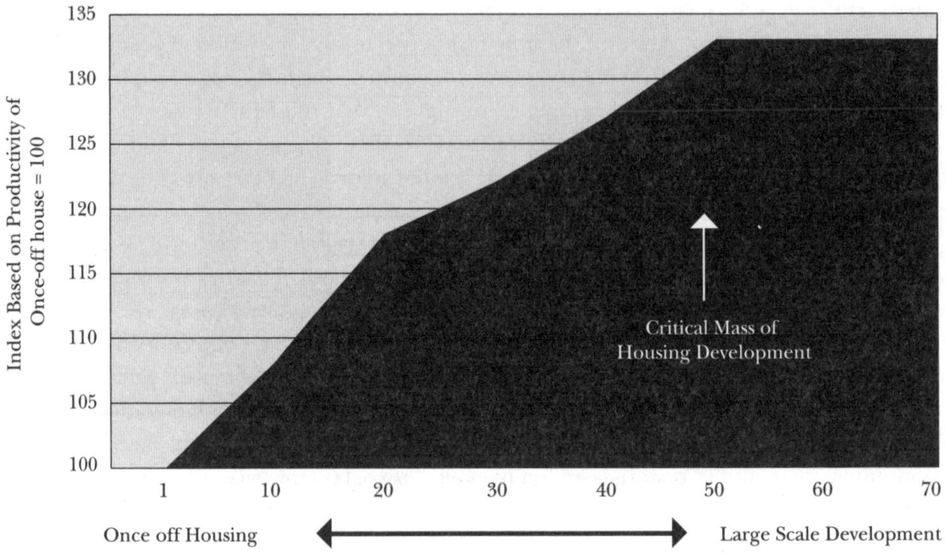

Source: Adapted from McKinsey Global Institute (1997).

The scale of a housing scheme is of critical importance to the productivity of an individual construction project. Research by the McKinsey Global Institute indicate that a once off house requires almost 33 per cent more hours worked than does a house of equivalent size on a large housing estate.[6] Further, estimates by McKinsey Global Institute (see Figure 7.4) suggest that productivity is maximised in developing housing projects with at least 50 units.

While there is a paucity of Irish statistics in this area, planning permission statistics would suggest that the number of units per new housing scheme in Ireland has increased by around 13 per cent from 1993 to 2003. In addition, data on planning permissions suggests that the average number of apartments in a new complex has almost doubled from ten units to 18 units per block over the same period.

There has been a move towards greater construction density in Ireland, reflected in a higher proportion of apartments and terraced housing of 33 per cent of total residential units completed in 2003, up from 24 per cent in 1993. Both market and regulatory forces have encouraged the shift to greater housing densities. First, higher land prices have led to reduced average plot sizes. Second, the introduction of the planning guidelines on residential density in 1999, by providing guidance on the benefits of higher residential density in appropriate locations, has prompted many local authorities to allow higher density levels when giving planning.

Figure 7.5: Composition of New Housing in Ireland by Type, 1994 - 2003

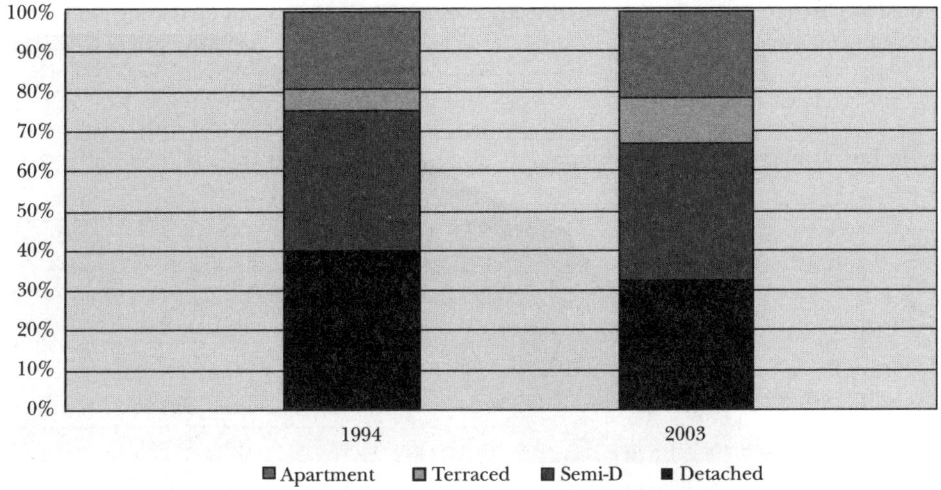

Source: DOEHLG, Housing Statistics, downloaded from www.environ.ie.

Despite increases in the scale of building schemes, the Irish housing market is still notable for the number of once off detached houses, particularly in rural areas, a reflection of our dispersed population structure and agrarian background. Supported by an accommodative planning system, almost 40 per cent of new housing in Ireland is once off.[7] This approach is impacting on productivity growth.

Further, dispersed housing settlements may have negative productivity implications on a host of other sectors including transport, utilities (electricity, postage, telephony, water, waste, etc.) and other services (e.g. health, education, etc.). There are, of course, a range of social, economic and environmental factors which are relevant to the debate on the regulation of rural land use, and productivity is just one of the factors to be considered.

7.4.3 Changes in Home Output

Increases in productivity levels of the Irish residential construction sector are reflected in three developments: more homes are being built per hour worked, the average home size in 2003 is significantly larger than in 1993, and the average home quality has increased over the period in question.

We estimate that the number of homes completed per worker increased by 27 per cent from 1993 to 2003. The average floor size of both houses and apartments has also increased by around 20 square metres from 1993 to 2003 (see Figure 7.6). For houses this represents an increase of around 20 per cent in terms of floor space. For apartments, the change is even more dramatic, with an average increase in floor space of 33 per cent. It requires less additional labour to increase the amount of aggregate residential floor size by building bigger houses than to build more houses, because large houses tend to have fewer fittings per square metre than small houses (e.g. sockets, lighting, toilets, staircases etc.), so increasing floor space is not very labour intensive.

It is unclear if house sizes will continue to increase in Ireland. On the one hand, Irish home buyers are better off today than in 1993, and are willing to devote a lot of that additional income to purchase larger homes. On the other, smaller family sizes and increasing land prices are forcing buyers and planners to economise on land, particularly in central urban locations.

Figure 7.6: Average Size of New Homes

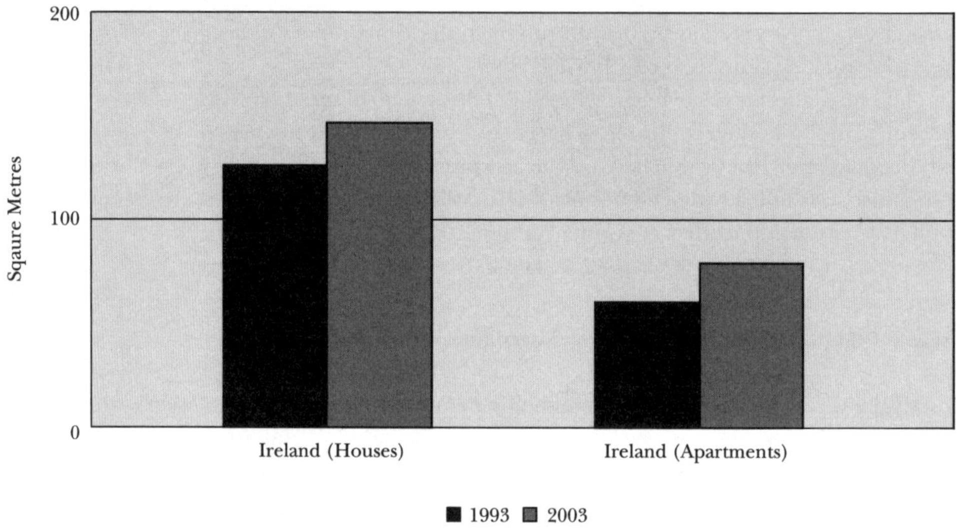

Source: Derived from CSO Planning Permissions, Q3 2005 and Q4 1999.

We assume based on industry interviews that house quality has improved by four per cent over the period 1993 – 2003.[8] This is, by necessity, an estimate, as changes in house quality are generally not measured. By way of illustration, if there had been no change in housing quality over the period under review, the total productivity increase would have been 23 per cent. Evidence from industry interviews suggests that the quality of once-off housing and local authority housing has improved over the period in question, though the quality of finish of some larger scale building projects, such as apartment blocks, has deteriorated. Examples of changes in quality include: disabled access, downstairs toilet facilities, ensuite bathroom facilities, durability, quality of finish, fittings, etc.

7.5 The Implications of Higher Productivity

How has higher productivity in the residential construction sector enhanced the competitiveness of the Irish economy? There are three inter-related mechanisms through which this could happen, namely, moderating house prices, increasing housing output, and releasing scarce labour resources that could be employed elsewhere in the economy.

7.5.1 Reducing House Prices

For most goods and services, greater productivity results in a lower cost to the final consumer. However, the period 1993 to 2003 has been one of extremely strong growth in house prices in Ireland. Figure 7.7 below assesses the role that growing labour productivity has contributed toward reducing housing costs. Two conclusions emerge:

The improvements in labour productivity of 27 per cent (2.4 per cent per annum) that have been identified over the period 1993 to 2003 have been more than offset by the growth in residential construction labour costs. A rapid increase in demand for housing has resulted in a large increase in land prices and profits in the construction industry, while government revenue from the housing sector has also risen commensurately.

Therefore, the productivity growth achieved has not resulted in reduced house prices in recent years. Nonetheless, if houses had been constructed in 2003 based on the lower 1993 productivity levels, they could have cost an average €28,500 more per unit to build in real terms. Of course, it is unlikely that all or any of this saving has been passed on to house purchasers, and may have had the effect of further raising profits and land prices instead.

Figure 7.7: Decomposition of Changes in House Prices, 1993 – 2003

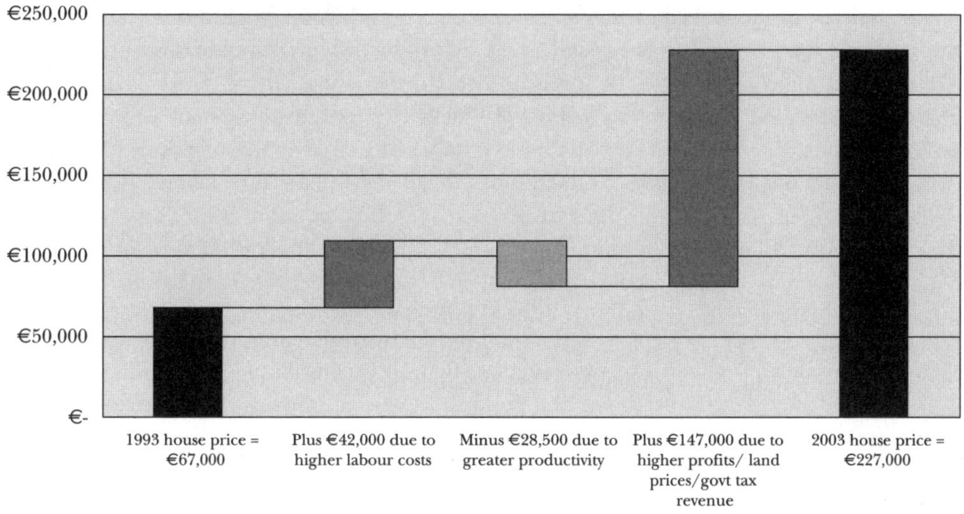

Source: Authors Calculations.

7.5.2 Increased Housing Output

We estimate that the increase in productivity in the residential construction sector over 1993 levels had increased the output of the sector by around 14,500 units per annum by 2003, based on 2003 employment levels. Cumulatively the productivity growth during the ten-year period has allowed the construction of over 80,000 additional new homes.

7.5.3 Releasing Scarce Labour Resources

An alternative way of examining the benefits of productivity is to calculate how much additional labour would have been required to produce the number constructed in 2003, at 1993 productivity levels.[9] Based on the estimates, over 40,000 additional workers would be needed to produce the 2003 level of output at 1993 productivity levels. This would have the effect of driving up wages, and using up scarce labour that is required elsewhere in the economy. In particular, the residential sector draws labour from other areas of construction such as commercial buildings and infrastructure construction.

7.6 Conclusion

The purpose of this chapter is to provide an assessment of the productivity performance of the Irish residential construction sector and its drivers since 1993. We estimate that the productivity levels of the Irish residential construction sector grew by 27 per cent from 1993 to 2003, mainly through improvements in technical efficiency, but also because of increases in the average size of building schemes. This could have affected the economy by moderating house price increases, increasing housing output, and releasing scarce labour resources that could be employed elsewhere in the economy.

Although the residential construction sector is one of the biggest employers in the economy, the statistical data needed to accurately assess its productivity performance is not available. An improved understanding of the industry through the availability of better data can help guide policies aimed at promoting further productivity growth. The estimate of productivity growth contained in this report is based on a number of simplifying assumptions which were necessitated by this lack of data. A much more detailed breakdown of labour utilisation by skill level and sub-sector within the construction sector is required. Further, very detailed data is currently collected from mortgage providers which could allow the development of a comprehensive new-housing quality survey, which could include indices tracking changes in house quality. However this data is currently not published. An additional issue to be addressed is the influence on average residential construction productivity of the share of apartments in total output, given the different construction methods used.

Notes

1 DKM (2005), "Economic Consultants, Review of the Construction Industry 2004 and Outlook 2005–2007", Estimate for 2005.

2 Productivity for some industries can be calculated in a number of ways, for example using a measure of physical outputs and inputs as in this report, or using value added in the industry divided by an appropriate deflator. Both methods should come up with the same answer, given the availability of all necessary data.

3 Productivity for some industries can be calculated in a number of ways, for example using a measure of physical outputs and inputs as in this report, or using value added in the industry divided by an appropriate deflator. Both methods should come up with a similar answer, given the availability of all necessary data.

4 BWA Associates (2006). The study is not based on data from a single year, but rather is based on a composite of data and surveys from 2000 to 2005.

5 BWA Associates (2006).

6 McKinsey Global Institute (1997).

7 Department of the Environment and Local Government (2001: 9-13).

8 This based on estimated labour input requirements for the observed quality improvements, in other words that a house in 2003 would require four per cent more labour than a corresponding house in 1993, assuming an identical level of productivity.

9 It should be noted that this is an alternative way of examining the benefits as discussed in the paragraph above, and is not additional to them.

References

BWA Associates (2006), *Benchmarking of Construction Efficiency in the EU Member States – Scoping Study.* Report commissioned by the Enterprise and Industry Directorate-General of the European Commission.

Department of the Environment and Local Government (2001), *Irish Spatial Perspectives: Rural and Urban Roles,* Dublin.

DKM Economic Consultants (2004), "Review of the Construction Industry 2004 and Outlook 2005–2007."

FÁS (2006), *Study of Project Management Skills in the Irish Construction Industry.* Report Commissioned for the FÁS Construction Industry Group.

McKinsey Global Institute (1997), *Boosting Dutch Economic Performance.*

CHAPTER 8

PRODUCTIVITY IN THE IRISH ROAD FREIGHT INDUSTRY

CIARÁN AYLWARD AND RONNIE O'TOOLE[1]

ABSTRACT

This chapter reports the results of a study into productivity in the Irish road freight industry. The results indicate that productivity in the industry, measured as tonne-kilometres per employee, increased by 22 per cent between 1995 and 2003. Increases in the average size and capacity of goods vehicles accounted for 14 per cent of that increase, with improvements in capital efficiency accounting for the remaining eight per cent. In other words, there were more large goods vehicles on the road in 2003 that were being utilised more efficiently than there were in 1995.

1 The views expressed are solely those of he authors and do not necessarily reflect the views of Forfás

8.1 Introduction

The purpose of this chapter is to provide an assessment of the productivity performance of the Irish road freight industry and the factors that influenced this performance. Our definition of the Irish road freight sector is based on the parameters outlined in the Central Statistics Office's Road Freight Transport Survey.[1] Broadly, the Irish road freight industry includes all firms that are mainly engaged in the transportation of freight by road, and firms engaged in renting vehicles with drivers for road freight transport.

We estimate that productivity in the industry, measured in tonne-km per employee, increased by 22 per cent between 1995 and 2003. Tonne-kilometres (tonne-km) is the recognised measurement of output for the road freight industry, and is calculated by multiplying the number of tonnes carried by a vehicle by the number of kilometres travelled.

Measuring the productivity performance or the efficiency of sectors that are predominately domestically traded has become increasingly important in Ireland. Since these sectors are only open to limited international competition, the services on offer can often be over priced, of poor quality and hinder the overall competitiveness of our economy. Productivity growth in the road freight sector can aid the Irish economy in three primary ways:

1. Productivity growth can help by ensuring the cost of transporting goods for industry via road freight remains competitive;
2. Productivity growth can improve the quality and speed of service being delivered;
3. Productivity growth has the potential to reduce the number of vehicles on our roads, which can in turn, lessen the welfare and monetary costs associated with traffic congestion.

Section 8.2 of this chapter presents an outline of the key characteristics of the sector and its importance to the Irish economy. Section 8.3 describes the choice of measure of productivity used in this study, while Section 8.4 decomposes the estimate of productivity into the roles played by improvements in carrying capacity and capital efficiency. Section 8.5 outlines some additional underlying factors that have influenced the industry's productivity performance, while Section 8.6 concludes.

8.2 The Irish Road Freight Industry

Some key characteristics of the road freight sector are as follows:

- The road freight industry is an important element in Ireland's economic growth and employment. With less than three per cent of freight transported by rail in 2003, the great majority of all freight is transported by road.
- Between 1995 and 2003, road freight output in terms of tonne-km trebled to almost 16 million while direct employment in the sector almost doubled from 7,784 to 15,658 employees.
- The rate of growth of road freight in Ireland, and across Europe, has generally been higher than the growth rate of the economy (Straw, 1999). This has been driven on the demand side by dispersion in retail and wholesale outlets, economic specialisation and external material sourcing, and logistics trends towards fewer warehouses. On the supply side, the cost of road freight services has fallen.

- The road freight industry in Ireland is characterised by a large number of small companies. There are about 5,000 licensed haulage operators in Ireland. Evidence would suggest that about 55 per cent of all operations are one vehicle firms with just four per cent of all operations having ten or more vehicles (Laoide-Kemp and O'Keefe, 2003).
- There are two broad categories of regulations that affect the road freight industry; regulations on traffic and vehicles (i.e. regulations on the carriage of hazardous substances) and regulations on the operation of the market (i.e. regulations on price and market access). Regulations on the operation of the market were largely removed in most OECD countries, including Ireland, by the early 1990s. There are still a significant number of regulations governing vehicle operation.
- The industry is fiercely competitive, and profit margins are low. Road freight operators are deemed to be price takers rather than price makers.
- The internationalisation of the road freight transport industry varies widely across countries, though is relatively small in geographically peripheral nations such as an island like Ireland.[2] International journeys accounted for 23 per cent of the total tonne-km of Irish registered vehicles in 2003.
- The industry is divided into the activities of 'hire or reward' vehicles (i.e. dedicated haulage companies who are not the owners of the goods being transported) and 'own account' vehicles (i.e. firms who transport their own goods with their own vehicles). In 2003, vehicles used mainly for 'hire or reward' accounted for 46 per cent of all registered goods vehicles, but transported 73 per cent of the total output measured in tonne-km.[3]
- Since 1995, there has been a decline in the percentage of goods being transported for agricultural purposes (i.e. foodstuffs, fertilisers and live animals); while there has been an increase in the percentage of goods being transported for manufacturing (i.e. chemical and metal products) and construction purposes (i.e. building materials and minerals).

8.3 Measure of Productivity

In this chapter, productivity is measured in tonne-km per employee per annum. Where it is difficult to find directly comparable measures of labour input (i.e. when comparing our performance relative to the UK), an alternative is used, namely tonne-km per vehicle per annum. Assuming that the ratio of hours worked to the number of vehicles does not differ greatly over time or between countries, these two measures should show very similar results.

Tonne-km per employee is a measure of actual output of the road freight industry, and is widely used for international comparisons of output and productivity in road freight. Its principal drawback is that it does not allow for the fact that transport companies might be adding value in other ways than merely moving more produce longer distances. For example, they might be providing more refrigerated trucks, which will protect produce from spoilage. In what follows, efforts are made to highlight such cases where improvements in quality may not be captured using tonne-km as a measure of productivity.

The most frequently used alternative measure of productivity in the road freight sector is value added per hour worked, which can roughly be calculated as the sum of wages and profits per hour worked.[4] This measure has a significant drawback. In a relatively wealthy country such as Ireland where wages are quite high, the measured value added per worker will be high, simply because the average wage received by a worker in freight will be high. Measured value added will be lower in a poorer country such as Russia, even if Russian freight workers have exactly the same efficiency as their Irish counterparts.

Attempts have been made to account for these differences through purchasing power parity adjustment, though these are generally recognised as being unsatisfactory for the analysis of specific industries.

8.4 Analysis of Productivity Changes, 1995-2003[5]

Output from the industry measured in terms of tonne-km tripled between 1993 and 2003, while direct employment only doubled, indicating a strong rise in output per worker. We estimate that productivity in the Irish road freight sector increased by 22 per cent between 1995 and 2003.

The sources of productivity changes in the road freight industry can be divided into two effects, namely the *Carrying Capacity Effect* and the *Capital Efficiency Effect.* In terms of the *Carrying Capacity Effect,* if drivers operate bigger vehicles with larger carrying capacities this will have a positive influence on productivity, assuming the same average laden factor. Capital efficiency on the other hand is a measure of how intensively vehicles are being used. As such, the *Capital Efficiency Effect* is when there is an increase in the amount of goods transported given a fixed level of carrying capacity.

The *Carrying Capacity Effect* made the greatest contribution to productivity growth in Ireland over the 1995 – 2003 period (14 percentage points), though the *Capital Efficiency Effect* also made a significant contribution (eight percentage points). As such, Irish good vehicles now have larger carrying capacities and are being worked more intensively than they were 1995. Figure 8.1 illustrates the sources of productivity improvement, while Sections 8.4.1 and 8.4.2 analyse the sources behind the improvement in the *Carrying Capacity Effect* and the *Capital Efficiency Effect* respectively.

Figure 8.1: Decomposition of Productivity Changes, 1995-2003

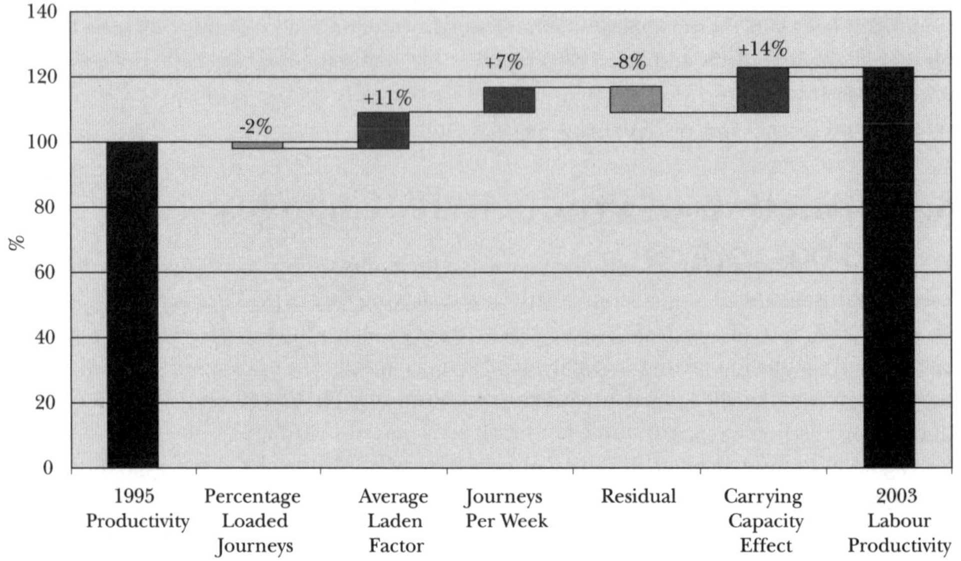

Source: Authors Calculations.

Despite this improvement, we also estimate that the productivity of the Irish road freight sector to be only 70 per cent of the UK level (measured as tonne-km per vehicle per annum). Irish goods vehicles have smaller carrying capacities, are emptier for longer, travel fewer kilometres and have lower average laden factors.[6] The longer average journeys length in the UK can only account for a small share of this differential.

The sources of the increase in Ireland's productivity improvements differ greatly from that observed in other European countries. A study by McKinsey Global Institute (MGI) on the causes of productivity improvements in the French and German road freight industries estimated that only 50 per cent of total productivity gains could be explained by the *Carrying Capacity Effect* (McKinsey, 2002). In Ireland, almost 65 per cent of the total improvements in productivity were explained by the *Carrying Capacity Effect.* The *Capital Efficiency Effect* played a much more important role in terms of increasing the productivity of the French and German freight industries than was the case in Ireland. This suggests that the French and German road freight industries have been able to extract efficiencies that the Irish road freight industry has not, and that there is still considerable room for improvement in Ireland.

8.4.1 The Carrying Capacity Effect

One way of improving the average size of load per driver is to increase the average vehicle size with larger carrying capacities. This is called the *Carrying Capacity Effect.* Our estimates indicate that the increase in carrying capacity accounted for most of the productivity gains in the sector. This section outlines how average vehicle size and carrying capacity increased between 1995 and 2003.

Goods Vehicles by Weight Category

In 1995, trucks in the two heaviest vehicle weight categories accounted for 21 per cent of registered goods vehicles and carried 65 per cent of total tonne-km.[7] By 2003, the number of vehicles within these two weight categories had increased to 34 per cent of registered goods vehicles, and carried almost 73 per cent of total tonne-km.

Goods Vehicles by Body Type

A change in the type of truck body being used in the industry also reveals that there has been a shift towards the use of larger vehicles with larger carrying capacities. Vehicles in the 'platform or sided' and 'box or van body' categories, categories that would generally be classified as being relatively small in terms of weight and carrying capacity, transported 80 per cent of total tonne-km in 1995. In 2003, these two categories transported just 26 per cent of total tonne-km. In contrast, the percentage of tonne-km being transported by vehicles with larger capacities, for example 'tipper trucks' and 'insulated or refrigerated box trucks', increased significantly during the same time period.

Figure 8.2: Percentage of Tonne-km Transported by Body Type, 1995-2003

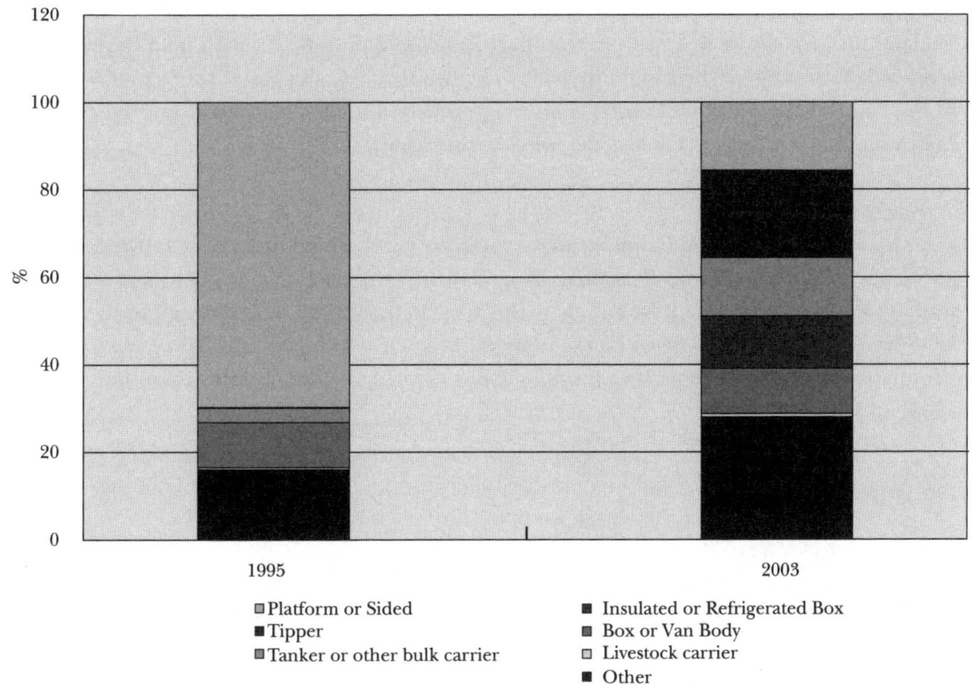

Source: CSO, Road Freight Transport Survey, various editions.

8.4.2 Capital Efficiency Effect

We estimate that goods vehicles were used eight per cent more efficiently in 2003 than they were in 1995. There are a number of factors that led to this improvement in the *Capital Efficiency Effect*. Some factors had a positive impact, some made no impact, while others had a negative impact.

Positive Impact

Average laden factor (+ 11%)

Our calculations suggest that the increase in the average laded factor (i.e. weight carried) made the most telling contribution towards improving capital efficiency. We estimate that the average goods vehicle, holding vehicle size constant, carried 11 per cent more tonnage in 2003 than in 1995. This was despite a large increase in the average truck size – in other words, the larger trucks in Ireland in 2003 were even fuller (as a percentage of their total capacity) than were smaller trucks in 1995.

The most probable explanation for this is to be found in the increase in the scale and number of Irish manufacturers, and the increased volume of imports over the course of the period 1995 to 2003. Against this is the trend towards an economy based on high value goods which are more time sensitive and therefore where the lower transport costs brought about by a more efficient utilisation of trucking capacity would be of less importance. For example, the increased demand for just-in-time deliveries in manufacturing firms in Ireland would tend to reduce the average laden factor of the freight industry. The average laden factor of heavy goods vehicles in the UK, Denmark and the Netherlands have remained stable or declined over recent years, indicating that Ireland has bucked the trend in this regard.[8]

Journeys per week (+ 7%)

An increase in the average number of journeys per week would indicate that goods vehicles are being used more intensively. We estimate that there has been a 7 per cent increase in the number journeys being made per week by the average Irish truck. The increase in the average laden factor in addition to this increase in the number of weekly journeys has resulted in there being more trucks in 2003 making more journeys carrying heavier weights than there were in 1995.

No Impact

Average length of haul (0%)

If a goods vehicle completes more long journeys per week, productivity measured in tonne-km would increase. While a potentially important factor, journey length is outside the control of the industry since it is influenced mainly by the geographic size and location of population centres and industry within a country.

The data suggests that the average length of haul has not increased in Ireland over the period 1995 to 2003. Data measuring the total vehicle-km travelled from a region of origin to region of destination (i.e. the total vehicle km travelled between the East and the South-West regions by goods vehicles), indicates that the length of haul has remained virtually unchanged between 1995 and 2003.[9] In 1995, the number of journeys that started and finished within the same region was 52.7 per cent. In 2003 that figure was virtually identical at 52.5 per cent.

Examining tonnage carried (as opposed to tonne-km) from region of origin to region of destination can provide us with some additional insights on how the movements of the freight fleet can influence productivity. The data indicates that on average approximately 78 per cent of total tonnes hauled started and finished within the same region. These figures have remained virtually unchanged between 1995 and 2003. This would suggest that the majority of tonnes carried in Ireland are generally transported relatively short distances, and that those vehicles that are travelling longer distances are generally carrying lighter loads.

Negative Impact

Empty Running (-2%)

Data on the percentage of journey time that a vehicle is empty indicates that the overall rate has increased slightly from 37 per cent in 1995 to 38 per cent in 2003. Examining the data by main use of vehicle provides some interesting results (see Figure 8.3). Rates of empty running for goods vehicles used by local authorities have deteriorated from 42 per cent to 51 per cent between 1995 and 2003, while rates for vehicles used in the building and construction industry have also deteriorated from 35 per cent to 46 per cent. In contrast, empty running rates for vehicles operating in the manufacture of drink, tobacco and food have all improved since 1995. This suggests that some freight sectors are operating more efficiently than others (see 8.5.1 for more detail).

Figure 8.3: Levels of Empty Running by Freight Sector, 1995-2003

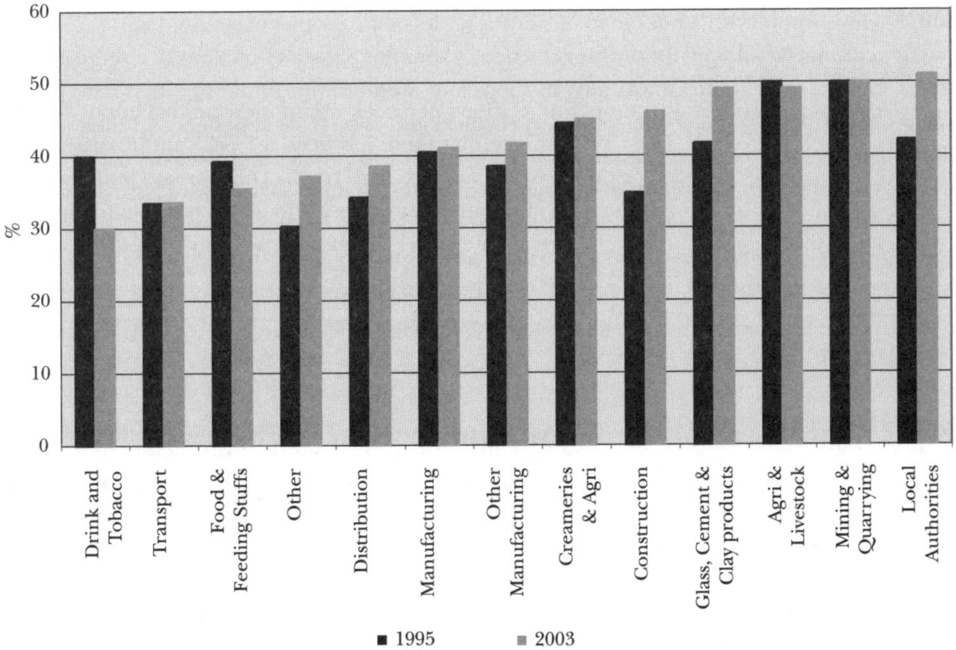

Source: CSO, Road Freight Transport Survey, various editions.

8.5 Underlying Influences

The previous section described the factors that directly influenced the productivity performance of goods vehicles over the period under investigation. Industry and statistical evidence indicates that there are other underlying influences on productivity growth, notably industry characteristics, that have a more indirect, yet significant impact on vehicle efficiency. In contrast to Section 8.4, it is not possible to accurately measure the influence that these factors had on determining our overall productivity growth rate of 22 per cent. This section categorises these factors based on whether they are thought to have had a positive or indeterminate influence on productivity growth.

Positive Impact

8.5.1 Distribution Centres

Distribution Centres (DC) for a set of products are warehouses or other specialised buildings that are stocked with products to be re-distributed to retailers or wholesalers. Historically goods were delivered by manufacturers and suppliers directly to individual stores. This resulted in multiple drops of relatively low volumes over dispersed locations and was an inherently sub-optimal operation in terms of the efficiency of freight haulage operations. The introduction of DC has meant that deliveries from manufacturers and suppliers are now limited to large volume deliveries directly into a DC. Within centres, the complete range of stock is available to dispatch, and an individual vehicle can typically leave a DC with the total daily delivery requirement for one to three stores within a small region. Thus the overall mileage required to supply a given store with a full range of stock is far less than it otherwise would be.

The centres have allowed for the introduction of complex logistics functions that reduce order times, give greater product availability in shops and minimise stockholding while also placing the logistics function under the control of retailers and away from suppliers and their agents. Furthermore, large retail organisations have been able to retain control of the supply chain while outsourcing the operation of the logistics function to third party logistics providers.

While smaller independent retailers are still served directly by local agents and suppliers, the vast majority of Ireland's multiples and symbol groups now operate through a DC, particularly in the retail sector. Indeed, the Irish outlets of some British owned retailers are served directly from DC located in the UK, through daily deliveries via ferries.

8.5.2 Information and Communication Technology (ICT)

Since 1995, one of the most significant technological developments in the road freight sector has been the increase in usage of the mobile phone and GPS technology (Global Positioning Systems). These developments have made it easier for haulage companies to track where their drivers/loads are at any given time. However, industry feedback would suggest that the level and extent of GPS usage in Ireland is still behind those levels in the UK. Evidence would also indicate that of those companies that are using GPS in Ireland, few are using the information to introduce practices that could promote more efficient practices. For example, GPS could provide haulage companies with information that could enable them to reduce levels of empty running by informing drivers at short notice that a load could be picked up close by.

Case studies emerging from the UK highlight the impact that more advanced ICT systems can have on improving fleet efficiency.[10] For example, trials established that Glanbia in the UK could save up to £200,000 a year by introducing a fleet management tracking system that makes sure that drivers can be re-routed quickly and efficiently, that drivers follow recognised routes and at authorised speeds and that vehicle idle time is reduced.[11] Driver habits also changed for the better as drivers began to return to the depot earlier, avoiding unnecessary overnight stays. The system also provided a warning if the trailer temperature fell outside a specific range and allowed the company to supply their customers with records of the transit temperature of goods. The UK Government is encouraging the greater adoption of ICT, or Intelligent Transport Systems as an integral part of its ten-year plan for a modern transport system.

No Impact/Indeterminate

8.5.3 Product Mix

Productivity performance can vary depending on what types of goods are being transported. Some bulky, heavy goods are relatively easy to transport compared to goods that have specialised transport requirements, for example, a requirement for temperature controlled vehicles. If there is a significant increase or decrease in the transport activity of a particular type of good, this can influence the aggregate productivity performance of the industry.

The Road Freight Transport Survey breaks down the overall output of the road freight industry (in terms of tonne-km) into 11 groups of different good categories. This tells us what percentage of the overall output is accounted for by the transport of different goods. Figure 8.4 outlines the transport activity by group of good. For simplicity, each of the 11 different good categories are grouped as being either 'Agricultural', 'Manufacturing' 'Building and Construction' or 'Mixed'.[12]

Figure 8.4: Percentage of Aggregate Industry Output (in Tonne-km) Transported by Group of Goods, 1995 and 2003

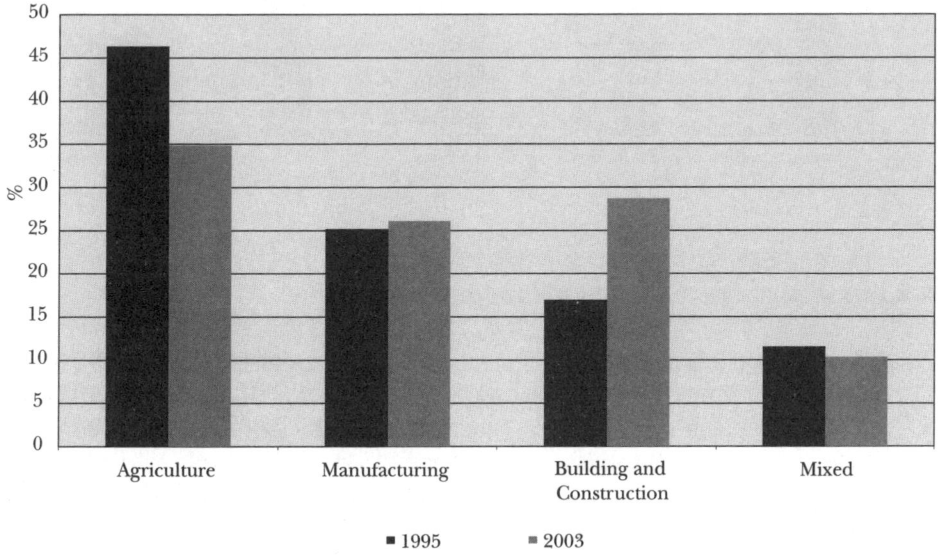

Source: CSO, Road Freight Transport Survey, various editions.

Transport activity (in tonne-km) in Agriculture fell by 25 per cent and by 10 per cent for Mixed goods between 1995 and 2003, while transport activity in Manufacturing rose by four per cent, and by almost 69 per cent in Building and Construction. The phenomenal growth of the construction industry has increased the use of vehicles with larger carrying capacities (i.e. tipper trucks, see Section 8.4.1), the main contributing factor towards productivity growth in the industry for the period 1995 to 2003 according to our earlier analysis. This may have artificially increased productivity growth in the industry.

8.5.4 Main Use of Vehicle

In terms of the main use of vehicle, goods vehicles are categorised as being used for either 'hire or reward' (HR) or for 'own account' (OA) transport.[13] Vehicles that were used for HR purposes performed 73 per cent of the total transport activity in both 1995 and 2003. Given that HR vehicles accounted for only 46 per cent of all relevant vehicles in 1995 and 2003, it is clear that they were used more intensively than vehicles used mainly for OA transport. Examples of how HR vehicles are working more intensively are illustrated in Figure 8.6.

Figure 8.5: Efficiency of HR versus OA Vehicles, 2003

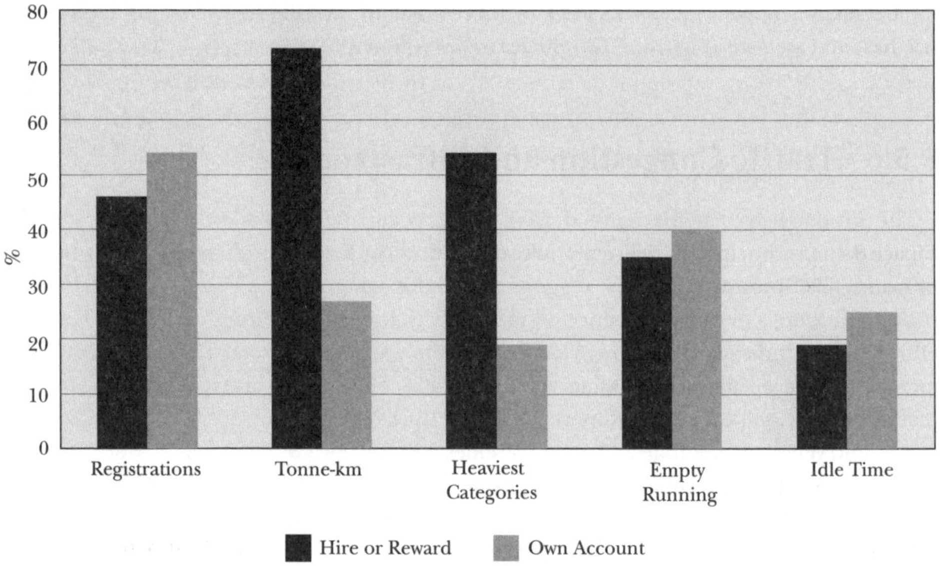

Source: CSO, Road Freight Transport Survey, various editions.

- **Kilometres and Tonnes Carried:** Despite the fact that HR vehicles accounted for only 46 per cent of all registered vehicles, they travelled 58 per cent of the total vehicle kilometres and were responsible for 59 per cent of the total weight of goods carried in 2003;
- **Efficient use of Large HR Vehicles:** In 2003, the 12,000 registered HR vehicles in the two heaviest weight categories carried over 54 per cent of total tonne-km transported. The 10,000 OA vehicles registered in the same weight category transported just 19 per cent of total tonne-km;

- **Empty Running:** In 2003, HR vehicles were empty for 35 per cent of the kilometres travelled; OA vehicles were empty for 40 per cent of the time;
- **Idle Time:** In 2003 HR vehicles were idle for 19 per cent of the time during any one survey week compared to 25 per cent of vehicles used mainly for OA purposes.

This analysis indicates that HR trucks were used more intensively between 1995 and 2003 than OA trucks. HR vehicles have larger carrying capacities; carry heavier loads, spent more time on the road and less time being empty or idle.

8.5.5 Average Fleet Size

In Ireland the road freight industry is characterised by a large number of small companies. There are about 5,000 licensed haulage operators in Ireland. As outlined in Section 8.2, evidence suggests that about 55 per cent of all operations are one vehicle firms with just four per cent of all operations having ten or more vehicles. The average Irish fleet size of three has changed little between 1995 and 2003.[14] As with Ireland, about half of all operators in the UK have just one vehicle, with the number of operators with large fleets being relatively small. In 2003, less than one per cent operators had fleets of over 100 vehicles. These operators, however, owned 13 per cent of all registered goods vehicles. The number of goods vehicle operators in the UK has fallen from 122,000 in 1994 to 102,000 in 2004 with the effect that the average fleet size has increased steadily, from 3.3 vehicles to 3.9 vehicles.[15]

8.5.6 Traffic Congestion and Infrastructure

The productivity benefits accrued from there being more vehicles with larger carrying capacities may be lost if deliveries are delayed because of traffic congestion and poor infrastructure. Industry feedback suggests that traffic congestion, particularly in the Dublin region, is having a negative influence on productivity. Indeed, data from the Dublin Transport Office (DTO) indicates that average car journey times during peak morning traffic in the city increased by seven minutes between 2002 and 2004, while additional data published in this year's Annual Competitiveness Report (ACR) measuring the average peak-hour speed of cars and motorcycles, ranks Dublin 28th out of 30 cities.[16] Bottlenecks in the access to major ports and road arteries can add significantly to the journey times for goods transport, and infrastructure such as the Dublin Port Tunnel should increase the efficiency of transport through the port.

Congestion can be reduced by either improving the standard of infrastructure or by reducing volumes of traffic. While there have been very large capital investment programmes that helped improve the quality of our road infrastructure, there has been a substantial increase in traffic volumes leading to congestion, particularly in urban areas. The total number of licensed vehicles, including both private and goods vehicles, increased by 53.4 per cent between 1995 and 2003. While the number of goods vehicles being licensed increased at a faster rate when compared to private vehicles during the eight-year period, good vehicles accounted for just 13 per cent of total licensed vehicles in 2003.[17]

8.6 Conclusions

The purpose of this chapter is to provide an assessment of the productivity performance of the Irish road freight sector. Our results suggest that productivity in the sector increased by 22 per cent between 1995 and 2003, mainly due to increases in carrying capacity with larger trucks being used, but also because of improvements in capital efficiency with increased load factors and improvements in logistics and supply chain management techniques. Despite the improvement, when compared with the UK, we estimate that the productivity performance of the Irish road freight sector to be only 70 per cent of the UK level. Irish goods vehicles have smaller carrying capacities, are emptier for longer, travel fewer kilometres and have lower average laden factors. In addition, the sources of the increase in Ireland's productivity improvements differ greatly from that observed in France and Germany where the road freight industry has been able to extract greater efficiencies than in Ireland.

Future productivity growth in Ireland's road freight sector will depend on the industries ability to extract such efficiencies. One area of future research is to determine the extent to which productivity growth is held back by the industry structure. In particular, would greater firm size allow for a better use of ICT and a reduction in empty running, and what role could a co-ordinating body (such as a professional or governmental body) usefully play in facilitating this? A further area of investigation could be the impact of congestion on productivity, for instance through looking at the trends in deliveries per day. The broader influence of infrastructure on productivity could also be examined, for instance by considering issues such as the provision of dedicated freight infrastructure (including the new Dublin Port Tunnel), or the possible impact of any expansion of rail freight on road freight productivity. Finally, the general role of further improvements in the road network and the experience on mainland Europe in this regard are also factors to be considered

Notes

1 The Road Freight Transport Survey covers Irish registered vehicles with an unladen weight of two tonnes and over. All activity of goods vehicles within the scope of the survey were engaged in the carriage of goods on the public road. Excluded therefore, was activity such as site work off the public road or work of a mainly service nature (e.g. carriage of personnel to or from places of work). The survey also includes international road transport (see Note 2 for definition of internationalisation).

2 Internationalisation, or international trade within an Irish context, is the carriage of goods by road by Irish registered goods vehicles between two places located in two different countries. International journey's accounted for 23 per cent of total tonne-km transported in 2003.

3 For this calculation we left out the smallest category of vehicle (2000-5000kg) because there is a disproportionately large number of 'own account' vehicles registered in this category when compared to the 'hire or reward' category. Since many of these vehicles are small jeeps and vans, we felt that many of these vehicles are not representative of the typical road freight vehicle, and thus would make the performance of the 'own account' vehicles appear worse that it actually is.

4 The concept of value added also includes indirect taxes paid to the Government.

5 Data on tonne-km (output) was taken directly from the Road Freight Transport Survey. Additional unpublished data from the survey was also made available to us and has been incorporated into our calculations. Employment data (input) for 1995 was not available from the CSO and is based on Forfás estimates. Data for 1996 1997 and 1998 was available from the CSO but has been unofficially adjusted by CSO. Employment data for 2002 is confidential and cannot be referenced publicly by Forfás. We are extremely grateful to Ken Moore and Caitriona O'Brien from the CSO for helping us compile the data used in this chapter

6 A more detailed outline of Ireland's comparative performance relative to the UK will be available in a more detailed version of this chapter that is due to be released in 2007.

7 The two heaviest weight categories are 10,001 – 12,500 kg and over 12,500 kg.

8 "Transport and Environment: Facing a Dilemma TERM 2005: Indicators Tracking Transport and Environment in the European Union", European Environment Agency 2006. Available online: www.iiiee.lu.

9 The regions defined in the Road Freight Transport Survey are the NUTS 3 regions of Ireland. An example of a NUTS 3 Region is the 'South West' region which contains the counties of Cork and Kerry.

10 The Department for Transport in the UK produced a 'Telematics Guide' report that provides information on how the road freight industry can use ICT to promote greater efficiency within the industry. This report, in addition to a number of other reports that examine how factors like skills and equipment can also improve efficiency, are available online on the Department for Transport's 'Freight Best Practice' website. Available at: www.freightbestpractice.org.uk

11 Glanbia installed BT Cellnets 'Pinpoint Fleet Management System', which uses TRACKER Networks Communicator technology. The telematics system allows Glanbia to monitor its vehicles around the clock by recording essential data such as vehicle location, mileage and speed, fuel consumption, driver hours and the temperature or goods in transit.

12 Agriculture = 'Agriculture products and live animals', 'Foodstuff and animal fodder' and 'Fertilisers'. Manufacturing = 'Petroleum products', 'Metal products', 'Chemicals' and 'Machinery and transport equipment'. Building and Construction = 'Building materials and crude manufacturing', 'Ores and metal waste' and 'Solid mineral fuels'. Mixed = 'Mixed loads'.

13 See Section 8.2 for an explanation of hire and reward and own account vehicles.

14 An estimation of the average fleet size in Ireland was calculated by dividing the number of vehicles licensed for hire or reward by the number of licensed operators. Data was sourced from the Department of Transport, Ireland.

15 Department for Transport, UK (2006), *Road Freight Statistics 2005*.

16 'Urban Transport Benchmarking'. Available online: www.transportbenchmarks.org.

17 Department of Environment, Heritage and Local Government data on 'Mechanically Propelled Vehicles under Current Licence'.

References

CSO (1996), *Road Freight Transport Survey 1995,* Central Statistics Office, Cork.

CSO (2004), *Road Freight Transport Survey 2003,* Central Statistics Office, Cork.

Laoide-Kemp, D. and O'Keefe, D. (2003), "Traffic Information Needs of the Freight Industry". Presented to the *International Road Haulage Association's* Annual Conference in Rochestown Park Hotel, Cork, Ireland, 7th March 2003. Available online: www.arup.ie/publications.htm.

McKinsey (2002), "Reaching Higher Productivity Growth in France and Germany: Sector Case – Road Freight", excerpt drawn from *Reaching Higher Productivity Growth in France and Germany,* published by McKinsey Global Institute. Available online: www.mckinsey.com/knowledge/mgi/.

Moylan, M., Oulton, N. and Vass, J. (1997), "Labour Productivity in Transport and Communications: International Comparisons", *NIESR Discussion Paper,* No.117, London.

NCC (2006), *Annual Competitiveness Report 2006,* National Competitiveness Council, Forfás, Dublin.

Straw, J. (1999), "Road Freight Transport in Europe – Some Policy Concerns and Challenges". Presentation to the *European Conference of Minsters of Transport,* Verona, Italy, 6th March 1999. Available online: www.cemt.org.

PART III

INSTITUTIONS AND REGULATION

INTRODUCTION

The productivity performance of a country depends critically on the institutional and regulatory environment of that country. In Chapter 9, O'Donnell and Cahill consider the role of institutions in shaping productivity and economic performance. They argue that good institutions are those that learn how to pragmatically identify constraints on productivity enhancement, and that the problem is not one of identifying specific 'missing' institutions per se. Further, they argue that some of the future challenges facing Irish society are in areas in which Ireland's record of institutional innovation, reform and delivery is not strong. The dominant theme from the next three papers in this section is that the most important factor for success in productivity performance is the competitive environment of the industry in question. In Chapter 10 Boyle and Evans set out the evidence of how strong competition supports productivity gains, in particular by encouraging innovative activity, more efficient business practices and technological diffusion. Chapters 11 and 12 report the impact of privatisation on productivity from an Irish and UK perspective respectively. Both papers come to the same conclusion - improvements in efficiency tend to be associated with the arrival of competition rather than privatisation per se. Finally, Watt and Scully in Chapter 13 discuss the regulatory burden in Ireland, and identify some potential areas for improving the Irish regulatory framework.

CHAPTER 9

THE INFLUENCE OF INSTITUTIONS

RORY O'DONNELL AND NOEL CAHILL

ABSTRACT

This chapter considers the role of institutions in shaping productivity and economic performance. It argues that some of requirement for higher productivity on which all are agreed—innovation, training, infrastructure, and utilities—seem to require further institutional change. And some of the increasingly recognised supply-side factors—life long learning, childcare, eldercare, educational disadvantage, health services, urban planning and tailored social services—take us into domains in which Ireland's record of institutional innovation, reform and delivery is not strong.

9.1 Introduction

This chapter considers the role of institutions in shaping productivity and economic performance. In Section 9.2, we survey the international literature on the role of institutions in productivity and economic development. While this strongly confirms the role of institutions, we suggest that there is no one compelling theory of economic development from which a comprehensive institutional design can be derived. Rather, the most convincing argument, and certainly the one most relevant to Ireland, is that development requires the successive removal of constraints, and good institutions are those that are good at learning how to identify and tackle constraints on productivity enhancement and business development. In Section 9.3, we discuss the role of institutions in Ireland. We draw attention to the role of institutional elements in Irish economic development, briefly characterise the evolution of institutions, and outline the argument that policy and institutional adaptation has been a key factor in Irelands success over the past decade and a half.

If our analysis affirms Ireland's overall approach to institution building and reform, it does not warrant complacency. The chapter closes by arguing that some of the requirement for higher productivity on which all are agreed — innovation, training, infrastructure, and utilities — seem to require further institutional change. And some of the increasingly recognised supply-side factors — life long learning, childcare, eldercare, educational disadvantage, health services, urban planning and tailored social services — take us into domains in which Ireland's record of institutional innovation, reform and delivery is not strong.

In our discussion, institutions embrace organisations as well as rules, norms and behavioural constraints. Our primary concern is on the broad contextual factors that influence productivity, many of which are usually classified as institutional influences.

9.2 Perspectives on Institutions and Economic Performance

In this section, we review analytical approaches that inform thinking in the role of institutions in economic growth and productivity. While we begin with the economic theory of growth, it is necessary to consider ideas from economic development, industrial sociology and political science.

9.2.1 The Neoclassical Growth Model

The neoclassical theory of economic growth, developed by Solow in the 1950s, used standard assumptions of diminishing returns (adding more capital to a given stock of labour yields diminishing increments of output) and constant returns to scale (doubling all inputs will double all outputs). Diminishing returns means that productivity cannot grow indefinitely on the basis of higher inputs (Solow, 1956). How can such a model explain the sustained growth in productivity that has characterised many rich countries for over two hundred years? Solow's answer was technological progress: diminishing returns could be offset by the flow of new technology, an exogenous factor in the model. The *Economist's* comment on the model is telling: "what it illuminated did not ultimately matter; and what really mattered (technological progress), it did little to illuminate".

9.2.2 Endogenous Growth Theory

In the 1980s, economists developed endogenous growth theory. While technological change was still seen as the key driver, it was incorporated in the theory, rather than treated as a gift of nature. This work was also motivated by the observation that national and regional growth patterns are correlated with a variety of economic, social and political variables, including many that are affected by government policies (Grossman and Helpman, 1994).

One set of models focused on the idea that investment in human or physical capital creates positive external benefits that increase the economy-wide productivity (Lucas, 1988). If these external effects are large enough they could offset diminishing returns on private investment and explain sustained productivity growth. The external benefits from physical investment mean that investment by one company reduces costs for another. The external effects of human capital mean one person's human capital affects the productivity of other people. In support of an external human capital effect, Lucas cited the observation that we know from ordinary experience that there are group interactions that are central to individual productivity: "most of what we know we learn from other people" (Lucas, 1988: 38). He cited Jane Jacobs (1969) who provided many examples of how the exchange of ideas enhances productivity in urban environments. Lucas invoked the external effects of human capital to explain why the pressure for migration from poor to rich countries appears to be much stronger than the tendency of capital to move to poor countries.

Endogenous growth theory was welcomed as capturing some widely observed features of real-world development processes. Productivity growth is influenced by policy, particularly subsidies to education and research. Where technological progress derives from private investment, "the institutional, legal, and economic environments that determine these investments must surely affect the pace and direction of technological change" (Grossman and Helpman, 1994: 27).

However, Nelson argued that while the theory formalises some observed realities, it omits other key insights from empirical research (Nelson, 2005). First, much research on technological advance has highlighted the inability of the actors involved to foresee the path of development, even in broad outline, and the surprises that occur along the way. Second, much research has pointed to the key influence of organisational and management practises on economic growth. Third, research suggests that a range of institutions — for example, financial systems, universities or institutions generally — are critical in explaining differences in national growth performance.

Nevertheless, the leading theorists of endogenous growth share Nelson's views on the centrality of institutions. For example, Romer has stated that: "new growth theory describes what's possible for us but says very explicitly that if you don't have the right institutions in place, it won't happen" (interview with *Reasononline,* December 2001). He suggests that in a developing country like the Philippines, the key question is: "what are the best institutional arrangements for gaining access to the knowledge that already exists in the rest of the world?"

A country like the US must ask "what are the best institutional arrangements for encouraging the production of new knowledge?" (Romer, 1994a: 21). Elsewhere, he says:

> For the nation as a whole, an effective institutional arrangement for supporting technological advance must therefore support a high level of exploration and research in both private firms and in universities. Moreover, it must support a high degree of interaction between these two domains. Both people and ideas must move readily between them (Romer, 1994b:5).

While endogenous growth theory does not provide a formal theory of institutions, its approach strongly points to their significance.

It is of interest that Helpman's recent survey of growth theory is entitled *The Mystery of Economic Growth,* and the mystery is, precisely, institutions:

> Although it has been established that property rights institutions, the rule of law, and constraints on the executive are important for growth, the exact ways in which they affect income per capita are not well understood. And the roles played by a host of other economic and political institutions, such as the structure of labour relations and the regulation of interest groups, are even less well understood. Yet an understanding of these features of modern societies is extremely important for greater insight into modern economic growth. Without it, it is difficult to pinpoint reforms that can help achieve faster growth in both developed and developing countries... The study of institutions and their relation to economic growth is an enormous task on which only limited progress has been made so far (Helpman, 2004: 141-142).

While growth theory has clearly taken increasing account of institutional factors, it seems that other analytical and policy perspectives must be taken into account also.

9.2.3 The 'Washington Consensus'

Economic doctrine has long had a certain affinity with the liberal theory of the minimal or 'night-watchman' state; from within these ideas, or for other reasons, in liberal societies, governments and other public institutions have persistently been active agents in the economy. Economists and others working in development have increasingly come to the view that access to international markets is a critical factor in facilitating the growth of less developed countries. The 'Washington Consensus' refers to a set of principles that shares something with both liberal thinking and development economics, but goes well beyond them. The term refers to a consensus view among the international institutions based in Washington (the World Bank, the IMF and others), particularly in their dealings with less-developed countries and transition economies in the past decade and a half. It holds that, in almost any circumstance, countries should adopt free trade, balanced budgets, privatisation, deregulation, tax reform and interest rate liberalisation.

Stiglitz and others have argued that the application of these principles has not had the positive effect on growth and prosperity which the doctrine would expect (Stiglitz, 2003). The limitations of the original Washington Consensus are widely accepted and a revised consensus has evolved, incorporating a number of institutional and social requirements for development. These include independent courts, flexible labour markets, central bank independence and adherence to international financial codes and standards (Rodrik, 2005). But the basic tenet, that the only institutions that are necessary are those that prevent distortion of markets, remains.

9.2.4 National Systems of Innovation

Following the Second World War, a high priority was attached to increasing research and development (R&D) investment. League tables of R&D became influential. However, over time evidence accumulated that innovation and its associated productivity gains depends not just on formal R&D but a range of other factors:

> In particular, incremental innovations came from production engineers, from technicians and from the shop floor. They were strongly related to different forms of work organisation. Furthermore, many improvements to products and services came from interaction with the market and with related firms, such as sub-contractors, suppliers and services... (Furthermore)... the external linkages within the narrower professional science-technology system were also shown to be decisive for innovative success with radical innovations (Freeman, 1995: 10-11).

From the research on these multiple sources of the innovation, the concept of a national system of innovation (NSI) emerged. Freemen defines it as "The network of institutions in the public and private sectors whose activities and interactions initiate, import, modify and diffuse new technologies" (Freeman, 1987). Lundvall highlights the role of relationships and the nation in his definition of the NSI: "The elements and relationships which interact in the production, diffusion and use of new and economically useful knowledge and are either located within or rooted within the borders of a nation state" (Lundvall, 1992). Nelson defines the NSI as "A set of institutions whose interactions determine the innovation of national firms" (Nelson, 1993).

Work on the NSI has evolved over time. It initially focussed on the institutions most directly involved in technological innovation (as in the Freeman definition above), but later research encompasses a wider range of institutions, including social and regional policy (see Lundvall and Tomlinson, 2000). Comparative studies led Freeman (1995) to argue that a variety of national institutions have powerfully affected the relative rates of technical change and economic growth in many countries.

The concept of the national system of innovation was used by Mjoset in his 1992 report for NESC, *The Irish Economy in a Comparative Institutional Perspective* (Mjoset, 1992). He traced Ireland's long-run development problem to the interaction between a weak national system of innovation and population decline through emigration. Other countries with similar structural characteristics, such as Denmark, had institutional arrangements that allowed them to build manufacturing industry on the base of grassland commodity production. Mjoset's analysis suggested a range of policy and institutional measures—including a strong emphasis on Porter's clusters — that would allow Ireland to build an effective NSI. The Government's recently published *Strategy for Science, Technology and Innovation 2006-2013* is a programme to strengthen Ireland's national system of innovation.

The proposition that a range of institutions influence learning and hence growth is now widely shared. However, the concept of the *national* system of innovation has been criticised by those who emphasise influences at levels other than the nation state, such as the regional level, the transnational corporation or the global market (Ohmae, 1990; and for a discussion of different levels of analysis, see O'Donnell, 1997). While all these levels are worth considering in the

Irish context, we focus here on multinational enterprises. They have been able to achieve high productivity operating in countries with different institutional environments. This suggests that the national institutional environment is not always a binding constraint on high productivity.

Teece sought to explain why enterprises operate internationally, when they could sell their knowledge, licence it, or exploit it solely in their home base. His answer is that firms' knowledge often cannot be codified. "Such know-how is tacit and is extremely difficult to transfer without intimate personal contact" (Teece, 1985: 29). In this situation, the establishment of a foreign subsidiary may be optimal. This is particularly the case if ongoing transfers are likely:

> If repeated transfers of technology are contemplated, intra-firm transfer to a foreign subsidiary (which avoids the need for repeated negotiations, contract specification, monitoring and enforcement) has advantages on how contractual difficulties arise. Better disclosure, easier agreement, better enforcement and more efficient transfer result. Here lies the incentive for developing the assets and investing in the creation of organisational infrastructure associated with horizontal direct foreign investment (Teece, 1985: 30).

This perspective, in conjunction with endogenous growth theory, provides a possible explanation for uneven distribution of technological and other know-how across the global economy. Achieving a return on R&D investment requires the establishment of a network of international subsidiaries. Hence, we have a world in which knowledge is transferred globally within multinationals, but it is not a world of perfect information or perfect competition.

9.2.5 Institutional Perspectives from Industrial Sociology and Comparative Politics

Not surprisingly, institutions are a major focus of study in sociology and political science. An influential study by the industrial sociologist, Peter Evans, explored the role of public institutions in promoting industrial development in Brazil, India and Korea (Evans, 1995). He distinguished between predatory and developmental states and argued that the developmental role of the state in the newly industrialising countries of East Asia could be traced to the structural characteristics of those states — their internal organisation and relation to society. Those states that most successfully promoted industrial transformation displayed what Evans called 'embedded autonomy'. Their corporate coherence gave them sufficient autonomy from vested business interests to pursue genuine national economic goals; at the same time they were embedded in dense networks with both business and civil society, which provided rich information and institutional channels for continual negotiation and renegotiation of goals and policies. The concept of the developmental state has been applied to a range of other countries and contexts (see Woo-Cummings, 1999).

Within comparative political science there is great interest in the institutions by which various countries address the pressures of international economic competition and mediate internal conflict. An example is Weiss's analysis of the way in which globalisation changes the nature of state capacity and puts various national institutional models under different kinds of pressure (Weiss, 1988). Her analysis is interesting from an Irish perspective — not so much for its substantive argument (it dates from 1988) but because of the categories she uses may have a certain relevance to Ireland's current institutional challenges. She distinguishes between the developmental states of East Asia and the 'distributive state' of Sweden. The former have great capacity for industrial transformation, but face pressures of social development and distribution.

The latter has achieved a high level of equality, but is somewhat threatened by globalisation (though not all would agree with this now). Her interest is in the possibility of institutional arrangements that could promote both industrial transformation and social cohesion. Writing in 1988, she argued that both Germany and Japan were 'dual states' — combining the capacity to promote both equity and industrial growth and transformation. Allowing for the structural and substantive differences between these countries and Ireland, and the fate of Germany and Japan since 1988, we argue in our closing section that there is a sense in which Ireland now faces the task of linking more adequately its institutions for economic and social development.

9.2.6 Context-Specific Institutions and Development Constraints

An interesting perspective on the institutions and policies that foster development has been developed by Dani Rodrik, a development economist at Harvard. Rodrik argues that certain first order economic principles that can be derived from neoclassical economics — protection of property rights, contract enforcement, market-based competition, appropriate incentives, sound money, debt sustainability — do not map into unique policy packages: "Good institutions are those that deliver these first order principles effectively. There is no unique correspondence between the functions that good institutions perform and the form that such institutions take" (Rodrik, 2005: 973).

Rodrik develops this argument with a thought experiment. Looking at countries' adherence to the policies of the Washington Consensus, can we predict which have achieved the best economic development? He argues that the East Asian countries of Taiwan and Korea, while benefiting from linkages with the global economy, departed significantly from the policy menu of the Washington Consensus. Neither country engaged in significant deregulation or liberalisation of their trade and financial systems until well into the 1980s. Both countries used more interventionist industrial policies than would be recommended by the Washington Consensus. China has gradually embraced market reforms but managed to initiate growth with initially quite modest reforms that introduced incentives within a planned economy. In the developing countries that most systematically embraced the Washington consensus agenda — Argentina, Brazil, Bolivia and Peru — growth in the past two decades has remained below its pre-1980 levels. In surveying cases of high growth, Rodrik contends that it is difficult to find cases where unorthodox policies have not played some role, with the possible exception of Hong Kong.

In explaining the relationship between tailored policies and growth Rodrik argues that the constraints on growth and capabilities vary across countries and over time. Countries can initiate growth if they can relax the most binding constraints, even if they do not undertake wholesale institutional reform. Growth itself can facilitate further institutional reform and reduce constraints on continuing growth. This argument for institutions tailored to circumstances does not imply that any institutions will work. Rodrik argues that there is a wide range of evidence across countries to support the view that "institutions that provide dependable property rights, manage conflict, maintain law and order, and align economic incentives with social costs and benefits are the foundation of long term growth" (Rodrik, 2003: 10).

In terms of industrial policy, like Evans, Rodrik argues that the key to developing growth-friendly policies is achieving the right balance between autonomy and embeddedness. The need for autonomy is straightforward. As economists frequently point out, industrial policy can easily lead to rent seeking or corrupt behaviour. A public system capable of acting in the country's interests is an essential requirement of industrial policy. However, embeddedness is also needed. If public officials are to understand the constraints on growth, they need to understand the concerns and constraints as seen by the business community:

> Too much autonomy for the bureaucrats and you have a system that minimizes corruption but fails to provide the incentives that the private sector really needs. Too much embeddedness for the business bureaucrats, and they end up in bed with (and in the pockets of) business interests. Moreover, we would like the process to be democratically accountable and to carry public legitimacy. Getting this balance right is so important that it overshadows, in my view, all other elements of policy design (Rodrik, 2004: 17).

Extending this argument, Sabel suggests that development policy is a social learning process (Sabel, 2005). It can be viewed as process of addressing successive constraints on development. An important type of constraint is the absence of certain public goods: for example, support institutions that help potential exporters determine where they should direct their efforts, training, quality certification, physical infrastructure and various stages of venture capital that new entrants are unlikely to be able to provide themselves (Sabel, 2005: 5). He says "The focus on relaxing successive constraints corresponds to a re-interpretation of the kinds of institutions that favour growth; and this re-interpretation in turn undermines the claim that growth depends on institutional endowments in the familiar sense of a single, well defined set of mutually supportive institutions" (ibid).

Growth requires continuing social learning. "The goal therefore is to create institutions that can learn to identify and mitigate different, successive constraints on growth, including of course such constraints that arise from defects in the current organisation of the learning institutions themselves" (Sabel, 2005: 6). Where these institutional interventions aim to shape entrepreneurial behaviour, they resemble traditional industrial policy, picking winners. But, says Sabel, that is as far as the similarity between industrial policy in the traditional sense and the process view goes. "Traditional industrial policy assumes that the state has a panoramic view of the economy, enabling it to reliably provide incentives, information and services that less knowledgeable actors cannot". There are no actors in the process or bootstrapping view with that kind of overarching vision. All vantage points are partial. "So just as private actors typically need public help in overcoming information limits and coordination problems, the public actors who provide that help themselves routinely need assistance in overcoming limits of their own".

International experience suggests that there is not one best set of institutions. Across currently rich countries in Europe, the US and Japan, there is comparatively little difference in productivity levels. In many respects, there are similarities in the roles played by institutions in protecting property rights and regulating product, labour and financial markets. However, there are also significant institutional differences between Europe, Japan and the US, as well as (smaller) differences in institutional arrangements between European countries. These differences are most evident in labour market institutions.

9.2.7 Regional Institutions and Quality of Life

Since the Irish economy has many of the characteristics of a regional economy, the determinants of regional growth are of interest (Krugman, 1997). Regional economies are often viewed as being driven by their export base — an incomplete theory, but one that captures some of the dynamics of regional growth. Regions that have, or develop, an export base in activities with favourable characteristics (strong demand, high level of skilled employment) will tend to enjoy strong income and employment growth. The shift in Ireland's export base from agriculture and related industries to one based on high-technology, software, financial and other internationally tradable services has had a profound effect on the Irish economy. The ability to reposition the economy in this way has been based on a wide range of factors.

A related perspective has been developed by Florida (2002). He sees 'creative activities' and creativity as the driving force in regional economic growth. His theory is consistent with endogenous growth theory, which places new knowledge creation at the heart of economic growth. Florida's focus is on the geography of creativity, in particular the role of urban regions in fostering it. He argues that regional prosperity depends on achieving a combination of what he terms the three Ts: technology (presence of high-tech companies), talent (employment of people in creative occupations) and tolerance (an attractive quality of life for the 'creative class', who seek culture, diversity, racial integration). Regions that have all three Ts are most successful in attracting new talent and generating new ideas, new enterprises and regional economic growth. Florida's analysis is mostly based on US regions and cities, but he cites Dublin as a city that is achieving the three Ts and, hence, dynamic growth.

If Florida's argument is convincing, his institutional recommendations remain somewhat general: "Building broad creative ecosystems that mobilize the creative talents of many is a complex, multifaceted activity". We are, he says, only beginning to understand how to do it. "It will take a long time and many local experiments" (Florida, 2002: xxiii). But it underlines the potential importance of quality of life in securing not only an adequate social dividend from Ireland's economic growth, but in sustaining growth potential itself.

9.3 Irish Institutions: Past, Present and Future

9.3.1 The Characteristics and Evolution of Ireland's Institutions

Without offering a comprehensive interpretation of the role of institutions in Irish development, a number of observations can be made. First, the institutions that shaped Ireland's outward-oriented economic development were significantly state-created or state-led, especially in the 1960s, 1970s and 1980s. In contrast to continental European countries, in earlier decades there were relatively few and weak associations in civil society in Ireland devoted to technical, scientific or business development. There were undoubtedly some strong religious and professional associations, but these were not particularly concerned with economic development or productivity enhancement. Their purposes and methods reflected the context in which they had developed — a protected economy and a closed society — in which the representation of interests and the provision of services was presumed to occur in a stable environment and to focus on the division of a roughly fixed national product.

Second, if some civic associations were too inwardly looking, another important nexus of institutions were insufficiently tailored to Irish realities. Because of the link with sterling and other historical connections, the monetary, financial and industrial relations systems bore the marks of the British regime. Indeed, in the 1960s and 1970s, reflecting the British experience, they became increasingly conflictual and inflation-prone.

Third, there was a very significant evolution of Irish institutions over the decades. Within a stable basic industrial policy, there were many institutional changes. Some organisations which were seen as important in the early days, such as the Institute for Industrial Research and Standards (IIRS), were no longer necessary as technical standards became increasingly international. Other functions were met by creation of new programmes and bodies. The European Monetary System (EMS), and eventually European Monetary Union (EMU), represented an historical shift in the institutional framework of monetary management and wage bargaining. Social partnership was a major institutional development that gave rise to behavioural changes in wage bargaining, industrial relations and public policy. The European internal market — by addressing non-tariff barriers to trade in goods and extending the common market to key services — prompted the creation of new regulatory institutions at both European and national level. In Ireland and elsewhere, there were deep changes in business organisation and technology as Japanese production techniques proved feasible in Western firms and new high-performance work practices were adopted by the, mostly American, IT and pharmaceutical firms investing in Ireland in the late 1980 and the 1990s.

It is notable that this evolution contains at least three strands: an EU-informed institutional framework for the regulation of markets, an American influence on business organisation and technology and the gradual creation of Irish institutions more suited to modern Irish realities. All three strands are supportive of Ireland's success in the international economy; they can be seen as creating the conditions in which Ireland's outward-looking strategy, which had mixed success in the decades after 1960, can really work.

The development of institutions tailored to Irish circumstances, and designed to address identified constraints, is particularly notable in two areas, industrial policy and social partnership.

9.3.2 Institutional Factors in Ireland's Industrial and Economic Development

Economic and social change in Ireland has been so profound, and institutional changes so multiple, that they lend themselves to various interpretations. Indeed, among those interpretations is the view that Ireland's experience, especially since the mid-1980s, reflects adherence to liberal or neo-liberal policies and institutions (Kirby, 2002). It is clear that several aspects of Irish policy and economic development are consistent with a liberal or Washington consensus view of the economy — the importance of free trade, the adoption of stable macroeconomic policies, the lowering of personal taxes, the independent regulation of utilities and privatisation of state enterprises.

In our view, the development of the Irish economy can be better understood as an example of what Rodrik and Sabel refer to as 'heterodox success'; this does, indeed, involve adopting a range of market-conforming policies, but combines these with institutions and policies that go beyond the minimalist prescription of neo-liberalism or the Washington consensus.

For a start, the Irish experience would appear to support Rodrik's view that *initiating* growth is easier than implied by the all-or-nothing institutional prescription of the Washington consensus. At the start of the 1960s Ireland still had high tariffs, capital controls, an inefficient industrial base built up under protection, weak domestic competition and state monopolies in transport and all of the network industries. Labour mobility between Ireland and the UK limited the extent to which Ireland's disadvantages could be offset by lower wages. Yet, there was a marked acceleration in Irish economic growth. Some key constraints on Irish growth were indeed released in the early 1960s — particularly lack of confidence and the balance of payments constraint — a process assisted by inward FDI by American companies.

Although highly reliant on the extension of free trade, and closely aligned to the strategies of transnational corporations, Ireland's industrial policy has been much more pro-active than implied by a purely liberal reading. Since the late 1950s, an important part of Irish public policy has been industrial and development policy. The policy aimed to re-orient indigenous enterprises to export and attract inward investment to Ireland. It had varying success in each of these tasks and there was ongoing debate on the rationale, feasibility and best method of state action to promote economic development (NESC, 1981, 1982, 1986; 1998; O'Malley, 1989; Mjoset, 1992, Industrial Policy Review Group, 2002). The experience since the late 1980s and recent research help us to see more clearly what role the state has played, and can play, in the Irish context. O'Riain distinguishes between the Asian 'bureaucratic developmental state' and what he calls the flexible or 'networked developmental state' (O'Riain, 2004). Ireland's flexible developmental State has developed the Irish economy by creating connections with the most modern networks of production and innovation. It does this by attracting high-tech firms to Ireland and fostering related indigenous networks of innovation, and encouraging them to internationalise.

This perspective allows us to see that the Irish state — through a complex and flexible set of agencies and policies — has played a key role in the economic progress of the past decade and a half. Under a fairly invariant industrial 'policy', the agencies have flexibly reconfigured the package of services that they offer, in dialogue with their client firms. The agencies and the firms seem to be jointly exploring the latest organisational and technical possibilities and teasing out how they can be applied in Ireland. The development agencies are in a complex form of interdependence — with Government Departments, universities and the social partners — which constitutes a form of external accountability. NESC argues that the idea of the networked developmental state "allows us to retain our focus on the challenge of developing a small peripheral economy that constituted the major task of independent Ireland, and remains relevant, while letting go of the overly statist outlook that sometimes goes with that focus, but which is no longer effective in an age of global information networks" (NESC, 2002: 7).

9.3.3 Social Partnership and the Institutions of Interest Mediation

Irish experience also seems to confirm the observation that initiating growth is easier than sustaining it. In reviewing Ireland's long-run economic development, NESC pointed out that although the Irish economy achieved significant economic growth, adjustment, modernisation and inward investment after 1960, these successes were qualified in important ways. Growth was not handled well, giving rise to inconsistent claims on the Irish economy. Awareness of the international environment was incomplete. The adjustment of indigenous enterprises to international competition failed more often than it succeeded. Job creation was insufficient, old jobs were lost at a remarkable rate and unemployment increased. High levels of savings and corporate profits were not matched by investment in the Irish economy. Inevitable adversities were allowed to become divisive and produced delayed and insufficient responses. Overall, there was an insufficient appreciation of the interdependence in the economy — between the public and the private sectors, between the indigenous economy and the international economy, and between the economic and the political (NESC, 1996: 21).

Social partnership seems to have had a significant influence on the Irish economy through a number of channels (NESC, 2002; 2003). First, the partnership approach has supported wage moderation, predictability and enhanced profitability. Second, partnership was an important element in Ireland's transition from a high-inflation, volatile and conflictual economy to a low-inflation, stable economy. Third, there was a supply side influence. By settling macroeconomic and distributional issues, partnership freed management, trade union, voluntary sector and government energies to focus on real issues affecting competitiveness and social cohesion, such as training, work practises, commercialisation of state enterprises, active labour market policy and many other supply-side issues.

9.3.4 The Role of Institutional Adaptation in Ireland's Recent Success

The role of institutions is seen by NESC as central in understanding Ireland's experience since the late 1980s. In its 2003 Strategy report, NESC argued that a critical aspect of vision is clear sight of how public policy, the social partners and others have influenced the economy and society, and how they can influence it in future. It noted that over recent decades NESC and others had developed a particular view of what a successful economy would look like, what role public policy has in promoting economic and social development, the nature and role of social partnership, the desirable and likely pattern of enterprise-level partnership, the contribution that EU membership can make and the social patterns and social policies that would be evident in a prosperous economy. "Our view on these issues was, in large measure, derived from study of the patterns of economic and social life, and public policy, found in the richer states that we aspired to catch up with, and was often described as a superior 'model'" (NESC, 2002: 36).

Now that a significant degree of economic and social catch up has been achieved, a more successful economy, society and public system looks significantly different from the model that was envisaged. Taken together, the slight deviation from the expected model or goal on many fronts—the role of the state, business development, social partnership, industrial relations, the EU and social policy and patterns—amounts to a significant deviation on all taken together. Ireland's experience, NESC argued, suggests that:

1. Ireland does not fit neatly into any existing model or category of socio-economic development;
2. Much greater economic and social progress occurred than was deemed possible within the models that informed earlier analysis;
3. Ireland has succeeded with an eclectic approach, that seeks to adopt the best features of different socio-economic models;
4. Many of the new economic and social possibilities were discovered by experimental problem-solving action involving government, the social partners and others; and
5. Changes in many parts of the economy, society and the state can amount to significant change in the whole.

Because of this, NESC rejects any one-dimensional view, that the changes in the past decade are due to a single factor, whether it be fiscal correction, tax reduction, inward investment, educational attainment, market liberalisation, high technology, European integration, labour supply, changes in social policy or indeed, social partnership itself:

> In contrast, the Council believes that the changes since the late 1980s—in the economy, business, public policy, enterprises, the EU and society — have been the product of widespread policy and institutional adaptation and experimentation. Although not derived from a preconceived plan or model, each change has been deliberate.
> It is the willingness and ability to change policies, arrangements and institutions that ultimately underlies Ireland's success. This is confirmed by the fact that Ireland continues to achieve less in precisely those areas where we have not adapted institutions, policies and arrangements (NESC, 2002: 37-38).

If this perspective is accepted, its poses the question: what policy and institutional adaptations are most important in securing Ireland's prosperity in the early decades of the 21st century?

9.3.5 What Now?

Our short review of international thinking strongly confirms the role of institutions in supporting productivity and prosperity. But it also suggests that there is no one compelling theory of economic development from which a comprehensive institutional design can be derived. Rather, the most convincing argument is that development requires the successive removal of constraints and good institutions are those that are good at learning how to identify and tackle constraints on productivity enhancement and business development. Our brief discussion of Irish institutions meshes with that analysis. The Irish economy performed poorly up to the late 1950s and it is widely accepted that institutional factors were critical in the subsequent success — but also in the intermittent failure — of Ireland's outward-looking strategy. Institutions played a role in identifying and mitigating constraints on economic development. Some of them evolved pragmatically in response to emerging problems. But other institutions — of political decision making, interest mediation, wage bargaining and macroeconomic management — considerably damaged economic performance, until they were recast around a shared understanding of Ireland's particular economic structure and position in the international system. Here also, there is no compelling international theory or model of social concertation, and our institutions work well when they are tailored and focused on learning.

This discussion suggests that Ireland must continue to create institutional arrangements that can identify and address constraints. We must continue close observation of international developments. We must continue to adapt institutions in a way that responds to changing conditions and suits Ireland's context. What is new is the range of factors that influence productivity and prosperity and, therefore, the spectrum of institutions that are relevant to the productivity challenge. If this argument affirms Ireland's overall approach to institution building and reform, it does not warrant complacency, for reasons we outline now.

Economic Constraints

There is considerable agreement on some of the economic constraints that need to be addressed to facilitate continued prosperity and increased productivity:

1. Innovation, on which the Government has recently published its *Strategy for Science, Technology and Innovation 2006-2013;*
2. A truly effective national training system that meets the needs of people at work and of enterprises;
3. Investment in infrastructure;
4. Stronger competition in several areas of the Irish economy to stimulate productivity and innovation among enterprises and reduce prices; and
5. Enhanced performance in the utility industries.

Some of the key requirements for productivity on which all are agreed — innovation, training, infrastructure and utilities — seem to require significant further institutional change if they are to be effectively delivered. The issue of productivity in the non-traded sector has received relatively little attention until recently in public policy. Productivity is below average in many parts of the non-traded sector and there is scope for public policy and industry bodies to promote innovation and best international practise.[1]

Social Constraints on Economic Performance

We are moving towards a new shared understanding of the Irish economy and a new view of the relationship between economic performance and social policy. While there was a real sense that the economic reality set limits to the social possibilities, it seems that the long-term strength of the economy now depends on effective social policy. The medium and long term strength of the economy seems to depend critically not only on the recently increased investment in physical infrastructure and scientific research, but also on a deepening of capabilities, even greater participation, internal as well as external connectivity, more social mobility and successful handling of diversity, including immigration. In short, social realities now set limits to economic possibilities.

The NESC is convinced that the development of a dynamic, knowledge-based economy has inherent social implications that can serve social justice and a more egalitarian society, *and* that the development of Ireland's welfare state—as outlined in its recent report, *The Developmental Welfare State*—is integral to sustaining the dynamism and flexibility of its economy. In a globalised world, the strength of Ireland's economy and the attractiveness of its society will rest on the same foundation – the human qualities of those who participate in them.

The wider set of supply-side factors which are critical to economy-wide productivity and prosperity include:

1. life long learning;
2. public transport;
3. childcare;
4. eldercare;
5. educational disadvantage;

6. health service;
7. urban planning; and
8. tailored social services.

Addressing this wide set of issues poses profound institutional challenges. These policies take us into domains in which Ireland's record of innovation, reform and delivery is not particularly strong (NESC, 2005b, Chapter 11).

Ireland is now confronted with the challenge of transforming its developmental state into a 'dual state' — a set of public institutions that achieve not only high productivity and competitiveness but also social solidarity and participation. Experience and analysis confirm that the exact institutional route to this is something we must work out for ourselves. Ireland's economy and 'networked developmental state' differ from even the most relevant comparators; its social situation and, yet to be created, 'developmental welfare state' will differ from that in the best performing countries, like Denmark. But experience and analysis — not least Ireland's surprising break-through — also suggest that we must now benchmark our businesses, technology and social outcomes against the best in the world. Benchmarking works best when combined with root-cause-analysis. So NESC's call to 'trust ourselves' and 'revise means and goals in the light of experience' is also a suggestion that we see ourselves as part of the worldwide quest for public institutions that achieve continuous improvement. Ireland will, almost certainly, not be on its own in discovering that a 'networked developmental state' and a 'developmental welfare state' are merely supportive of, and also dependent on, a 'developmental society'.

Notes

1 The recently published Forfás report on the construction sector provides an example of what could be done to address productivity in a non-traded area.

References

Evans, P. (1995), *Embedded Autonomy: States and Industrial Transformation*, Princeton University Press, Princeton N.J.

Florida, R. (2002), *The Rise of the Creative Class*, Basic Books, New York.

Forfás (2006), *Productivity in Residential Construction*, Forfás, Dublin.

Freeman, C. (1987), *Technology and Economic Performance, Lessons from Japan*, Pinter, London.

Freeman, C. (1995), "The 'National System of Innovation' in Historical Perspective", *Cambridge Journal of Economics*, 19, 5-24.

Grossman, G. M. and Helpman, E. (1993), "Endogenous Innovation in the Theory of Growth", *Journal of Economic Perspectives*, 8: 23-44.

Helpman, E. (2005), *The Mystery of Economic Growth*, Harvard University Press, Cambridge, MA.

Hollingsworth, J.R. and Boyer, R. (1997), "Co-ordination of Economic Actors and Social Systems of Production" in Hollingsworth, J.R. and R. Boyer, *Contemporary Capitalism: The Embeddedness of Institutions,* Cambridge University Press, Cambridge.

Industrial Policy Review Group (2002), A Time for Change: Industrial Policy for the 1990s, Dublin: Stationery Office.

Kirby, P. (2002), *The Celtic Tiger in Distress: Growth and Inequality in Ireland,* Palgrave, London.

Kitschelt, H., Lange, P., Marks, G. and Stephens, J.D. (1999), *Continuity and Change in Contemporary Capitalism,* Cambridge University Press, Cambridge.

Lucas, R. E. (1988), "On the Mechanics of Economic Development", *Journal of Monetary Economics,* 22: 3-42.

Lundvall, B.A. (1985), "Product Innovation and User-Producer Interaction" *Industrial Development Research Series,* Vol. 31, Aalborg University Press, Aalborg.

Lundvall., B.A. and Tomlinson, M. (2000), "On the Convergence and Divergence of National Systems of Innovation", Aalborg University, Department of Business Studies.

Mjoset, L. (1992), *The Irish Economy in a Comparative Institutional Perspective,* National Economic and Social Council, Dublin.

Nelson, R. (2005), *Technology, Institutions and Economic Growth,* Harvard University Press, Cambridge, MA.

NESC (1981), *Industrial Policy and Development: A Survey of the Literature,* National Economic and Social Council, Dublin.

NESC (1982), *A Review of Industrial Policy* National Economic and Social Council, Dublin.

NESC (1993), *A Strategy for Competitiveness, Growth and Employment,* National Economic and Social Council, Dublin.

NESC (1993), *A Strategy for Competitiveness, Growth and Employment,* National Economic and Social Council, Dublin.

NESC (1996), *Strategy into the 21st Century,* National Economic and Social Council, Dublin.

NESC (1998), *Sustaining Competitive Advantage: Proceedings of NESC Seminar, Policy* National Economic and Social Council, Dublin.

NESC (1999), *Opportunities, Challenges and Capacities for Choice,* National Economic and Social Council, Dublin.

NESC (2002), An *Investment in Quality: Services, Inclusion and Enterprise—Conclusions and Recommendations,* National Economic and Social Council, Dublin.

NESC (2003), *An Investment in Quality: Services, Inclusion and Enterprise,* National Economic and Social Council, Dublin.

NESC (2005a), *The Developmental Welfare State,* National Economic and Social Council, Dublin.

NESC (2005b), *ESC Strategy 2006: People, Productivity and Purpose,* National Economic and Social Council, Dublin.

North, D. (1990), *Institutions, Institutional Change and Economic Performance,* Cambridge University Press, Cambridge.

O'Donnell, R. (1997), "The Competitive Advantage of Peripheral Regions: Conceptual Issues and Research Approaches", in Brian Fynes and Sean Ennis eds. *Competing From the Periphery: Core Issues in International Business,* Oak Tree Press, Dublin.

O Riain, S. (2004), *The Politics of High-Tech Growth: Developmental Network States in the Global Economy,* Cambridge University Press, Cambridge.

Rodrik, D. (2005), "Growth Strategies" in P. Aghion and S.N. Darlauf, *Handbook of Economic Growth Volume 1A,* Amsterdam: Elsevier.

Rodrik, D. (2003), "What Do We Learn from the Country Narratives", in D. Rodrik, *In Search of Prosperity: Analytical Narratives of Economic Growth,* Princeton University Press, Princeton.

Rodrik, D. (2004), "Industrial Policy for the Twenty-First Century", Paper prepared for UNIDO.

Romer, P. (1990), "Endogenous Technological Change", *Journal of Political Economy,* 98: S71-S102.

Romer, P. (1994a), "The Origins of Endogenous Growth Theory", *Theory of Economic Perspectives,* Vol. 8, No.1, 3-22.

Romer, P. (1994b), "Beyond Classical and Keynesian Economic Theory", *Policy Options,* July-August 2004.

Sabel, C. (2005), "Bootstrapping Development: Rethinking the Role of Public Intervention in Promoting Growth", Paper presented to the *Protestant Ethic and Spirit of Capitalism Conference,* Cornell University, Ithaca, New York.

Solow, R. (1956), "A Contribution to the Theory of Economic Growth", *Quarterly Journal of Economics,* 70: 65-94.

Stiglitz, J. (2003), *Globalisation and its Discontents,* Norton, New York.

Teece, D.J. (1986), "Transaction Economic and the Multinational Enterprise: an Assessment", Journal of Economic Behaviour and Organization, 7: 21-45.

Weiss, L. (1988), *The Myth of the Powerless State: Governing the Global Economy in a Global Era,* Polity Press, Cambridge.

Woo-Cummings, M. (1999), *The Developmental State,* Cornell University Press, Ithaca, New York.

CHAPTER 10

COMPETITION AND PRODUCTIVITY

DAVID BOYLE AND JOHN EVANS[1]

ABSTRACT

The body of research linking competition and productivity has been growing in recent years and there appears to be a strong positive association. This chapter sets out the economic evidence in support of the thesis that strong competition supports productivity gains by encouraging innovation activity, more efficient business practices and technological diffusion. By way of example, the chapter discusses the Irish air travel and electricity sectors in-dept. In it's conclusions, the chapter emphasises the problems in the non-traded sectors of the economy in terms of competition and productivity.

1 David Boyle and John Evans are staff at the Policy Division of the Competition Authority. Views expressed here are our own and do not necessarily represent those of the Competition Authority.

10.1 Introduction

The motivation for competition policy is often framed in terms of monopoly (or market) power. Anyone with even a passing interest in competition policy is aware of the 'monopoly example'. Monopolies are 'bad' because they can charge the monopoly price (or equivalently, the monopoly margin over cost). The monopolist's power, and therefore the harm it can cause to society, arises because the consumer's only choice is to buy or not buy. By contrast, in a competitive market, each firm's market power is weakened because consumers have other choices – the fact that the consumer can choose to buy from different firms disciplines each of them in such a way that the price they can charge approaches the cost of producing whatever good or service is at issue. This result is often referred to as the allocative efficiency property of competitive markets. It is not however the only, or perhaps even the most important efficiency property of competitive markets.

Competitive markets are also characterised as being both productively and dynamically efficient. Recent studies on gains from competition have been focussing increasingly on 'productive efficiency' and 'dynamic efficiency', which can be broadly defined in terms of productivity growth through innovations (Ahn, 2002).[1] In short, productive efficiency gains come from productivity enhancing innovations which introduce new and better production methods, and successful innovations will eventually raise the level and growth rate of productivity in the long run. As with the previous example, harm to society tends to arise where competition is weak. Weakly competitive markets tend to be less productively or dynamically efficient, or in other words, productivity levels and growth rates tend to be less in weakly competitive markets.

The overall harm to society can be ascertained by considering briefly the determinants of economic growth. Economic growth is typically attributed to three factors: (i) capital accumulation; (ii) labour force growth; and (iii) multi-factor productivity. In other words, increasing factor inputs such as capital and labour, and enabling them to work together in more productive combinations, allow for the creation of greater wealth. To the extent that the degree of competition affects factor productivity, economic growth and therefore societal prosperity, now and into the future, is also affected. This line of reasoning yields a very powerful motivation for competition policy.

The remainder of this chapter is structured as follows. In Section 10.2 we first provide some intuition on the relationship between competition and productivity, attempt to extend this intuition to more formal treatments of the issue and bring out the empirical evidence to underline key points. In Section 10.3 we consider two contrasting illustrative examples – the Irish air travel and electricity sectors. In Section 10.4 we attempt to draw out some general policy principles and in Section 10.5 we conclude with a discussion of the role of competition policy.

10.2 The Relationship between Productivity and Competition

10.2.1 Some Intuition

The relationship between competition and productivity is in some respects not a straightforward one. Nonetheless, a rudimentary understanding of what is often termed the 'competitive process' provides a compelling intuition.

A useful starting point is to consider first the concept of 'rivalry' among firms. Rivalry refers to the interaction of firms in a market, i.e., the manner in which firms compete for custom based on price, quality and other product or service dimensions that the consumer values. Rivalry may be more or less vigorous and is determined by many factors. The simplest, but often deceptive characterisation of rivalry involves market structure. That is, markets with more firms tend to be more rivalrous. The concept of rivalry is however essentially a static one.

Concepts of the competitive process are more complete when dynamic effects are incorporated. Specifically, firms over time seek to (i) improve the way in which they produce goods or services, i.e., they seek out more efficient ways of operating and/or (ii) provide better or new goods and services. The first effect influences the productivity of the firm directly. Improving the manner in which a firm produces may involve employing labour and capital in more productive combinations, it may involve the adoption of new technologies or it may involve shifting the boundaries of the firm. The second effect influences productivity to the extent that the firm supplying new and innovative products operates at an intermediate stage of production, its 'new or improved' goods or services, to the extent that they are taken up, allow downstream firms to operate more productively.

Central to this dynamic notion of competition is the process of entry and exit. The threat of entry and the possibility of failure are strong drivers of competition. Weak rivalry, and the associated high profits and/or inefficient practices will over time induce entry by more efficient firms. Incumbents will either adapt or fail. When this process is effective, dynamic competition ensures greater productivity.

10.2.2 A More Formal Understanding

While this intuitive understanding of how competition can drive productivity is useful, formal studies of productivity tend to distinguish three different processes (Pilat, 1996: 108-109): (i) innovation activity; (ii) efficiency and; (iii) technological diffusion. Each of these processes is influenced by competition.

Productivity gains through 'innovation activity' refer to the development of new products and processes. Innovative activity and research and development (R&D) advances are central for productivity growth. The manner in which the degree of competition affects incentives to innovate is complex and much debate remains amongst economists. On the one hand, weak competition tends to weaken incentives to innovate because the firms in question do not need to. Empirically, the majority of recent studies conclude that a low degree of competition as expressed in high concentration rates is not conducive to innovation activity (Symeonides, 1997). On the other hand, very strong competition may also weaken incentives to innovate. This occurs because a firm considering investing in R&D activity must consider the costs associated with making a risky R&D investment that may or may not be successful as well as the potential return from the R&D activity. In extremely competitive markets where the results of R&D, i.e., the new product or process, can be easily copied, the returns from R&D activity are reduced leading to reduced incentives to innovate in the first place. It is this line of reasoning which motivates the rationale for patents and licences.

Recent empirical studies undertaken by the OECD take an entirely different approach from the more conventional analysis of the relationship between competition and innovation which primarily focuses on the relationship between concentration levels and innovation. Recent studies search for a correlation between the level of anti-competitive product market regulation and innovation across entire national economies. Jaumotte and Pain (2005) show that all else being equal, anti-competitive regulations (other than Intellectual Property Rights) have a significant negative correlation with both R&D intensity and patenting. The study analysed various policy levers and their effects on business R&D spending and found removing or reducing anti-competitive regulation was the second most effective lever for raising the level of R&D spending. In fact, the authors concluded that the low levels of such anti-competitive regulations in Australia, the UK and the US have helped to raise the intensity of R&D in each of those countries by ten per cent or more above the OECD average.

The 'efficiency' process refers to the reduction of productive inefficiency. Exposing inefficient firms to competition forces them to improve their methods of production. Competition provides the stimulus to adopt or invest in new technology or find more cost efficient ways of producing. Studies on the relationship between competition variables and inefficient behaviour conclude that in most countries efficiency in an industry declines beyond a certain level of concentration, suggesting that high levels of concentration are detrimental to efficiency (Caves et al., 1992).

'Technological diffusion' as a source of productivity gains refers to the process whereby firms adopt new technologies or processes developed elsewhere and is distinct from the efficiency channel which typically involves more efficient use of existing technology. Diffusion of technology is also considered a key factor for improving productivity. The McKinsey Institute have carried out numerous studies on productivity and conclude that the degree to which firms implement modern technology is directly related to their exposure to competition.[2] Firms in markets sheltered from competition have little incentive to invest in new technology and improve efficiency, the result being lower productivity than under conditions of competition. An OECD study concluded technology diffusion often accounts for more than half of Total Factor Productivity (TFP) (OECD, 1996).

10.2.3 Comment

In summary, the general consensus from the research on the relationship between competition and productivity to date seems to conclude that competition has a number of distinct effects. First, competition stimulates innovation as firms invest in the development of new products or production methods. Second, competition encourages efficiency improvements. As firms face competition they must reduce costs in order to compete for custom. This is achieved by finding quicker or more efficient methods of production. Third, competition promotes diffusion of technology as firms seek to improve productivity by adopting processes or products which may have been developed by market leaders. This diffusion process is prominent in markets which are open to international competition.

10.3 Two Illustrative Examples

In this section we provide two examples where the considerations outlined in the previous section can be seen in practice. The importance of the transport and electricity sectors for an economy are widely recognised. The European Commission (2002: 26) described these sectors as "*.... the arteries of the Internal Market, the lifeblood of competitiveness, when they under-perform, so does the rest of the economy. If they are efficient, all other sectors benefit.*"

10.3.1 The Irish Air-Travel Industry

A cursory analysis of the air-travel industry in Ireland over the past two decades illustrates the effect that effective dynamic competition can have on productivity and how consumers and the economy more generally can benefit. In particular, the history of Aer Lingus is an interesting example of how a once primed national champion can become an effective competitor, not just on a domestic but also on an international stage.

Liberalisation of the Airline Sector

The process of liberalisation of the Irish travel sector was a long one but two distinct phases can be distinguished. The first phase commenced in 1986 with the decision by regulatory authorities to allow Ryanair to challenge British Airways and Aer Lingus for the Dublin to London route. The second phase resulted from the European Commission decision to fully deregulate the airline industry in 1997.

The first phase of liberalisation allowed, most notably, Ryanair to compete directly with the national carrier, Aer Lingus. At first Ryanair employed the traditional airline business model and, until restructuring in 1990, made losses. The restructured Ryanair employed a new low cost business model that was closely based on that of the original low fares airline, Southwest Airlines in the U.S. The low cost model involved minimising costs and maximising efficiency through operating from uncongested secondary airports with a single aircraft-type fleet and getting maximum utilisation from each aircraft through fast turnarounds and high load-factors. The Ryanair business model was in stark contrast with that of Aer Lingus who operated the more traditional airline model. While throughout the 1990s, consumers benefited from lower prices and greater choice, Aer Lingus, tried to compete, lost money, and were rescued by the government. In 1993, Aer Lingus had debts of €16 million and were incurring losses of €1 million a week. Aid in the region of £175 million was approved by the European Commission subject to conditions (Chari, 2004).

The second phase of liberalisation involved the opening of European markets to competition. The first steps towards this phase of liberalisation were taken in 1987 when rules were adopted that allowed the European Commission to enforce competition rules (Articles 81 and 82 EC) in the EU air transport sector and to adopt certain group exemptions. Many inter-airline agreements which were commonplace in the industry were now considered anti-competitive and therefore illegal under EU law. Competition was not fully realised until 1993 when all price controls were removed.[3]

Aer Lingus' Turnaround

The removal of the restrictive barriers which were commonplace in the industry resulted in increased competition for Aer Lingus. Following the shock to international air travel caused by the events of September 11th, 2001, many governments across Europe faced calls to financially support their national carriers. The decision of the European Commission not to allow airlines to receive state aids provoked fears we had seen the last of the 'national champion'. Table 10.1 below provides some details on Aer Lingus' perfomance between 1999 and 2005.

Table 10.1: Aer Lingus Performance 1999 - 2005[4]

	'99	'00	'01	'02	'03	'04	'05
Staff	7044	6624	6833	5245	4281	3906	3,475
Aircraft	38	38	39	32	34	33	33
Passengers (m)	6.5	6.9	6.3	6.2	6.6	6.9	8.0
Turnover (€m)	1134.2	1372.5	1097	958	888	906	883
Profit (€m)	71.6	79.9	-50.4	63	83	107	72.4
Turnover/staff (€)	161,016	207,201	160,544	182,650	207. 428	231,951	254,100
Turnover/craft (€m)	29.8	36.1	28.1	29.9	26.1	27.4	26.7
Turnover/passenger (€)	174	199	174	155	135	130	110
Profit/staff (€)	10,165	12,062	-7,375	12,011	19,387	27,394	20,834
Profit/craft (€m)	1.8	2.1	-1.2	2.0	2.4	3.2	2.1
Profit/passenger (€)	11.0	11.5	-8.0	10.2	12.5	15.39	8.6
Passenger/craft	171,000	182,000	162,000	194,000	194,000	211,000	244,000
Passenger/staff	923	1041	922	1182	1542	1779	2313
New Routes	No new routes, entered one world alliance	+4: Balt/Wash, London (Gat), Munich, Stockholm	-2: Baltimore, Newark Total 42	+9: Barcelona, Nice, Malaga, Alicante, Faro, Geneva, Prague, Vienna, Cork to Malaga.	+6: Palma, Tenerife, Toulouse, Bologna, Lisbon, Jersey.	Total 65 (24 new European routes since 2001)	16 new routes operated in 2005.

The restructuring of Aer Lingus is evident from the table. For example, Aer Lingus since 2001 has reduced staffing levels by almost 50 per cent and the number of craft they operate by approximately 15 per cent. The Aer Lingus model now looks more like the low cost airline model. Increases in efficiency and associated productivity gains are evident from the passenger/craft and passengers/staff figures. The average number of passengers/craft increased by almost 50 per cent between 2001 and 2005. The passengers/staff figures are even more impressive, increasing by approximately 150 per cent over the same period. While these are not ideal measures, they do indicate a substantial rise in TFP. This example illustrates how effective competition and a pro-competitive approach to regulation can drive efficiency and productivity gains.

Vigorous competition has also driven Aer Lingus not just to use existing capital more intensively, but also to adopt new technologies. For example, Aer Lingus has installed new check in systems that make it possible for passengers to check in without queuing. Ryanair have now introduced an online self check in system.

Apart from the direct effects on productivity, competition in the air travel sector has clearly benefited consumers. The cost of air travel is down and consumers have a much broader range of destinations and carriers. The knock-on effects of increased competition in the air travel industry are visible across various sectors of the economy including the export and tourism markets, which contributes to our overall growth. Transport is an essential input for many sectors and industries; Ireland is now a convenient place to do business due to the cost and frequency of flights to and from Ireland.[5] Passenger traffic through Dublin Airport is indicative. Inward (outward) traffic has increased by 216 per cent from 3.67 million passengers in 1995 to 8.07 million passengers in 2005.[6]

10.3.2 The Irish Electricity Sector

The impetus to liberalise the Irish electricity sector came from Europe. The principal objective behind the ongoing programme is to introduce greater competition into EU electricity markets by integrating national and regional energy markets into a single European market. Vertically and horizontally integrated companies, incorporating all the functions of the electricity supply chain (i.e., generation, transmission, distribution and supply) have historically controlled energy markets in Europe. As was the case in Ireland, these companies tended to be in public ownership and often had monopoly rights conferred on them by statute. The primary challenge facing the liberalisation programme lies in tackling these national and regional monopolies. The Irish experience of electricity market liberalisation has so far largely been a negative one, precisely because of the failure to tackle the former statutory monopolist.

Liberalisation of the Electricity Sector in Ireland

The launch of the EU electricity market liberalisation programme began with the adoption of the 'First Electricity Directive' in December 1996, Directive 96/92/EC. The second piece of important community legislation aimed at liberalisation was the 'Second Electricity Directive', Directive 2003/54/EC. Together, these pieces of EU legislation attempt to remove legal monopolies in the Member States by requiring a degree of vertical disintegration of the electricity supply chain, i.e., decomposition of generation, transmission, distribution and supply, along with market opening in generation and phased market opening in supply.

The rate of progress of liberalisation in Ireland has been slow. There has been market opening at the generation level but, despite significant initial interest from potential entrants, the ESB Group's market share remains high at approximately 77 per cent with the remainder of the market largely being accounted for by Viridian.[7] At the transmission level, there has been legal unbundling of the transmission system assets, but ownership of the assets remains with the ESB Group. At the supply level, as with generation, entry has been limited with the former statutory monopolist supplying 74 per cent of the market in total.[8]

Generation and supply are two areas of the Irish market in which competition is possible.[9] While the requirements for liberalisation as set out in the directives have been complied, the success of liberalisation can only really be assessed in light of the emergence of competition in the sector. The reality is that competition has not materialised and further, the prospect of it eventually appearing, at present, seems remote.

The Impact of Liberalisation

Unsurprisingly, one of the implications of weak competition in the electricity sector is inefficiency (or low productivity). Deloitte (2005) in a review of the electricity sector in Ireland, find evidence of (i) higher than average non- fuel costs; and (ii) poor plant availability at the ESB. Together it is estimated that these two factors lead to approximately €100 million per annum additional cost compared to a generation segment operating at the international benchmark (Deloite, 2005: 10).

One of the main determinants of non-fuel costs are payroll and maintenance costs. Staffing levels and operation and maintenance costs of many ESB generation facilities compare favourably with benchmarks. However, staffing costs are notably above benchmarks. In general ESB PG staff costs are in the region of 20-30 per cent higher than benchmark generating stations in the UK (ibid). Very often in monopoly industries high profits are siphoned off in the form of higher wages for staff.

'Plant availability' refers to the average level of generating capacity available compared to the stock of generating capacity and it is considerably below benchmark levels. Deloitte (2005) note that plant availability for 2005 was 80 per cent compared to the benchmark of 90 per cent. Poor plant availability and low intensity capital usage is indicative of the low productivity levels at the ESB group. Deloitte (2005) also note that rapidly rising demand has outstripped the growth in generation capacity leading to a situation where old and poorly performing generating plants are kept on the system leading to higher costs. In an effectively functioning competitive market, entry of more efficient firms with modern generating plants would have occurred.

Overall Irish electricity prices for industrial electricity users are 22 per cent higher than the EU average, for small domestic users the prices are 51 per cent higher than the EU average, placing us with the third and second highest electricity prices, respectively, in Europe (Deloitte, 2005: 216-218). Other countries in the EU have seen steady or falling energy prices whereas the National Competitiveness Councils (NCC) *Annual Competitiveness Report 2005* notes that electricity costs for Irish firms escalated by almost 42 per cent between July 2000 and January 2005 (NCC, 2005: 45).

The 1990's saw sectors such as the technology sector and pharmaceuticals and chemicals become the frontrunners in boosting Irish productivity and growth. These industries are extremely reliant on a secure and competitively priced energy supply. Their position is now threatened. Introducing and actively promoting competition is crucial for continued economic growth.

10.3.3 Comment

In some respects the two examples described above are not that dissimilar. First, up until recently both Aer Lingus and the ESB were state owned. Second, both sectors were highly regulated. Third, both sectors have experienced severe supply-side shocks (i.e. oil/gas prices and the events of September 11th, 2001).

However, in other respects the examples described are worlds apart. In the first, regulatory reform was effective in introducing competition. In the airline sector, new firms with new business models were allowed to enter and compete. This forced productivity improvements on the part of all operators with attendant benefits passed on to consumers in the form of greater choice and better value. Benefits were also realised outside the sector with export and tourism markets in particular flourishing.

In the electricity sector, largely because of the manner in which we chose to pursue the EU liberalisation programme, effective competition has not emerged. The consequence has been low productivity at the former statutory monopolist and steadily rising electricity prices. The high costs are being and will continue to be felt throughout the economy, by consumers and business alike.

10.4 Policy Environment

10.4.1 Traded vs. Non-traded Sectors

The NCC's *Annual Competitiveness Report* highlighted evidence of weaker productivity growth in sectors of the Irish economy less exposed to international competition (NCC, 2005: 5). That portion of the economy not exposed, or only exposed in a very limited fashion, to international competition is often referred to as the non-traded sector.

Competition in the non-traded sector is determined domestically, not imported. The implication is that the non-traded sectors tend to be less competitive and, for the reasons outlined in Section 10.2, this has implications for productivity. For example, Forfás (2005) compared hourly output per worker for thirteen countries with that of the US and the results highlighted that Irish productivity in the provision of utilities is substantially below that of the US and our European peers (NCC, 2005: 33).

As discussed in the context of the electricity example from Section 10.3, the implications of weak competition, and attendant low productivity, go beyond the sector or market in question. Goods and services produced in the non-traded sector are often inputs for other sectors of the economy, including those exposed to international competition. Poor performance in the non-traded sector, not only affects consumers to the extent that they are paying higher prices, but also competitiveness.

Various factors influence a firm's decision to invest in a particular country, including taxation policy, level of education and most importantly input costs. Much of Ireland's huge productivity growth in the 1990's can be attributed to foreign investment; spiralling input costs will deter firms setting up business in Ireland in the future. The electricity sector is part of the non-traded goods market and is an example of where weak competition is putting a strain on the traded sector.[10]

Continued globalisation and the enlargement of the EU imply greater competition for new investment. Higher prices for non-traded goods significantly hamper our chances of attracting investment in the future. During Irelands growth period in the 1990's a key factor in attracting firms to Ireland was our favourable corporate tax system. As this is currently being phased out we will have to compete to a greater extent on the basis of factors such as input costs.

Policy makers and governments have a role in ensuring that non-traded sectors are as competitive as possible. This is achieved in two main ways. First, policies aimed at generating competition domestically should be pursued. Second, by pursuing policies aimed at opening up non-traded sectors to international competition.

10.4.2 Good vs. Bad Regulation

Another area where policymakers can have significant influence is in the area of market regulation. There are two main considerations. First, regulation affects the cost of doing business directly, e.g., compliance costs. Second, regulation can affect the competitive dynamic in a market. For example, not only can regulation limit rivalry in a market, it can also significantly affect dynamic competition by stifling innovation or limiting entry and exit.

Regulation that supports competition rather than hinders it is desirable. Two principles are worth bringing out here. First, regulation should be kept to the necessary minimum and there should be a rolling back of regulation where competition can be established through structural reform. One weakness in the Irish policy approach to regulation so far has been the reluctance to use structural remedies in regulated markets to overcome efficiency and competition concerns. Successive governments have avoided structural reform making difficult and expensive conduct regulation unavoidable. Structural remedies reduce the regulatory burden and improve market performance. Decisions not to separate Cablelink from Telecom Eireann, not to restructure Telecom Eireann prior to privatisation, and not to restructure the ESB have undoubtedly contributed to higher prices for energy and poor broadband infrastructure.

Second, regulatory decision making should be both expert and transparent so as to reduce regulatory error and capture. Regulatory impact analysis can be a valuable tool in achieving this.

10.4.3 National Champions

Ireland has a legacy of providing state protection across a range of markets including energy, communications, and transport. Such regulation rarely if ever brings net benefits for the economy. It prevents entry and in the process reduces incentives for incumbents to reduce costs and improve efficiency. National champion-type policies are a form of state protection.

National champion advocates argue that applying the principles of competition policy in small economies can be harmful because firms are precluded from achieving the necessary scale to compete internationally. The implication of this argument is that industrial policy would be designed to encourage national champions, to which normal competition rules would then not apply. There are, however, several reasons why the trade-off between competition and other policy goals in industrial policy can be considered small, or even non-existent.

While monopoly profits could in theory have a beneficial effect by providing a source of funding for the investment necessary to allow a national champion to compete internationally, a number of criticisms of this argument can be made. First, capital markets, rather than monopoly profits derived from domestic consumers, are a more efficient source of funds for investment abroad, and almost certainly result in more sound investment. Funds raised on capital markets, either via bonds or equity, impose obligations, controls and incentives on the shareholders and management of firms. By contrast where a firm has access to monopoly profits there is much less incentive to encourage sensible investment at home or abroad. Second, the argument rests on the assumption that monopoly profits will in fact be available for investment. This assumption ignores the fact that monopolies are typically inefficient and that monopoly rents are often dissipated by rent seeking behaviour or through rent sharing with input suppliers such as labour. Third, the discipline earned by intense competition in the domestic market is the best stimulus to success abroad. Firms that have to compete domestically know how to cut costs, operate efficiently, please customers and win business.

10.4.4 Comment

Effective dynamic competition in the non-traded sectors of the economy is crucial, not just because productivity in the non-traded sectors is important in itself, but also because the products or services at issue are often necessary inputs for firms operating in the traded sector. As prices rise in the non-traded sectors so too does the cost of doing business in Ireland. For example, much of Ireland's growth over the last ten years comes from pharmaceutical and chemical industries, as previously mentioned these industries are heavily reliant on competitively priced energy; having the second highest electricity prices in Europe does not strengthen our case when trying to attract or maintain foreign direct investment.

Regulation needs to be proportionate to the market failure present, expert and transparent. The air travel sector provides a prefect example of how the removal of anti-competitive regulation can boost productivity.

Unfettered competition in domestic markets allows the market, rather than history or the State, to select the most productive suppliers. Firms which are exposed to competition in domestic markets are much more likely to be able to compete successfully on international markets. Exposing Aer Lingus to competition in domestic markets forced efficiency and productivity improvements, and highlights how a once inefficient incumbent can be transformed into one of the most successful airlines in Europe.

10.5 Concluding Comment

The body of research on the link between competition and productivity has been growing in recent years and there appears to be a strong positive association. Strong competition tends to support productivity gains by encouraging innovative activity, more efficient business practices and technological diffusion. The relationship between competition policy and productivity is much less extensive. The likely reason for this is that on the one hand the relationship between competition and productivity is an indirect one and on the other, that the relationship between competition and competition policy is difficult to measure.

In a narrow sense, competition policy relates to activities of competition authorities. By enforcing competition law, reviewing mergers and advocating for reform of legislation and regulation that inhibits competition, competition authorities seek to eliminate the creation of market power by: (i) illegal means (e.g., by targeting cartel behaviour, exclusionary conduct on the part of dominant firms and prohibiting anticompetitive mergers); or (ii) legal means (e.g., by counteracting rent seeking activities of special interests who often seek shelter from competition through legislation and regulation).

A broader interpretation of competition policy can go much further than the activities of competition authorities and can encompass the activities of policy makers throughout the economy. Three overlapping areas are of particular importance. First, regulatory policy should seek to encourage competition by ensuring that regulations are proportional to the market failure they address and by seeking to implement structural rather than expensive behavioural solutions where appropriate. Regulation can be a valuable policy instrument in sectors where competition is absent due to market failures that cannot be corrected by the market. However, regulation can also have adverse affects when it acts as a barrier to competition by inhibiting entry or stifling innovation. Problems such as regulatory capture, regulatory lag and regulatory creep place huge cost burdens on both business and tax payers.

Second, enterprise policy should seek to ensure that domestic markets are conducive to dynamic competition and not on the creation or protection of national champions. Competition in domestic markets or the non-traded sectors is essential as it allows the market, rather than history or the State, to select the most productive suppliers. Policy should reflect this and aim to promote market conditions that are conducive to competition. Competition policy aims to ensure that competition works well for consumers. This contrasts with protectionism, or protecting 'infant industries', or the creation of 'national champions', all of which are focused on producers rather than on what the consumer wants. The Department of Enterprise, Trade and Employment (2003: 34) acknowledges this in the course of its description of the transformation of the economy from the 1960s-1980s by saying: "*notwithstanding the shift to foreign direct investment, the legacy of past protectionist policies was an industrial base that was uncompetitive in European and global markets*". Any enterprise policy choice that has the effect of protecting producers from competition runs the risk of repeating this mistake.

Third, market liberalisation programmes should be pursued vigorously and particularly in relation to the non-traded sectors of the economy. The non-traded portion of the economy is an important determinant of national productivity, but precisely because it is non-traded, competition tends to be weaker than in more exposed sectors. Because the outputs from our traded sectors are very often inputs for our traded sectors, inefficiency in the non-traded sector acts like a tax on production and tends to place a drag on national competitiveness. There must be willingness on behalf of Government to not only adopt but to vigorously implement European Commission directives and regulations on liberalisation and promoting competition.

In a recent report by the OECD on Australia, which has a mature and effective competition policy regime, the OECD estimated that effective competition policy in Australia added two and a half percentage points to GDP, which would equate in the Irish situation to gains in the order of €3.5 billion. It added $7,000 to the average household income in Australia and made the Australian economy more robust towards internal and external shocks. In Ireland, the gain per household would be in the order of €2,500. Unlike Australia however, there is a substantial legacy of anticompetitive regulation and therefore these figures likely substantially underestimate the true costs to Irish businesses, consumers and the economy more generally.

Notes

1 Other studies of the relationship between dynamic efficiency and competition include Spence (1984), Vickers (1995) and Evans and Schmalensee (2001).
2 See, for example, McKinsey Institute (1993) and McKinsey Institute (1995). See also Lewis (2004).
3 Council Regulation (EEC) No 2408/92 of 23 July 1992 on access for Community air carriers to intra-Community air routes.
4 Source: Aer Lingus Annual Reports.
5 Ireland's trade surplus has increased from approx €18 million in 1990 to €88 million in 2005. Source: CSO.
6 Source: CSO.
7 The ESB Group, in generation, consists of three main entities: ESB Power Generation (PG), Hibernian Wind and Synergen. Viridian Group is an Irish energy business that owns Northern Ireland Electricity (NIE), Energia and Huntstown Power Station.
8 ESB PES and ESB IE are wholly owned subsidiaries of the ESB Group. ESB IE is a supplier in the liberalised portion of the market.
9 The transmission and distribution markets are considered natural monopoly markets.
10 The Energy regulator has recently approved further price increases which vary from 19.4 per cent for domestic users to 19.6 per cent for small and medium enterprises and 21 per cent for large industrial customers.

References

Ahn, S. (2002), "Competition, Innovation and Productivity Growth, A Review of Theory and Evidence", *OECD Economics Department Working Papers,* No. 317.

Caves, R.E. et al. (1992), *Industrial Efficiency in Six Nations,* MIT Press, Cambridge, MA.

Chari, R.S. (2004), "State Aids in the Airline Sector: A Comparative Analysis of Iberia and Aer Lingus," TCD Policy Institute. Blue Paper 13.

Deloitte (2005), *Review of the Electricity Sector in Ireland: Final Report,* Department of Communications, Marine and Natural Resources.

Department of Enterprise Trade and Employment (2003), *Review of Industrial Performance and Policy 2003,* Department of Enterprise Trade and Employment.

European Commission (2002), *The Internal Market- Ten Years Without Frontiers,* European Commission.

Evans, S. and Schmalensee, R. (2001), "Some Economic Aspects of Antitrust Analysis in Dynamically Competitive Industries", *NBER Working Paper Series,* No. 8268.

Gonenc, R. and Nicolletti, G. (2001), "Regulation, Market Structure and Performance in Air Passenger Transportation", *OECD Economic Studies* No. 32, 2001/I.

IBEC/Amárach Consulting (2005), *National Survey of Energy Provision,* IBEC/Amárach Consulting.

Jaumotte, F. and Pain, N. (2005), "From Ideas to Development: The Determinants of R&D and Patenting", OECD, ECO/WKP(2005)44, *Economics Department Working Paper,* No. 457/49 (2005).

McKinsey Institute (1993), *Manufacturing Productivity,* McKinsey Global Institute, Washington D.C.

McKinsey Institute (1995), *Sweden's Economic Performance,* McKinsey Global Institute, Stockholm.

Lewis, W. (2004), *The Power of Productivity,* McKinsey Institute. University of Chicago Press.

National Competitiveness Council (2005), *Annual Competitiveness Report 2005,* Forfás.

OECD (1996), *Technology, Productivity and Job Creation,* OECD Paris.

Pilat, D. (1996), "Competition, Productivity and Efficiency", *OECD Economic Studies,* No 27. 1996/11.

Small Firms Association (2005), *5th Annual Business Survey,* Small Firms Association.

Spence, M. (1984), "Cost Reduction, Competition, and Industry Performance", *Econometrica,* Vol.52, No.1.

Symeonides, G. (1997), "Innovation, Firm Size and Market Structure: Schumpeterian, Hypotheses and Some New Themes", *OECD Economic Studies,* No. 27, Vol. 1996111.

Vickers, J. (1995), *Concepts of Competition,* Oxford Economic Papers, 47.

CHAPTER 11

PRIVATISATION AND PRODUCTIVITY PERFORMANCE IN IRELAND

DONAL PALCIC AND EOIN REEVES

ABSTRACT

This chapter presents an analysis of privatisation in Ireland. It discusses the sale of state owned enterprises, the contracting out of refuse collection services and Public Private Partnership (PPPs). The analysis of the sale of state owned enterprises demonstrates a clear pattern of improved performance prior to change of ownership. The post-privatisation productivity performance is not as clear-cut, with the specific case studies highlighting the importance of product market competition as a driver of sustained productivity growth. This lesson also emerges from an examination of the experience of the contracting out of services - strong competition for contracts is an important determinant of whether efficiency gains accrue.

11.1 Introduction

Although the term 'privatisation' was originally used to describe economic policies of the National Socialist Party in Germany during the 1930s (Bel, 2006) it only gained popular international currency in the late 1970s and early 1980s when newly elected governments in countries such as Great Britain, France and New Zealand commenced programmes of divestiture of state owned enterprises (SOEs). The scale of such programmes worldwide has been enormous and it is estimated that at the turn of the new millennium the volume of privatisation had exceeded €1 billion dollars. However, global privatisation activity has not been confined to the sale of SOEs, as the term has been applied to a range of other public sector reforms including liberalisation, de-regulation and contracting out. This wide application of the term 'privatisation' highlights a need for clarity about its precise meaning and scope.

Starr (1988) provides a useful working definition of privatisation as any shift in the production of goods and services from public to private. According to Starr this more focused definition of privatisation includes the following sub-categories:

1. The cessation of public programmes and disengagement of government from specific kinds of responsibilities. At a less drastic level, the restriction of publicly produced services in volume, availability, or quality which may lead to a shift by consumers toward privately produced and purchased substitutes (called 'privatisation by attrition' when a government lets public services run down);
2. Transfer of public assets to private ownership, through the sale or lease of public land, infrastructure, and enterprises; and
3. The withdrawal of government from production but not the financing of services, for example, through contracting-out or vouchers.

This chapter presents an analysis of privatisation in Ireland, covering variants of the reform covered by Starr's (1988) typology, namely the privatisation of SOEs, the contracting out of refuse collection services and PPPs. The extent of privatisation activity varies across these three categories but in all cases these reforms have been adopted for the purpose of raising efficiency, defined usually in terms of achieving higher productivity and lower-cost production. The following sections examine the impact of the three forms of privatisation on these aspects of performance.

11.2 Privatisation of State Owned Enterprises

The rationale behind the adoption of privatisation programmes worldwide varies from country to country.[1] Of the numerous factors put forward for industrialised countries, the most common are: (1) public enterprises are inefficient and privatisation will lead to increased efficiency; (2) technological developments in markets such as telecommunications no longer justifies monopoly provision of services and the consequent requirement for liberalisation of utility markets in EU countries; (3) the sale of SOEs can raise useful sums of money for the Exchequer and remove the burden of loss-making public enterprises; and (4) the privatisation of public enterprises through flotation on the stock market can help the development of domestic capital markets and widen domestic equity ownership.

When privatisation policies initially came into vogue, economic arguments in favour of the reform were based on theories of government failure such as agency, public choice and property rights theory. These focused on aspects of structure, control and incentives in SOEs compared to private enterprise and argued that performance is superior in the case of the latter. Empirical evidence has however failed to conclusively support predictions from these theories.[2] This points to the limitations of theories that focus entirely on ownership (rather than including, for example, product market competition) as a determinant of performance. The broad conclusion to be drawn from this literature is that the case for private ownership is confined to sectors where markets are competitive and does not apply in the case of natural monopolies or heavily regulated industries (Boardman and Vining, 1989; Martin and Parker, 1997).

Numerous empirical studies on the effects of privatisation on the financial and operating performance of divested firms have been carried out in recent years and on the whole the evidence can be considered mixed. In general, the empirical literature can be divided into two main groups; broad based international studies which by and large find that privatisation leads to improved performance; and more comprehensive country-specific studies that find more ambiguous results and suggest that privatisation does not necessarily lead to an improvement in company performance, with other factors such as competition and regulation proving to be significant determinants of performance.[3]

The first Irish privatisations took place in 1991 and since then the privatisation programme has developed gradually. To date, ten SOEs have been privatised and these sales have had a significant impact on the Irish economy. Table 11.1 provides details on the companies sold and the amounts raised thus far.

Table 11.1: Privatisation of Irish State-Owned Enterprises 1991-2006

Company	Year	Sector	Exchequer Proceeds (€m)	Method of Sale
Greencore	IPO in April 1991	Sugar/Food	210.65	IPO and Placements
Irish Life	IPO in July 1991	Insurance	601.93	IPO and Placements
B&I	1992	Shipping	10.80	Trade Sale
Irish Steel	1994	Steel	0	Trade sale
Eircom	IPO in July 1999	Telecoms	6,399.91	Trade sale and IPO
ICC Bank	Jan 2001	Banking	322.27	Trade Sale
TSB Bank	April 2001	Banking	408.35	Trade Sale
INPC	May 2001	Energy	20.00	Trade Sale
ACC Bank	December 2001	Banking	154.60	Trade Sale
Aer Lingus	September 2006	Air Transport	200.00	IPO
Total			**€8,328.51**	

Note: IPO = initial public offering; (2) At time of writing, Aer Lingus had just been floated. The proceeds for Aer Lingus given above are a conservative estimate based on the IPO price of €2.20.

Of the various reasons put forward in support of privatisation, the goal of improving the performance of SOEs has been most prominent.[4] The measurement of performance is however complex and the choice of performance indicator can be problematic. Ideally, economists seek to measure firm performance in terms of both allocative and productive efficiency. Productive efficiency is achieved when a firm produces its output at minimum cost while allocative efficiency is concerned with achieving the level of output valued most highly by society. In practice, allocative efficiency is not easy to measure and most of the empirical work carried out to date on the impact of privatisation on firm performance concentrates on the measurement of productive efficiency. The two most common indicators of firm-level efficiency in the literature are productivity and profitability and the following section analyses the pre- and post-privatisation performance of SOEs privatised in Ireland between 1991 and 2006.

Profitability measures are unsuitable where enterprises operate in imperfectly competitive markets, which is the case for most SOEs.[5] Consequently, productivity measures are preferred but these are also subject to limitations. Labour productivity measures can be biased for reasons such as the use of output rather than value-added as a numerator and the prevalence of contracting out labour intensive services (Parker, 2003). In addition, labour productivity measures based on output to employment ratios do not take account of the impact of other inputs such as capital on output and care needs to be taken when interpreting these partial productivity results.

As well as the complications inherent in performance measurement, our study of the performance of privatised companies in Ireland is further hindered by the following:

1. Six of the ten privatised companies were sold by trade sale and absorbed into the operations of the acquiring company, thus rendering an analysis of post-privatisation performance impossible; and
2. Aer Lingus was sold very recently and therefore no post-privatisation data is available.

With these factors in mind the following section analyses the pre and post-privatisation (where possible) performance of the ten SOEs divested to date.

11.2.1 Pre-privatisation Performance

Since the ten privatised companies operate in different sectors and differ in terms of size and historical performance, an aggregate analysis of their performance requires the use of basic indicators that can be applied across all companies. For the purpose of this study we restrict our analysis to two basic profitability indicators: Profit Before Interest, Tax and exceptional items (PBIT) and Return On Capital Employed (ROCE); and one productivity indicator, namely Labour Productivity. The results presented below analyse the five years prior to privatisation for all companies and are presented as five-year average annual rates of growth.[6]

Table 11.2: Pre-privatisation Performance of SOEs: Average Annual Rates of Growth

Company	Labour Productivity	PBIT	ROCE
Irish Life	-1.40	-	-
Greencore	14.36	20.09	2.46
B&I	8.92	-63.92	-124.15
Irish Steel	1.67	- 135.15	-183.32
Eircom	8.18	0.41	2.61
ACC	2.31	8.25	-6.89
ICC	5.78	22.45	1.38
TSB	-	11.25	-0.46
Aer Lingus	6.36	5.18	-0.37

Notes: (1) ROCE figures for ACC, ICC and TSB are ROA figures (ROA = PBIT ÷ Total Assets); (2) Output indices used to calculate labour productivity in the case of Irish Life, ICC and ACC were based on total income figures instead of turnover; (3) B&I figures are four-year averages as data for 1991 unavailable; (4) Employment figures are unavailable for TSB, hence no labour productivity analysis could be carried out.

Greencore (formerly Irish Sugar) improved their performance dramatically prior to its flotation in 1991. The company implemented a significant rationalisation programme during the 1980s, halving the number of employees and closing two loss-making plants. The impact of these decisions is reflected in the impressive labour productivity and PBIT growth figures provided in Table 11.2.

An analysis of PBIT and ROCE was not possible in the case of Irish Life due to various changes in the company's accounting policies over the pre and post-privatisation periods examined. The measurement of performance in the insurance industry is highly problematic, requiring sector-specific indicators commonly based on actuarial valuations. The method of valuation adopted by the company prior to privatisation was the *surplus arising* measure.[7] Between 1984 and 1989 this figure grew by an annual average of 3.3 per cent. In addition, Sweeney (1990) notes that the company increased the funds under its management tenfold in the decade prior to divestiture. Although, the labour productivity result for Irish Life in Table 11.2 is negative, it must be recognised that it is based on annual total income figures, which do not reflect the future value of many of the company's investments.

Turning to both B&I Line and Irish Steel, despite implementing significant rationalisation programmes prior to privatisation, which is reflected in the positive growth rates for labour productivity; both companies continued to perform poorly in terms of profitability. The decision to sell both companies was taken on the basis that the only other alternative would have been liquidation and their sale would ensure the companies continued as going concerns.

Eircom (formerly Telecom Éireann), the national telecommunications company, was privatised through flotation on the stock market in 1999. In 1996, the company entered into a strategic alliance with the Comsource consortium, which acquired a 20 per cent stake in Eircom.[8] Given that this effectively started the privatisation process, 1996 is thus taken to be the year of privatisation for the purpose of our analysis and the results provided for Eircom refer to the five years prior to this date. Prior to 1996, the company implemented a programme of rationalisation, which included a significant reduction in employees, the impact of which is evident in the strong labour productivity growth of 8.1 per cent. The poor growth in PBIT is explained by a large increase in depreciation charges and other operating costs over the period examined.

Table 11.2 shows that prior to their divestiture in 2001, the three state banks experienced significant growth in profits. However, the more informative Return On Assets (ROA) ratio indicates that underlying performance was less impressive for both the TSB and ACC. ICC Bank showed considerable improvement across every indicator prior to privatisation. Although the pre-privatisation period for all three state banks was characterised by an improvement in efficiency and profitability, it must be borne in mind that all three banks were small players in the Irish banking sector, lacking the scale necessary for sustained improvements in performance. In addition, the ACC and ICC banks had benefited from decades of government subsidisation which may exaggerate their true underlying performance (Sweeney, 1990).

The Initial Public Offering (IPO) of government shares in Aer Lingus in September 2006 is the most recent privatisation to take place. The government originally decided to sell the airline in December 1999; however the plan was put on hold after a number of strikes by employees and the negative impact on company performance after the September 11th attacks in the US in 2001. The decision to finally float the airline on the stock market was taken in early 2006, with the government opting to retain a stake of 28 per cent in the company.

Significantly improved performance was recorded by Aer Lingus after 2001, with the company implementing a rationalisation programme involving a reduction in the workforce of over 1,500 staff in 2002, and employees securing a 14.9 per cent shareholding in the company.[9] Marked improvements in performance have been sustained with Aer Lingus cutting costs further in order to compete with low-cost competitors such as Ryanair. Overall, the workforce has been reduced by approximately 3,000 since 2001 as a result of restructuring and redundancy plans and this is reflected in the strong growth in labour productivity shown in Table 11.2. While the growth figures for PBIT are positive, the growth in ROCE was negative on average over the period analysed.

In general, with the exception of the two loss-making firms, B&I Line and Irish Steel, the pre-privatisation period for the companies examined was one of improved performance in terms of labour productivity and profitability. The key underlying reason for improved performance in the non-financial public enterprises has been the implementation of significant rationalisation programmes as the companies restructured their businesses along more commercial lines. The observed trend of improved performance prior to privatisation is consistent with the findings from similar studies carried out in other industrialised countries.[10]

11.2.2 Post-privatisation Performance

Our analysis of post-privatisation performance is restricted to Irish Life, Greencore and Eircom as post-privatisation data is unavailable for the other seven SOEs that were sold. The results presented below cover the five-year period after the divestiture of each company and are expressed as five-year average annual rates of growth.

Over the five-year period after privatisation, Greencore recorded lower average rates of growth across all indicators compared to the pre-privatisation period. Whilst growth in labour productivity and PBIT improved, the gains were not as impressive as before privatisation and the important ROCE indicator decreased on average over the period analysed. It is noteworthy that since 1997 the company's share price has consistently under-performed the overall ISEQ index and this can be attributed to problems with a major acquisition in the US sugar industry and perceived uncertainty about plans to diversify away from its core sugar business.

Table 11.3: Post-privatisation Performance of Privatised SOEs: Average Annual Rates of Growth

Companies	Labour Productivity	PBIT	ROCE
Irish Life	1.23	-	-
Greencore	7.67	9.42	-0.66
Eircom	5.67	2.10	-5.82

Note: The output index used to calculate labour productivity in the case of Irish Life is based on total income data rather than turnover.

In the case of Irish Life, pre-privatisation improvements were sustained following its divestiture in 1991. The *embedded value* method of actuarial valuation was adopted by Irish Life from 1990 onwards and in the five years after divestiture this measure grew by 7.3 per cent on average.[11] In addition, the company's share price performed well, never falling below its IPO price level after 1993 and increasing significantly in the period prior to the company's merger with Irish Permanent in 1999. Funds under management increased by close to 60 per cent, from approximately €6.1 billion in 1992 to €9.7 billion in 1996, reflecting strong business growth.

Post-privatisation gains in Eircom's labour productivity were not as impressive as those recorded pre-1996, mainly due to increases in employment in the rapidly expanding mobile division, Eircell. Although the rate of growth in PBIT improved from 0.4 to 2.1 per cent, the more important ROCE measure decreased significantly after 1996. It must be noted that the 5-year averages above do not provide an accurate overview of the post-1996 period in Eircom. The post-flotation years, 1999-2001, account for much of the deterioration in performance shown in Table 11.3. Significant improvements across all indicators were in fact recorded in the years 1996-99 prior to divestiture.

There are a number of reasons for improved performance prior to full privatisation in 1999. Chief among these was the establishment of an independent communications regulator in January 1997 and the full liberalisation of the telecommunications market in December 1998.[12] Indeed impending liberalisation had been one of the main reasons why Eircom entered into a strategic alliance in 1996. Eircom held an effective monopoly position in its core product markets throughout the 1990s, however during the mid-1990s the company improved its performance significantly in an effort to prepare for the threat of competition. The company also benefited from the transfer of advanced technology and other expertise from its strategic alliance partners as well as major growth in mobile telephony during the late 1990s.

The privatisation of Eircom led to a marked turnaround in the performance of the company. The collapse of the company's share price after the dot-com bubble burst in effect led to the de-merger of the company just two and a half years after its flotation. Eircell, the most profitable division in the firm, was sold to Vodafone in May 2001 and this was shortly followed by the sale of the remaining fixed-line business to the Valentia telecommunications consortium. Since 2001, Vodafone Ireland has continued to grow its business and has emerged as the most profitable division of the international Vodafone group.[13] Over the same period, Eircom has changed ownership twice with the company refloating on the stock market in 2004 and then taken over in 2006 by the Australian company Babcock and Brown. Although Eircom has improved its performance in terms of profitability since 2001, it must be noted that this is mainly due to massive cuts in capital expenditure and a large amount of labour shedding. Whether reductions in capital expenditure result in a trade-off between short term improvements and deteriorating performance in the long-run is a question that will require further analysis in the future.

The Irish privatisation experience to date provides no evidence of a simple relationship between ownership and performance. With the exception of the two loss-making firms, pre-privatisation improvements in performance were recorded in all cases suggesting that commercialisation measures carried out in public enterprises have had more of an impact than privatisation *per se* in the case of Ireland. Where post-privatisation evidence on performance is available it is largely disappointing, especially in the case of Eircom.[14] Both Eircom and Greencore were dominant in their markets at the time of sale. Eircom enjoyed an approximate 80 per cent share of the fixed-line market while holding the larger share of the mobile market duopoly. Greencore held control of the Irish EU sugar quota after divestiture. The post-privatisation record of both companies suggests that product market competition is a hugely important determinant of enterprise performance.

The case of Eircom in particular highlights problems that arise when a regional economy privatises telecommunications infrastructure. From a strategic perspective the post-privatisation experience in the case of Eircom has been characterised by significant reductions in capital expenditure and failure to grant access to its network. The latter issue has impeded the rollout of broadband services, which are vital in the context of a regional economy. The government's recent decision to re-enter the telecommunications market by investing in broadband capital raises obvious questions about the rationale behind earlier decisions to privatise.

11.3 Contracting Out and Public Private Partnership

Privatisation activity in Ireland has not been confined to the divestiture of shares in high profile SOEs such as Aer Lingus and Eircom. For a number of years, there have been examples of privatisation in the form of government withdrawal from the production but not necessarily the financing of private services. The cases considered in this paper are:

1. The contracting out of local authority services, focusing on the case of refuse collection; and
2. The adoption of public private partnerships for purpose of providing physical infrastructure and related public services.

11.3.1 Contracting Out

Despite the traditional role of the state as both a funder and provider of public services most governments have a tradition of buying in certain goods and services from the private sector (e.g. road-building, house building). What emerged in the late 1970s and early 1989s however, was a widespread rapid growth in market-based reforms, which altered the traditional role of the state. Deakin and Walsh (1996) described the emergence of the 'contract-state' at the centre of a process of reinvention of the state's functions "separating out a 'core' of policy making and direction and retaining only a minimal 'periphery' of residual delivery functions that are defined as essential but cannot for whatever reason be discharged elsewhere" (Deakin and Walsh, 1996: 33).

In many countries the role of the state was largely altered to an enabling one, with the state responsible for service delivery but not necessarily producing them itself. Conferring monopoly rights of service provision on a private producer need not necessarily reduce economic welfare. The theory of contestable markets developed by Baumol et al. (1982) suggests that efficient production and delivery of goods and services depends on the contestability of the market rather than competition within it. According to these writers, a market is contestable if there is freedom of entry and exit because sunk costs are low. Under such conditions, a firm that must purchase assets (e.g. plant and equipment) in order to enter the industry can sell the assets if it consequently decides to leave the industry without incurring a loss on the transaction. These conditions create a threat of entry that drives down prices and guarantees efficiency. If there is perfect contestability the price set in the market will equal the average cost of production even in the limit case of one monopoly firm in the market. The implication of this theory for public services is that if supply is perfectly contestable the government should procure the good through contracting (Vining and Weimer, 1990).

Supported by the predictions of such theories, governments around the world turned to privatisation in the form of contracting out services. The undoubted pioneer of such policies was the UK where The Local Government Act 1988 compelled local authorities to put certain 'blue collar' services up for tender. Similar policies were adopted in countries such as Holland, Sweden, New Zealand and Australia where contracting out was mostly encouraged rather than compulsory.

In the case of Ireland, local authorities have traditionally made extensive use of external sources for service provision (for example, major capital projects such as roads and water/ sewerage). Such arrangements can be distinguished from privatisation, as they are not characterised by a transfer from traditionally public to private provision. A prominent case of privatisation has been refuse collection services where it has been noted that due to financial pressures on local authorities the "domestic refuse collection service has been contracted out, franchised or privatised in many areas, in the latter case the local authority withdrawing from the service and allowing private contractors take over and charge for the service" (Coughlan and de Buitleir, 1996: 103).

Reeves and Barrow (2000) conducted the only detailed analysis of the impact of privatisation on the efficiency of refuse collection services in Ireland. Their study was based on data gathered in a survey of Irish local authorities that had either retained the provision of refuse collection services in-house or contracted out the service over the years 1993-1995. Using data on service costs, quantity (e.g. number of households) and service characteristics (e.g. frequency of collection), multivariate statistical analysis was conducted. This approach, which enabled control of relevant service characteristics, revealed significant savings for contracting authorities in the region of 45 per cent on average. Although the analysis found that the best non-contracting authorities performed as well as the best contracting ones, the incidence of efficiency was much greater amongst authorities that contracted out the service. The study also examined the source of these efficiency gains and concluded that lower costs incurred by private contractors were partly attributable to more flexible work practices (e.g. smaller crew sizes). While these represent real productivity gains, some cases reported the existence of poorer working conditions in the private sector (e.g. lower health and safety standards and the employment of underage labour). The latter sources of cost savings have obvious redistributive consequences and reduce the extent to which measured cost savings improve overall economic welfare.

The finding that sizeable cost savings are accrued following the contracting out of refuse collection services is consistent with findings from a host of similar studies from different countries (see Domberger and Jensen, (1997) for a review). Although such savings can be reduced by transaction costs (e.g. the costs of organising procurement and monitoring contracts), such costs tend to be manageable in the case of refuse collection services because asset specificity is low and quality is relatively easy to measure. It is however noteworthy that there is evidence from other countries of initial cost savings disappearing over time. Dijkgraaf and Gradus (2006) suggest that the problem of reduced savings is in part attributable to the increased concentration of suppliers in this market. This is relevant in the case of Ireland where the Competition Authority (2005) has noted increased market power in some local refuse collection markets in Ireland. However, this phenomenon is occurring in markets where local authorities no longer contract out but have withdrawn entirely from service provision. The evidence from studies on the effects of contracting out indicate that if efficiency gains are to be sustained this requires periodic competition for contracts that are well specified and enforced.

11.3.2 Public Private Partnerships

In recent years the Irish Government has adopted PPPs as an important element of efforts to address Ireland's acute deficit of economic infrastructure. Although there is no commonly accepted definition of PPP, the model adopted in the Irish case has mainly involved contractual agreements between the public and private sectors whereby the private sector takes responsibility for designing, planning, financing, constructing and/or operating infrastructure projects normally provided through traditional procurement mechanisms by the State. Compared to the contracting out of public services, this form of PPP constitutes a more extensive form of privatisation as it involves the withdrawal of government from its traditional role of providing and financing investment in infrastructure and the provision of related public services.

To date, different variants of the PPP model have been adopted across a range of sectors. In the case of roads for example, the National Roads Authority (NRA) is at various stages of implementing ten PPP concessions. In these cases the private contractor is contracted to design, build and operate the routes (usually for a 25 to 30 year period). Most of the projects are financed by a mix of public and private finance and the private sector recoups its investment from tolls levied on road-users on the basis of a revenue sharing agreement with the NRA.[15] In the case of schools, the Design, Build, Operate and Finance (DBOF) model is being used to procure school buildings and services (excluding education services). Typically the private contractor designs, builds and operates the school over a 25-year period. The contractor takes responsibility for financing the project and recoups its investment via a structure of payments from the exchequer over the duration of the contract. In the water and wastewater sector the preferred model of procurement has been Design, Build and Operate (DBO). Other PPP models being adopted or under consideration include: Design, Build, Finance and Maintain (DBFM), in prisons and Design, Build and Finance (DBF) in the housing sector.

Proponents of PPP, in Ireland and elsewhere, assert that the model offers a better alternative to traditional procurement methods, which are often beset by cost and time overruns.[16]

For example, the Department of Finance (2001: 3) asserts that the goals and benefits of PPP include the following:

1. Speedy, efficient and cost-effective delivery of projects;
2. Value for money for the taxpayer, *inter alia,* through optimal risk transfer and risk management; and
3. Efficiencies from integrating design and construction of public infrastructure with financing, operation and maintenance/upgrading.

The international evidence in support of these claims is however scarce. As PPP contracts are typically based on durations of 25-30 years, *ex-post* evaluations are not possible. Hence, studies on the cost efficiency (value for money) of PPP are confined to pre-implementation appraisals. Among the studies that provide supporting evidence in terms of value for money are Anderson and LSE Enterprise (2000), National Audit Office (NAO) (1998: 1999) and Fitzgerald (2004). However, there is a significant and growing literature, which questions the thrust of the findings in these studies. For example, Shaoul (2005) provides an extensive review of empirical studies covering the health, transport and education sectors that query whether the projects covered demonstrated value for money. Other writers have raised issues of concern in relation to estimates of value for money. These include: (1) difficulties in quantifying risk transfer which is a key determinant of estimated value for money (Ball et al, 2001; Hodge, 2004); (2) the complexities of the financial modelling required to appraise Value for Money (VFM) (Quiggin; 2004, Shaoul, 2003); and (3) the problem of bias towards PPP options (Spackman, 2002; Heald, 2003).

In Ireland, the only PPP project that has been subjected to in-depth analysis is the contract for five secondary schools. In this case, the private sector consortium (Jarvis Project Limited) was contracted to design, build, operate and finance the schools over a 25-year period. The schools opened in 2003 and in June 2004 the Comptroller and Auditor General (C&AG) published its Value for Money Report on the project. The C&AG have estimated that the public sector obligations under the contract amount to €283 million (€150 million in net present value terms). It reported that the initial value for money exercise conducted by the DOES estimated that PPP would yield cost savings of six per cent compared to traditional procurement. On the basis of their examination however, the C&AG highlighted a number of significant errors in the original value for money exercise. Having corrected for these errors the C&AG estimated that the PPP would be between 13 per cent and 19 per cent more expensive than under traditional procurement. The C&AG also accounted for elements of the deal that changed after the value for exercise (namely, changes in interest rates and treatment of VAT). Including these elements ultimately led the C&AG to conclude that the final PPP deal was in the range eight per cent to 13 per cent more expensive than under traditional procurement.

The C&AG described a number of important failings in the procurement process that potentially led to sub-optimal decisions at important junctures. While space does not permit a detailed discussion of these issues it is worth noting that they exemplify one of the principal shortcomings of the PPP that is the potentially high transaction costs involved in PPP.[17] Transaction costs are the costs of using the market. In the context of PPPs these can be thought of as the costs of organising the tendering process, designing and executing contracts, monitoring contract performance and enforcing contract terms where failures occur. The latter are likely to be significant in the case of a complex procurement process such as PPP, yet they are rarely, if ever, included in estimates of value for money.

Overall the efficiency effects of the PPP model of procurement are unclear. While features such as risk transfer give PPP the potential to deliver efficiency gains the evidence in support of the model is scarce. Moreover the transaction costs incurred under PPP tend to be ignored and require greater consideration if the PPP model is to be applied appropriately.

11.4 Conclusions

The last fifteen years or so have witnessed an appreciable degree of privatisation activity in Ireland as Irish governments follow the global trend of reducing direct government provision of goods and services across a range of sectors. Although the reasons for such change differ from case to case, the general objective of privatisation has been to improve the efficiency of service delivery.

The sale of SOEs tends to be the most high-profile measure of privatisation with governments often choosing to sell shares to the public. The extent of privatisation in the Irish SOE sector has been significant with the public sector withdrawing entirely from sectors including banking, steel, sugar, shipping and telecommunications. The analysis conducted in this paper demonstrates a clear pattern of improved performance prior to changes in ownership. In most cases firms prepared for privatisation by implementing cost-cutting measures including significant labour shedding. The post-privatisation impact is not as clear-cut. The cases of Greencore and especially Eircom highlight the importance of product market competition as a driver of efficiency gains. In this respect the distinction between static and dynamic efficiency gains merits attention. The incidence of improved performance in the years before and after privatisation is indicative of static efficiency gains, which are inherently once-off. Dynamic efficiency gains depend on factors such as ongoing investment in research and development and improved processes and management. While the relationship between privatisation and dynamic efficiency will take time to establish, the post-privatisation experience at Eircom provides grounds for concern about the case for privatisation in this respect as the company has implemented significant cuts in capital expenditure with Ireland consequently ranking close to the bottom of European rankings of broadband penetration.

Competition is an important determinant of whether efficiency gains are accrued as a result of privatisation, not just in the case of SOEs but also in the case of other public services. This is exemplified in the case of contracting out local authority services where the evidence in the case of refuse collection demonstrates the scope for productivity improvements where there is strong competition for contracts and where transaction costs are low.

The question of transaction costs is critical in the case of more complicated public procurement like PPP. The early evidence from Ireland illustrates the difficulties associated with implementing a significant programme of PPP. These include problems with sustaining competitive tensions in the context of long-term contracts as well as difficulties in forging agreements based on optimal risk allocation.

Looking ahead it appears that privatisation will continue to be an important tool of public policy in Ireland over the coming years. The Irish experience to date however shows that privatisation *per se* is not necessarily a panacea for any public sector inefficiencies. The findings reported in this chapter suggest that policymakers ought to bear in mind that the effectiveness of future privatisation policies will depend on factors including the underlying economic characteristics of each activity, the technological characteristics of its production and the supporting institutional frameworks.

Notes

1 See for example, Miller (1995); OECD (2003).
2 For comprehensive reviews of comparative studies of public versus private sector performance see Vickers and Yarrow (1988) and Martin and Parker (1997).
3 See Megginson and Netter (2001) for a detailed review of empirical evidence.
4 Space does not permit a review of the rationale behind the development of the Irish privatisation programme, however this is discussed in detail in Reeves and Palcic (2004).
5 In the case of Ireland however, with the exception of Eircom, most privatised companies operate under mainly competitive conditions.
6 The INPC is not included in our analysis. The instability of the international oil market within which the company operated caused wide fluctuations in company profits in the years preceding privatisation. Consequently rates of growth measures are not instructive.
7 Under the 'surplus arising' method, all the expenses associated with new business are written off in year one and a conservative view is taken on future liabilities. No allowance is made for future profits on new business.
8 The Comsource consortium consisted of KPN (Netherlands) and Telia (Sweden).
9 Employees were given an additional 9.9 per cent stake; workers had already been granted a five per cent shareholding in 1994 as part of a previous restructuring programme.
10 For example Megginson et al. (1994) and Martin and Parker (1997).
11 The embedded value method attempts to calculate the profits which will arise on new business written during the period by projecting the profits that will be earned over the life of the policy and discounting it back to give a present value for these profits.
12 At the same time a CPI-X price cap (similar to the one used for British Telecom in the UK) on a basket of Eircom services was introduced with responsibility for the implementation of the price cap given to the newly created regulator.
13 Vodafone Ireland's Average Revenue per User (ARPU) in March 2006 was the highest of the 18 countries in which the Vodafone group operates.
14 In addition, the Irish Steel Company was closed in 2001, just five years after being taken over by Indian firm, ISPAT. The company claimed mounting losses and a failure to control costs as the principal reason for its closure.
15 For example, in the case of the N4 Kilcock-Kinnegad PPP, the NRA website (www.nra.ie) states that for infrastructure with an estimated value of €550 million, excluding land and preparatory costs, the state will pay €152 million, excluding land and preparatory costs.
16 Problems with traditional procurement have highlighted in two influential studies. One Danish study by Flyvberg et al. (2002) examined 258 large transport infrastructure projects covering 20 countries. The vast majority of these projects were procured by conventional means and costs were underestimated in 90 per cent of cases. Another major study, published by Matt MacDonald (2002) examined the outcome of 50 large infrastructure projects in the UK. They reported that time overruns exceeded the estimated duration by 17 per cent and capital costs exceeded estimates by 17 per cent on average.
17 See Reeves and Ryan (2007) for a discussion of these aspects of the C&AG's findings.

References

Arthur Andersen and LSE Enterprise (2000), *Value for Money Drivers in the Private Finance Initiative,* Treasury Task Force, HM Treasury, London.

Baumol, W.J., Panzar, J. and Wilig, R.D. (1982), *Contestable Markets and the Theory of Market Structure,* Harcourt Brace Jovanovich, New York.

Bel, G. (2006), "The Coining of "Privatization" and Germany's Nationalist Socialist Party." *Journal of Economic Perspectives,* 20, 187-194.

Boardman, A. E. and Vining, A. R. (1989), "Ownership and Performance in Competitive Environments: A Comparison of the Performance of Private, Mixed, and State-Owned Enterprises." *Journal of Law and Economics,* 32, 1-33.

Comptroller and Auditor General (2004), *The Grouped Schools Pilot Partnership Project.* Stationery Office, Dublin.

Coughlan, M. and de Buitleir, D. (1996), *Local Government Finance in Ireland.* Institute of Public Administration, Dublin.

Deakin, N. and Walsh, K. (1996), "The Enabling State: The Role of Markets and Contracts". *Public Administration,* 74, 33-48.

Department of Finance (2001), *Framework for Public Private Partnerships.* Stationery Office, Dublin.

Dijkgraaf, E. and Graadus, R.H.J.M. (2006), "Collusion in the Dutch Waste Collection Market", paper presented to *Workshop on Local Government Restructuring: Privatization, Public-Private Cooperation,* Universitat de Barcelona, Barcelona, 12-14 June.

Domberger, S. and Jensen, P. (1997), "Contracting Out by the Public Sector: Theory, Evidence, Prospects" *Oxford Review of Economic Policy,* 13, 67-78.

Fitzgerald, P. (2004), *Review of Partnerships Victoria Provided Infrastructure,* Melbourne, Review of Partnerships Victoria.

Flyvbjerg, B., Holm, M.S. and Buhl, S. (2002), "Underestimating Costs in Public Works Projects – Error or Lie? *Journal of the American Planning Association,* 68, 279-295.

Ball. R., Heafey, M. and King, D. (2001), "Private Finance Initiative – A Good Deal for the Public or a Drain on Future Generations?" *Policy and Politics, 29,* 95-108.

Heald, D. (2003), "Value for Money Tests and Accounting Treatment in PFI Schemes" *Accounting, Auditing and Accountability Journal,* 16, 342-271.

Hodge, G.A. (2004), "The Risky Business of Public-Private-Partnerships" *Australian Journal of Public Administration,* 63, 37-49

Martin, S. and Parker, D. (1997), *The Impact of Privatisation: Ownership and Corporate Performance in the UK*, London, Routledge.

MacDonald, M. (2002), *Review of Large Public Procurement in the UK*, London, HM Treasury.

Megginson, W. L., Nash, R. C. and Van Randenborgh, M. (1994), "The Financial and Operating Performance of Newly Privatized Firms: An International Empirical Analysis." *The Journal of Finance,* 49, 403-452.

Megginson, W. L. and Netter, J. M. (2001), "From State to Market: A Survey of Empirical Studies on Privatization." *Journal of Economic Literature,* 39, 321-389.

Miller, A. N. (1995), "British Privatization: Evaluating the Results." *The Columbia Journal of World Business,* 30, 82-98.

National Audit Office (1998), *The Private Finance Initiative: The First Design, Build, Finance and Operate Roads Contracts,* HC 476, Session 1997-98, London, Stationery Office.

National Audit Office (1999), *Examining the Value for Money Deals Under the Private Finance Initiative,* HC 739, Session 1998-99, London, Stationery Office.

OECD (2003), *Privatising State-owned Enterprises: An Overview of Policies and Practices in OECD Countries,* Paris, OECD.

Parker, D. (2003), "The UK's Privatisation Experiment: The Passage of Time Permits a Sober Assessment." *CESifo Privatisation Experiences in the EU Conference,* Cadenabbia, Italy.

Quiggin, J. (2004), "Risk, PPPs and the Public Sector Comparator". *Australian Accounting Review, 14,* 51-61.

Reeves, E. and Barrow, M. (2000), "The Impact of Contracting Out On the Costs of Refuse Collection Services: The Case of Ireland." *Economic and Social Review,* 31, 129-150.

Reeves, E. and Palcic, D. (2004), "Privatization Policy and Enterprise Performance: The Case of Ireland." *Annals of Public and Cooperative Economics,* 75, 525-548.

Reeves, E. and Ryan, J. (2007), "Piloting Public Private Partnerships: Expensive Lessons from Ireland's Schools Sector." *Public Money and Management,* (*in press*).

Shaoul, J. (2005), "A Critical Financial Analysis of the Private Finance Initiative: Selecting a financing method or reallocating economic wealth?" *Critical Perspectives on Accounting,* 16, 441-471.

Shaoul, J. (2003), "A Financial Analysis of the National Air Traffic Services Public Private Partnership." *Public Money and Management,* 3, 185-194.

Spackman, M. (2002), "Public-Private Partnerships: Lessons from the British Approach." *Economic Systems,* 26, 283-301.

Starr, P. (1988), "The Meaning of Privatization." *Yale Law and Policy Review,* 6, 6-41.

Sweeney, P. (1990), *The Politics of Public Enterprise and Privatisation,* Dublin, Tomar.

The Competition Authority (2005), "Alleged Excessive Pricing by Greenstar Recycling Holdings Limited in the Provision of Household Waste Collection Services in Northeast Wicklow", *Enforcement Decision Series,* No. E/05/002.

Vickers, J. and Yarrow, G. (1988), *Privatization: An Economic Analysis,* Cambridge, MA, MIT Press.

Vining, A.R. and Weimer, D.L. (1990), "Government Supply and Government Production Failures: A Framework Based on Contestability", *Journal of Public Policy,* 10, 1-22.

CHAPTER 12

PRIVATISATION: LESSONS FROM THE UK

DAVID PARKER

ABSTRACT

This chapter outlines the development of privatisation as a policy in the UK, analyses the impact that privatisation had on UK economic performance and points to some lessons that Ireland might learn from the experience. The lessons for Ireland of the UK experience are that as part of a wider programme of opening up the economy to market forces, privatisation can lead to efficiency gains, from which consumers and taxpayers benefit. However these efficiency gains are not guaranteed. Improvements in efficiency tend to be associated with the arrival of competition and better regulation rather than privatisation per se.

12.1 Introduction

By the mid-1970s it was common to label the UK 'the sick man of Europe'. The growth of GDP between 1950 and 1973 averaged 2.4 per cent. This contrasted with growth rates of five per cent in Germany and four per cent in France (Crafts, 2002: 44). At the time the UK had a large state sector with nationalised industries accounting for around 11 per cent per cent of GDP and eight per cent of employment. The returns on investment in the nationalised industries were depressingly low. Earnings before interest and tax are estimated to have ranged between –0.4 per cent and 1.1 per cent in the period 1972-82 (Brittan, 1984:128). In part this was because Governments interfered with the prices set by the nationalised industries in a futile attempt to hold down inflation. In 1975 inflation in the UK peaked at around 22 per cent. Accumulated government subsidies, capital write-offs and other payments to the nationalised industries from the mid-1950s are said to have totalled nearly £8 billion. By 1997 as a result of the privatisation programme the nationalised industries accounted for only around two per cent of GDP and public sector employment had fallen by over 1.5 million.

May 1979 saw the Election of a Conservative Government under the leadership of Margaret Thatcher. Between 1974 and 1979 the previous Labour Government had extended state ownership with nationalisation of the aerospace and shipbuilding industries, the taking into state ownership of the country's largest vehicles manufacturer British Leyland, the establishment of the British National Oil Corporation to control North Sea oil extraction, and an Industry Act in 1975, which amongst other things set up the National Enterprise Board (NEB). The role of the NEB was to invest taxpayer funds in industrial enterprises. Both Rolls-Royce, taken into state ownership in 1971 after going into receivership, and British Leyland similarly rescued from bankruptcy in 1975, came under the supervision of the NEB.

Although the Conservatives' 1979 Election Manifesto made only modest promises on denationalisation, between May 1979 and May 1997, first under Margaret Thatcher and then under John Major, the UK experienced the world's first large-scale privatisation experiment. Nor did the re-election of a Labour Government in 1997 see it come to an end. Although Labour had opposed every one of the Conservatives' privatisation measures, under Tony Blair as Prime Minister privatisation has been extended with the sale of organisations such as National Air Traffic System and Qinetiq, a defence research establishment, and the promotion of Public-Private Partnerships (PPPs). By April 2003, 564 private-financing deals had been agreed with a capital value of £35 billion (Financial Times, 2003).

This chapter looks at the UK's experience of privatisation and points to some lessons that Ireland might learn from the experience.

12.2 Development of Privatisation as Policy

In 1979 an initial reason for the sale of state-owned assets was the Exchequer's need to raise funds to sustain high levels of public expenditure without further tax rises. However, once the budgetary pressures began to ease in the early 1980s, attention turned to the wider economic benefits. The economic benefits claimed were higher productivity in the private sector, widening share ownership so as to create 'popular capitalism', and reducing the power of the trade unions. In the 1970s the trade unions toppled governments and strikes were prevalent. Union power was centred in the public sector including the nationalised industries.

During the first Conservative Government, from May 1979 to June 1983, the Conservatives denationalised British Aerospace, the international telecommunications operator Cable and Wireless, Amersham International a specialist producer of radioactive chemicals, the country's largest ports operator Associated British Ports, Britoil incorporating the oil and gas exploration and production activities of the British National Oil Corporation, and the National Freight Corporation. Shares in each of these industries were sold through the stock market, often in tranches with just over 50 per cent sold initially. An interesting exception was the National Freight Corporation, involved in road haulage and storage, which was transferred to the private sector in February 1982 through a management and employee buyout. In all cases small shareholders were encouraged to buy shares, as part of the Government's strategy to extend property ownership. In addition to this programme of privatisation, the Government also encouraged the nationalised industries to sell off subsidiary activities and the NEB was run down. These privatisations typically took the form of direct sales of businesses to other companies, usually referred to as 'private sales' or 'trade sales'.[1]

The election of the second Thatcher Government in June 1983 saw privatisation step up a further gear. Between 1983 and 1987 receipts totalling £10.4 billion were raised from the sale of nationalised industries, the most important being British Telecom, British Gas, British Airways, Rolls-Royce, parts of British Leyland, the National Bus Company, and shipbuilding and ship repair yards. The 1987-97 Conservative Governments went even further, privatising airports, the Scottish Transport Group, water, electricity, coal and most controversially, the railways.

Where outright privatisation was deemed not possible for the present time, Government developed a programme of competitive tendering for public services, such as refuse collection, cleaning and catering, in central and local government and the National Health Service (NHS). This was extended in the later 1980s with the introduction of compulsory competitive tendering for a range of local government work and the transfer of the running of the Royal Dockyards to private contractors. However, privatisation of the welfare state remained almost entirely 'out of bounds'. Suggestion in September 1982 that the Government was contemplating privatisation of the NHS led to a speedy denial from Mrs Thatcher. Thatcher was well aware of the public's fondness for the welfare state.

Table 12.1 lists the main privatisations in the UK between 1979 and 1987 and Figure 12.1 details the amounts raised each year from privatisation receipts and the number of transactions. As can be seen, public offers (stock market flotation's) dominated in terms of privatisation revenues. Receipts peaked in the early 1990s with the sale of the electricity industry. Although privatisation receipts never amounted to more than about three per cent of total government revenues each year, the Exchequer benefited during the 1980s and 1990s from a useful privatisation income totalling around £70 billion (over $100 billion).[2] Moreover, because the Government was no longer at risk from having to finance the losses of the nationalised industries and gained tax revenues from the higher profits earned by the industries once in the private sector, the gains to the Exchequer were much larger. However, balanced against this is the criticism that the Government 'sold the family silver' too cheaply. Certainly investors in privatisation stock made some spectacular capital gains (Parker, 1997). For example, by the end of the first day of stock market trading in BT shares the potential gain was 86 per cent.

Table 12.1: The UK's Major Privatisations, 1979-1987

	Date of sale (where more than one date is given the shares were sold in tranches)
British Petroleum	October 1979 September 1983 November 1987
British Aerospace	February 1981 May 1985
Cable & Wireless	October 1981 December 1983 December 1985
Amersham International	February 1982
National Freight Corporation Britoil	February 1982 November 1982 August 1985
Associated British Port Holdings	February 1983 April 1984
Enterprise Oil	July 1984
Jaguar	August 1984
British Telecommunications	December 1984 December 1991 July 1993
British Shipbuilders and Naval Dockyards British Gas	1985 onwards December 1986
British Airways	February 1987
Rolls-Royce	May 1987
BAA (British Airports Authority)	July 1987
British Steel	December 1988
Anglian Water	December 1989
Northumbrian Water	December 1989
North West Water	December 1989
Severn Trent	December 1989
Southern Water	December 1989
South West Water	December 1989
Thames Water	December 1989
Welsh Water	December 1989
Wessex Water	December 1989
Yorkshire Water	December 1989
Eastern Electricity	December 1990
East Midlands Electricity	December 1990
London Electricity	December 1990
Manweb	December 1990
Northern Electric	December 1990
NORWEB	December 1990
SEEBOARD	December 1990

	Date of sale (where more than one date is given the shares were sold in tranches)
Southern Electric	December 1990
South Wales Electricity	December 1990
South Western Electricity	December 1990
Yorkshire Electricity	December 1990
National Power	March 1991
PowerGen	March 1991
Scottish Hydro-Electric	June 1991
Scottish Power	June 1991
Trust Ports	1992-97 (various dates)
Northern Ireland Electricity	June 1993
British Coal	December 1994
Railtrack	May 1996
British Energy	July 1996
AEA Technology	September 1996
Train Operating Companies	Various dates in 1996/7
National Air Traffic Services	July 2001

Figure 12.1: Total Privatisation Revenues and Transactions, UK, 1977-2005

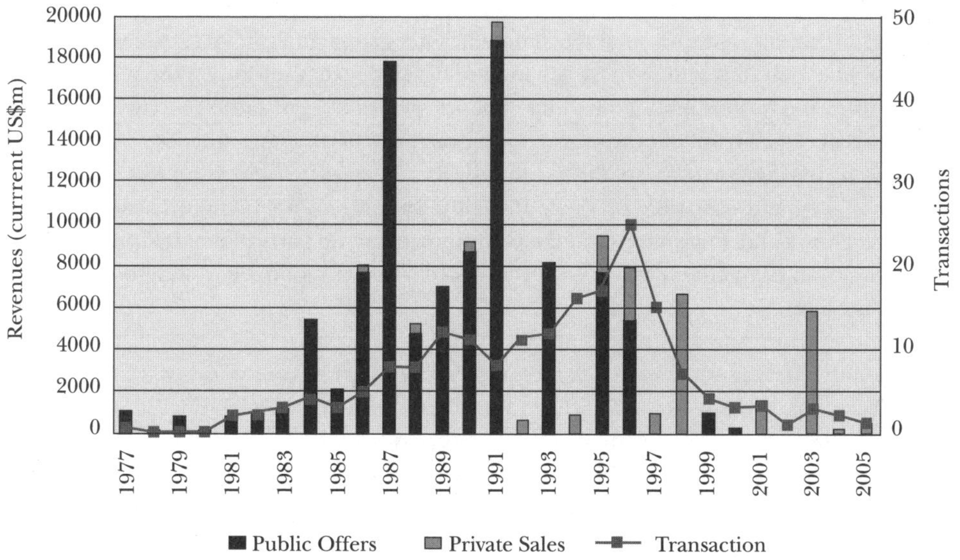

Source: Available online at: www.privatizationbarometer.net.

12.3 Privatisation and UK Economic Performance

For an economist, the litmus test for privatisation is whether the industries performed much better than they would have done had they stayed under state ownership. This requires a consideration of the 'counterfactual' or what would have been their economic performance had they remained nationalised. This must ultimately be a matter of conjecture. However, it is the case that under Thatcher the nationalised sector as a whole performed much better in terms of productivity and profitability, in no small part because the management were mandated to improve efficiency rather than pursue political or social objectives. For example, the British Steel Corporation saw manning fall from 191,500 in 1979 to 53,720 in 1988, immediately before privatisation. Over the same period, labour productivity rose by almost 18 per cent per annum. In British Airways between 1981 and privatisation in 1987 employment fell by 30 per cent and labour productivity rose annually by around 8.6 per cent a year (Martin and Parker, 1997).

Perhaps these efficiency gains would not have occurred if the management had not been preparing for privatisation. In which case the gains can be credited to privatisation; but some industries that stayed in the state sector in the 1980s, such as the Post Office and the National Coal Board, also saw efficiency improvements (Bishop and Kay, 1988; Bishop and Thompson, 1992). For example, Total Factor Productivity (TFP) in the Post Office rose by some 3.7 per cent per annum between 1979 and 1988 (Bishop and Kay, 1988: 45). Perhaps the safest conclusion is that state industries can perform well when Government concentrates on managing them as commercial concerns and not as political poodles. Whether Governments can be relied on to do so for long, however, is quite another matter.

So the counterfactual is tricky. Less problematic is the record of performance in the privatised industries since their transfer to the private sector. A number of studies have been undertaken, some by this author, and they generally show efficiency gains. However, in some cases the gains were not markedly different to those achieved under nationalisation and, more unequivocally, the gains in the former monopoly public utilities (telecoms, gas and electricity) tend to be associated with the arrival of competition rather than privatisation per se.

Under nationalisation a number of the industries were given monopoly powers even though there was no sound economic rationale for not permitting competition, coal mining comes immediately to mind. Once privatised the Government had no particular reason to protect the industries from competition and even the so-called 'natural monopolies' were opened up to new competitors.

The Government was criticised for privatising British Telecom in 1984 and British Gas in 1986 as monopoly enterprises – in both cases breaking up the industries before sale was contemplated but rejected, particularly as the Boards of these enterprises strongly objected to the idea. So when later, in 1990-91, the electricity industry was sold it was vertically unbundled in England and Wales to create two competing non-nuclear generating companies, National Power and PowerGen, a nuclear generator (which initially remained state owned but was privatised as British Energy in 1996), National Grid owning the high-voltage transmission system, and 12 regional electricity companies primarily concerned with local distribution and retail sales. At the same time, generation was opened up to new entrants and by 1999 electricity sales to all consumers had become competitive. Similarly, in the 1990s the Government encouraged more competition in telecommunications and gas supply.

The result of competition is evident especially in the labour productivity figures in Table 12.2. In the cases of both British Telecom and British Gas the largest efficiency gains occurred in the 1990s with the arrival of competition and regulatory tightening, discussed below (although there were also some impressive gains in the run up to privatisation too).[3] It can also be seen from the figures in this table that the growth in TFP, which takes account of other inputs notably capital, is more modest. This suggests that the industries after privatisation undertook capital for labour substitution. They also contracted out a number of activities, taking the labour involved off their books. Both trends are consistent with the notion of over-manning when state owned, probably because of the stronger power of the trade unions. Since privatisation the power of the trade unions has been much diminished, and with it the UK's previously depressing record of man-days lost through strikes.

Table 12.2: Productivity Growth in British Telecom and British Gas (annual percentage change)

	Late 1970s/ early 1980s	Mid 1980s	Post-privatisation	Mid 1990s
British Telecom:				
Labour Productivity	2.8	8.7	4.3	15.0
TFP	7.1	4.8	2.9	4.7
British Gas:				
Labour Productivity	2.7	7.1	2.6	6.0
TFP	0.8	3.5	0.1	-1.3

Note: The dates given are approximate; for more details of the dates and the methods of calculation, see Martin and Parker (1997: 63).

Where the quick development of competition proved difficult, the Government resorted to establishing a new regulatory structure. It was recognised that regulating prices and services from government departments, as had occurred under nationalisation, would leave the industries open to political manipulation and would be likely to frighten away private investors. In consequence, when the privatisation of the first of the monopoly industries, British Telecom, was planned, the decision was taken to set up a quasi-independent regulatory agency, the Office of Telecommunications (Oftel), headed by a Director General. Oftel's responsibilities were set down in statute and a licensing system was introduced to regulate BT and new entrants into the industry. Amongst the licence terms was the regulation of pricing, which took the form of a price cap based on the retail price index minus an 'X' efficiency factor (RPI-X) (Littlechild, 1983). Although it would have been possible for Ministers to have interfered in the regulation, in practice the regulatory offices were given a high degree of independence. This regulatory model was later extended to gas, water, airports, electricity and the railways.

It was therefore, in the absence of competition, that these regulatory agencies had the task of encouraging management to raise economic efficiency in a number of the privatised industries. Economic regulators suffer from inadequate information about the regulated firm's potential revenues and efficient costs so as to achieve the prices and outputs that would exist were the industry fully competitive (Helm, 1995; Parker, 1998). Nevertheless, the new regulatory bodies in the UK quickly built up a reputation for effective intervention to protect consumers. At the same time, their skill in identifying the scope for efficiency gains grew and with it their pressure on management to achieve efficiency. The initial price caps at privatisation were set through negotiation between the corporations, government departments and their respective financial advisors, but always with an eye to achieving a successful sale. However, once the price caps came up for renewal, typically after five years (although sometimes less), each regulator acted to tighten the cap.

For example, at privatisation British Telecom's price cap was set at RPI-3 per cent, which was raised to 4.5 per cent in 1989, 6.2 per cent in 1991 and then to 7.5 per cent in 1993. The effect was to put increasing pressure on the management in these privatised industries to achieve efficiency improvements. In addition, over time new competition did develop, so that the privatised monopolies were eventually faced by a double squeeze involving competition *and* regulation, until such time as regulation could be safely removed. Regulation of British Telecom's prices was finally abolished in August 2006. The regulation of electricity and gas retail prices had been removed a few years earlier.

With the arrival of competition, the privatised industries were subject to normal competition law in the UK, relating to market power, restrictive practices and mergers. This necessitated the Government revisiting competition policy to ensure that the competition authorities in the UK, the Office of Fair Trading and the Competition Commission, and the regulatory agencies such as Oftel (now Ofcom) could work seamlessly to promote and protect competition. The UK strengthened its competition laws in 1998 and 2002.

The figures in Table 12.2 above, showing labour and TFP growth in British Telecom and British Gas therefore reflect both the results of growing competition *and* more effective regulation during the 1990s. Privatisation has not led to the withering away of the state in the UK, but rather to a reformulated role for government as a market regulator rather than a direct service provider (Cook, 1998; Parker, 1999).

Consumers have gained from the efficiency improvements. In most of the UK public utilities prices and tariffs have fallen since privatisation. For example, between 1984 and 1999 average real charges in telecommunications fell by around 48 per cent on average; although this change certainly resulted from technology and competition in addition to ownership change and regulation. Turning to gas, between 1986 and 1997 domestic gas bills fell by an average of 2.6 per cent a year, again in real terms. After 1997 the gradual introduction of competition in domestic gas supplies led to further cuts of up to 20 per cent. Real industrial and commercial gas prices fell over the same period by about five per cent a year. In the electricity market the decline in charges for domestic consumers in England and Wales between 1990 and 1999 was around 26 per cent in real terms for domestic consumers, while the reduction for industrial and commercial consumers was even larger, totalling between 25 per cent and 34 per cent (Parker, 1999; Littlechild, 2000: 32-33). The main exception to this impressive track record on charging occurred in the water and sewerage industry, where prices rose. Higher charges were levied to fund the modernisation of the water and sewerage system after years of under investment when in the state sector and to meet the requirements of new EU water quality directives.

It is important, however, to acknowledge that the above figures are averages and conceal disparities in the distribution of the welfare gains between different consumer groups (Waddams Price and Hancock, 1998; Waddams Price and Young, 2003). State ownership is associated with cross-subsidies and 'no undue discrimination' clauses that lead to uniform pricing. Since privatisation, users with lower marginal costs, usually large users or industry, have tended to receive bigger reductions in charges than smaller, often poorer consumers, which are individually more costly to serve (NAO, 2001). The result is that lower income groups have received smaller welfare gains from privatisation and in some cases may even have lost out.

Service quality changes since privatisation are particularly difficult to summarise. However, there is little evidence that price reductions following privatisation have been at the expense of service quality. The industry regulators police service quality and penalise quality reductions where competition is restricted and in competitive markets it will not be in the interests of firms to compromise on the quality that consumers expect. An exception may relate to long-term investment. It has been suggested that privatisation of electricity may have driven firms to reduce their capital investment programmes to reduce costs, leading to less reserve capacity to meet peak load demands or emergencies. Recent blackouts in London may be a result of such action. The black outs occurred when technical faults took capacity off-line and the electricity supplier had insufficient alternative supplies.

Economists distinguish between static efficiency gains and dynamic efficiency gains. Static gains involve the firm moving towards its efficiency frontier or achieving the level of productive efficiency that it should be able to attain given existing inputs, input prices and technology. Dynamic efficiency gains are more concerned with efficiency improvements associated with technological development and management changes, including changes to production processes and supply chains. In other words, it might be possible for an industry to register efficiency gains at the time of privatisation and immediately afterwards that simply reflect de-manning and the selling off of under-utilised land and buildings - and this did occur in the UK. But maintaining continuing efficiency gains, and therefore long-term international competitiveness, requires investment and management effort directed into improving products and production processes.

Assessing the impact of privatisation in terms of dynamic efficiencies is particularly problematic and not well investigated for the UK. The achievement or failure to achieve dynamic efficiency gains, by their very nature, may not show up for many years. But there are a number of possible indicators. The first is expenditure on research and development. Figure 12.2 show the amounts spent on Research and Development (R&D) in British Telecom both before and in the ten years after privatisation. What is clear from these figures is that privatisation led to less spending on R&D. Expenditure as a percentage of turnover fell from 2.6 per cent immediately before privatisation to around 1.8 per cent in the early 1990s. However, this does not mean necessarily that the technological capability of BT has therefore declined. Perhaps privatisation may simply have led to the ending of wasteful R&D; perhaps since privatisation the company has achieved a better return on its R&D investment.

Figure 12.2: BT Expenditure on R&D, 1979-80 to 1993-94

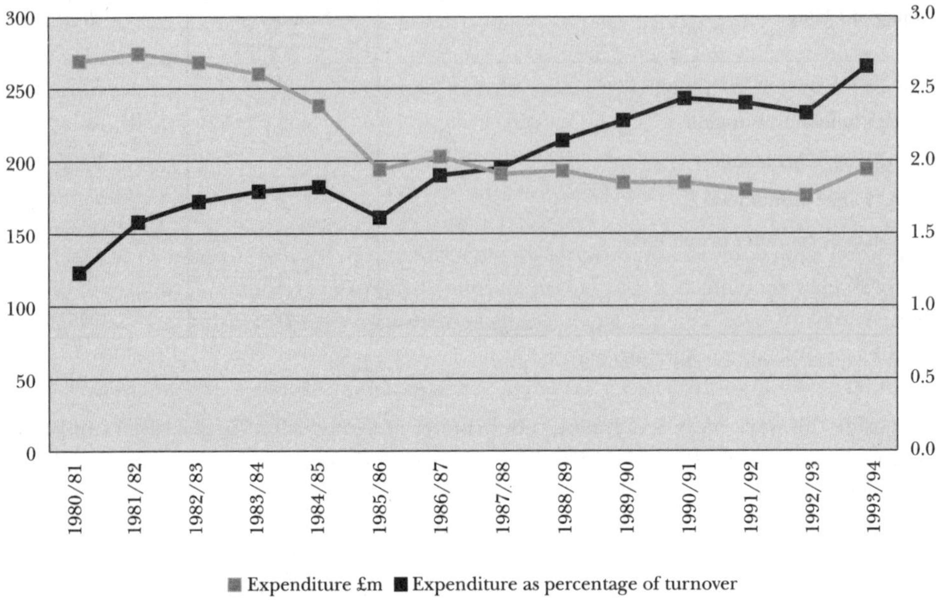

Source: BT, Annual Report & Accounts, various; Parker (1994).

More generally, anecdotal evidence suggests that in privatised companies R&D has been expected to achieve greater, shorter-term, commercial payoffs, leading to less spent on 'blue sky' research. But we cannot be sure and if it has occurred the long-term economic effects are difficult to gauge.

Another indicator is to look at processes within firms. In a piece of major research by this author and colleagues changes in the management of procurement were investigated (Harris, Parker and Cox, 1998; Cox, Harris and Parker, 1999). Twenty-eight privatised firms in the UK were included in the research and evidence was gathered that there had been substantial changes in the structure of procurement in most in the three years before or following privatisation (see Table 12.3). In many there had been the introduction of a more professional approach to procuring goods and services including the introduction of 'leading-edge' procurement practices. Whereas under state ownership procurement had often been a 'Cinderella' activity, professional procurement managers had been recruited from the private sector to champion these new and more effective procurement methods. This had led to improved supplies and lower costs; although arguably in many cases there was an over emphasis on cost reduction rather than using procurement strategically to gain competitive advantage.

Table 12.3: Changes in the Structure of Procurement in UK Privatised Industries

Timing of Change	Number of Companies	%
More than 3 years before privatisation	2	7
0-3 years before privatisation	5	18
During year of privatisation	3	11
0-3 years after privatisation	9	32
More than 3 years after privatisation	7	25
No change	2	7
Total	**28**	**100**

Source: Cox, Harris and Parker (1999:51).

Alongside this work on procurement, other studies of management in privatised companies have revealed a new attention to satisfying the consumer. Whereas previously the consumer may have had no choice but to buy from the nationalised industry, the introduction of competition necessitated the building of new competencies in consumer marketing. Other changes to improve responsiveness to the market included the installing of new accounting and IT systems (Parker, 1995; Martin and Parker, 1997; Cragg and Dyck, 1999). In general, this evidence (albeit tentative) is consistent with management pursuing dynamic efficiency gains after privatisation.

However, the failure of a number of privatised shipyards, mines and steel works, the collapse of Rover cars, the liquidation of Railtrack and the need for government financial support for British Energy to prevent its collapse in 2001, are just some examples confirming that privatisation is not a panacea for economic failure. Moreover, most of the UK's electricity industry, much of its water industry, and privatised companies such as Amersham International, Associated British Ports and most recently the British Airports Authority, have come under foreign control. This suggests that foreign managers have seen greater potential for efficiency gains than British managers. Privatisation alone does not reverse national failings in management competency.

12.4 Lessons for Ireland

Ireland has had its own privatisation programme since the late 1980s (Barrett, 1998). However, there are still some useful lessons that can be learned from the UK experience.

Firstly, government departments in the UK were slow to recognise that privatisation might not lead to adequate incentives to improve efficiency in the absence of competition. Although the Treasury pressed on departments the importance of competition, agendas in departments tended to be focussed on achieving a quick and easy sale. For reasons of self-interest the management of state industries did not want to be transferred to the private sector along with a much tougher competition and were therefore strongly opposed to any industrial restructuring. Also, selling enterprises with monopoly powers raised more revenue because future monopoly profits were capitalised in the sale price. However, the statistical work undertaken on the performance of privatised industries post-privatisation suggests that competition is important if economic efficiency gains are to be achieved and perhaps more important than ownership change per se.

Secondly, where effective competition is not possible, at least for some time, the Government must regulate to protect consumers. This requires the establishment of a new regulatory regime. The role of regulation should be two fold: first, to protect consumers from monopoly abuse and second, to promote competition wherever possible, perhaps even by tilting the playing field in the favour of new entrants into the industry. Once competition develops it needs to be protected because there is an incentive for producers to merge to reduce competition and raise their market power. This necessitates Government revisiting its competition laws to ensure that they are adequate to protect competition in the privatised utilities and to ensure that the regulatory regimes and competition authorities work consistently.

Thirdly, consumers in the UK have benefited from more competition and lower prices, especially for telephone calls and fuel. They have also benefited since privatisation from improved service quality. The UK's experience confirms that private profit making is not incompatible with good public services. However, regulators have to act to ensure that the benefits of privatisation flow down to the poorest who can be the most expensive to serve. In private-sector markets businesses are interested in the most profitable consumers.

Finally, the longer-term economic benefits from privatisation will come from dynamic efficiency gains. While there is some evidence that since privatisation management has tackled some of the deficiencies under nationalisation in, for example procurement and marketing, the impact of privatisation on research and development and the country's technological capability is much less clear. The possibility that privatised firms will be overly 'short termist' in their investment programmes because of pressures from the capital market for quick returns should not be dismissed.

12.5 Conclusions

In the UK, of the major nationalised industries in 1979 only the Post Office escaped largely unscathed from the privatisation experience. It seems that Margaret Thatcher had nervousness about privatising the 'Royal Mail' and more pragmatically Conservative Governments were mindful that the rural constituencies from which most of their MPs came might well lose out from privatisation. Typically, urban post cross-subsidises more expensive mail collection and delivery in rural areas. Since 1997 the trade unions have opposed any suggestion from the Labour Government that private capital should be introduced into the Post Office. Nevertheless, it is difficult to believe that the Post Office can remain an entirely state-owned organisation into the future. A lacklustre service and a lamentable record of industrial disputes is a reminder of what the public suffered from more widely in the 1970s under nationalisation.

Privatisation in the UK resulted from growing disquiet about the performance of the nationalised industries and indeed of the economy as a whole. Since the mid-1980s the UK has recorded GDP growth figures equivalent to and sometimes in excess of those of other EU Member States - although not Ireland. However, this cannot be put down simply to privatisation. Rather it resulted from much wider economic reforms involving controls on public spending, tax cuts, more flexible labour markets and deregulation; a reform package of which privatisation was but one part, although an important part. The lessons for Ireland from the UK experience are that as part of a wider programme of opening up the economy to market forces privatisation can lead to efficiency gains, from which consumers and taxpayers benefit. However, these efficiency gains are not guaranteed. In particular, where competition remains restricted there needs to be an appropriate institutional response in terms of effective state regulation.

Notes

1 The Government also sold its majority shareholding in the company BP, starting in October 1979. The final share sale occurred in November 1987.

2 To this might be added the sums raised by state industries selling off subsidiaries and surplus land and buildings which were usually retained by the industries. However, the Government was then able to adjust the level of loan financing they obtained through Government. Similarly, local authorities gained receipts from the sale of council housing to the tenants under legislation introduced in 1980 which gave tenants the right to buy on privileged terms.

3 Saal and Parker (2000) study performance in the water and sewerage industry, where competition is strictly limited by the technology of provision, and find that tighter regulation is associated with efficiency gains.

References

Barrett, S. (1998), "The Importance of State Enterprises in the Irish Economy and the Future for Privatisation", in D. Parker (ed.) *Privatisation in the European Union: Theory and Policy Perspectives,* London: Routledge.

Bishop, M. and Kay, J. (1988), *Does Privatization Work? Lessons from the UK,* London: London Business School.

Bishop, M. and Thompson, D. (1992), "Regulatory Reform and Productivity Growth in the UK's Public Utilities", *Applied Economics,* Vol.24, 1181-90.

Brittan, S. (1984), "The Politics and Economics of Privatization", *Political Quarterly,* Vol.55, 109-128.

Cook, P. (1998), "Privatization in the UK", in D.Parker (ed.) *Privatisation in the European Union: Theory and Policy Perspectives,* London: Routledge.

Cox, A., Harris, L. and Parker, D. (1999), *Privatisation and Supply Chain Management: On the Effective Alignment of Purchasing and Supply after Privatisation,* London: Routledge.

Crafts, N. (2002), *Britain's Relative Economic Performance 1870*-1899, London: Institute of Economic Affairs.

Cragg, M. and Dyck, I.J.A. (1999), "Management Control and Privatization in the UK", *RAND Journal of Economics,* Vol.30, No.3, 475-97.

Financial Times (2003), "Big Expansion Planned in PFI Projects", 11 June, p.6.

Harris, L., Parker, D. and Cox, C. (1998), "UK Privatisation: Its Impact on Procurement", *British Journal of Management,* Vol.9, Special Issue, 13-26.

Helm, D. (1995), *British Utility Regulation: Principles, Experience and Reform,* Oxford: Oxford

University Press.

Littlechild, S.C. (1983), *Regulation of British Telecommunications' Profitability*, London: HMSO.

Littlechild, S.C. (2000), *Privatisation, Competition and* Regulation, Occasional Paper 110, London: Institute of Economic Affairs.

Martin, S. and Parker, D. (1997), *The Impact of Privatisation: Ownership and Corporate Performance in the UK*, London: Routledge.

NAO (2001), *Giving Domestic Customers a Choice of Electricity Supplier*, Report by the Comptroller and Auditor General, HC 85 Session 2000-2001, London: Stationery Office.

Parker, D. (1994), "A Decade of Privatisation: the Effect of Ownership Change and Competition on British Telecom", *British Review of Economic Issues*, Vol.16, No.40, 87-113.

Parker, D. (1995), "Privatisation and Agency Status: Identifying the Critical Factors for Performance Improvement", *British Journal of Management*, Vol.6, 29-33.

Parker, D. (1997), "Price Cap Regulation, Profitability and Returns to Investors in the UK Regulated Industries", *Utilities Policy*, Vol.6, No.4, 303-15.

Parker, D. (1999), "Regulating Public Utilities: Lessons from the UK", *International Review of Administrative Sciences*, Vol.65, 117-31.

Saal, D. and Parker, D. (2000), "The Impact of Privatisation and Regulation on the Water and Sewerage Industry in England and Wales: A Translog Cost Function Model", *Managerial and Decision Economics*, Vol.21, 253-68.

Waddams Price, C. and Hancock, R. (1998), "Distributional Effects of Liberalising UK Residential Utility Markets", *Fiscal Studies*, Vol.19, No.3, 295-319.

Waddams Price, C. and Young, A. (2003), "UK Utility Reform: Distributional Implications and Government Response', in Ugaz, C. and Waddams Price, C. (eds.). *Utility Privatization and Regulation: A Fair Deal for Consumers?* Cheltenham: Edward Elgar.

CHAPTER 13

THE IMPACT OF REGULATIONS IN IRELAND

ROBERT WATT AND DEREK SCULLY[1]

ABSTRACT

Regulations can have a negative impact on economic behaviour and productivity. The challenge for policymakers is to balance estimated costs with the potential benefits of regulations. One of the key issues is to identify the areas which have the most significant impact on business. This chapter reports new research on the issue of the regulatory burden in Ireland, and identifies some potential areas for improving the Irish regulatory framework.

1 Both authors are economists working for Indecon International Economic Consultants. We would like to thank Alan Gray and Sean Lyons for helpful comments. The views expressed are those of the authors and do not necessarily reflect those of Indecon.

13.1 Introduction

Policymakers and representatives of the business sector in Ireland have been concerned to ensure that the regulatory burden on Irish firms does not represent a source of competitive disadvantage. This has led the Government to introduce more systematic evaluations of proposed regulation through the Regulatory Impact Assessment (RIA) process, and to introduce a more thorough review of the stock of regulations. We argue in this chapter that regulations have a cost that can have a negative impact on economic behaviour and productivity. However, the challenge for policymakers is to balance estimated costs with the potential benefits of regulations. One of the key issues for policymakers is to identify the areas which have the most significant impact on business. We report new research on this issue and identify some potential areas for improving the regulatory framework in Ireland.

It is important to distinguish administrative regulation from the economic regulation of certain sectors such as electricity and telecommunications, which are not focus of this chapter. Nor do we focus on regulations that place quantitative restrictions on entities or explicitly restrict market entry. These regulations tend to impose the most severe costs on society and would include, for example, the current pub licensing regime. Finally, there is the issue of the impact of labour market regulations on the functioning of labour markets. We do not address this issue as this chapter is focussed on the impact of regulations of an administrative nature that affect firm behaviour.

13.2 Regulations and Productivity

Regulations are usually introduced in order to achieve some specific social or economic objective although they sometimes have unintended impacts. Regulations are defined by the OECD as "...A set of 'incentives' established either by the legislature, government, or public administration that mandates or prohibits actions of citizens and enterprises.... Regulations are supported by the explicit threat of punishment for non-compliance" (OECD, 2004). This definition includes regulations in a variety of different areas such as taxation compliance, consumer protection, health and safety and employment standards and protection.

Regulations impacting on the business sector require firms to alter their behaviour and also to invest both time and money. The cost of doing so is often referred to as the compliance cost and it is seen as the burden on firms of the regulation. This burden directly adds to costs. By adding to costs, regulation can negatively impact upon productivity and can also divert resources away from more productive activities. Of course, the fact that regulations have an economic cost is not a sufficient argument against all regulations as they have potential benefits, and a judgement would have to be reached on these relative costs and benefits.

Existing research also suggests that the burden of certain regulations falls disproportionately on small business. As small developing businesses tend to be innovators and are increasingly seen as engines of economic growth, the impact of regulations on Small and Medium Size Enterprises (SMEs) requires careful evaluation. Specifically, regulations on the SME sector could increase entry costs and affect overall levels of competition and innovation with implications for productivity.

Reflecting the linkages between regulations and economic performance, the development of appropriate regulatory policy is seen as an area of importance for policymakers. In an attempt to deliver the Lisbon Agenda, the European Commission has identified better regulation as a means for promoting better jobs and growth in Europe (European Commission, 2005). This is mirrored in a number of countries such as, for example, the UK which has put in place the Better Regulation Task Force. In Ireland, RIAs are being used to assess the costs and benefits of proposed regulations and the Government has recently established the Better Regulation Group to advise on policy towards regulation.

13.3 Defining the Costs of Regulations

Numerous regulations govern the actions of businesses. We are concerned with regulations in the areas set out below. They cover the tax compliance costs, environment regulations, health and safety etc.

1. Tax compliance (including income tax/corporation tax, VAT and excise duty);
2. Collection of taxes and levies;
3. Annual accounts;
4. Environmental legislation;
5. Statistical information;
6. Trade-related (e.g. tariff collection);
7. Legislation dealing with quality of goods and services and consumer protection;
8. Employment contracts and employee participation;
9. Equality; and
10. Working conditions (including health and safety)

In the UK, the Better Regulation Task Force has taken compliance costs to be the sum of both recurring and non-recurring costs, relating to the regulation. The recurring costs are taken to be the additional ongoing costs for business brought about by the existence of the regulation, including the costs associated with assigning staff to complete forms, often referred to as the red-tape or administrative burden. Non-recurring costs, or policy costs, are those costs specifically undertaken to achieve the goal of the regulation. This is likely to include one-off purchases of plant and machinery, as well as training for staff.

Further insights on this issue can be gleaned from the model in Figure 13.1, called MISTRAL, which was developed in the Netherlands as a method of measuring the administrative burdens associated with regulation. Within this framework it is possible to consider the administrative burden legislation is placing on an individual firm. The first box relates to the administrative procedures undertaken by the business. These are made up of administrative activities all firms have an interest in undertaking, such as maintaining accounts, stock control and sales administration (box two), as well as administrative procedures businesses are required to undertake under national or international legislation (box three).

The diagram defines all efforts businesses have to make in order to comply with legislative obligations as administrative burdens even though some of these would have been carried out by the firm regardless of the existence of the regulation (box four). These represent a burden on businesses as the regulation generally does not allow the business to undertake this activity within their own timetable but rather when the legislation dictates, an example of this is the preparation of a firm's annual accounts. Those activities in the final box represent administrative procedures firms would not undertake if not required to do so by regulation.

Figure 13.1: Classifying Small Business Administrative Procedures

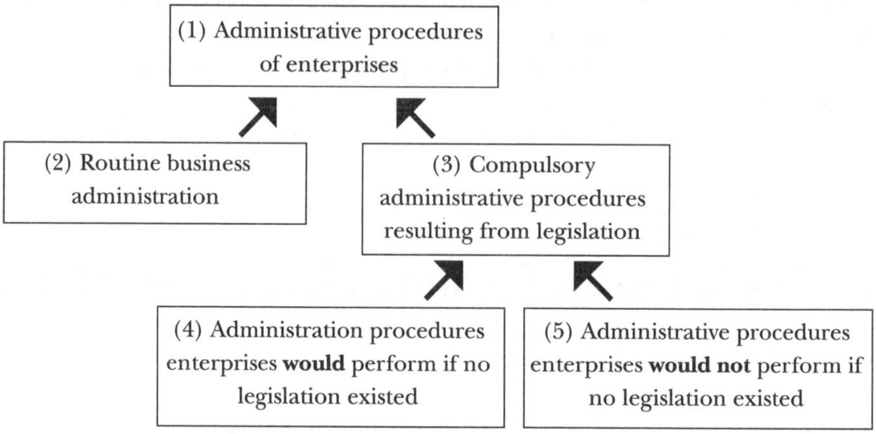

Source: Based on ENSR (1995), Figure 14.1.

Of course, estimating these costs is not easy. One model that is used across Europe to estimate the cost of administrative burdens is the Dutch Standard Cost Model. This approach can be identified as falling within the expenditure evaluation approach methodology and thus relies on the experience of firms in assessing costs. This model has already been used in Denmark and the Netherlands and it is the proposed approach for assessing the administrative burden of regulation in the UK (Better Regulation Task Force, 2005).

Under this approach the administrative burden caused by each individual regulation is separately identified and is reported in a monetary value. The approach is simple: the number of businesses affected by the regulation is multiplied by the hourly tariff of those workers required to meet the information obligation of the regulation and this is further multiplied by the number of hours required to meet the administrative obligation in a given year. The formula for this approach is given in Figure 13.2.

Figure 13.2: Standard Cost Model

Cost of Regulation (SCM) = N x W x T
N = number of businesses affected by the regulation
W = the hourly wage of those involved in meeting the information obligation
T = the number of hours taken to meet the administrative obligation in a year

This approach does not claim to establish the true administrative burden of a particular piece of regulation but rather a stylised estimate and when summed to the estimates of all other regulations, provides the government with an overall picture of regulation. This enables policymakers to identify key areas where action should be taken to reduce the regulatory burden.

Based on these approaches the Dutch Bureau of Economic Policy analysis (April 2004) estimated the Dutch Administrative Burden to be 3.6 per cent of GDP. The Better Regulation Task Force report assumes this to be similar for the UK, with tax and employment regulations accounting for the most significant element of this. This is clearly a significant cost and offers the potential for policymakers to ease these costs through improved regulation. The cost of regulation in Ireland would depend on Irish circumstances which may differ from the Netherlands and the UK. However, it is reasonable to assume that the cost burden of regulation for the Irish economy is significant.

Finally, research in the US indicates that the regulatory burden falls disproportionately on small businesses (Hopkins, 1995). The cost of compliance per employee is significantly larger for firms with 1-20 employees compared to firms with more than 500 employees. This difference is largely attributable to economies of scale.

13.4 The Rationale for and Benefits of Regulation

Policymakers are aware that regulations impose a cost, and it is assumed that this is justified given the benefits. In the first instance, the benefits ought to be clearly aligned with the rationale for the regulatory intervention. The principal justification for regulatory intervention from governments is a need to address some form of 'market failure'. Market failure occurs when markets do not bring about economic efficiency or are not working optimally i.e., there is a Pareto sub-optimal allocation of resources in a market/industry. Put in simple terms this means that the market is not allocating scarce resources efficiently and total social welfare is not being maximised. In such a situation it is acknowledged that government intervention in the market may be in the public interest.

Regulation is, however, only one of a number of possible responses to market failure. Regulation can take the form of minimum standards, the imposition of taxes, standards, directives or quotas and as well as other interventions and can be a result of a national government intervention or from an international body (e.g. the European Commission). In general, regulations tend either to aim at *protecting* consumers or employees from the consequences of market failure or at *preventing* the market failure from occurring at all.

There are four broad categories or reasons for market failure, namely:

1. Asymmetric information;
2. Externalities;
3. Public goods; and
4. Monopoly.

Asymmetric information may arise when sellers or providers of a good have information which is not available to the buyers or purchasers. In this regard, economists distinguish between 'search goods' and 'experience goods'. The former are goods that can be inspected by either touch or sight prior to purchase. Experience goods are goods the quality of which cannot be discerned prior to purchase. The distinction between search and experience goods has important implications for the ability of consumers to make judgements on them. Some goods may also constitute what is known as 'credence goods'. This is a good whose quality cannot be fully assessed before or after consumption. Asymmetric information between buyers and sellers is likely to be more pronounced with credence than experience goods.

In cases where sellers possess information that consumers do not but would use in making a decision on whether to consume the good or not, a government may intervene by introducing regulations stipulating that the seller must provide that additional information. Some examples of interventions of this kind include drug companies being required to put generic names on drugs in order to cut search costs for users and rules prohibiting publication of false information.

Externalities arise in situations where "the unregulated price of a good does not reflect the true cost or benefit to society of producing the good." Thus the potential market failure arising from externalities is that the social optimum output or level of consumption diverges from the private optimum. In the case of negative externalities, regulations may be used to bring private costs more closely into line with social costs (e.g. environmental taxes) or restrict social costs to a given level (e.g. imposition of employment standards). These would include health and safety regulations, employment standard type regulations and environmental regulations and would cover the bulk of administrative type regulations.

Breyer (1982) considers a number of justifications for regulation, and these are consistent with the benefits identified above. He also outlines a number of additional cases in which regulation may be justified. These included:

1. Unequal bargaining power;
2. Rationalisation;
3. Moral hazard, whereby "someone other than the buyer pays for the buyers purchase";
4. Paternalism; and
5. Scarcity.

In summary, the case for regulation is to address the principal sources of market failure identified above. Taken together, a legitimate purpose of regulation is to assure standards of competence, performance, ethical behaviour and personal accountability in a market. What is important, however, is to examine the impact of any regulations, i.e., costs and benefits, and to evaluate the key issue of proportionality. The potential benefits of regulation include consumer protection, fair-trading, optimal resource allocation and maintaining service standards.

13.5 The Burden of Regulations in Ireland

It is important to examine whether the regulatory burden in Ireland is increasing, or whether it is a source of competitive disadvantage. Data on the relative burden of regulations is limited but there is some interesting survey evidence from a recent World Bank survey. One issue the survey assesses is the difficulty attached to starting up a business. This may be measured in terms of the number of procedures involved, the time in days that it would typically take to complete the total number of procedures, and an estimate of the cost of setting up a business as a percentage of income per capita. Table 13.1 presents the findings on setting up a business in the countries studied where Ireland performs well with a mid-to-low table rating of 5.3 per cent of income per capita and, with a low number of four procedures required.

Table 13.1: A Comparative Assessment of Starting a Business

Country	Procedures (number)	Time (days)	Cost (% of income per capita)
Greece	15	38	24.6
Poland	10	31	22.2
Spain	10	47	16.5
Italy	9	13	15.7
Portugal	11	54	13.4
Netherlands	7	11	13.0
Belgium	4	34	11.1
Slovenia	9	60	10.1
Austria	9	29	5.7
Ireland	4	24	5.3
Germany	9	24	4.7
Finland	3	14	1.2
France	7	8	1.2
Sweden	3	16	0.7
United Kingdom	6	18	0.7
United States	5	5	0.5
Denmark	3	5	0.0

Source: World Bank: 'Doing Business Report', 2005.

From the same survey Table 13.2 presents the findings on the estimated difficulty, rigidity and cost of employing individuals in each of the studied countries. Ireland ranks low in terms of the cost of hiring as a percentage of salary, coming fourth from bottom. Denmark has the lowest ranking, while Belgium and France rank top, with employers in Belgium spending over half of the salary for a position on hiring costs.

Table 13.2: A Comparative Assessment of Hiring Workers

Country	Difficulty of Hiring Index	Rigidity of Employment Index	Hiring cost (% of salary)
Belgium	11	20	55.0
France	78	66	47.4
Sweden	28	43	33.4
Italy	61	57	32.6
Spain	67	66	31.6
Austria	11	44	31.3
Greece	78	66	30.0
Poland	11	37	25.8
Portugal	33	58	23.8
Finland	44	48	22.2
Germany	44	55	21.3
Slovenia	61	64	16.6
Netherlands	28	49	15.6
Ireland	28	33	10.8
United Kingdom	11	14	8.7
United States	0	3	8.5
Denmark	11	20	0.7

Source: World Bank: 'Doing Business Report', 2005.

The regulatory burden arising from tax issues is often mentioned as a concern for business and the main cost according to UK and Netherlands studies. The findings are presented in Table 13.3 and show that Ireland ranks fifth from bottom with eight tax payments and an estimated cost of 76 hours. France, Switzerland, Finland and the United Kingdom rank lower in terms of the estimated burden. The tax system in the Netherlands seems to be most burdensome, with compliance requiring an estimated 700 hours.

Table 13.3: A Comparative Assessment of Annual Tax Payments

Country	Payments (number)	Time (hours)
Netherlands	22	700
Italy	20	360
Slovak Republic	31	344
Portugal	7	328
United States	9	325
Austria	20	272
Slovenia	29	272
Greece	32	204
Poland	43	175
Belgium	10	160
Denmark	18	135
Sweden	5	122
Germany	32	105
Ireland	8	76
France	29	72
Switzerland	25	63
Finland	19	..
United Kingdom	22	..

Source: World Bank: 'Doing Business Report', 2005.

Finally, data is also available based on a EU commissioned study, which suggests that Irish SMEs are less prone to see administrative regulations as the major constraint on their business performance than are firms in other European countries (see Table 13.4). The results indicate that five per cent of SME's identified administrative regulations as a barrier compared to nine per cent for Europe as a whole. In addition, firms in Ireland cite other issues as a more significant barrier to business performance.

Table 13.4: Major Constraint on Business Performance cited by SMEs in 2003 (% of SMEs)[2]

	Ireland	European average
Lack of Skilled Labour	17%	13%
Access to Finance	11%	10%
Implementing New Technology	1%	3%
Implementing New Forms of Organisation	3%	2%
Quality Management	2%	1%
Administrative Regulations (on environment, health, safety)	5%	9%
Infrastructure (road, gas, electricity, communications)	5%	4%
Purchasing Power of Customers	31%	36%
Other	12%	8%
None at all	12%	13%
Don't know /No answer	2%	1%
Total	**100%**	**100%**

Source: Categories are exclusive. Weighted data, ENSR Survey 2003 among 7,837 SMEs in 19 European countries.

Despite the relatively favourable ranking for Ireland on selected regulations, there are concerns about the impact of some specific regulations and the overall scale of burdens facing certain sectors.

Next we consider the types of regulations that may be most significant. This could assist in identifying those areas where the attention of policymakers ought to focus, in considering the stock of regulations. Quantitative research on how different types of regulation affect businesses is relatively scarce in Europe and in Ireland specifically. However, in the field of employment regulation there is some survey evidence. In 2001, the ENSR survey included a module on the perceived effects of employment regulations. Like other European firms, Irish SMEs ranked health and safety regulations highly among sources of administrative burden. However, employment related taxes were ranked higher still by Irish firms, whereas their European counterparts tended to see these as relatively less significant. In contrast, European firms gave a much higher ranking to social security and pension requirements and restrictions in working hours than Irish firms did.

Table 13.5: Field of Employment Regulations in Which Administrative Burdens are Highest (% of SMEs)[3]

	Ireland	European Average
Employment Related Taxes	32%	12%
Health & Safety Protection for Workers	28%	30%
Social Security & Pension Requirements	4%	14%
Employment Contracts	4%	3%
Dismissal Law	3%	3%
Collective Bargaining	3%	2%
Sector-specific Requirements for Licences/Certificates	3%	5%
Restriction on Working Hours	1%	6%
Worker Participation Law	0%	1%
Don't Know/No Answer	22%	23%
Total	**100%**	**100%**

Source: Categories are exclusive. Weighted data, ENSR Survey 2001 ENSR Survey among 7,662 SMEs in 19 European countries.

In addition to scoring employment regulation by the significance of burdens imposed, the survey explores to what extent regulation affects firms' behaviour. On the question of how far administrative burdens have an affect on firms' hiring decisions (Table 13.6 below), Irish responses were much closer to the European average. About half of SMEs felt that employment regulations had no effect on hiring decisions. Among those firms that reported some effect, Irish SMEs tended to report a more limited effect than the European average. Similar questions in the survey sought to discover how far employment regulations affected the extent of outsourcing and the use of temporary staff. As with hiring decisions, most firms reported that these activities were not affected by regulation.

Table 13.6: Influence of Administrative Burdens of Employment Regulations on Hiring of Employees (% of SMEs)[4]

Response	Ireland	European Average
Not at all	47%	47%
A Little	24%	18%
Considerably	10%	12%
Much	2%	9%
Very much	6%	8%
Don't know/No Answer	10%	5%
Total	**100%**	**100%**

Source: Categories are exclusive. Weighted data, ENSR Survey 2001 ENSR Survey among 7,662 SMEs in 19 European countries.

Indecon, in conjunction with Lansdowne Market Research, compiled recent findings on regulatory compliance costs for small firms in Ireland for a recent Forfás study. Table 13.7 presents a summary of the views of respondents as to the burden of key regulations. Based on the findings, a number of the regulations are considered to be either a significant burden or a very significant burden by a large percentage of respondents. These would include health and safety regulations, VAT administration, employment regulations, income tax administration and environmental regulations. In each case, between 44 per cent and 47 per cent of respondents viewed these regulations as a very significant or significant burden.

Table 13.7: Respondents' Views on Burden on Principal Regulations (% of Firms)

	Very Significant Burden	Significant Burden	Neither	Insignificant Burden	Very Insignificant Burden	Don't Know
Health and Safety Regulations	11	34	7	41	6	1
VAT Administration	10	37	6	40	3	4
Employment Regulations	7	38	2	41	6	6
Income Tax Administration	7	39	7	33	7	7
Environmental Regulations	6	38	7	43	4	2
Corporate Taxation Administration	3	32	12	35	8	13
Corporate Governance	1	25	9	38	13	14

Source: Indecon and Lansdowne Market Research.

Respondents were also asked their views on which regulations are associated with the highest administrative burden (Table 13.8). The findings show that the most burdensome regulations in terms of compliance are: health and safety protection for workers (16 per cent); dismissal law (14 per cent) and employment related taxes (14 per cent). Other potential options listed received considerably lower rankings.

Table 13.8: Respondents' Views on Regulations with Highest Administrative Burden (% of Firms)

Health and Safety Protection for Workers	16
Dismissal Law	14
Employment Related Taxes	14
Restrictions on Working Hours	7
Social Security and Pension Requirements	3
Worker Participation Law	1
Collective Bargaining	1
Sector-specific Requirements Regarding Licenses and/or Certificates	1
Employment Contracts	9
Don't Know	34

Source: Indecon and Lansdowne Market Research.

Of course, the fact that health and safety and employee regulations are most costly for firms does not imply that regulations in these areas should be abolished, but it could provide a guide to policymakers on where more detailed work may be required.

13.6 Policy Issues

It is important to realise that there will always be a burden imposed by regulation. If the actions of a firm were not altered by the regulation, then the purpose of the regulation would be questionable, due to its failure to bring about a specified objective. This type of regulation is unnecessary and is an example of 'bad regulation'. The goal of the policymaker therefore should be to minimise disproportionate regulations based on five principles (Better Regulation Taskforce, 2005):

1. Proportionality – regulations should be implemented only when necessary and favourable to alternatives and they should be appropriate to the risks posed with the associated costs minimised;
2. Accountability – the objective of the regulation should be clearly justifiable and subject to scrutiny;
3. Consistency – regulations should be a coordinated set of policies wherein overlaps are minimised and that are implemented and enforced in an equal and fair manner;
4. Transparency – as well as regulations being open to scrutiny, it is important that all interested parties are informed of and given the opportunity to contribute to policy objectives to be achieved through regulation; and
5. Targeting – regulations should be focussed on a clear and achievable objective with full knowledge of the likely impacts on specific groups and designed such as to minimise potential side effects.

These five principles of good regulation aim to minimise the burden of regulation. Good regulation will not only minimise the associated policy costs of complying with the regulation but they will also minimise the administrative burden placed on businesses. This is the motivation behind the Government's Better Regulation work and the development of RIA's which focus on ex-ante assessments of proposed regulations. The RIA process is a relatively new concept which is being extended across Government departments and agencies. It is too early to assess the effectiveness of this process, but it is having an impact on how proposed regulations are being considered. Methodological and resource constraint issue notwithstanding, RIAs are a key part of policy development in this area.

There is also a greater role for policy in terms of reviewing the stock of existing regulations and improving enforcement. Some of these issues are discussed in subsequent paragraphs.

13.6.1 Enforcement

A significant contributing factor to the administrative burden of regulation is the time and effort exerted by businesses attempting to keep up to date with new regulations and how changes in their business could create further regulatory issues for them. To alleviate this burden more, better and easily accessible information should be made available to businesses informing them of their regulatory requirements as a result of the introduction of a new regulation. The provision of more and better information will not only reduce the time and effort spent by businesses attempting to understand their regulatory requirements but it may also reduce the expenditure by these firms on obtaining this information from a private source.

In respect of this issue, and other areas of Government activity, there is greater scope to examine the benefits of e-Government. Accessing information electronically or engaging directly with the Government via e-mail can bring substantial benefits. There are already positive from recent developments, such as the Revenue Online System (ROS) and recent changes in the payment system for meter taxation. Extending these initiatives in to other areas could provide further benefits.

Just as businesses require more and better information in order to minimise the burden imposed on them by regulation, for the regulation to be effective, firms must also understand the incentives associated with compliance. In the absence of clear penalties associated with non-compliance and vague guidelines as to when businesses are to be liable to pay penalties, it can result in an inefficient use of resources thus increasing the burden of regulation on businesses.

Over recent years policy makers have begun to consider alternatives to the classic 'command and control' style of regulation, and in some cases have adopted clearly targeted regulation that is proportional to the risks posed. The implementation of risk based regulation places the most significant burden on those businesses that work in the areas that pose greatest risk of harm. The burden is proportional to the risk and as such it minimises the burden of compliance on those businesses whose activities do not pose a considerable harm or a threat to the objective of the regulation. A number of EU transport directives have adopted a risk-based approach in favour of the classic command and control style, with the effect that all transport businesses are not subject to the same regulations or penalties. In the case of businesses that transport chemical materials, those that handle more harmful or dangerous materials, such as nuclear materials, are subject to more stringent regulations whereas those transporting chemicals that do not pose a considerable threat to individuals or the environment do not have to comply with such stringent regulations. Risk based regulations therefore reduce the misallocation of resources for businesses in a particular industry by no longer requiring low risk businesses to over-invest in compliance but instead requiring high risk businesses to incur the majority of the burden.

13.6.2 Exemptions

The targeting of regulation is an important principle for policymakers and is best informed by an ex-ante examination of the likely impacts of a proposed regulation, such as a RIA. Considering the likely impact of a regulation on the market as a whole may lead the policy maker to falsely assert that the burden of regulation on businesses is not disproportionate to the objectives of the regulation. However this approach has significant flaws as it treats all businesses affected by the regulation equally and thus will understate the burden of regulation on small businesses in a sector containing small, medium and large sized businesses, provided there are fixed costs associated with the regulation. Many of the administrative burdens placed on businesses by regulation, such as completing financial accounts and filing returns with the revenue, may not vary proportionally with firm size and as a result may place a particular burden on small businesses. Exemptions have been used both in Ireland and many other countries in order to relieve this excess burden on small businesses and both the exemptions and their thresholds represent a clear opportunity for policy makers to better target regulations to achieve their objective in an efficient a way as possible.

13.6.3 Abolishing Regulations

The previous suggestions have been applicable to both new and existing regulation, but there is also merit in considering abolishing regulations. This is also relevant when policy makers are assessing the alternatives to adopting new regulations. The 'do nothing' option is one that should always be considered alongside the options for regulation. The statute books in many countries contain regulations that were developed at the beginning of the twentieth century, that are still in force but whose focus has been altered significantly through technological and general advancements such that they are out-dated, in some cases irrelevant or covered by new regulations, but still impose a burden on businesses. A full review of active regulations, such as that proposed in the UK by the Better Regulation Task Force, would uncover the ineffectual, out-dated and duplicated regulations that impose burdens on businesses. This could lead to the abolishment or simplification of the regulatory compliance process. New regulations should be subject to such scrutiny after an initial period, to assess the impact of the regulation. If the regulation has not been operating as was envisaged, then its abolition should be considered as an alternative to modifying the existing the regulation.

The Standard Cost Model, discussed in earlier sections, has a role to play in assessing the costs of certain regulations. This has been used successfully in both the Netherlands and the UK. While it is an expensive tool to apply, its selected use in reviewing certain regulations can assist policymakers in Ireland. Once again, after a reasonable period has elapsed, it would be useful to review the applicability and effectiveness of this methodological approach in an Irish context.

13.7 Conclusions

Inappropriate regulations result in an increase in costs and damage productivity and competitiveness. Appropriately targeted regulations can have distinct benefits and the key issue for policymakers is to ensure that there is an economic justification for any regulations introduced and that they are framed in a manner which minimise the negative impact on economic welfare.

Notes

1 Of course, this can be interpreted to justify government action, even where there is no clear case of market failure.

2 The question posed in the survey was "Which of the following factors has been the major constraint on your business performance over the last two years?".

3 The question posed in the survey was "Governments may require enterprises to keep registers or submit information, etc. In which ONE of the following fields of employment regulations are such administrative burdens highest?".

4 The question posed in the survey was "To what extent do these legal administrative burdens in the field of employment regulations influence your decision to hire employees?"

References

Better Regulation Task Force (2005), "Regulation – Less is More".

Breyer, S. (1982), *Regulation and its Reform*, Harvard University Press.

European Commission (2005), "Implementing the Community Lisbon programme: A Strategy for the Simplification of the Regulatory Environment", COM (2005) 535.

Hopkins, T.D. (1995), "Profiles of Regulatory Costs", Report to the US Small Business Administration, Office of Advocacy.

OECD (1994), "The OECD Reference Checklist for Regulatory Decision-Making: A Draft Recommendation of the OECD", Paris.

PART IV

AGGLOMERATION ECONOMIES

INTRODUCTION

Policymakers have long assumed that inward investment can bestow large economic benefits, not only in terms of new investment but also an inflow of new foreign knowledge and technology. This has led to greater importance being given to the notion of industrial clusters. This view of agglomeration economies based on industrial clusters derives largely from the work of Michael Porter, which is reviewed in detail by Doyle and Fanning in Chapter 14. The chapter concludes, however, that there is little evidence that such clusters have had a significant effect on productivity growth in Ireland. The review of the international evidence by Görg in Chapter 15 also finds that the evidence is at best mixed. O'Leary argues in Chapter 16 that agglomeration effects may be due to much broader considerations than suggested by a focus on clusters. For example, the advantages of urbanisation may be important - a well functioning city, with a high degree of economic and social diversity, might be a fertile seed-bed for the development of new ideas. Finally, Andreas Kopp in Chapter 17 analyses the macroeconomic productivity effects of road investment in 13 western European countries and shows that the rate of return for many countries on past investment has been low.

CHAPTER 14

PRODUCTIVITY SPILLOVERS FROM MULTINATIONAL COMPANIES

HOLGER GÖRG[1]

ABSTRACT

Many host country governments assume that inward Foreign Direct Investment (FDI) can bestow large benefits to the economy, bringing not only new investment that boosts national income but also an inflow of new foreign knowledge and technology. The purpose of this chapter is to review the evidence of the importance of these productivity spillovers from inward FDI. It finds that the international evidence on productivity spillovers is mixed. It argues that the most plausible interpretations for the lack of consistent findings are that, firstly, characteristics specific to individual countries can influence the extent to which spillovers happen, secondly, individual firms' level of absorptive capacity is important and thirdly, focusing purely on horizontal spillovers misses important vertical channels of knowledge transfer, in particular through backward linkages, which may bestow larger external effects.

1 The author is grateful to Aoife Hanley for helpful comments on an earlier draft.

14.1 Introduction

FDI by multinational companies is undoubtedly one of the most visible and, at the margin, arguably most important aspects of economic globalisation. As the latest United Nations' *World Investment Report* shows, annual flows of FDI were around $700 billion with the total stock being around $9 trillion in 2004 (UN, 2005). In that year, Europe was host to almost half of the world-wide inward FDI stock and, within the continent; Ireland is an important player in that regard. In terms of the absolute level of inward FDI stock it is the seventh most important host country in Europe. Taking account of the small size of the economy, Ireland's ratio of inward FDI stocks to GDP equals 126.3 in 2004, being second only to Luxembourg among European countries (UN, 2005).

Many host country governments assume that inward FDI can bestow large potential benefits to the economy, bringing not only new investment that boosts national income but also an inflow of new foreign knowledge and technology. This may lead to spillovers to the local economy, resulting in higher productivity and overall economic growth. These external effects from multinationals to domestic firms are generally referred to as 'productivity spillovers' or 'technology spillovers'. The expectation of such positive effects has led many governments to actively attract multinational companies and the associated FDI into their economies, with policies ranging from creating more liberal investment environments to providing substantial public subsidies. While it is difficult to obtain reliable data on such financial incentives, Head (1998) reports that the government of Alabama paid the equivalent of $150,000 per employee to Mercedes for locating its new plant in the state in 1994. Across the Atlantic the UK government provided an estimated $30,000 per employee to attract Samsung to the northeast of England in the late 1990s and $50,000 per employee to attract Siemens (Girma et al., 2001).

It seems reasonable to ask whether such policy intervention can be justified. While the answer to such a question would involve some detailed cost-benefit analysis a simpler but nevertheless very important issue is whether the assumption that FDI brings with it spillovers that foster productivity growth stands up to scrutiny. This contribution attempts to provide some discussion of this question, focussing on the evidence provided from econometric analysis of micro level data.[1]

Hence, the purpose of this chapter is to discuss the evidence on such productivity spillovers. In order to do so it is structured in the following way. In Section 14.2 the theoretical rationale for why multinationals may give rise to productivity spillovers is discussed. Also, the empirical evidence that examines whether multinationals are indeed more productive than domestic firms (as implied by the theory) is presented. Section 14.3 examines the empirical evidence that attempts to measure the magnitude of spillovers from multinationals in econometric analyses for a number of countries, while Section 14.4 focuses on the specific evidence for the Republic of Ireland. It also discusses a number of alternative approaches to measuring other potential spillovers from multinationals to domestic firms in Ireland. Section 14.5 concludes by setting out briefly the policy implications of the current research.

14.2 Multinationals' Spillover Potential

Before discussing the evidence on productivity spillovers it seems pertinent to start off by presenting the basic intuitive framework as to why multinationals can be a source of such effects.

In general, the availability of new foreign knowledge through inward FDI may benefit domestic firms as these can learn the technology from the multinationals, allowing them to upgrade their own production process and as a result increase productivity. The theoretical argument for why one may expect such productivity spillovers from multinationals is straightforward.

Given the foreign multinationals' limited knowledge of the local market, and the distance from their parent firm, they are generally at a disadvantage compared with local firms in the host country (Caves, 1996). Hence, multinationals will only be able to locate profitably abroad if they have some sort of offsetting advantage. This takes the form of a 'firm specific asset' (FSA), such as superior production technique, know-how or management strategy, which has at least to some extent the characteristics of a public good and enables the firm to locate profitably abroad (Markusen, 2002). Most importantly, these FSA can be transferred at low or zero cost between subsidiaries of the same firm.[2] The possibility of productivity spillovers then arises because multinationals may find it difficult to protect a leakage of the FSA in the host country, as other firms may somehow 'learn' about, for example, the production technology or management strategy. They can then apply it in their own firm, thus allowing them to improve technology and ultimately productivity. The public good characteristics imply that once the FSA is out on the external market it can be used by other firms, due to it being at least to some extent non-rival and non-excludable.

The inability of the multinationals to protect the asset is due to a number of reasons. Firstly, domestic firms may just imitate the multinationals in terms of products, production techniques or management techniques. Secondly, labour may move from multinationals to domestic firms, taking with them some of the knowledge of the FSA. Thirdly, domestic firms supplying to or purchasing inputs from multinationals may be exposed to the superior technology and, hence, be able to upgrade their own production techniques. Fourthly, competition from multinationals may force domestic rivals to up-date production techniques to become more productive and competitive. This is frequently referred to as a 'competition effect'. As Aitken and Harrison (1999) point out, however, this competition effect may also reduce productivity in domestic firms, if multinationals attract demand away from their domestic competitors, forcing domestic firms to reduce output and, hence, productivity.

While this appears to be a very intuitive and plausible theoretical proposition, the question is whether it also stands up to empirical scrutiny. The first step in evaluating this is to start off by considering the importance of FSA. If these are indeed crucial then one should observe that multinationals use 'superior' technology compared to their domestic competitors. The use of technology is, of course, difficult to observe and measure, but it should arguably be correlated with a number of other measurable firm characteristics, and in particular with productivity. If a firm uses a superior technology one would, all other things equal, expect it to show higher levels of labour or Total Factor Productivity (TFP) than its rivals.

There is a large body of evidence that looks at the question as to whether multinationals indeed have higher levels of productivity than domestic firms, as would be predicted by the 'firm specific asset argument'. For example, Doms and Jensen (1998) and Girma and Görg (2007) provide discussions of this issue and evidence for the US and the UK to the extent that multinationals indeed have a productivity advantage compared to domestic firms, even when taking into account other firm characteristics such as sector, size of the firm, etc.

A number of studies have also undertaken comparisons of firm characteristics between domestic firms and foreign multinationals for Ireland.[3] For example, Barry et al. (1999) use data from the Irish Census of Production, as well as data available from Forfás, to show that, on average, foreign multinationals based in Ireland are larger, have higher labour productivity (measured as net output per worker) as well as higher profits, employ more skilled workers and spend more on Research and Development (R&D). Furthermore, decomposing productivity growth using plant level data from the Central Statistics Office, Ruane and Ugur (2005a) provide evidence that foreign owned firms in Ireland have far higher levels of labour productivity growth than domestic-owned firms.[4]

It is important to point out that most of the literature, including the studies looking at Irish data, compares foreign-owned multinationals with domestic-owned firms. This is understandable for a number of reasons, most importantly the policy concern with inward investment and the availability of data for many countries distinguishing foreign and domestic firms. However, it must be made clear that the theoretical argument relates to multinationals per se (and not only to foreign multinationals) compared to non-multinationals in the domestic economy. Hence, the former category includes domestic multinationals as well (with subsidiaries in foreign countries), and the theory predicts that these firms should also have FSA that allow them to use superior technology, and show higher productivity, than purely domestic non-multinational firms. This idea has been picked up in a number of recent studies. For example, Girma et al. (2004) use data from the Forfás Annual Business Survey of Economic Impact (ABSEI) for the year 2000 and find evidence that Irish-owned multinationals are more productive (in terms of labour productivity) than Irish exporters and purely domestic market oriented Irish firms.[5]

What we can take from this discussion is that there are plausible theoretical reasons for why there may be spillovers from multinationals, and that the evidence also suggests that these firms indeed have 'superior characteristics' – hence, the potential for spillovers should be taken as given. The next section looks at the vast empirical evidence amassed in international studies that directly examines productivity spillovers from multinationals, before discussing in more detail the case of Ireland in Section 14.4. Note that the literature referred to in the next sections investigates purely whether there are spillovers from foreign multinationals to domestic firms, neglecting completely the possibility of spillovers emanating from domestic-owned multinationals.

14.3 International Evidence on Productivity[6]

When it comes to examining productivity spillovers from multinationals, i.e., the transfer of knowledge from foreign to domestic firms, it is important to point out that these are difficult to measure since, as Krugman (1991: 53) puts it, "knowledge flows [...] leave no paper trail by which they may be measured and tracked". The approach adopted in the empirical literature therefore largely avoids the (arguably difficult to answer) question as to how exactly productivity spillovers actually take place, but focuses on the simpler issue of whether or not the presence of multinationals affects productivity in domestic firms.

Over the last thirty years, a large empirical econometric literature has developed, starting with Caves (1974), Globerman (1979) and Blomström (1986) using data for Australia, Canada and Mexico, respectively. Since then, their empirical models have been extended and refined in studies covering a large number of countries, although the basic approach is still, by and large, similar. Most econometric analyses are undertaken in a framework in which labour productivity or TFP of domestic firms is regressed on a range of independent variables. To measure productivity spillovers from foreign multinationals a variable is included which proxies the extent of foreign firms' penetration of an industry in order to gauge the importance of multinationals in the sector. This variable is usually calculated as the share of employment or sales in multinationals over total industry employment/sales in a given sector. In other words, the regression allows for an effect of FDI on productivity of domestic firms in the same industry. If the regression analysis yields a positive and statistically significant coefficient on the foreign presence variable, this is taken as evidence that positive intra-industry (or horizontal) spillovers have occurred from multinationals to domestic firms. Most studies use either the contemporaneous level of foreign presence or relatively short lags as their explanatory variables. If anything, therefore, these studies usually measure short-run effects of foreign presence on domestic productivity.

A large body of evidence has been amassed in terms of studies of productivity spillovers for many developing, transition and developed countries.[7] Early papers such as Caves (1974), Globerman (1979) and Blomström (1986) generally find positive spillover effects. However, their results have to be taken with a grain of salt as they use cross sectional data (i.e., for a number of firms or industries for one particular year) for their analysis. As Görg and Strobl (2001) discuss, the use of this data may lead to biased and, hence, unreliable results.[8] Focussing on studies using panel data it is apparent that, though much econometric work has been done in it provides, at best, mixed results as to the importance of spillovers.

While a number of authors (Haskel et al. (2002) for the UK and Keller and Yeaple (2003) for the US) find unambiguously positive spillovers, several studies (such as Aitken and Harrison, 1999 for Venezuela or Konings, 2001, for Bulgaria) find negative effects of the presence of multinationals on domestic firms' productivity. Furthermore, a number of papers find no statistically significant impact on average of multinationals on domestic productivity (e.g., Girma and Görg, 2006 for the UK and Konings, 2001, for Poland). There is some supportive evidence from case studies of spillover benefits to domestic firms (e.g., Moran, 2001) although there is, even at that level, disagreement in particular instances.[9]

The most plausible explanation for negative effects of multinational presence on domestic firms' productivity is that foreign firms reduce their productivity through competition effects, as suggested by Aitken and Harrison (1999). They argue that domestic firms compete with multinationals (which have lower marginal costs due to their firm-specific advantage) on domestic product markets. When multinationals enter, they steal business away from the domestic firms, which due to increasing returns to scale reduce their output and are forced up their average cost curve, reducing productivity as a result. Note that this argument is not necessarily inconsistent with the idea that competition can act as one of the channels through which positive spillovers are transmitted. Some firms may experience negative competition effects in the short run (moving up a given average cost curve), while other firms may improve efficiency (shifting down their average cost curve) because of increased competition in the short run as well as the long run.[10]

There are also other explanations for a failure to find evidence of positive aggregate spillovers in the short run. Firstly, there may be lags in domestic firms' learning from multinationals, which short-run analyses do not pick up. Secondly, spillovers may be localised as geographic proximity may be important for technology transfer. Hence, they may not be picked up in the standard regression analysis. Thirdly, multinational firms may be able to guard their firm-specific advantages closely, preventing leakages to domestic firms and, therefore, spillovers as well. These explanations are straightforward and plausible and require little comment.

A further explanation that is discussed by Lipsey and Sjöholm (2005) is that countries, and firms within countries, differ in their ability to benefit from spillovers. They argue that there may be instances, particularly in developing or transition countries, where the domestic industry is too small or too backward to be able to learn from multinational firms. Since it is difficult to control for such country characteristics in studies using data for only one country, the empirical literature has paid more attention to the notion that only a subset of firms may be able to capture positive spillovers. The basic idea is that only domestic firms that have a certain level of ability are able to assimilate the knowledge available from multinationals. More specifically, the more backward a domestic firm is in its level of technology compared to the multinational, the less likely it is to have the appropriate level of human and physical capital, and know how, it needs to benefit from spillovers.

This explanation has received substantial support in the empirical literature. For example, Kokko et al. (1996) using firm-level data for Uruguay find evidence for productivity spillovers to domestic firms with moderate technology gaps (measured as the difference between the domestic firm's labour productivity and the average labour productivity in foreign firms) but not for firms that use considerably lower levels of technology. Also, Girma (2005) and Girma and Görg (2006) find support for the hypothesis that only firms with some minimum level of absorptive capacity benefit from productivity spillovers in their analysis using British establishment level data.

Arguably, and this has been put forward in the recent literature as another explanation for the lack of evidence on positive spillovers, a simple search for purely horizontal spillovers misses a much more complex picture of knowledge diffusion. If multinationals prevent the transfer of their firm-specific knowledge to domestic competitors in the same industry, there is no scope for intra-industry knowledge spillovers. It is possible, however, that multinational firms voluntarily or involuntarily help to increase the efficiency of domestic suppliers or customers through vertical input-output linkages. Multinationals may provide technical assistance to suppliers to help them raise the quality of the intermediate products they produce, or they may simply insist on high quality standards for local inputs, providing incentives for local suppliers to upgrade their technology.[11] Multinationals may also provide active assistance or passive guidelines to domestic customers on the most effective way to use the products the firms supply.

Several recent studies have empirically investigated vertical spillovers. The most frequently cited of those is Javorcik (2004) who develops the idea that spillovers are more likely to occur through vertical relationships, rather than horizontally as has been the predominant view in the literature. Using firm level panel data for Lithuania for 1996 – 2000 she finds evidence consistent with her conjecture. Domestic firms in sector *j* increase their productivity following the presence of multinationals in industries which are being supplied by *j*. She refers to this as spillovers through backward linkages. While the evidence on such backward linkages is robust to a number of amendments, there is no robust evidence that domestic firms benefit from horizontal spillovers from multinationals. Blalock and Gertler (2003) also find results suggesting positive productivity spillovers through backward linkages in their analysis of Indonesian plant-level panel data. They do not find evidence for horizontal spillovers, however. Furthermore, Girma et al. (2005), using UK firm-level data, find that vertical linkages are important for spillovers, and that there are substantial differences in such spillover benefits, depending on whether multinationals are export or domestic-market oriented.

14.4 Evidence for Ireland

This section focuses on the evidence for spillover effects from multinationals in Ireland. Few would doubt that the influx of FDI over the last three decades has been an important factor for the Irish growth experience (e.g., Sachs, 1997; Barry, 1999) not least since multinationals, due to their being on average more productive than domestic firms (as pointed out in Section 14.2) contribute to higher aggregate productivity growth in the economy. However, there remains the question as to whether the more productive multinationals also contribute spillover benefits to local firms. Perhaps surprisingly, there is little formal econometric evidence addressing this issue and linking the presence of foreign multinationals to productivity growth in domestic firms at the micro level.

Ruane and Ugur (2005b) implement the conventional approach of measuring productivity spillovers for the Irish economy. They use plant level panel data available from the Irish Central Statistics Office for manufacturing industries covering the period 1991 to 1998. They regress labour productivity (defined as net output per worker) on the employment share of foreign-owned firms in the same industry (defined alternatively at the two, three and four digit level) and control for capital intensity, skill intensity as well as firm specific time invariant effects. They do not find any statistically significant evidence for productivity spillovers from these regressions.

In alternative estimations, they use a similar set up but include the *level* of employment in foreign-owned firms in the industry (rather than employment *share*) as the 'spillover variable', controlling additionally for total employment in domestic firms also. They argue that this may perhaps be a more appropriate approach to measuring spillovers in the Irish case, as the employment *share* of foreign owned firms changed only marginally over the period analysed (due to an increase in the level of domestic employment), while the *level* of employment in foreign multinationals increased substantially. It is noteworthy that, from these estimations they find robust evidence for horizontal spillovers based on the 4-digit definition of the industry, however, not for two or three digit definitions. In other words, only when industries are defined very narrowly do they find evidence for spillovers. This may reflect that spillovers vary substantially across narrowly defined sectors and that they cannot be detected when aggregating industries.

Barry et al. (2005) provide a similar analysis based on plant level data from the Forfás Irish Economy Expenditure Survey for the period 1990 to 1998.[12] They estimate equations regressing alternatively labour or TFP in domestic firms on the employment share in foreign owned firms in the same two digit industry – in other words, sectors are fairly widely defined. Similar to the first set of regressions in Ruane and Ugur (2005b) they fail to detect any evidence for positive spillovers in their estimation.

While the two aforementioned studies are applications of the traditional spillover studies as found in the literature, Görg and Strobl (2003) present an alternative way of examining these. Their approach is based on the idea that an increase in productivity through spillovers will, all other things being equal, reduce a host country firm's average cost of production and, hence, increase profitability. Profitability, in turn, has long been regarded as a main determinant of firm survival. Hence, technology spillovers from multinationals and the associated increase in productivity should lead to a higher probability of survival for host country firms.

They test their hypothesis using data from the Forfás Employment Survey covering the period 1973 to 1996. The advantage of using this data set is that it covers virtually the whole population of manufacturing plants in Ireland.[13] In the empirical analysis, using a Cox proportional hazard model they find that, controlling for other plant and sector specific effects, the presence of multinationals (measured as the foreign employment share) has a life enhancing effect only on domestic plants operating in high technology sectors. This suggests that there may be productivity spillovers taking place in these industries. They do, however, not find any evidence for such effects on the survival of domestic plants in low technology industries.[14] Their interpretation of these results is that firms in low tech sectors may not have the necessary absorptive capacity to utilise the relevant knowledge from multinationals and, hence, are not able to benefit from spillovers, an issue discussed in Section 14.3.

Görg and Strobl (2002) and Barrios et al. (2005) develop another alternative approach to gauge the effect of multinationals on the development of domestic plants in Ireland. They apply and extend a theoretical approach by Markusen and Venables (1999), which argues that multinationals, through developing backward linkages with domestic suppliers increase markets for these firms and, hence, increase their profits in the short run. This can lead to a further entry of new domestic firms in supplier industries, which will drive down the price of supplies, also increasing the scope for the entry of new domestic firms in final good industries.

In line with this idea, Görg and Strobl (2002) and Barrios et al. (2005) investigate econometrically whether the entry rate of domestic firms in an industry is positively related to the presence of multinationals (again measured as foreign employment share) in the same industry. Both studies use data from the Forfás Employment Survey since 1973. Supporting their theoretical expectation they find evidence that the presence of multinationals indeed has a positive effect on the entry rate of domestic firms. This is taken to indicate that spillovers from multinationals encourage Irish entrepreneurs to set up new firms, either in supplier or in final good industries.[15]

14.5 Conclusions

As was seen in Section 14.3, the international evidence on productivity spillovers from multinationals is mixed. The most plausible interpretations for the lack of consistent findings are that, firstly, country characteristics matter, secondly, individual firms' level of absorptive capacity is important (i.e., they must posses a certain ability before they can usefully apply the knowledge from a multinational) and, thirdly, focusing purely on horizontal spillovers misses important vertical channels of knowledge transfer, in particular through backward linkages, which may bestow larger external effects.

This provides important implications for policymakers as it suggests that policy can be usefully targeted at these issues in order to maximise spillover benefits, rather than focusing solely on attracting ever more multinationals into the economy. In order to assist domestic firms to strengthen their absorptive capacity government could aim to improve R&D and, more generally, innovation activity, as well as targeting training and general skill upgrading activities in the economy. Hence, innovation, education and training policies are likely to be key to facilitating spillovers. In order to boost vertical spillovers policy can be aimed at encouraging multinationals to generate linkages with the domestic economy.[16] Here government can usefully act as a provider of information to potential new inward investors, on availability and location of sub-suppliers. Another potential area where government can act in this regard is to ensure quality standards of and competition among local suppliers.

For the Irish case, the few papers that applied the 'traditional approach' of measuring spillovers do not come up with overwhelming and unambiguous support for positive effects. Given that Ireland is widely regarded as having benefited from inward investment it is unlikely that it is a country that is, in Lipsey and Sjöholm's words "unable to learn from foreign-owned firms" (2005: 40). Also, the evidence from the 'alternative approaches' discussed in Section 14.4 suggests that there are positive effects on the development of domestic firms. Hence, multinationals can be regarded as having brought important spillover benefits to domestic firms in the Irish economy. What is a plausible interpretation of the results in the spillovers studies is that, in line with the findings of the international literature, they do not take adequate account of the importance of absorptive capacity and vertical linkages.

The finding by Görg and Strobl (2003) that only firms in high tech industries benefit from multinationals in terms of having higher probabilities of survival is in line with the argument that firms are more likely to benefit from technology spillovers if they have the necessary absorptive capacity to do so. However, a simple distinction between high and low technology sectors is arguably a crude way of measuring absorptive capacity; further research into this direction should be fruitful in order to gauge the importance and magnitude of spillovers for different types of domestic firms with heterogeneous levels of absorptive capacity. As regards the role of vertical linkages, multinationals in Ireland have relatively strong backward linkages with the local economy and one would, therefore, expect a potential for vertical spillovers.[17] Hewitt-Dundas et al. (2002) provide an interesting analysis as regards the importance of linkages. They report results from a survey, which asked managers of foreign-owned plants based in Ireland about their input-sourcing behaviour, and the perceived impact they had on the performance of local suppliers.[18] They find, *inter alia*, that knowledge gaps exist between the multinationals and their best local suppliers, suggesting that there is a potential for knowledge spillovers. They also present some case study evidence of how these knowledge transfers take place. Furthermore, they report that a large proportion of multinationals argue to have had a significant impact on the performance of their local suppliers through knowledge spillovers.

Hence, the policy implications from the research on Irish data are similar to those from the international studies: targeting absorptive capacity and vertical linkages is crucial. However, more evidence should be useful to get a better idea of the precise importance of absorptive capacity and vertical linkages in Ireland, to inform policymakers and allow targeting policies appropriately.

Notes

1 There is a related literature which investigates whether inward FDI fosters economic growth using macro-level data. For example, Borensztein et al. (1998) and Alfaro et al. (2003) show that inward FDI can have positive growth effects if countries have a certain level of human capital or well developed financial markets.

2 For example, the know-how available in the microchip producer Intel can be seen as a FSA. This can be easily transferred within the firm, from the parent in the US to subsidiaries abroad.

3 In the datasets used, foreign firms are generally defined as those with at least 50 percent foreign ownership.

4 The data for foreign multinationals have of course to be taken with a grain of salt due to the possibility of the figures being distorted through transfer pricing. However, the evidence for Ireland, taken together with the large body of international evidence, can still be taken to suggest that foreign owned multinationals are 'better' along a number of firm characteristics than their domestic owned counterparts, even if the accurate level of foreign firms' advantage is unclear.

5 Their findings are in line with recent heterogeneous firms models which predict that among firms, the most productive will choose to become multinationals, less productive firms export and the least productive ones serve purely the domestic market (Helpman et al., 2004).

6 This section draws on earlier work by Görg and Strobl (2001) and Görg and Greenaway (2004).

7 See Görg and Greenaway (2004) for a review of this literature.

8 They argue that panels, using longitudinal firm or plant level data are the most appropriate estimating framework for two reasons. Firstly, longitudinal data studies allow one to investigate the development of domestic firms' productivity over a longer time period, rather than relying on one data point. Secondly, they allow one to investigate spillovers after controlling for other factors. Cross sectional data, in particular if they are aggregated at the sectoral level, fail to control for time-invariant differences in productivity across sectors which might be correlated with, but not caused by, foreign presence. Thus coefficients on cross-section estimates are likely to be biased. For example, if productivity in the electronics sector is higher than, say, the food sector, multinationals may be attracted into the former. In a cross section, one would find a positive and statistically significant relationship between the level of foreign investment and domestic productivity, consistent with spillovers, even though foreign investment did not cause high levels of productivity but rather was attracted by them.

9 For example, Larrain, Lopez-Calva and Rodriguez-Claré (2000) conclude that the location of Intel in Costa Rica has had positive effects on the local economy, while Hanson (2000) argues that there is little evidence for spillovers from Intel on domestic firms.

10 Evidence for positive effects of competition are found by Kokko (1996) for Mexico and Driffield (2001) for the United Kingdom.

11 Moran (2001) provides a number of case studies which show that this happens frequently in practice.

12 In comparison to the CSO data used by Ruane and Ugur (2005b), which include all industrial local units with three or more employees, their data set only includes a sample of plants with at least 20 employees.

13 One of the disadvantages is that only employment is recorded; hence, there is no possibility of using data from this survey for productivity analyses.

14 Their classification of industries is based on the OECD definition of high and low tech industries.

15 This is in line with earlier evidence provided by Cogan and Onyemadum (1981) which look at new domestic spin-off companies from foreign multinationals in the Irish electronics industry.

16 It is important to point out that this is not imply a supporting argument for the use of local content requirements, as these may have more harmful than beneficial effects – inter alia, they are likely to deter multinationals from investing in the country in the first place (Görg and Greenaway, 2004).

17 See Görg and Ruane (2001) for recent evidence using plant level data for the electronics industry from the Forfás Irish Economy Expenditure Survey.

18 An additional interesting point about the paper is that it includes a comparison of data for the Republic and Northern Ireland.

References

Aitken, B.J. and Harrison, A.E. (1999), "Do Domestic Firms Benefit from Direct Foreign Investment? Evidence from Venezuela", *American Economic Review*, Vol. 89, 605-618.

Alfaro, L., Areendam, C., Kalemli, K.O. and Sayek, S. (2003), "FDI and Economic Growth: The Role of Local Financial Markets", *Journal of International Economics.*

Barrios, S., Görg, H. and Strobl, E. (2005), "Foreign Direct Investment, Competition and Industrial Development in the Host Country", *European Economic Review*, 49(7): 1761-1784.

Barry, F. (1999), *Understanding Ireland's Economic Growth*, London: MacMillan.

Barry, F., Bradley J. and O'Malley, E. (1999), "Indigenous and Foreign Industry: Characteristics and Performance", in Barry, F. (ed.), *Understanding Ireland's Economic Growth*, London: MacMillan: 45-74.

Barry, F., Görg, H. and Strobl, E. (2005), "Foreign Direct Investment and Wages in Domestic Firms in Ireland: Productivity Spillovers versus Labour-market Crowding Out" *International Journal of the Economics of Business*, 12(1): 67-84.

Blalock, G. and Gertler, P. (2003), "Technology from Foreign Direct Investment and Welfare Gains through the Supply Chain", mimeo, Cornell University, Ithaca, N.Y.

Blomström, M. (1986), "Foreign Investment and Productive Efficiency: The Case of Mexico", *Journal of Industrial Economics*, 35(1): 97–112.

Borensztein, E., De Gregorio, J. and Lee, J.W. (1998), "How Does Foreign Direct Investment Affect Economic Growth?", *Journal of International Economics* , 45(1): 115–35.

Caves, R.E. (1974), "Multinational Firms, Competition, and Productivity in Host-Country Markets", *Economica*, 41(162): 176–93.

Caves, R.E. (1996), *Multinational Enterprise and Economic Analysis.* Second Edition. Cambridge: Cambridge University Press.

Cogan, D. and Onyemadum, E. (1981), "Spin-Off Companies in the Irish Electronics Industry", *Irish Journal of Business and Administrative Research*, 3(2): 3-15.

Driffield, N. (2001), "The Impact on Domestic Productivity of Inward Investment in the UK", *The Manchester School*, 69(1): 103–19.

Girma, S. (2005), "Geographic Proximity, Absorptive Capacity and Productivity Spillovers from FDI: A Threshold Regression Analysis", *Oxford Bulletin of Economics and Statistics.*

Girma, S. and Görg, H. (2006), "The Role of the Efficiency Gap for Spillovers from FDI: Evidence from Quantile Regressions", *Open Economies Review*, forthcoming.

Girma, S. and Görg, H. (2007), "Multinationals' Productivity Advantage: Scale or Technology?", *Economic Inquiry*, forthcoming.

Girma, S., Görg, H. and Pisu, M. (2005), "Exporting, Linkages and Productivity Spillovers from Foreign Direct Investment". mimeo, University of Nottingham.

Girma, S., Görg, H. and Strobl. E. (2004), "Exports, International Investment and Plant Performance: Evidence From a Non-Parametric Test", *Economics Letters*, 83, 317-324.

Globerman, S. (1979), "Foreign Direct Investment and 'Spillover' Efficiency Benefits in Canadian Manufacturing Industries", *Canadian Journal of Economics*, 12(4): 42–56.

Görg, H. and Greenaway, D. (2004), "Much Ado About Nothing? Do Domestic Firms Really Benefit From Foreign Direct Investment?", *World Bank Research Observer*, 19(2): 171-197.

Görg, H. and Ruane, F. (2000), "An Analysis of Backward Linkages in the Irish Electronics Sector", *Economic and Social Review*, 31(3): 215-235.

Görg, H. and Strobl, E. (2001), "Multinational Companies and Productivity Spillovers: A Meta-Analysis", *Economic Journal*,111 (473): F723–39.

Görg, H. and Strobl, E. (2002),"Multinational Companies and Indigenous Development: An Empirical Analysis", *European Economic Review*, 46(7): 1305-1322.

Görg, H. and Strobl, E. (2003), "Multinational Companies, Technology Spillovers and Plant Survival", *Scandinavian Journal of Economics*, 105(4): 581–95.

Hanson, G.H. (2001), "Should Countries Promote Foreign Direct Investment?", G-24 Discussion Paper 9, UNCTAD, Geneva.

Haskel, J., Pereira, C. and Slaughter, M. (2002), "Does Inward Foreign Direct Investment boost the Productivity of Domestic Firms?", *NBER Working Paper* 8724, Cambridge, Mass: National Bureau of Economic Research.

Head, K. (1998), Comment on "Comparing Wages, Skills, and Productivity between Domestically and Foreign-Owned Manufacturing Establishments in the United States". In Baldwin, R., Lipsey, R. and Richardson, J.D. eds., *Geography and Ownership as Bases for Economic Accounting*, Chicago, Chicago University Press.

Helpman, E., Meltiz, M.J. and Yeaple, S.R. (2004), "Export versus FDI with Heterogeneous Firms", *American Economic Review*.

Hewitt-Dundas, N., Andreosso-O'Callaghan, B., Crone, M., Murray, J. and Roper, S. (2002), "Knowledge Transfers from Multi-national Plants in Ireland – A Cross-border Comparison of Supply Chain Linkages", Working Paper No. 72, Northern Ireland Economic Research Centre, Belfast.

Javorcik, B. (2004), "Does Foreign Direct Investment Increase the Productivity of Domestic Firms? In Search of Spillovers through Backward Linkages", *American Economic Review.*

Keller, W. and Yeaple, S. (2003), "Multinational Enterprises, International Trade, and Productivity Growth: Firm-Level Evidence from the United States", GEP Research Paper 03/03, University of Nottingham, United Kingdom.

Kokko, A., Tansini, R. and Zejan, M. (1996), "Local Technological Capability and Productivity Spillovers from FDI in the Uruguayan Manufacturing Sector", *Journal of Development Studies,* 32: 602–11.

Konings, J. (2001), "The Effects of Foreign Direct Investment on Domestic Firms: Evidence from Firm Level Panel Data in Emerging Economies", *Economics of Transition,* 9(3): 619–33.

Krugman, P. (1991), *Geography and Trade,* Cambridge, MA: MIT Press.

Larrain, F., Lopez-Calva, L. and Rodriguez-Claré, A. (2000), "Intel: A Case Study of Foreign Direct Investment in Central America", Center for International Development Working Paper 58, Harvard University, Cambridge, Mass.

Lipsey, R. and Sjöholm, F. (2005), "The Impact of Inward FDI on Host Countries: Why Such Different Answers?" in Moran, T., Graham, E. and Blomström, M. (eds.): *Does Foreign Direct Investment Promote Development?,* Washington, D.C.: Institute for International Economics.

Markusen, J. (2002), *Multinational Firms and the Theory of International Trade,* Cambridge, MA, MIT Press.

Markusen, J. and Venables, A. (1999), "Foreign Direct Investment as a Catalyst for Industrial Development" *European Economic Review* 43: 335-356.

Moran, T. (2001), *Parental Supervision: The New Paradigm for Foreign Direct Investment and Development,* Washington, D.C.: Institute for International Economics.

Ruane, F. and Ugur, A. (2005a), "Labour Productivity and Foreign Direct Investment in Irish Manufacturing Industry: A Decomposition Analysis", *Economic and Social Review,* 36(1): 19-43.

Ruane, F. and Ugur, A. (2005b), "Foreign Direct Investment and Productivity Spillovers in Irish Manufacturing Industry: Evidence from Firm Level Panel Data", *International Journal of the Economics of Business,* 11(3): 53-66.

Sachs, J. (1997), "Ireland's Growth Strategy: Lessons for Economic Development", in Gray, A. (ed.): *International Perspectives on the Irish Economy,* Dublin.

United Nations (2005), *World Investment Report 2005: Transnational Corporations and the Internationalization of R&D,* United Nations: Paris.

CHAPTER 15

REGIONAL POLICY AND AGGLOMERATION ECONOMIES IN IRELAND

EOIN O'LEARY

ABSTRACT

In this chapter O'Leary extends the definition of agglomeration beyond a focus on industry clusters, defining six kinds of potential agglomeration economies. He concludes that agglomeration economies have had a positive impact in Irish industries, though not through the channels that have up to now been considered important. For example, the advantages of urbanisation may have been underestimated by policymakers - a well functioning city, with a high degree of economic and social diversity might be a fertile seed-bed for the development of new ideas. O'Leary then considers the implications this analysis has for the role of spatial policy in promoting the competitiveness of Irish industries

15.1 Introduction

Since the emergence of regional divergence during the 1990s, regional policy is back on the Irish policy agenda. The National Spatial Strategy 2002-2020 was the first major regional policy statement by an Irish government in decades. In an analysis of the sources of regional divergence during the 'Celtic Tiger' boom, I have previously shown that strong regional living standards divergence during the period 1993 to 1999 was driven both by the emergence of the 'demographic dividend' and by regional productivity divergence, which in turn, was driven from the manufacturing sector. I went on to argue that future growth in regional and therefore national living standards hinges on continued productivity growth in internationally competitive industries based in Irish regions (O'Leary, 2002/03).

My objective in this chapter is to reflect on the role that might be played by agglomeration economies and diseconomies in the future productivity trends of Irish regions. I begin by asking what has happened to the trend in regional divergence between 1999 and 2003. This is followed by a consideration of a number of scenarios that might shape future trends in regional divergence or convergence. I then turn to the role that might be played by six kinds of agglomeration economies in driving regional productivity. The importance in the Irish context of considering the different kinds of agglomeration economies, many of which have been ignored, is discussed. The chapter ends with an outline of the implications for policymakers.

15.2 Regional Divergence Post 'Celtic Tiger'

The early years of the new millennium marked a slowdown in the 'Celtic-Tiger' growth rates of the 1990s. It is therefore interesting to check what effect this slowdown had on the rate of Irish regional divergence. Figure 15.1 shows the trend in the degree of regional divergence in the official measure of living standards from 1991 to 2003 (the most recent year for which we have official regional data). The regions considered are seven Regional Authority Areas with Dublin and the Mid-East regions amalgamated.[1] It should be noted that this measure, Gross Value Added (GVA) per capita, is far from ideal owing to the significant levels of profit repatriations from Ireland. Divergence is measured as the trend in the coefficient of variation in GVA per capita.

The results show that the divergent trend strengthened after 1999. According to O'Leary (2002/03) the rate of GVA per capita divergence during the 'Celtic Tiger' period, 1993 to 1999, was + 4.4 per cent per annum. Between 1999 and 2003, the results reveal a trend of + 3.5 per cent per annum. Strong regional divergence should be a cause for concern for policymakers. In the present context, the question arises as to whether regional productivity differences have continued to be a source of this strengthening divergence.

Figure 15.1: Dispersion of Regional GVA per Capita, 1993-2003.

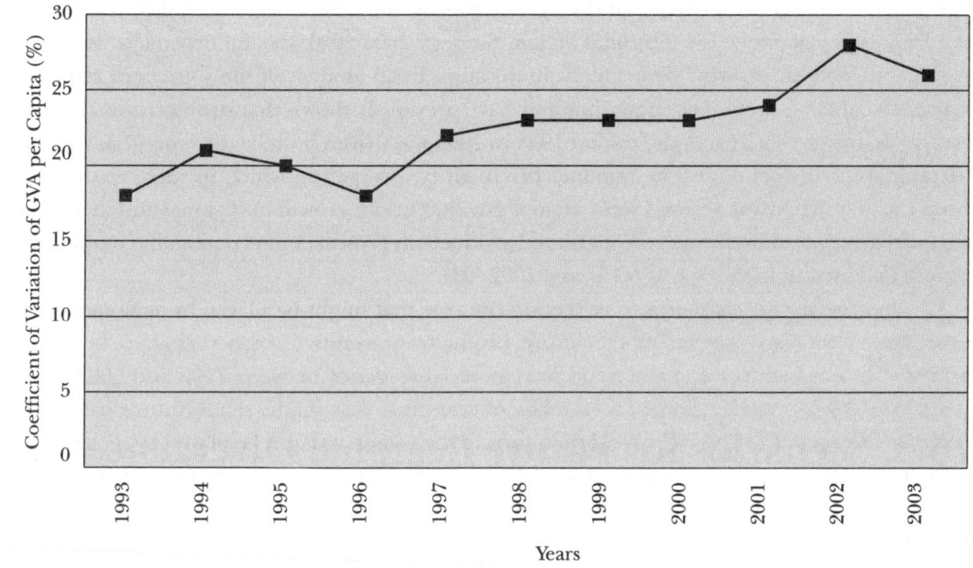

Source: O'Leary (2002/03) and Central Statistics Office (2006).

O'Leary (2002/03) showed that productivity divergence was a major source of the strong living standards divergence between Irish regions from 1993 to 1999. The rate of labour productivity divergence during this period was + 3.6 per cent per annum. Table 15.1 shows the relative levels of labour productivity in 1999 and 2003. These results indicate that between these years the rate of productivity divergence strengthened considerably to + 7.5 per cent per annum. It is noticeable that the Border, Midlands and West (BMW) regions have failed to catch up on the national average. However, the main feature is the very strong performance of the South-West, which increased its lead to nearly 30 percentage points on Dublin/Mid-East. This result is undoubtedly affected by the practice of transfer pricing, particularly by the pharmaceutical industry based in the Cork area. O'Leary (2003a) attempted to adjust Irish regional productivity estimates for transfer pricing and showed relatively minor alterations to the overall divergent trend between 1979 and 1996. However, the method used is fairly crude and the results are probably time dependent. In order to clarify the extent of Irish productivity divergence post 'Celtic-Tiger' more work needs to be conducted to improve the accuracy of Irish regional output estimates.

However, notwithstanding these measurement issues, it appears that productivity divergence remains one of the main sources of the increasing divergence of living standards after the 'Celtic Tiger'. Before considering the role that might be played by agglomeration economies and diseconomies, the discussion now turns to possible future scenarios of Irish trends in regional divergence or convergence.

Table 15.1: Relative Levels of GVA per Worker and Coefficient of Variation among Irish Regions (%): 1999 and 2003

Regions	1999	2003
Border	82	82
Midlands	70	67
West	77	71
Dublin/Mid-East	112	108
Mid-West	89	89
South-East	87	88
South-West	118	137
Coefficient of Variation	20	26

Source: Central Statistics Office (2006).

15.3 Scenarios for Future Regional Divergence/ Convergence Trends

O'Leary (2003b) proposed two scenarios in order to consider whether the increasing trend in Irish regional divergence is likely to continue over the next decade or so. The first, a regional convergence scenario, involves a productivity slowdown in relatively rich regions such as Dublin/Mid-East and the South-West with relatively poor regions, such as the Border and the Midlands being successful at exploiting their catch-up potential. The second, a regional divergence scenario, assumes the rich regions will grow richer with the poor regions stagnating. These scenarios are presented in Table 15.2.

The first scenario may appeal to the neo-classical convergence mechanism which assumes diminishing marginal returns to capital accumulation or to technological catch-up. Convergence, despite implicit assumptions to the contrary from Honohan and Walsh (2002) in their commentary on the causes of the 'Celtic Tiger' boom, cannot be regarded as automatic, even if the national policy obstacles to it are removed. The second scenario invokes the theory of cumulative causation and the more recent 'new growth' literature, which envisages that rich regions may have advantages over poor regions as a result of increasing returns to such factors as education, 'learning by doing' or research and development.

It might appear as if the second scenario describes the evolution of Irish regional disparities over the past decade. However, more research needs to be undertaken in order to determine whether 'rich' regions have benefited from increasing returns. In addition, research is required to examine the extent to which 'poor' regions have failed to exploit their growth potential. There is a significant research agenda here that generally remains unexplored. This is partly due to the absence of detailed regional data from official sources. This research is important for understanding the probability that either scenario, or indeed a combination of them, might transpire in future.

Table 15.2: Regional Growth Scenarios

	'Rich' Regions	**'Poor' Regions**
Scenario 1: Regional Convergence	Experiencing Productivity Slowdown	Exploiting Catch-Up Potential
Scenario 2: Regional Divergence	Benefiting from Increasing Returns	Falling Behind

Source: Based on O'Leary (2003b).

Of particular interest in this chapter, is the geographical dimension to our understanding of the future drivers of productivity growth in Irish regions. O'Leary (2003b) suggested that under scenario 1, the Williamson (1965) hypothesis may be invoked as this suggests that as countries catch-up regional disparities may initially increase, due to the emergence of growth poles, but may subsequently lessen as urban diseconomies emerge. For scenario 2, agglomeration economies in rich urban centres may be the cause of increasing returns facing these regions. In order to further explore the issues involved here, the next section considers the nature of agglomeration economies and diseconomies.

15.4 Defining Agglomeration Economies and Diseconomies

This section draws heavily from an important article on the subject by John Parr (2002).[2] Parr argues that, despite the burgeoning interest in the subject of agglomeration economies, "a certain vagueness continues to surround [it]" (2002: 151). An agglomeration economy may be defined as an increase in the productivity or a decrease in the unit cost of a business, consequent on the concentration of economic activity at a given location. Parr defines agglomeration economies as particular kinds of internal and external economies of scale, scope and complexity. Figure 15.2 depicts agglomeration economies as a subset of these economies (see shaded areas).

Figure 15.2: Agglomeration Economies (Shaded Areas) in the Context of Internal and External Economies of the Business

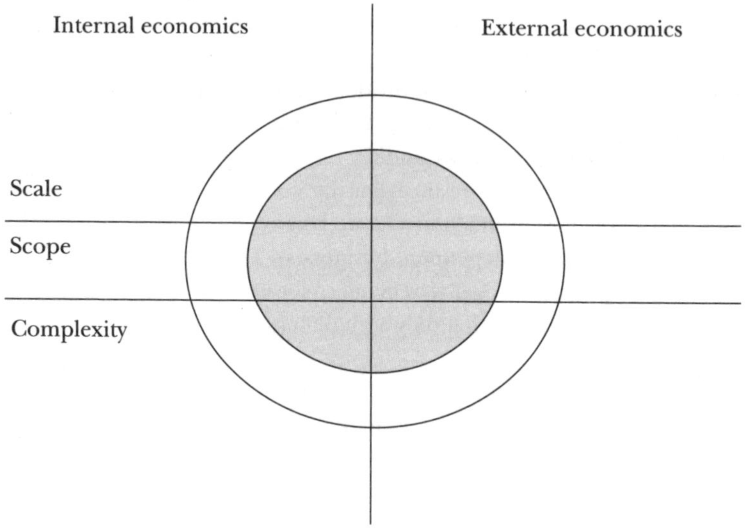

Source: Parr, (2002: 159).

Following Parr (2002), we can define each of the six kinds of agglomeration economies.

1. *Internal economies of scale* refer to productivity gains in the business as a result of increases in its production of a given product. This may involve mergers or acquisitions (i.e. horizontal integration). It is an agglomeration economy if it results in the concentration of production at a given location;
2. *Internal economies of scope* relate to the scope or diversity of production by a business. This results where the production by a given business of two or more different products occurs at a lower cost than would be the case in separate businesses. The efficiency gain results from a shared input in the business. It is an agglomeration economy where this shared input is restricted to a specific location;
3. *Internal economies of complexity* might apply where a business's production involves several technologically separable stages. They occur where the undertaking of various stages of production of a product by a single business result in higher productivity than if the stages were carried out in separate businesses. This vertically integrated business experiences an internal agglomeration economy where the stages are co-located;
4. *External economies of localisation* refer to the common location of a number of independent businesses in the same industry. They are best thought of as economies of scale in that they arise due the common location of like businesses. Originally identified by Marshall (1892) who pointed to the three classic sources of localisation economies as being the availability of (i) a skilled labour pool; (ii) a range of auxiliary trades and specialized services; and (iii) knowledge spillovers. Porter's discussion of clusters most closely resembles this form of agglomeration economy, although he puts more emphasis on businesses competing with each other (1990 and 1998);

5. *External economies of urbanisation* relates to the common location of businesses belonging to different and unrelated industries. Sources of urbanisation economies include the availability of a range of public utilities and services, transportation and communications infrastructures, the existence of a variety of business services and the plentiful supply of labour of different kinds. These economies, which are often associated with Jacobs (1960), are best regarded as a function of the scope or diversity of production that might prevail in an urban setting. Productivity in individual businesses is increased as a result of the presence of public and private services and infrastructures that could only be available in cities where sufficient demand exists; and
6. *External activity-complex economies* result from the common location of a particular set of businesses that exist in a production chain. This might refer to backward or forward linkages from a business to independent business(s). This is an agglomeration economy if the business enjoys productivity gains by being co-located with suppliers or buyers. It differs from a localisation economy in that only a single business is involved.

For each of the six kinds of agglomeration economies considered above it is possible to think of agglomeration diseconomies. Thus, the potential exists for internal diseconomies of scale, scope or complexity where for example technological and/or management difficulties within the business result in lower productivity at a specific location. Similarly, external diseconomies may occur. For example, urban diseconomies associated with factors such as congestion or pollution might outweigh any of the positive effects of an urban location. The key point is that agglomeration economies and diseconomies may co-exist so that the key objective facing a business is to maximise the former and minimise the latter.

In outlining Parr's classification of agglomeration economies this section has begun to highlight some important issues for Irish policymakers. The next section continues by assessing the relevance of Parr's classification to Ireland's internationally competitive industry.

15.5 Agglomeration and the Irish Economy

This section first provides a brief overview of Irish internationally competitive industry. It then considers the extent to which Parr's classification may be important for our understanding of the importance of spatial issues for the competitiveness of these industries.

A list of Ireland's internationally competitive industries might include industries such as pharmaceuticals, electronics, medical devices, financial services, software and perhaps food.[3] These industries are dominated by foreign-owned multi-national businesses using Ireland as an export-platform. Although there may be a number of individual businesses in a sector, broadly defined, these businesses are seldom in direct competition with each other. The small size of the domestic market ensures that indigenous businesses have to export at an early stage in their evolution in order to become competitive.

In assessing the relevance of Parr's classification to these industries, four points are made. The first is to note the possibility that agglomeration economies of scale are not necessarily external to the business. It is possible that internal economies of scale are evident in many of the very large foreign-owned businesses in sectors such as pharmaceuticals and electronics. Thus for example, due to increased division of labour, the Pfizer plant in Cork may benefit from productivity gains associated with increased production of its key ingredient of 'Viagra'.

Possibilities also exist for internal economies of scope, where for example the Pfizer plant might use immobile machinery to produce other drugs.

It is equally plausible to think of these businesses benefiting from internal economies of complexity, where various stages of production, which might otherwise be located in other plants in the corporation, are present in the Irish plant. Thus, the Dell computer plant in Limerick might benefit as a result of the manufacturing and distribution stages of its computer operation being located there.[4] The key issue is that in both cases the benefits arise from within the business and are not attributable to the particular aspects of the external environment that are usually associated with agglomeration economies. This has important implications for policymakers which will be discussed later.

Second, in relation to external economies of localisation it is worthwhile to consider the extent to which the three classic sources identified by Marshall might be present in Irish industries. In relation to labour, there is little doubt but that the availability of a young skilled labour force has made an important contribution to the 'Celtic Tiger' phenomenon. However, 'skilled' here typically refers to workers with formal educational qualifications. In order to qualify as a 'skilled labour pool' the skills would, to a significant extent, need to be specific to the particular industry concerned. While the foundations for such skills may be acquired in formal education it is likely that experience acquired 'on-the-job' is the key. Such skills may be said to be in the local/regional economy, and therefore available as an external economy, if there is significant churning in the labour market as workers move between businesses or found new businesses in the same industry.

Thus, the key question for localisation analysis is to determine the extent to which this occurs in Irish industry. In the case of the Irish Pharmaceutical industry for example, Van Egeraat's (2006) evidence suggests that skills that are available externally have been acquired in third level institutions and not 'on-the-job'. On the other hand, in the Dublin software industry, where businesses are smaller and are increasingly founded as entrepreneurial spin-offs from existing businesses, skills might be more transferable (Crone, 2004).

Regarding the presence of forward and backward linkages, compared to the features of a classic localisation economy, it is likely that fewer possibilities exist for linkages with foreign-owned businesses in Ireland. This is because as subsidiaries these businesses are typically part of vertically integrated corporations who often source suppliers in the home country and distributors on mainland Europe. Gallagher, Doyle and O'Leary (2002) conclude, from a survey of the literature, that there is limited evidence of linkages in Irish internationally competitive industry. This is supported by the findings of Barry, Gorg and Strobl (2003) for Irish manufacturing.

Turning to the notion of knowledge spillovers, which is the third source of external economies of localisation. Since knowledge spills-over from workers and via external linkages it is likely that, given the preceding argument, fewer possibilities might exist here. In this regard a survey on innovation in Irish based high-technology sectors has shown that although strong interaction with suppliers and customers takes place, it does so over four hours average driving time (Jordan and O'Leary, 2005). This might suggest that in the Irish case geographical proximity may not be crucial for innovation and competitiveness of these businesses. However, as with the other two sources of localisation, more research needs to be conducted in order to more fully determine the extent of localisation economies in Irish industry.

Third, urbanisation economies have tended to be overlooked in much of the Irish discussion about agglomeration. This may be explained by the discussion failing to make a distinction between localisation and urbanisation economies. A notable exception is the detailed study by Van Egeraat of the Irish pharmaceutical industry who concludes by stating that "to the extent that agglomeration economies have influenced the location of the drug-substance industry, these have been, and to a large extent still are, mainly urbanisation economies"(2006: 21). This industry is concentrated in the urban centres of Dublin and Cork. The benefits associated with these locations are the availability of labour supply with third level qualifications and the quality of life available in these population centres.[5] Clearly a significant and important research agenda might be followed in order to understand the relative importance of these kinds of external agglomeration economies in other Irish industries.

In addition, the presence of urbanisation diseconomies and their effect on these industries should be investigated. For example, the effects of rising land values and congestion in Dublin might mitigate the agglomeration economies to be achieved by industries located there. This is what is envisaged in the Williamson (1965) hypothesis mentioned under scenario 1 above.

Finally, the possible existence of *activity complex economies* should be considered in the Irish case. This might refer to businesses supplying inputs to or distributing the output of a given business. This may be relevant for some of the foreign-owned assembly plants based here. A case in point might be the Intel plant in Kildare, which was accompanied by its independent suppliers when they first located there (O'Sullivan, 2000: 281). This form of agglomeration may arise as a result of large vertically integrated businesses out-sourcing key inputs or services to independent operations. If benefits accrue to these businesses being local, then an agglomeration economy is present.

Before considering the implication of the above discussion for policymakers, it is worth investigating further causes of the concentration of foreign-owned industry in Irish towns and cities. One possibility is the so-called demonstration or reputation effects, associated with Krugman (1997), which results in businesses mimicking each others location decisions. Barry, Gorg and Strobl (2003) have shown that these effects, which in their purest form are not agglomeration economies, may also be important determinants of US business's entry into Ireland. Other possibilities include factors unrelated to geography, such as Ireland's cost competitiveness relative to other countries and government policies. It is therefore important to establish not only the relative importance of each type of agglomeration economy, but also the importance of these other factors which may have played a key role.

15.6 Implications for Irish Policymakers

This section begins by showing how Irish regional and enterprise policies are not integrated. It then proceeds to show what policymakers can learn by assessing the relevance of Parr's classification to Ireland's internationally competitive industry.

As a response to Ireland's increasing regional divergence the National Spatial Strategy (2002) was formulated. This proposed an urban hierarchy model, consisting of eight gateways and nine hubs. I have argued that this strategy is more concerned with distribution rather than the mainstream policy goals of growth and competitiveness (O'Leary, 2003b). While I support the urban-hierarchy approach followed in the National Spatial Strategy (2002), too many gateways and hubs were identified. The size of the country will probably only sustain five or six urban centres. However, there is little appetite in Irish regions for developing distinctive policies on economic development. The Regional Planning Guidelines, which gave effect to the National Spatial Strategy in Ireland's regions, were remarkably similar in identifying the same kinds of industries in high-technology knowledge-based sectors.

When it comes to enterprise policy it seems as if little importance is attached to spatial issues. This can be seen for example in the Enterprise Strategy Group report which only once refers to the necessity of implementing the National Spatial Strategy and this is in the context of addressing the infrastructural deficits. Crucially the strategy is not seen as one of the five key sources of future competitive advantage (ESG, 2004: 97-8). It is noteworthy however that despite this, enterprise policymakers have for nearly two decades attached importance to the notion of clusters and networks, which are often thought of as being effected by geography.

The Culliton Report (1992) was the first to stress the importance of local or regional clusters around internationally competitive businesses for improved national competitiveness, and in particular for embedding foreign-owned industry. These prescriptions were strongly influenced by the work of Porter (1990 and 1998). More recently, Forfás recommended that the Government focus on inter-firm networks as a key building block in the development of the innovation capacity of Irish industry (ESG, 2004: 7). The Enterprise Strategy Group also advocated networks involving industry, academic and public sector co-operation to drive the development of knowledge and expertise (ESG, 2004: 53).

It is worthwhile to consider why enterprise policymakers pay scant attention to spatial strategy within the country while at the same time advocating the importance of clusters and networks for future Irish growth and competitiveness. It may be that agglomeration economies are held to have been relatively unimportant to the success of Irish-based industry. Instead, the main causes have been attributed to stable macro-economic policies, low corporation tax and favourable demographics (see for example Kennedy, 2000-01).

The discussion in the last section has highlighted that agglomeration economies are not just limited to localisation economies, as is often implied in the enterprise policy discussions on the issue. A consideration of Parr's classification reveals five other sources of agglomeration, some of which may be crucially important as we face future challenges, such as increasing the innovation performance of Irish-based industry.

In relation to skilled labour, there is a continuing emphasis in policy circles on the importance of formal educational qualifications. For example, the recently launched *New Strategy for Science, Technology and Innovation to 2013* (2006) envisages a doubling of the number of PhD's. From a business perspective the key issue is that educational qualifications, even at PhD level, only provide the basis for the key skills, crucial to the competitiveness of the business, that are necessarily acquired on-the-job. There is no certainty that businesses would have a preference for entrants with higher qualifications such as PhD's. Instead they may prefer to train employees on-the-job. This implies that the benefits attributable to these skills are internal to the business. However, the above discussion implies that these are internal agglomeration economies. So in addition to supporting the development of external agglomeration economies arising from formal educational qualifications, policymakers should also focus on the support of in-employment training. This might better equip the key workers in these businesses to contribute to their enhanced competitiveness in their Irish location. If so, the 'New Strategy' should be re-appraised.

There are examples of Irish subsidiaries of foreign-owned enterprises where local management pursues strategies of developing multiple capabilities in their workforce. The purpose is to enable the subsidiary to be a location for more than just basic assembly for the corporation, thus more deeply embedding it in its Irish location.[6] This is an example of an internal economy of complexity which is also worthy of policy support. Unfortunately, due to the restricted nature of existing enterprise policy instruments, which are based predominantly on 'clusters' or 'networks', these opportunities may be missed.

The imperative of enhancing the innovation performance of Irish industry also has implications for the way policymakers think about supporting external agglomeration economies. There is some international evidence suggesting that diversity might be more conducive to innovation than specialisation (Gordon and McCann 2005; Feldman and Audretsch, 1999). Urbanisation rather than localisation may be important. A well functioning city, with a high degree of economic and social diversity, might be a fertile seed-bed for the development of new ideas. Given that the objective of the New Strategy for Science, Technology and Innovation to 2013 is to develop Ireland as a knowledge economy with a critical mass of creative people (Florida and Tingali, 2004), it might be important for policymakers to consider whether these kinds of urbanisation economies may be developed in Irish cities. The small size of Irish urban centres implies that the level of diversity evident in some of the world's larger cities are clearly not possible here. This does not mean that there are no productivity benefits to be experienced from economic and social diversity in Irish cities. In addition there is considerable scope to bring about improvements in the more mundane aspects of urban living in Ireland, such as transport infrastructure and quality of life aspects in and around urban centres.

There is much evidence suggesting that innovative Irish businesses source ideas through interaction, especially with customers and suppliers. Our survey on innovation in Irish–based high-technology sectors has shown that although strong interaction with suppliers and customers takes place, it does so over long distances (Jordan and O'Leary, 2005). This highlights the importance for innovation of facilitating international interactions by Irish-based business. Thus, once again policies to improve transport and communications infrastructures may have a crucial role to play.

15.7 Final Comment

The discussion has shown, given the size of the country and the dominance of internationally competitive industry by large foreign-owned multi-national businesses, that policymakers should consider other kinds of agglomeration economies, besides localisation economies, as important drivers of Irish regional productivity growth. The scale, scope and complexity of these businesses imply that internal agglomeration economies might warrant attention. In addition, urbanisation economies and external activity-complex economies may also warrant attention from policymakers. Policy failures here might result in agglomeration diseconomies with negative effects on productivity growth in Irish regions.

Successful policy therefore requires collaboration from all Government departments concerned with agglomeration issues. Given the imperative of developing these policies in Irish urban centres it might be important to address the existing over-centralisation of power in Dublin. Genuine decentralisation of governance might enable Irish cities to develop policies that allow them to better reach their growth potential. The problems of high land values and congestion in Dublin, which as a consequence is already witnessing the flight of creative people, point to the growing urgency of addressing these questions.

I have argued before that, given the emergence of a regional problem, Ireland's future growth depends more than ever before on the growth of regions outside Dublin. If all Irish regions, including Dublin, reach their full growth potential then our future prosperity will be assured.[7] In order to meet these challenges policymakers might have to undergo a significant change of mind-set in order to think regionally rather than nationally.

Notes

1 The seven regions are: Border, Midlands, West, Dublin/Mid-East, Mid-West, South–East and South-West. The first three of these NUTS 3 regions represent Ireland's Border, Midlands, West (BMW) NUTS 2, Objective 1 region in transition.
2 The paper won the Moss Madden Memorial Medal in 2002 which is a prestigious award of the British and Irish Section of the Regional Science Association International.
3 This list, which is based on Gallagher, Doyle and O'Leary (2002) who constructed it using the 'revealed comparative advantage' method applied to 1998 data, is suggestive and not meant to be exhaustive.
4 If the distribution stage was situated in another facility of the Dell Corporation on mainland Europe, then the Limerick plant would be benefiting from an internal economy that is not attributable to agglomeration.
5 Interestingly Van Egeraat concludes that factors such as environmental and regional planning policies were more important than agglomeration economies in explaining the concentration of this industry in Dublin and Cork (2006).
6 For example, O'Gara (1996) describes how Pepsi-Cola developed the capability of sourcing shared services in its bottling facility in Cork.
7 Paradoxically, as this involves the most optimistic aspects of the two scenarios depicted in Table 15.2 above, it could correspond to continued regional divergence. However, policymakers and the public at large surely have a revealed preference for growth rather than regional balance.

References

Barry, F., Gorg, H. and Strobl, E. (2003), "Foreign Direct Investment, Agglomerations and Demonstration Effects: An Empirical Investigation", *Review of World Economics/Weltwirtschaftliches,* 139, 4, 583-600.

Central Statistics Office (2006), *County Incomes and Regional GDP: 2002,* Central Statistics Office, 17th August.

Crone, M. (2004), "Celtic Tiger Cubs: Ireland's VC-Funded Software Start-ups", paper presented at the *Institute for Small Business Affairs,* National Entrepreneurship and SME Development Conference, Newcastle-Gateshead, 2-4 November.

Culliton, J. (1992), *A Time for Change: Industrial Policy for the 1990s,* Report of the Industrial Policy Review Group, Dublin.

Department of Enterprise, Trade and Employment (2006), *Strategy for Science, Technology and Innovation 2006-2013,* Stationery Office, Dublin.

Department of the Environment and Local Government (2002), *National Spatial Strategy for Ireland 2002-2020: People, Places and Potential,* Stationery Office, Dublin.

Enterprise Strategy Group (2004), *Ahead of the Curve: Ireland's Place in the Global Economy,* Forfas, Dublin.

Feldman, M. and Audretsch, D. (1999), "Innovation in Cities: Science-based Diversity, Specialization and Localized Competition", *European Economic Review,* 43: 409-429.

Florida, R. and Tingali, I. (2004), "Europe in the Creative Age", February 2004.

Forfás (2004), *Innovation Networks.* Forfás, Dublin.

Gallagher, L., Doyle, E. and O'Leary, E. (2002), "Creating the Celtic Tiger and Sustaining Economic Growth: A Business Perspective". Quarterly Economic Commentary, *Economic and Social Research Institute,* Dublin, Spring, 63-81.

Gordon, I. and McCann, P. (2005), "Innovation, Agglomeration and Regional Development", *Journal of Economic Geography,* 5, 523-543.

Honohan, P. and Walsh, B. (2002), "Catching Up With the Leaders: The Irish Hare", *Brookings Papers on Economic Activity,* 1(1), 1-57.

Jacobs, J. (1960), *The Economy of Cities,* Random House, New York.

Jordan, D. and O'Leary, E. (2005), "The Roles of Interaction and Proximity for Innovation by Irish High-Technology Businesses: Policy Implications", *Quarterly Economic Commentary.* Summer, 86-100.

Kennedy, K. (2000/01), "Symposium on Economic Growth in Ireland: Where has it Come, Where is it Going? Reflections on the Process of Irish Economic Growth", *Journal of the Statistical and Social Inquiry Society of Ireland,* Vol XXX. 123-139.

Krugman, P. (1997), "Good New from Ireland: A Geographical Perspective" In Gray A.W, Editor. *International Perspectives on the Irish Economy,* 38-53, Indecon: Dublin.

Marshall, A. (1892), *Economics of Industry,* MacMillan, London.

O'Gara R. (1996), "How Can the Shared Services Centre at Pepsi Cola International Cork Produce Marketing or Technological Linkages as a Contribution to Achieving Sustainable Competitive Advantage?", MBS (Business Economics) Dissertation, University College Cork.

O'Leary, E. (2003a), "Aggregate and Sectoral Convergence Among Irish Regions: The Role of Structural Change: 1960-96", *International Regional Science Review,* 26 (4), 483-501.

O'Leary, E. (2003b), "A Critical Evaluation of Irish Regional Policy". In Eoin O'Leary (Editor). *Irish Regional Development: A New Agenda,* The Liffey Press, Dublin, 1-37.

O'Leary, E. (2002/03), "Sources of Regional Divergence in the Celtic Tiger: Policy Responses", *Journal of the Statistical and Social Inquiry Society of Ireland,* XXXII: 1-32.

O'Sullivan, M. (2000), "Industrial Development: A New beginning?" In O'Hagan, J.W., (ed.) *The Economy of Ireland: Policy and Performance of a European Region,* 8th edition, Gill and MacMillan, Dublin: 260-285.

Parr, J. (2002), "Missing Elements in the Analysis of Agglomeration Economies", *International Regional Science Review*, 25(2): 151-168.

Porter, M. (1998), "Clusters and the New Economics of Competition", *Harvard Business Review*, Nov-Dec, 77-90.

Porter, M. (1990), *The Competitive Advantage of Nations*, MacMillan, London.

Van Egeraat, C. (2006), "The Pharmaceutical Industry in Ireland: Agglomeration, Localisation or Simply Spatial Concentration?" *NIRSA Working Paper Series*, 28, February, National Institute for Regional and Spatial Analysis, Maynooth.

Williamson, J.G. (1965), "Regional Inequality and the Process of National Development: A Description of the Patterns", *Economic Development and Cultural Change*, Vol 13, 3-45.

CHAPTER 16

THE ROLE FOR CLUSTERS IN IRISH ECONOMIC DEVELOPMENT POLICY

ELEANOR DOYLE AND CONNELL FANNING

ABSTRACT

Irish policymakers interest in the concept of industrial clusters dates back to the Culliton Report, which recommended the promotion of industrial clusters focused on niches of national competitive advantage. This view of agglomeration economies based on industrial clusters derives largely from the work of Michael Porter. Given the widespread use in the term 'cluster', Doyle and Fanning review the evolution of this concept, and outline the international and Irish evidence regarding the existence of Porterian clusters. The authors conclude that while there is little evidence that such clusters have had a significant effect on productivity growth in Ireland, the research to date has been inadequate, and has been hampered by a lack of appropriate data.

16.1 Introduction

This chapter focuses on the concept of 'clusters' as a tool for economic analysis and guiding development policy. It has been widely used in many policy reports, for example in the Culliton Report, and referred to in many Irish business support programmes as desirable or necessary to improve productivity. This line of thought has been heavily influenced by Michael Porter, especially by his Competitive Advantage of Nations (1990). Yet the notion of the cluster is often used with different connotations to that meant when the term was used and defined by Michael Porter. Indeed from the nine inclusions of 'cluster' in the Enterprise Strategy Group Report (2004) it is not at all obvious that either the meaning or implications of the cluster concept, in Porter's terms, were intended. In research circles, the concept has also proved problematic and generated a substantial literature debating its merits and shortcomings.[1]

The context in which the cluster is founded and from which it takes its meaning must be understood to appreciate its purpose and its usefulness as a tool of analysis. We explain the concept as grounded in the work of Michael Porter, from its introduction in 1990 through to its current and ongoing progression. The setting of the cluster within a theory for economic development that is being developed by Porter is also provided.

International and Irish evidence from the array of research generated by cluster-based analyses is summarised. The mainly negative findings on clusters evident in Irish studies is re-examined in the light of our discussion of the relevance and purpose of using clusters as a lens through which to view economic and business development. Some implications for development in policymaking in Ireland are outlined.

16.2 Porter's Clusters – Definition and Foundations

Irish policymakers interest in the cluster concept dates back to 1992 with the publication of the *Culliton Report,* which recommended the promotion of industrial clusters focused on niches of national competitive advantage. Culliton's views were based on Michael Porter's 1990 book, The Competitive Advantage of Nations, where the cluster was introduced in the context of national competitiveness.

Porter's focus was on why a nation becomes "the home base for successful international competitors in an industry?" (1990: 1). In answering the question, Porter observed that:

> A nation's successful industries are usually linked through vertical (buyer/supplier) or horizontal (common customers, technology, channels, etc.) relationships...The phenomenon of industry clustering is so pervasive that it appears to be a central feature of advanced national economies (Porter 1990: 149).

For the purposes of this chapter, the definition of clusters used follows Porter, as cited above and in later work, where he outlines two specific elements constituting a cluster:

> Critical masses - in one place - of unusual competitive success in particular fields...Clusters are geographic concentrations of interconnected companies and institutions in a particular field. Clusters encompass an array of linked industries and other entities important to competition (1998: 78).

Porter observed that competitive success of companies in particular 'fields' coincided with strong clusters. Porter is unequivocal in defining success in terms of productivity and productivity growth relative to rivals. The above definitions correspond to the question Porter wished to answer regarding the location of successful international competitors. Although Porter set out to identify the causes of national competitive advantage, it is not the only context in which the cluster has relevance. Clustering is appropriate for considering related but distinct issues of industry and regional development that include business and/or industry origins, evolution and decline.

The nature of interconnection can vary across cluster members, which makes a simple definition challenging, but the impact of interaction is seen in the contribution made to cluster members' individual and overall competitiveness. A cluster may include producers of goods or services, their specialised suppliers, service providers and any associated institutions, from industry or trade associations to universities and standard-setting agencies, normally within the boundaries of a country or across a region. Cluster members may compete with other members in their field or support the competitiveness of other cluster members by resource-sharing. A key feature of Porter's cluster concept is that co-operation as well as competition underlies cluster activities allowing member firms to have higher productivity than would otherwise be possible.

The essence of the cluster concept has its roots in work on what Marshall, as far back as 1890, called 'externalities of specialised industrial locations' (Marshall, 1920). Somewhat paradoxically in the current context of increasingly globalised markets, firm location and interdependence are significant explanations of their competitive performance according to cluster theory. Location is one of the few sources of differentiation that competitors outside a cluster are unable to imitate. Porter's cluster concept includes elements of location, competition, co-operation and strong relative performance in a manner that was not otherwise conceptualised, but recognising that: "most past theories address particular aspects of clusters or clusters of a particular type" (1998: 208).

Furthermore, by grounding the concept in productivity, a link appears across Porter's separate research streams at the level of firms[2], industries[3] and locations[4] in a comprehensive and integrated framework.

16.3 Identifying Clusters

The cluster can be considered from the business-based perspective on social structure offered by Herbert Simon.[5]

> A mythical visitor from Mars approaches the Earth from space, equipped with a telescope that reveals social structures. The firms reveal themselves, say, as solid green areas with faint interior contours marking out divisions and departments. Market transactions show as red lines connecting firms, forming a network in the spaces between them. Within firms (and perhaps even between them) the approaching visitor also sees pale blue lines, the lines of authority connecting bosses with various levels of workers...No matter whether our visitor approached the United States or the Soviet Union, urban China, or the European Community, the greater part of the space below it would be within the green areas, for almost all of the inhabitants would be employees, hence inside the firm boundaries. Organizations would be dominant feature of the landscape. A message sent back home, describing the scene, would speak of 'large green areas interconnected by red lines'.

Extending this thought experiment, 'the large green areas' delineating firms would be further connected by market, technology or resource relationships - not necessarily market transactions - that not only allow but stimulate and facilitate firms to improve productivity, innovation and enhance the business environment.

Artefacts of clusters may be found in countries, states, regions, counties, or cities. Clusters may occur in small local industries or large international industries. They characterise small or large economies and tend to be most developed in advanced economies. In practice, precisely how and how well clusters function varies across regions as well as across industries within regions.

The identification of cluster boundaries goes beyond standard industrial reporting or classification systems commonly used to delineate industries from each other (e.g. Standard Industrial Classification (SIC)). This point is central to analysing any economic region using the cluster concept because the general purpose of classification systems is to provide a framework for the collection, tabulation, presentation and analysis of data. Their purpose is not to describe the structure of economic activity, or economic interactions in a location, or to assist in identification of the determinants of successful business or industries. For example, two businesses producing the same product may be classified into separate industries because the product may be both the principal product of one business and the secondary product of another or because industries may be defined in terms of the production process used (Nijhowne, 1997). Businesses using a vertically integrated production process may produce the same product as others in their industry that purchases the unfinished product and further process it. Some of the tension between classification systems of economic activity and how economies actually function based on businesses' operations, activities and relationships are addressed in the cluster concept.

Since such standard classifications do not identify the value-adding cross-industry transactions or linkages that characterise the activities of many firms, moving from the cluster concept to its measurement is difficult. This is reflected in how Porter's methods for cluster identification and measurement have developed and progressed over time (consider Porter, 1990 and Porter, 2003). Researchers grappling with using the cluster concept are invariably faced with the challenge of dealing with the information and data available to them, usually provided in the format of 'standard' industry classifications, and attempt to interpret it or reorganise it in a manner appropriate to the cluster concept and identifying a cluster in particular locations.

16.4 Cluster Origins in the Economic Environment

The identification of locations with a distinctive business environment that influences how individual businesses choose to compete is a novel feature in Porter's work. The cluster emerges from Porter's analysis of the quality of the economic environment of a location for business and an appreciation of the concept requires that it be placed in this broader context. The factors that Porter included in his 'Diamond' framework for competitive advantage (the microeconomic business environment of firms and clusters) presented in Figure 16.1, facilitate or hinder the development of successful firms and clusters.

Both 'chance' (i.e. contingency), and 'Government' lie outside the 'Diamond' but impact on the business environment in determining business performance "in important ways" (Porter 1990: 73) and are also included here. Each 'Diamond' element may influence the other elements to generate an environment conducive, or not, to successful business performance. The cluster emerges 'naturally' as the result of interactions of 'Diamond' factors in a location and "the nature and depth of clusters varies with the state of development of the economy" (Porter 2005: 47). The cluster is intrinsically linked to and defined by the system of features described by the 'Diamond'.

Figure 16.1: Porter's 'Diamond' Framework: Microeconomic Business Environment

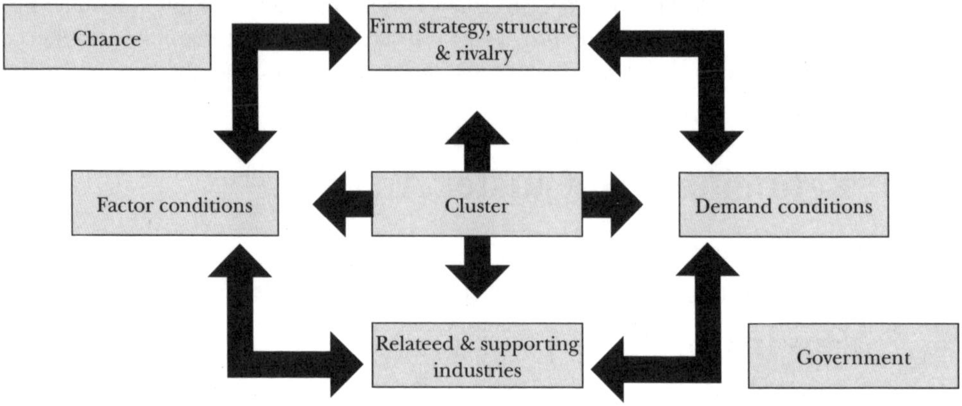

Source: Adapted from Figure 3.1: The Determinants of National Advantage, Porter, (1990: 72).

Porter (1998: 13) states that his "core set of ideas about competition ... contains a consistent perspective". This is echoed in the emphasis of his contributions to the Global Competitiveness Programme of the World Economic Forum on location where he views the sophistication of companies operations and strategies and 'Diamond' conditions as the core features or determinants of competitiveness (Porter, 2004). So while average industry profitability is determined by the international structure of an industry (as in a 'Five-Forces' type analysis), local business conditions and operational and strategic decisions determine the relative productivity/profitability of resident businesses vis-à-vis competitors. Clusters fit into this perspective as their main benefits generate higher productivity for constituent firms, a better environment for innovation and productivity growth and stimulation of new business formation that serve to embed successful firms in their locations.[6]

Those interested in local and regional economic development are aware of the abundance of cluster studies in which the word 'cluster' often has a meaning or definition other than that employed by Porter. Spatial definitions (agglomeration, urbanisation and localisation) lack the integration of competition, cooperative and strategic elements that are encompassed in the 'Diamond' perspective. Such studies emphasise our central point - a localised concentration of economic activity or employment in one or more classification codes (e.g. NACE 21211: Manufacture of corrugated paper and paperboard and corrugated board containers) is not the same as an industry cluster.

Porter argues that where strong clusters exist, they enhance productivity. Yet not every firm operates, or is presumed to operate, within what may be classified as a strong or active cluster. For a group of interrelated firms to qualify as a cluster four conditions must be met:[7]

1. **Proximity**: Firms must be close enough geographically to allow for positive spillovers to be enjoyed and/or for resources to be shared;
2. **Market Relationship**: Firms must have a common goal (e.g. meeting the needs of the same market), or requiring highly skilled specialised labour in a specific field to benefit from interaction;

3. **Active Interaction**: Active relationships must be developed for positive cluster effects to emerge; and
4. **Critical Mass:** A sufficient number of participants must engage in active interactions before any meaningful or significant impact on company performance results. The number depends on the particular cluster, its location, its target market etc.

16.5 Refinement in Cluster Analysis

Porter (2003) extended his approach to analysing regional performance, according to the cluster concept, using a specially assembled US dataset. He does not attempt to test any particular hypotheses in this work but to examine the facts and relationships that have been contained in many theories such as how employment growth, industry composition, cluster activity and patenting rates across regions are related to levels and variations in performance, as measured by wages.

Regions were differentiated according to their structure of local, resource-dependent and traded industries. Local industries are defined as those that have similar shares of employment across most regions and represent over two thirds of US private sector employment. Resource-dependent industries tend to be located where resources are accessible and compete with other domestic or international locations but represent less than one per cent of employment. Traded industries' locations (approximately one third of US employment) are not dependent on resources but are based on "broader competitive considerations, and employment concentration varies markedly by region" (Porter 2003: 559).

Porter found traded industries to be more geographically concentrated than local industries. Acknowledging that knowledge spillovers and other positive externalities that characterise clusters are difficult if not impossible to measure directly, Porter used the locational correlation of employment to identify pairs/groups of tightly linked industries, using judgement to identify clusters across industries and to avoid spurious relationships. Overall 41 traded clusters were identified averaging 29 industries in each, each with its own geographic employment configuration.

Marked differences were found in the mix of clusters in different regions (with regions' wages strongly affected by their traded clusters that sell products or services across regions or internationally). Regional wage differences were driven by relative wages in traded industries while the mix of clusters in a region appeared less important in determining regional performance than relative wage levels. Only very recently have attempts been made to use Porter's latest methods to systematically identify and map clusters in a comparable and internationally transferable manner.[8]

16.6 International Evidence on Cluster Initiatives

Internationally and across states and cities, practitioners and policymakers have embraced the cluster concept with a range of efforts aimed at improving regional growth and competitiveness. One evaluation of such projects is provided in The Cluster Initiative Greenbook based on a 2003 survey reporting on 250 cluster initiatives.[9] The survey addressed issues such as the settings in which cluster initiatives evolved, the objective(s) pursued, the process as it unfolded, and the drivers of good performance. The majority of initiatives were quite recent. Of the initiatives active in 2003, almost three quarters were initiated in 1999 or later.[10]

Initiatives were largely focused on technology-intensive sectors including IT, medical devices, production technology, communications equipment, biopharmaceuticals and automotive. The link with technology-intensive sectors/firms is reasonably logical since innovation processes can be well understood from a cluster perspective. Modern innovation is characterised as non-sequential interactions between combinations of companies, research institutions and universities. This is at variance with the 'traditional' approach where innovation was carried out by corporate research and development departments that turned basic research of universities into new applied products and processes. Vitally, however, clustering is not limited to such industries or sectors as it is the type of interactions between members and their effects that define the cluster, and not the end productive economic activity defined in terms of goods or services provision.

Survey results from Solvell et al. (2003) indicate that the goals of cluster initiatives were quite varied (see Table 16.1). Each of these factors targets one of the following six categories: (1) Research and networking; (2) Cluster expansion; (3) Innovation and technology; (4) Education and training; (5) Commercial co-operation; and (6) Policy action. Most clusters were observed to target objectives within at least four of the above six goals. One-third of cluster initiatives were instigated by government, slightly less (27 per cent) by industry or jointly in 35 per cent of cases. Financing of the initiatives came mostly from government (54 per cent), jointly from government and industry (25 per cent) or solely from industry (18 per cent).

Table 16.1: Goals of Cluster Initiatives (1 indicates the goal of greatest importance)

1. To foster networks among people	2. To provide technical training
3. To promote expansion of existing firms	4. To provide management training
5. To establish networks among firms	6. To diffuse technology within the cluster
7. To facilitate higher innovativeness	8. To enhance production processes
9. To promote innovation and new technologies	10. To lobby government for infrastructure
11. To attract new firms and talent to the region	12. To improve FDI incentives
13. To create a brand for the region	14. To improve regulatory policy
15. To promote cluster exports	16. To provide incubator services
17. To provide business assistance	18. To lobby for subsidies
19. To assemble market intelligence	20. To co-ordinate purchasing
21. To analyse technical trends	22. To conduct private infrastructure projects
23. To improve firms' cluster awareness	24. To establish technical standards
25. To promote formation of spin-offs	26. To reduce competition in the cluster

Source: Figure 2 in Solvell et al. (2003).

Having engaged in cluster initiatives, 85 per cent of respondents agreed that the competitiveness of the cluster was enhanced and 89 per cent agreed that they helped the cluster to grow. In the case of 81 per cent of initiatives, the goals set at their outset were met. In four per cent of instances respondents were disappointed with reports of insignificant change.

Although cluster initiatives appear to offer potential for economic improvement, three key challenges were identified;

1. Setting objectives and monitoring performance;
2. Organising the clusters initiative process over time; and
3. Integrating the cluster initiative in a broader microeconomic policy agenda.

The tendency for cluster initiatives to achieve their stated goals is related to the extent to which these three issues are addressed.

16.7 Irish Clusters: Evidence and Implications

Several cluster-based studies have been carried out for Ireland, particularly in the last decade as international interest in cluster policy has mushroomed. The main studies include those summarised in Table 16.2.

The conclusions provide no convincing argument to support the existence of strong clusters in Ireland. In further support for this view, Ireland's ranking in terms of cluster development was 27th of 110 countries in 2005, based on survey responses regarding supplier quantity, supplier quality, the local availability of process machinery and research services.[11] This was somewhat lower than the Irish ranking of 21st for the Global Competitiveness Index, which indicated relative growth prospects over the next five to eight years.[12]

Two issues are raised by the cluster research conducted to date. First, two of the three cases addressed in Irish research (popular music and Irish dairy processing) cannot be regarded as competitive, as acknowledged by the authors.[13] The failure to meet one potential requirement in applying a cluster approach, the 'market test' of competitive success, is a potential difficulty in studies that set out to apply a Porterian analysis to Irish clusters. The selection of non-competitive sectors in several studies implies the odds were stacked against finding clusters from the outset. It is also worth noting that the most unambiguously competitive industry (Software) was also found to be the most clustered. Second, in using data provided in standard classification formats, efforts to apply the cluster concept were absent from the studies. Properly grounded cluster analysis goes beyond the identification of backward or forward linkages or identifying where geographical concentrations of activities exist.

Table 16.2: Irish Cluster Studies and Findings[14]

Authors	Focus	Findings
Donnellan (1994)	Examination of extent of clustering in Irish manufacturing and link to performance.	Evidence of clustering in food and wood & printing only. Little association to performance.
O'Connell, Van Egaraat, and Enright (1997)	'Diamond' analysis of Irish dairy processing industry to investigate presence or extent of cluster activity.	"An Irish dairy cluster supported by an Irish 'Diamond' functioning as a system leading to innovation and sustained growth has not developed" (p.79).
Clancy and Twomey (1997)	'Diamond' analysis of Irish popular music industry to investigate presence or extent of cluster activity.	Absence of a clear competitive advantage.
O'Gorman, O'Malley and Mooney (1997)	'Diamond' analysis of Irish indigenous software industry to investigate presence or extent of cluster activity.	Industry is relatively successful and internationally competitive (p.52). "good reasons for concluding that the ... industry can be regarded as part of a clustering phenomenon (p.50). "not quite a fully developed "cluster" in Porter's strict sense of the term" (p.54).
Clancy, O'Malley, O'Connell, and Van Egaraat (2001)	Examines importance of clusters and relevance of Porter's 'Diamond' in Ireland using three case studies.	Summary of three studies above.
O'Malley and Van Egaraat (2000)	Assessment of clustering activity in Irish indigenous industries (broader analysis than above).	Limited evidence of clusters.
Gallagher, Doyle and O'Leary (2002)	A 'Diamond' analysis of business or micro- foundations of Irish competitiveness.	Cluster emerging in software, electronics and telecoms equip. industries. Weak cluster in indigenous meat & dairy industries.

A conclusion common to many studies is that Irish industrial policy should not be focused on the development of clusters and that the search for an alternative model for Irish industrial development should proceed, as relative success has been experienced by the Irish economy without the presence of established clusters.[15] However, in the context of research to date, and the lack of availability of Irish cluster-based data, research of the Porter type has yet to be conducted for Ireland. Without such analyses, it must be premature to conclude that a cluster-based approach to development is not relevant for policymaking purposes.

The scale of multinational contribution to Irish economic activity has been identified as problematic in applying the cluster concept since Porter largely excluded such plants and sectors in identifying clusters, although observing their potential to contribute to determining the competitive advantage(s) of a location. In his more recent work he emphasises that: "Productivity is the goal, not whether firms operating in the country are domestic or foreign-owned" (Porter, Ketels and Delgado, 2006: 52).

However, it is a matter for debate whether relevant commentary on related issues from 1990 may still have relevance.

> A development strategy based solely on foreign multinationals may doom a nation to remaining a factor-driven economy. If reliance on foreign multinationals is too complete, the nation will not be the home base for any industry...The result of not developing more advanced forms of competitive advantage is a cap on economic development: rapid progress can be made, but it only goes so far...In Singapore and Ireland, my view is that the shift has been too little and too late. Neither nation has truly committed to the slow process of developing a broader base of indigenous firms (Porter, 1990: 679).

A further obstacle to applying Porter's theory has been identified as the potential requirement to include relevant other countries – including, for example, the sources of productive factors, market destinations, home-base countries of multinational subsidiaries located in Ireland - in a super 'Diamond' given Ireland's small open economy nature.[16] Notwithstanding the profuse academic literature generated by such views, a review of Porter (1990) reveals that Denmark and Singapore, both small economies and the latter one of the most open in the world, were included in his analyses and subjected to analyses based on 'Diamond' and cluster approaches.

16.8 The Value and Challenges of Cluster-Based Analysis

The three issues at the heart of cluster-based analyses - competitiveness, productivity and innovation - can usefully be considered by perceiving the economy as organised around clusters. These issues are also central to policy concerns, as evident in Europe's goal of becoming the world's most competitive and dynamic knowledge-based economy in the world by 2010 (as stated in the Lisbon goals). There appears to be a broad consensus that sound macroeconomic performance is necessary but insufficient to achieve productivity improvements across the EU and microeconomic issues are increasingly centre stage in policy discussion on competitiveness improvements. The sources or explanations of performance, and its absence, may be found from the examination of clusters and the characteristics of location, competition and co-operation that define them which are grounded in the microeconomic features of an economy, as organised in the 'Diamond' framework of locational characteristics.

The analysis of economies as systems of clusters, based on 'Diamond' conditions, affords policymakers an explicit framework on which to organise focussed policies and launch initiatives across main cluster players, from companies, to state agencies, universities, labour unions or industry associations, based squarely on how businesses conduct their competitive and co-operative activities. Cluster analysis focuses on important inter-firm linkages, complementarities, and spillovers in terms of technology, skills, information, marketing (among others) that describe the ongoing dynamic process of how firms compete.[17] Such linkages and the actual and potential external benefits clusters can generate point to a scope for joint actions by companies, industry groups and/or government to support cluster development.

Despite the research conducted to date, it is our view that a comprehensive cluster analysis, following Porter, of the Irish economy has yet to be carried out. The limited information and evidence available indicates that Porterian clustering is not a widely experienced phenomenon in Ireland. Indeed, we could go so far as to say that a relatively small number of indigenous Irish firms are successful in the international economy. At the same time, it is clear that a considerable share of economic activity based in Ireland leverages competitive advantages effectively on national and international markets but the extent to which these advantages are grounded in elements of location, competition and co-operation remains to be examined.

This might lead to support for the conclusion that clustering is not a relevant policy direction for Ireland. Alternatively, it may be the case that temporary favourable factors, other than strong clustering, more than made up for its absence in the Irish experience. Improvements in economic management and rapid expansion in labour supply for which demand developed, largely due to production by multinational enterprises, are once-off sources of growth associated with the Celtic Tiger. It should be remembered, however, that despite these important recent contributions to growth, Irish productivity per worker averaged 3.5 per cent per annum between 1995 and 2004, similar to the figure over the period from 1947 to 2000.[18] To explore how such rates can be at least maintained, in tandem with full employment, in an economy that has exhausted its catch-up potential, clustering may well prove to be a fruitful strategy.

16.9 Conclusions

A cluster-centred view of economic development poses particular challenges for policymakers. It makes redundant the notion that any specific industry or sector should be targeted by industrial policy since all clusters have the potential to contribute to prosperity and emphasises that business support programmes should best be structured to enhance the competitiveness of groups of related firms rather than individual businesses. Cluster-based thinking accords contributory roles to domestic and foreign companies which are both important in securing productivity improvements. The role of the policymaker in cluster-based economic development is to relax any identified impediments or constraints to productivity and to emphasise and enhance the cross-company linkages and complementarities that facilitate and generate business competitive advantage. This almost certainly implies a role for more cluster initiatives at sub-national and local levels and the development of trust not only by leaders and members of such initiatives in the policy sphere but also in the businesses that populate clusters since they are conduits for information and inputs on the barriers they face to developing their cluster.

For cluster-based economic growth, it is not the role of policymakers to impose cluster development on un-cooperative businesses. Should businesses themselves view clustering as a feasible and beneficial activity that could increase their probability of achieving competitive success, then facilitation could be provided through state and business representative agencies with requisite responsibilities for supporting business development.

To examine the potential of cluster-based economic development, there is a need to identify existing, emerging and potential clusters, which cannot be done using available data and probably not through desk-research alone, pointing to the need for researchers to engage hands on with businesses and with policymakers in the cluster debate.

Notes

1 For example see Martin and Sunley (2003).
2 See Porter (1985).
3 See Porter (1980).
4 See Porter (1990).
5 See Simon (1991: 27).
6 See Porter, Ketels and Delgado (2006: 54).
7 Ketels (2004).
8 For examples see the Cluster Mapping Project for the US developed by Michael Porter at the Harvard Business School and the Cluster Mapping Report for Sweden commissioned by the Swedish Programme for the Development of Innovation Systems and Clusters. The Cluster study of the UK commissioned by the Department for Trade and Industry (2001) is based on the methods outlined in Porter (1990).
9 Solvell et al. (2003).
10 One (anonymous) Irish cluster initiative is included in the survey. For more details on the survey see Solvell et al. (2003: 32-33).
11 From the annual Executive Opinion Survey for the *Global Competitiveness Report* of the World Economic Forum.
12 It is also considerably lower than the Irish ranking of 19th on the Business Competitiveness Index, which is constructed to reflect the sustainability of current productivity levels.
13 For example see (Clancy, 2000: 12).
14 Only studies considering Porter-type clusters are included.
15 O'Connell, Van Egaraat and Enright, 1997; Clancy and Twomey, 1997; O'Gorman, O'Malley and Mooney, 1997; Clancy, O'Malley, O'Connell and Van Egaraat, 2001.
16 As in Rugman and D'Cruz (1993).
17 For examples of the range of cluster-based studies see Van der Linde (2002).
18 Kennedy (2001) Table 1 presents historical data.

References

Clancy, P. and Twomey, M. (1997), "Clusters in Ireland: The Irish Popular Music Industry: An Application of Porter's Cluster Analysis", *National Economic and Social Council*, Research Series Paper No. 2, November.

Clancy, P., O'Malley, E., O' Connell, L. and Van Egeraat, C. (2001), "Industry Clusters in Ireland: An Application of Porter's Model of National Competitive Advantage to Three Sectors", *European Planning Studies*, Vol. 9, No. 1, 7-28.

Claros, A., Porter, M. E. and Schwab, K. (2006), *The Global Competitiveness Report 2006-7*, Palgrave Macmillan, 43-77.

Culliton, J. (1992), *A Time for Change: Industrial Policy for the 1990s*; Report of the Industrial Policy Review Group, Stationery Office; Dublin.

Donnellan, N. (1994), The Presence of Porter's Sectoral Clustering in Irish Manufacturing, *Economic and Social Review*, Vol. 25, No. 3, 221-232.

ESG (2004), *Ahead of the Curve, Ireland's Place in the Global Economy*, Report of the Enterprise Strategy Group, Forfás.

Gallagher, L., Doyle, E. and O'Leary, E. (2002), "Creating the Celtic Tiger and Sustaining Economic Growth: A Business Perspective", *Quarterly Economic Commentary*, Economic and Social Research Institute, Spring, 63-81.

Kennedy, K. (2000/1), "Reflections on the Process of Irish Economic Growth", *Journal of the Statistical and Social Inquiry Society of Ireland*, XXX, 123-139.

Ketels, C. (2004), "European Clusters, Structural Change in Europe 3 – Innovative City and Business Regions", Hagbarth Publications, 1-4.

Marshall, A. (1920), *Principles of Economics*, Eighth edition, Macmillan and Co. Ltd., London. Original published 1890.

Martin, R. and Sunley, P. (2003), "Deconstructing Clusters: Chaotic Concept or Policy Panacea?" *Journal of Economic Geography*, 3, 5-35.

Nijhowne, S. (1997), "Alternative Aggregations and the Standard Industrial Classification: A note." paper presented at the 12th meeting of the *Voorburg Group on Services Statistics*, Copenhagen, September.

O'Connell, L., Van Egaraat, C. and Enright, P. (1997), "The Irish Dairy Processing Industry: An Application of Porter's Cluster Analysis", *National Economic and Social Council*, Research Series Paper No. 1, November.

O'Gorman, C., O'Malley, E. and Mooney, J. (1997), "Clusters in Ireland: The Irish Indigenous Software Industry: An Application of Porter's Cluster Analysis", *National Economic and Social Council*, Research Series Paper No. 3, November.

O'Malley, E. and Van Egeraat, C. (2000), "Industry Clusters and Irish Indigenous Manufacturing: Limits of the Porter View". *Economic and Social Review*, 31(1), 55-79.

Porter, M. E., Ketels, C. and Delgado M. (2006), "The Microeconomic Foundations of Prosperity: Findings from the Business Competitiveness Index", chapter 1.2 in *Lopez-Global Competitiveness Report 2006-2007.*

Porter, M.E. (2004), "Building the Microeconomic Foundations of Prosperity: Findings from the Business Competitiveness Index", chapter 1.2 in Porter, M.E., Schwab, K.,

Sala-i-Martin, X. and Lopez-Claros, A. (2003), *The Global Competitiveness Report 2003-2004*, Oxford University Press, 29-56.

Porter, M. E. (2003), "The Economic Performance of Regions", *Regional Studies*, 37, 6&7, 449-478.

Porter, M. E. (1998), "Clusters and the New Economics of Competition", *Harvard Business Review*, Nov.-Dec, 77- 90.

Porter, M. E. (1990), *The Competitive Advantage of Nations*. Free Press, New York. Republished with New Introduction, 1998 (1990).

Porter, M. E. (1985), *Competitive Advantage: Creating and Sustaining Superior Performance*. Free Press, New York. Republished with New Introduction, 1998.

Porter, M. E. (1980), *Competitive Strategy: Techniques for Analyzing Industries and Competitors*. Free Press, New York. Republished with New Introduction, 1998.

Rugman, A.M. and D'Cruz, J.R. (1993), "The 'Double Diamond' Model of International Competitiveness: The Canadian Experience", *Management International Review*, Vol. 33, No. SPI/2, 17-39.

Simon, H.A. (1991), "Organizations and Markets", *The Journal of Economic Perspectives*, 5, 2, Spring, 25-44.

Solvell, O., Ketels, C.H. and Lindqvist, G. (2003), *The Cluster Initiative Greenbook*, The Competitiveness Institute/Vinnova: Gothenburg.

Van der Linde, C. (2002), *Findings from Cluster Meta-Study*. Boston: Institute for Strategy and Competitiveness, Harvard Business School.

CHAPTER 17

AGGREGATE PRODUCTIVITY EFFECTS OF ROAD INVESTMENT: A REASSESSMENT FOR WESTERN EUROPE

ANDREAS KOPP[1]

ABSTRACT

Economists have long been interested in the productivity effects of infrastructure investment, and this research has been an important input into budget allocations for investment in transport infrastructure. This chapter analyses the macroeconomic productivity effects of road investment in 13 Western European countries. This chapter shows that the rate of return for many countries on past investment, while positive, has been quite low at around five per cent. Assuming that infrastructure investment is subject to falling returns, the return on future investment in Europe is likely to be even lower. This does not necessarily apply to Ireland which has a relatively undeveloped stock of road infrastructure, suggesting that future road investments are likely to have higher returns than elsewhere in Europe.

1 The author is grateful for the valuable comments received from two anonymous referees.

17.1 Introduction

Transport infrastructure investment, and road infrastructure investment in particular, are seen by a major part of the general public and by many political decision makers as a central instrument to promote regional or national economic growth. Large-scale investment in the road network formed part of long-term growth policies in the US under the Dwight D. Eisenhower System of Interstate and Defence Highways, which was launched in 1956 and led to over 80,000 miles of highways by 1980 (Federal Highway Administration, 1976). In 1998, the Transportation Equity Act was signed, assigning $203 billion to improve the national highway infrastructure. Of this amount, $176 billion was allocated for highway construction (Chandra and Thompson, 2000).

The European Council of October 2003 called on Member States to "...promote investment in networks and knowledge". It highlighted "the importance of speeding up the roll-out of European transport, energy and electronic communications networks and of increasing investment in human capital". These are crucial steps to boost growth, better integrate an enlarged Europe and improve the productivity and competitiveness of European businesses on global markets (Commission of the European Communities, 2003)". The Community budget contributes €700 million annually to fund up to ten per cent of Trans-European Network (TEN) projects. The Structural Funds are foreseen to provide €29.2 billion for transport infrastructure while Cohesion fund resources can mobilise up to €1.5 billion per year for infrastructure investment. Furthermore, the Commission is considering setting up an innovative Guarantee Instrument to facilitate private sector funding through Public Private Partnerships (PPPs) for TEN transport projects. The European Investment Bank (EIB) supports the Growth Initiative with a €50 billion TEN Investment Facility to be allocated to TEN's priority projects. In addition, the EIB reinforces its financing capacity under the Structured Finance Facility which, inter alia, supports the TEN projects. On the national level, transport infrastructure investment is considered to be of equal importance to increase economic growth.

The strong role assigned to transport infrastructure investment as a vehicle for economic growth appears to be worth critical examination for at least two reasons. There is no strong growth theory foundation for the hypothesis that an increase in transport infrastructure investment would lead to an immediate and lasting increase in growth rates of economic activity. Rather, according to the exogenous growth theory, an increase in the investment rate (which does not necessarily result from an increase in transport infrastructure investment) leads to an increase in income levels (Barro and Sala-i-Martin, 1995). Some variants of endogenous growth theory do provide a link between transport infrastructure investment and growth rates. The link is established by the effects of transport infrastructure investment on urban form and the size distribution of cities, and the resulting agglomeration economies (Lucas, 1988; Black and Henderson, 1999; Lucas, 2001; Lucas and Rossi-Hansberg, 2002). However, the links from transport infrastructure investment to economic growth are less direct than claimed in public debates, and related arguments are rarely used in policy discussions.

There is no clear, empirical evidence that transport infrastructure investment leads to higher growth or even to a higher level of income. Some authors interpret the strong correlation between public capital and macroeconomic productivity, which was found for the US, as evidence that infrastructure generally provides valuable services to the private sector and that, in particular, the slowdown in US public investment after the early 1970s explains a substantial proportion of the concomitant productivity slowdown.[1] Other authors have argued that public capital is endogenous, in that higher public investment is due to the public sector response to an increased demand for infrastructure services resulting from higher aggregate income.[2] Sectoral and regional disaggregation have led to smaller, positive but more robust effects (see the review in Cohen and Morrison Paul, 2004). A number of studies have looked into issues which complicate the estimation of public infrastructure investment effects, such as the existence of spatial spillovers from public infrastructure investment in geographically linked areas and the temporal dependence of estimated infrastructure effects. Kelejian and Robinson (1997) allowed for spatial lags of dependent and independent variables along with spatial correlation of the error terms. Holtz-Eakin and Schwartz (1995) consider interstate spillovers in a production model based on long lags to accommodate long-run adjustment, and Boarnet (1998) measured cross-county spillovers using a Cobb-Douglas production function approach.

Among the studies which addressed the more specific question of whether road infrastructure investment increased productivity, Carlino and Voith (1992) found that the productivity of US states was higher the greater the density of highways. Holtz-Eakin and Schwartz (1995) could not confirm the strong positive productivity effects of transport infrastructure on the state level. Holtz-Eakin and Lovely (1996) succeeded in relating output growth to the positive effect transport infrastructure investment had on the number of firms in the manufacturing industry, without observing a direct effect on manufacturing productivity.

Within the production function approach, Canning (1999) and Canning and Bennathan (n.d.) have used a different method to solve the problem of the endogeneity of public capital. It is based on the non-stationarity of the data for output per worker and capital stock per worker. This means that the production function may represent a long-run, co-integrating relationship. They use this fact to apply the panel data co-integration methods of Kao and Chiang (2000). Using this method, two assumptions are made. It is assumed that production functions are identical for all countries, and that the relationship between investment and income varies across countries. This allows each country in the sample to have its own short-run investment dynamics, to give consistent estimates of the parameters of the production function which are robust to reverse causality.

This chapter is related to the study of Fernald (1999). He tried to give an answer to the question of how changes in road stock affected the relative productivity performance of US industries from 1953 to 1989. His argument is based on the hypothesis that if roads contribute to industries' productivity, industries which use roads intensively should benefit more from their expansion. Given the complemenarity between vehicle use and road use, and the lack of direct measures for industrial road use, vehicle use is employed as a direct measure of road intensity. The basic result of Fernald's study is that changes in road growth are associated with larger changes in productivity growth in industries which are relatively vehicle-intensive. This finding supports the hypothesis that industries with more than average vehicles benefited more than proportionately from road building. This result, in turn, suggests that the correlation between aggregate productivity and infrastructure reflects causation from changes in road stock to changes in productivity. If roads did not contribute to aggregate productivity at the margin, but governments just built more roads as aggregate income rose, one would not expect any particular relationship between an industry's vehicle intensity and its relative productivity performance when road growth changes. The results do not, however, support the idea that public investment offers a continuing route to increasing income. The US industry data are consistent with the view that the massive road-building of the 1950s and 60s offered a one-off boost to the level of productivity, rather than an instrument to continuing rapid growth in productivity.

This chapter differs from Fernald's (1999) paper in that different congestion levels between countries are taken into account. Moreover, we add bilateral trade between the European countries to the picture. The productivity enhancing effect of road infrastructure investment does not only depend on national road infrastructure stocks, but also on the accumulated road investment in trading partner countries. In contrast to the Fernald study where all industries use the same national road infrastructure, the countries studied here use different national infrastructure and use the roads of the trading partners. We distinguish the Western European countries by their transport intensity, as well as their use of labour and capital. The next section sets out the conceptual framework for the empirical analysis. Section 17.3 explains some data and econometric issues, and the results of the empirical analysis are presented in Section 17.4. In Section 17.5 we make some concluding remarks.

17.2 Conceptual Background

This section provides the conceptual background of the estimation equation. The estimation makes use of data on transport infrastructure investment in 13 Western European countries, for which transport infrastructure investment data are available for the years 1975 to 2000. The estimation function relates that part of national value added growth which cannot be explained by increased usage of private inputs to the services derived from road stock available to national road users. Road stock services are not only dependent on national road stocks but also on foreign roads to the extent that they are used for international trade. Moreover, the road services depend on the number of vehicles and the level of congestion.

The derivation of the estimation equations starts out from a macroeconomic production function. This function relates the individual country's gross output to labour inputs, the capital stock of private firms and the input of transport services. The transport services are in turn produced by combining road services and vehicles. With the assumption of decreasing marginal productivities of vehicles and of infrastructure stock, use of vehicles per kilometre of road infrastructure could be used as a proxy to account for congestion. As the demand for road services cannot be directly observed, the complemenarity with the demand for vehicles is used to estimate the contribution of road stock to the growth in gross output.

To be able to use the value added statistics, instead of having to use gross production statistics which are unavailable for some of the panel countries, the Divisa index of value added growth as a function of gross output growth and the growth of intermediate goods' input is used. The value added growth equation is used to derive the value added residual that cannot be traced back to the growth of capital, labour and vehicles. This residual is a linear function of the growth of road services and a technology shock.

The growth in national road service consumption depends first on the increase in domestic road stock and on the increase in the road stock in foreign countries weighted by the respective shares of the partner country in the total of bilateral trade. Secondly, the availability of road services depends on the level of congestion, proxied by the number of vehicles per kilometre of road infrastructure.

With an estimation equation derived in this way, there would still be an endogeneity problem. In other words, the empirical analysis could still suffer from transport infrastructure investment growth being induced by higher national incomes rather than the growth of road services contributing to income growth. To address the endogeneity problem, the country-specific technology shocks are broken down into a component that represents a joint random income shock of the entire group of countries in the panel and a country-specific random deviation from this average. This deviation is by construction orthogonal to the national productivity shocks and hence to government expenditures on transport infrastructure.

The income growth which is not explained by the expansion of the use of private inputs is computed as a Tornquist index of value added growth, both for the country group and for individual countries. The final estimation equation assesses the difference of income growth between individual countries and the panel of Western European economies as a function of differences in transport infrastructure growth, taking into account differences in transport requirements per unit of output of the different countries.

17.3 Data and Econometric Issues

The empirical analysis includes Western European countries for which data on all the variables involved are available. The largest gaps in the data were found for transport infrastructure investment, and for the real value of vehicle stock. The countries in the sample are Austria, Belgium, Finland, France, Germany, Italy, the Netherlands, Norway, Portugal, Spain, Sweden and the UK.

A major part of the data used was taken from the OECD's STAN (Structural Analysis) database (OECD, 2004e). This holds for gross production figures, value added, gross capital stock figures and the data on labour compensation. The employment figures in terms of hours worked have been taken from the OECD Productivity database (OECD, 2004d). The changes in vehicle stock were computed from the STAN figures on the production of motor vehicles, trailers and semi-trailers, subtracting exports and adding imports. The vehicle stock figures were calculated by applying the permanent inventory method and using the depreciation rate of 25.3 per cent proposed by Joergensen and Yan (1991b). The long-term interest rate reported in the OECD Outlook (OECD, 2004c) is used as the required rate of return on capital. Lacking information on the relevant taxes and subsidies, the user cost of capital is approximated by the sum of the discount rate and the required rate on return to capital. The total cost of vehicle capital divided by nominal value added gives the share of the vehicle capital cost in value added which is used to compute the Tornquist index of productivity growth. Nominal figures have been deflated using the deflator for private capital investment provided by the OECD Economic Outlook (OECD, 2004c).

Very few ECMT (European Conference of Ministers of Transport) member countries provide data on transport infrastructure stocks. The road stock figures are computed by applying the permanent inventory method to the ECMT data (ECMT, 2004b) on transport infrastructure investment. Following Boskin et al. (1989), it is assumed that roads depreciate geometrically at a rate of 1.9 per cent per year. Constant national currency values for road stock are calculated by using the deflator for government investment, reported in the OECD Economic Outlook (OECD, 2004c). As mentioned above, the variable 'road services' takes account of international trade relations and congestion. Bilateral trade coefficients are based on the bilateral trade data provided by the STAN Bilateral Trade Data Base (OECD, 2004a; 2004b). Congestion is depicted by dividing the constant currency value of road stock by the number of vehicles. The data on the number of vehicles are collected in the ECMT Statistical Report on Road Accidents (ECMT, 2004a).

Wherever absolute national currency values have had to be added up or compared, they have been made commensurable by using the Purchasing Power Parity (PPP) conversion factors of the OECD Economic Outlook (OECD, 2004c).

17.4 Results

For all the countries in the sample, the Tornquist index of productivity increased during the period from 1975 to 2000 (see Figure 17.1), Portugal, Finland and Sweden having the greatest overall increase of Total Factor Productivity (TFP). The increase in the index was highly volatile, but decreased on average over the whole period, as can be seen from Figure 17.2.

The transport infrastructure investment data show that the absolute numbers for transport infrastructure investment, and road infrastructure in particular, are highly volatile. Moreover, the share of transport infrastructure investment, including all modes, in GDP is secularly decreasing for the western European countries. They do, however, show a continuous increase in road stock which is, however, unable to keep pace with GDP growth. For road stock, this implies continuous growth, as shown by Figure 17.3, but at substantially decreasing rates (see Figure 17.4).

Figure 17.1: Tornquist Index of Real Productivity

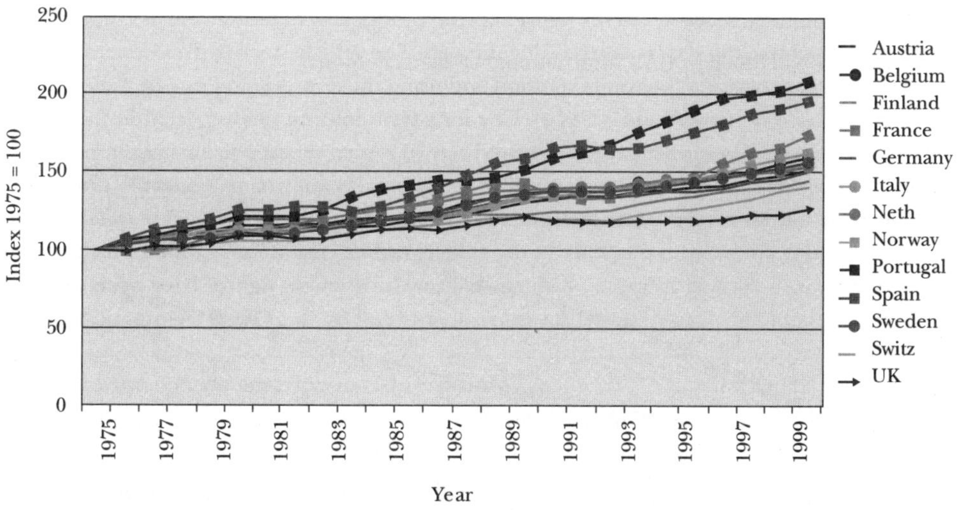

Figure 17.2: TFP Growth

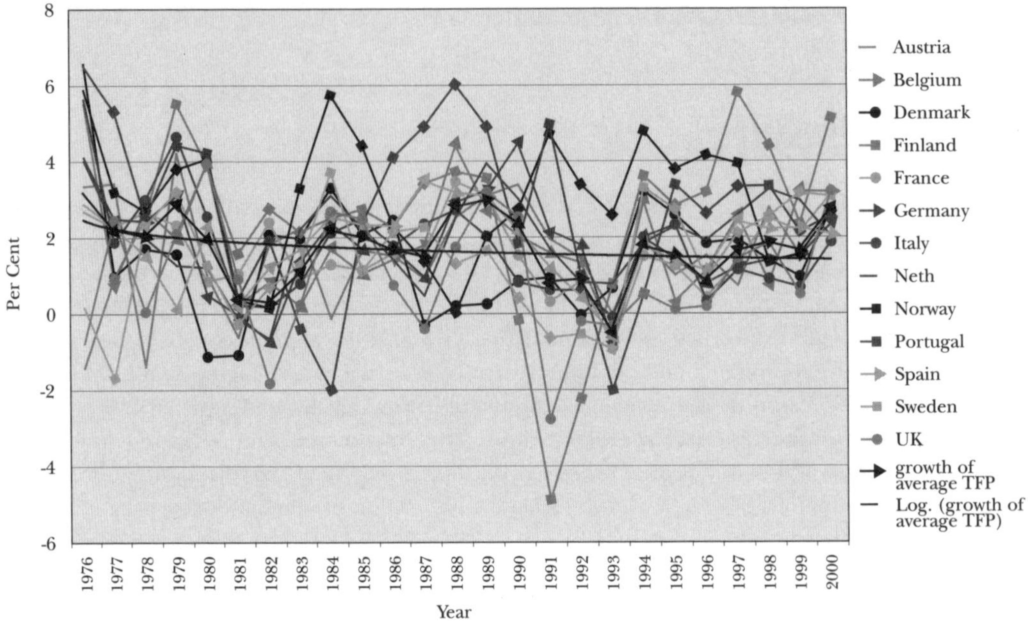

Figure 17.3: Road Stock in 1975 International Dollars (millions)

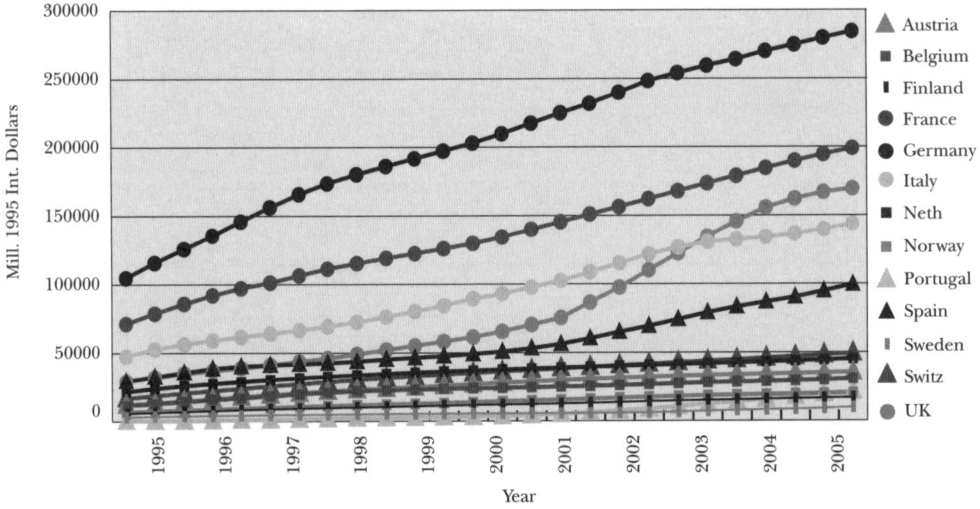

Figure 17.4: Growth Rates of Capital Stock

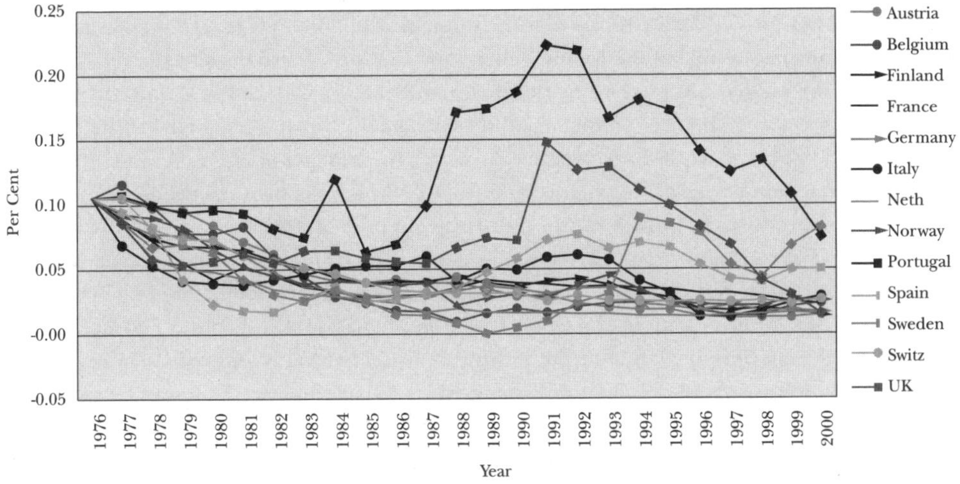

We estimate the relationship between the growth of road services and the change in the Tornquist index of value added by using a fixed-effects model. That is, we allow for country-specific, unobserved characteristics influencing the relationship between road infrastructure investment and macroeconomic productivity effects, which are assumed to be constant over time.

Whether road infrastructure investment has an impact on macroeconomic productivity growth is determined by the sign of the parameter ϕ. With a positive sign, we obtain an indication that infrastructure investment has a positive influence on productivity growth. In the first regression, we estimate the difference between national growth of TFP, measured by the Tornquist index of national value added, and the average TFP growth of the group of Western European countries overall (difftfp) as a function of the national shares of vehicle expenditures in value added multiplied by the growth rate of national road services (prod1) and the average vehicle share in national value added multiplied by the growth rate of the overall road services (prod2).

Table 17.1: Fixed Effects Regression 1

(Independent variables for national and international road stock).

Number of obs. = 300

difftfp	Coefficient	Standard Error	t	P > $\|\|t\|\|$	95 p.c. Confidence Interval
prod1	.7143729	.1921074	3.72	0.000	.3362493 1.092497
prod2	-2.478365	.49504	-5.01	0.000	-3.452749 -1.503981
constant	.2947857	.0294078	10.02	0.000	.2369025 .352669

R-sq: within = 0.0882
between = 0.0266
overall = 0.0458
F test that all $U_i = 0$: F(11,286) = 53.41 Prob > F = 0.0000

Table 18.1 shows difftfp as the dependent variable, prod1 and prod2 as the explanatory variables, the estimation coefficients of the latter, the t values, the P values and the 95 per cent confidence intervals. The table shows that the estimation coefficients have the expected signs (i.e., ϕ is positive), as both, national vehicle shares in value added and the average vehicle share in average value added are positive by definition and the coefficient for the product of the national vehicle share and the national road services is positive, and negative for the product of the overall vehicle share and the overall road stock. An increase in national road services by investment in national road infrastructure improves, *ceteris paribus*, national productivity growth relative to the productivity growth of the country group. All coefficients are highly significant and the F-test shows desired results. However, as can be seen from the reported coefficients, the share in the variation of productivity growth explained by road investment is very low.

Estimating the difference in productivity growth on the national and country group levels as a function of the difference between the products of vehicle shares and road services on the national and international levels does not change the fundamental results, as can be seen from Table 17.2. The ratio of production elasticities (i.e., ϕ) of road stock and vehicle stock remains positive. The significance of the estimation coefficient is, however, slightly decreased and the regression coefficient is even smaller than in the first model.

Table 17.2: Fixed Effects Regression 2

Difference between vehicle share weighted national and international road stock
Number of obs. = 300

difftfp	Coefficient	Standard Error	t	P > $\|\|t\|\|$	95 p.c. Confidence Interval
diffprod	.6563709	.1964768	3.34	0.001	.2696527 1.043089
constant	.2159342	.0223437	9.66	0.000	.1719559 .2599126

R-sq: within = 0.0374
between = 0.0266
overall = 0.0282
F test that all $U_i = 0$: F(11,287) = 50.81 Prob > F = 0.0000

The third estimation model adds a time dummy to estimation model 2. This improves the performance of the estimate in that the statistical significance of the estimated ϕ is improved and the regression coefficients are increased. The low coefficient for the time variable suggests that there is no problem of spurious correlation, due to the independent and dependent variables following the same time trend.

Table 17.3: Fixed Effects Regression 3

Difference of vehicle share weighted national and international road stock and year dummy
Number of obs. = 300

difftfp	Coefficient	Standard Error	t	P > $\|\|t\|\|$	95 p.c. Confidence Interval
diffprod	.7982335	.1919924	4.16	0.000	.4203362 1.176131
year	.0139947	.0029731	4.71	0.000	.0081427 .0198466
constant	-27.6085	5.911197	-4.67	0.000	-39.24347 -15.97353

R-sq: within = 0.1066
between = 0.0266
overall = 0.0528
F test that all $U_i = 0$: F(11,286) = 54.46 Prob > F = 0.0000

Including the time dummy leads to the result that road infrastructure services have a positive effect on productivity growth. According to the result in Table 17.3, the variance in growth of road services explains about ten per cent of the variance of the growth of TFP. The results do not suggest that there is an overall shortfall of road infrastructure investment. The rates of return for country i, which using a Cobb-Douglas function, can be computed by the expression $\phi s_{vi} * \frac{Y_i}{G_i}$, i.e., by multiplying the ratio of transport elasticities of vehicles to road services with the vehicle share in value added and the ratio of value added to road services, is on average about five per cent. This result is remarkably close to what Fernald (1999) obtained for the United States of America, using a sectoral panel.

17.5 Concluding Remarks

This chapter has argued that investment in road infrastructure indeed has positive macroeconomic productivity effects. The results of the paper do not, however, justify a general conclusion that national road infrastructure investment levels should be increased.

The rate of return implied by the above analysis does not seem to be high (for many countries around five per cent). A relatively low rate of return might not necessarily be due to too high a level of investment but could be due to a misallocation at the local level. As demand for transport services is highly unequally distributed over space and even over time, local road infrastructure investment projects might have high expected rates of return, even if the overall implied rate of return is low.

The greater income that can be achieved with the given resources may be associated with greater external costs, in particular in the form of environmental damage. On the other hand, the under provision of transport infrastructure services leads to external costs in the form of time costs, which are not reflected in the national accounts data used here. While it is certainly true that GDP is an imperfect welfare measure, further research is required to identify how the impact of transport infrastructure on income differs from the impact on welfare.

An analysis such as the above can, however, give a broad indication as to an appropriate level of infrastructure investment, at least based on the hypothetical assumption that the assignment of investment resources to individual projects is rational. To link the above macroeconomic analysis to planning tools to allocate regional infrastructure resources and cost-benefit analysis at the project level is a matter for future research.

Notes

1 Aschauer (1989, 1990) started the discussion on the productivity effects of public investment. His finding of large positive productivity effects being caused by public investment has been confirmed by Munnel (1990, 1992), Nadiri and Manuneas (1994), Kocherlakota and Yi (1996), Morrison and Schwartz (1996) as well as Duggal et al. (1999).

2 See, for example, Aaron (1990), Hulten and Schwab (1991a), Holtz-Eakin (1994) as well as Sturm and de Haan (1995).

References

Aaron, H. J. (1990), Discussion. In A. H. Munnel (ed.), *Is there a Shortfall in Public Capital Investment?,* Boston, Mass.

Aschauer, D. A. (1989), "Is Public Expenditure Productive?", *Journal of Monetary Economics,* 23: 177-200.

Aschauer, D. A. (1990), Why is Infrastructure Important? In A. H. Munnel (ed.), *Is there a Shortfall in Public Capital Investment?,* Boston, Mass.

Barro, R. J. and Sala-i-Martin, X. (1995), *Economic Growth,* New York.

Basu, S. and Fernald, J. G. (1997), "Returns to Scale in U.S. Production: Estimates and Implications", *Journal of Political Economy,* 105: 249-83.

Black, D. and Henderson, V. (1999), "A Theory of Urban Growth", *Journal of Political Economy* 107: 252-84.

Boarnet, M. G. (1998), "Spillovers and Locational Effects of Public Infrastructure", *Journal of Regional Science,* 38: 381-400.

Boskin, M. J., Robinson, M. S. and Huber, A. M. (1989), Government Saving, Capital Formation, and Wealth in the United States 1947-85. In Lipsey, R. E. and Tice, H. S. (ed.), *The Measurement of Saving, Investment, and Wealth,* Chicago.

Bougheas, S., Demetriades, P. O. and Morgenroth, E. L. W. (2003), "International Aspects of Public Infrastructure Investment", *Canadian Journal of Economics,* 36: 884-910.

Canning, D. (1999), "Infrastructure's Contribution to Aggregate Output", *World Bank Policy Research Working Paper,* 2246, Washington, D.C.

Canning, D. and Bennathan, E. (n.d.), The Social Rate of Return on Infrastructure Investment. mimeo, World Bank.

Carlino, G. A. and Voith, R. (1992), "Accounting for Differences in Aggregate State Productivity", *Regional Science and Urban Economics,* 22: 597-617.

Case, A., Rosen, H. and Hines Jr, J. (1993), "Budget Spillovers and Fiscal Policy Interdependence: Evidence from the States", *Journal of Public Economics,* 52: 285-307.

Chandra, M. and Thompson, E. (2000), "Does Public Infrastructure Affect Economic Activity? Evidence from the Rural Interstate Highway System", *Regional Science and Urban Economics* 30: 457-490.

Cohen, J. P. and Morrison Paul, C. J. (2004), "Public Infrastructure Investment, Interstate Spatial Spillovers, and Manufacturing Costs", *Review of Economics and Statistics,* 2 (86): 551-560.

Commission of the European Communities (2003), *"A European Initiative for Growth-Investing in Networks and Knowledge for Growth and Jobs".* Final Report to the European Parliament Brussels.

Duggal, V. G., Saltzman, C. and Klein, L. R. (1999), "Infrastructure and Productivity: A Nonlinear Approach", *Journal of Econometrics,* 92: 47-74.

ECMT (2004a), *Statistical Report on Road Accidents 2002 CD Rom ed.* Paris.

Fernald, J. G. (1999), "Roads to Prosperity? Assessing the Link Between Public Capital and Productivity", *American Economic Review,* 89: 619-38.

Hall, R. E. (1990), Invariance Properties of Solow's Productivity Residual. In P. Diamond (ed.), *Growth/Productivity/Unemployment: Essays to Celebrate Bob Solow's Birthday,* Cambridge, Mass.

Holtz-Eakin, D. (1994), "Public Sector Capital and the Productivity Puzzle", *Review of Economics and Statistics,* 76: 12-21.

Holtz-Eakin, D. and Lovely, M. E. (1996), "Scale Economies, Returns to Variety, and the Productivity of Public Infrastructure", *Regional Science and Urban Economics,* 26: 105-123.

Holtz-Eakin, D. and Schwartz, A. E. (1995), "Spatial Productivity Spillovers from Public Infrastructure: Evidence from State High-Ways", *International Tax and Public Finance,* 2: 459-68.

Hulten, C. R. and Schwab, R. M. (1991), "Public Capital Formation and the Growth of Regional Manufacturing Industries", *National Tax Journal,* 44 (4): 121-34.

Jörgensen, D. W. and Yan, K.-Y. (1991), *Tax Reform and the Cost of Capital,* Oxford.

Kao, C. and Chiang, M. (2000), On the Estimation and Inference of a Cointegrated Regression in Panel Data. In B. H. Baltagi (ed.), *Nonstationary Panels, Panel Cointegration, and Dynamic Panels. Advances in Econometrics,* Vol. 15, Amsterdam.

Kelejian, H. and Robinson, D. (1997), "Infrastructure Productivity Estimation and Its Underlying Econometric Specification: A Sensitivity Analysis", *Regional Science and Urban Economics,* 76: 115-31.

Kocherlakota, N. R. and Yi, K.M. (1996), "A Simple Time Series Test of Endogenous vs. Exogenous Growth Models: An Application to the United States", *Review of Economics and Statistics,* 78 (1): 126-34.

Lucas, R.E. (1988), "On the Mechanics of Economic Development", *Journal of Monetary Economics,* 22: 3-42.

Lucas, R.E. (2001), "Externalities and Cities", *Review of Economic Dynamics,* 4: 245-74.

Lucas, R.E. and Rossi-Hansberg, E. (2002), "On the Internal Structure of Cities", *Econometrica* 70: 1445-76.

Mankiw, N.G. (1992), "The Optimal Under Provision of Public Goods", Harvard University Working Paper Cambridge, Mass.

Morrison, C. J. and Schwartz, A. E. (1996), "State Infrastructure and Productive Performance", *American Economic Review,* 86: 1095-1111.

Munnel, A. H. (1990), "Does Public Infrastructure Affect Regional Economic Performance?" In A. H. Munnel (ed.), *Is there a Shortfall in Public Capital Investment,* Boston, Mass.

Munnell, A. H. (1992), "Policy Watch: Infrastructure Investment and Economic Growth", *Journal of Economic Perspectives,* 6: 189-98.

Nadiri, M. I. and Mamuneas, T. P. (1994), "The Effects of Public Infrastructure and R&D Capital on the Cost Structure and Performance of U.S. Manufacturing Industries", *Review of Economics and Statistics,* 76 (1): 22-37.

OECD (2004a), *BTD Old Bilateral Trade Database in ISIC, Rev. 2 1970-1995.* Paris.
— (2004b), *BTD STAN Bilateral Trade Database in ISIC, rev. 3.* Paris.
— (2004c), *OECD Economic Outlook. Annual and Quarterly Data.* Paris.
— (2004d), *Productivity Database. 2004 edition.* Paris.

Sturm, J. E. and de Haan, J. (1995), "Is Public Expenditure Really Productive?", *Economic Modelling,* 12 (1): 60-72.

United States Department of Transportation (1976), Development of the Interstate Program, America's Highways, 1776-1976. Federal Highway Administration, Washington, D.C.

PART V

PRODUCTIVITY AND THE KNOWLEDGE ECONOMY

INTRODUCTION

The concept of the 'knowledge economy' is based on the idea that science, research, technology and innovation play an important role in creating knowledge in modern economies, and that the use of computers and the Internet have a role in generating, sharing and applying knowledge. This section reviews the various disparate elements that come under this definition, and asks what evidence exists to confirm their economic importance. Kavanagh and Doyle in Chapter 18 review the compelling evidence in support of the view that increased human capital boosts growth, individual earnings, and firm level productivity. Turning to R&D, Czarnitzki and O'Byrnes (Chapter 19) conclude that R&D expenditure generates significant private and social returns. The social returns are substantially higher than the private returns due to the 'spill-over' of research findings. They also find that countries which lag behind in R&D performance can benefit most from these spillovers, as long as they have sufficient absorptive capacity. Dagg (Chapter 20) sets out how the R&D performance of Ireland is evolving. In terms of ICT, in Chapter 21 Mundschenk shows that while ICT can have a very positive effect on productivity, particular characteristics of the European economy have prevented Europeans from taking full advantage of it. In a review of four case studies in Chapter 22, Maddox and Boyle show that the success of an organisation in optimising its ICT use depends on the strategic vision for ICT within that organisation.

CHAPTER 18

HUMAN CAPITAL AND PRODUCTIVITY IN THE IRISH CONTEXT

CATHERINE KAVANAGH AND ELEANOR DOYLE

ABSTRACT

Human capital has long been regarded as one of the main drivers of growth and productivity in an economy. This chapter analyses and outlines the theoretical and empirical findings linking human capital to productivity growth at a macroeconomic level. There is compelling evidence in support of the view that increased human capital boosts growth, individual earnings, and firm level productivity. While the impressive gains in labour productivity experienced in Ireland since the 1990s were underpinned by a steep rise in educational attainment, educational outcomes today, while broadly in line with OECD averages, are still below the results achieved by the best performers in the OECD.

18.1 Introduction

One of the most important macroeconomic issues is how to improve living standards, i.e., GDP per capita, over time. It is now widely recognised that the main driver of living standards in the long term is productivity growth.

But what drives productivity? Levels and growth rates of productivity depend on many factors of which human capital – in essence, a skilled labour force - is just one, but an increasingly important one. This observation has attracted considerable recent attention not least because of the ability of policymakers to influence it through investment in education and training.

With global, demographic and technological change, it has been argued that the links between human capital and productivity are now more important than ever (Bergheim, 2005; Leitch, 2005). Product markets have become more global, increasing the elasticity of both product and labour demand. The growing availability of high-technology capital has created new products and production systems that may require workers to have greater cognitive skills and to be more adaptable and efficient learners.[1] Economic growth increasingly depends on the synergies between new knowledge and human capital, which is why large increases in educational and training investment have accompanied major advances in technological knowledge in all countries that have achieved significant growth over the past decade.[2]

Despite the consensus that human capital impacts on productivity, the extent and nature of the relationship remains unclear. There are at least three ways of defining the impact or returns to investment in human capital: (1) the productivity or growth effects – sometimes referred to as macro effects; (2) the returns to the individual; and (3) the firm level effects. The first highlights the impact of human capital investment on macroeconomic growth and productivity. The second is made up of the costs and benefits to the individual and is net of any transfers from the state and any taxes paid. The third attempts to estimate any additional externalities or spillover effects at the level of the firm.[3] The purpose of this chapter is to provide an insight into the literature that examines these separate effects of human capital on growth and productivity.

The chapter is structured as follows. Section 18.2 outlines the theoretical and empirical findings in the literature linking human capital to productivity and growth at the macroeconomic level. The following section reviews the basic tenets of human capital theory and provides some empirical evidence that demonstrates compelling support for positive rates of return to education and training for the individual. Section 18.4 reviews the strand of literature that links human capital and firm level productivity. A brief overview of Ireland's human capital record in a comparative context is offered in Section 18.5 and Section 18.6 provides a conclusion and some policy considerations.

18.2 Human Capital, National Growth and Productivity

There are many definitions of human capital in the literature. However, one of the most useful and widely used is that by the OECD (2001), which states that human capital is the "knowledge, skills, competencies and attributes embodied in individuals that facilitate the creation of personal, social and economic well-being." Hence, the knowledge and skills that a worker has – which can be acquired or added to from education and training – generates a stock of productive capital. Education, experience and abilities of an individual have an economic value for the individual, for employers and for the economy as a whole.

18.2.1 Theoretical Foundations

There are two main strands to the literature that attempt to link human capital to growth and productivity. The first is based on the seminal work of Robert Solow in 1956. Solow's model is based on a production-function approach to the economy where output (Y) depends on inputs of capital (K) and labour (L) and exogenous technological advances.[4] Solow shows that economic growth is driven by the improvement of productivity via technological advancement. Hence, improving the efficiency of labour, through a better skilled workforce, is an example of how growth can be generated within the Solow framework, although Solow does not specifically explain how the process of growth is determined.

The second strand is based on the new growth theories by Lucas (1988) and Romer (1986; 1990). These models emphasise the endogenous determination of growth rates which are determined within the model (and can thus be affected by government policies), instead of being driven by exogenous technical change. Human capital affects growth in at least two ways: increases in education and training have the potential to spillover to other individuals, making other workers more productive; and better educated and trained workers are more productive, have more knowledge and make better use of firms' capital investments. The approach also emphasises the higher rate of innovation that can be generated by having more educated workers generating new ideas.

Empirically, the theoretical frameworks propose the following outcomes. The first view proposes that the level of output depends on the level of human capital and this implies that output growth depends on the rate at which countries accumulate human capital over time. Hence, a one-off permanent increase in the stock of human capital (e.g. average years of education in the population) will give rise to a one-off increase in productivity growth.[5]

The second views human capital as enhancing the absorption and innovation of new technologies. Human capital stocks (levels of education) are thus linked to productivity growth, and a one-off permanent increase in the level of human capital is associated with a permanent increase in the growth rate of productivity.[6]

There is no consensus among academics about which theory most accurately describes the process of economic growth. However, there is consensus that improvements in human capital provide a boost to growth by making workers more productive and/or more flexible.

18.2.2 Empirical Evidence

We can summarise the following key points from the empirical literature as follows:[7]

- There is compelling international evidence indicating that investment in education increases growth and productivity. For example, increasing average education in the population by one year has a positive impact on productivity of between three and six per cent (and perhaps seven per cent, based on new growth theories).[8]
- Third level education is relatively more important for growth in OECD countries than primary or secondary education, between 1960 and the 1990s (Gemmell, 1996).

- It appears that the stage (primary, secondary, tertiary), level (are all years of education equally valuable? Does the impact of expanding a stage of education (say, higher education) depend on the initial levels of attainment in that stage?) and type (e.g. engineering versus arts degree, academic versus vocational) of education all matter for growth (Judson, 1998).
- There is some evidence (albeit small) that efficiency of educational resource allocation matters for growth (Judson, 1998).
- Human capital also contributes indirectly to growth through its positive impact on physical capital (Barro, 1991; Gemmel, 1996; Benhabib and Spiegel, 1994).
- There is evidence that the rate of technology transfer is enhanced by human capital (Griffith, Redding and Van Reenen, 2000; Cameron, Proudman and Redding, 1998; Benhabib and Spiegel, 1994).
- The effects of training on productivity growth at the national level are not addressed in the literature. The debate would benefit greatly from such research.
- There are wider social benefits associated with increased investment in human capital, such as improved health (Barro and Lee, 1994; Rose and Taubman, 1979; Fuchs, 1979; Schultz, 1963; 1981; Becker, 1993), reduced crime possibilities (Blundell et al., 1999; Johnson, 2004), greater social cohesion (Green et al., 2003), fertility (Barro, 1991 and Barro and Lee, 1994), lower infant mortality (Barro and Lee, 1994), and greater voter participation (Dee, 2003).

18.3 Human Capital, Productivity and Returns to the Individual

The idea that education and training constitute an investment in individuals that is analogous to investment in machinery was first espoused by Adam Smith in 1776 in his book, The Wealth of Nations.[9] However, it is the writings of Mincer (1958; 1962; 1974), Schultz (1961), and Becker (1962) that underpin the theoretical and empirical foundations of human capital.

18.3.1 Theoretical Foundations

Human capital theory suggests that differences in human capital lead to differences in productivity and hence to differences in earnings. The process of acquiring skills is analogous to an investment decision. Like other investment decisions, it requires the outlay of resources now (costs) for expected returns in the future (benefits), and like other investments, it is the prospect of these returns that motivates the individual to undertake such investment.

The costs to the individual of investment include psychological, social and monetary costs (e.g. difficulty with learning, costs of going to college, loss of earnings when not working, etc.). The private benefits to the individual are the expected financial rewards from work, i.e., an individual will expect higher earnings over their working life because investment in education and training equips them with skills that improve their productivity and make them more attractive to employers as a result.[10]

Human capital theory postulates that an individual, when deciding to invest in education and training, will perform a sort of cost-benefit analysis, considering the benefits of education and training, net of costs. Various other factors will also influence the individual's decision: investment is more likely when the person is young, when the expected earnings are higher and when the initial investment costs are lower.[11]

18.3.2 Empirical Evidence: The Returns to Education

There is a significant amount of research indicating that education and earnings are positively linked. In all countries, including Ireland, graduates of tertiary level education earn substantially more than upper secondary and post-secondary non-tertiary graduates. In many countries, upper secondary and post-secondary non-tertiary education forms a break point beyond which additional education attracts a particularly high premium. Earnings differentials between tertiary and upper secondary education are generally more pronounced than those between upper and lower secondary or below (OECD, 2005).

The theory itself gives rise to earnings functions that attempt to explain the observed differences in earnings between individuals.[12] There is a vast and varied literature on the internal rates of returns using these earnings functions, and some of these have been estimated with a good degree of success.[13] Blundell et al. (1999), Card (1999) and more recently Harmon et al. (2003) offer good summaries of this literature.

Some of the key findings are as follows.

- Education and earnings are positively linked. In all countries, including Ireland, graduates of tertiary level education earn substantially more than upper secondary and post-secondary non-tertiary graduates.
- The main measure of human capital used in the empirical literature is education, captured by the years of schooling of the individual. Analyses using this measure of human capital throw up rates of return to the individual of an additional year of education in the range five to fifteen per cent.
- Although there is wide variation in cross country studies, the most recent international evidence suggests a return to a year of schooling is in the range of seven to nine per cent for males and about eight to ten per cent for females. It is higher for Ireland: between nine to eleven per cent for males and about 14 per cent for females.[14] These returns for Ireland are significant and represent a high return on investment, relative to any other form of investment. They are central to any assessment of the impact of Exchequer investment on education.
- Individuals have different levels of ability and when estimates of the rate or return to schooling are adjusted for this, they are somewhat lower. Nevertheless, there is an "unambiguous positive effect on the earnings of an individual from participation in education" (Harmon et al., 2003: 150).
- Some tentative evidence suggests the return to education may not be linear; there may be a bonus for higher levels of educational attainment such as a degree (Denny and Harmon, 2001; Skalli, 2001) – this may also be true for Ireland, but further research is required.

18.3.3 Empirical Evidence: The Returns to Training

Training and up-skilling are just as important as initial education. In ten to fifteen years from now, the bulk of the labour force will still be composed of individuals who are currently in the labour market. Furthermore, due to population ageing and the effect of policies aimed at prolonging working life, most of these individuals will have completed their initial education many years before and rapid technological change will have made part of their competencies obsolete. The education and training they receive after they have started their working life is therefore crucial for both output growth an individual career prospects (OECD, 2003).

Although less empirical evidence exists on the impact of training on productivity, the limited data available indicates that on-the-job training is an important source of the increase in earnings that workers get as they gain experience at work. The returns of on-the-job training are commonly found to be quite high, at between five to ten per cent.

The following is a summary of the key points from the literature:

- People with higher ability and with higher educational attainment are more likely to participate in training, suggesting a strong complementarity between the components of human capital; early ability, qualifications and knowledge (acquired from formal education) and skills and competencies (acquired from training on the job) (see Blundell et al., 1999).
- Women, part-time workers and older workers are less likely to receive training than other groups. However, the returns to training for working women may be greater than for working men (see Booth, 1991; Greenlagh and Stewart, 1987).
- International evidence indicates there are significant returns to investment in formal training for the individual: higher earnings in the range of five to ten per cent have been observed (see Blundell et al., 1999; Smith, 2001; Groot, 1995). Despite the positive effects of training, there is some evidence of under provision.[15]
- There is very limited evidence on the returns to training in Ireland but the studies that do exist, indicate it is positive (Denny and Harmon, 2000).[16] Also, surveys of Irish training show that large firms train more than small firms, foreign enterprises provide more employee training than their indigenous counterparts, and training is concentrated among those who are already highly qualified.
- Individuals benefit in other ways from training, in addition to increased earnings. Training is associated with the likelihood of promotion (Bishop, 1990), reduced probability of unemployment, and reduced likelihood of quitting (Dearden et al., 1997; Lillard and Tan, 1992; Booth and Satchell, 1994; Blundell et al., 1996 for men; and Lynch, 1991 for company-provided formal on-the-job training).
- Firms are generally slow to invest in training that equips workers with transferable skills, for fear of poaching. With specific training, firms are more likely to invest as they can reap some of the benefits when the worker becomes more productive as a result of training. There is some evidence that the content of training is important; computer training seems to have a greater impact on productivity, as least in the non-manufacturing sector in the US (Black and Lynch, 1995; 1996).
- There is evidence that training also benefits the firm; in the UK a one percentage point increase in training is associated with an increase in the value-added per hour of about 0.6 per cent (Dearden et al., 2005).[17] However, evidence from the US and New Zealand is not as conclusive.

- More highly skilled workers are more likely to adapt to change and are more likely to be a direct source of innovation (Bosworth and Wilson, 1993; Chapman and Tan, 1990).

18.4 Human Capital and Firm Level Productivity

Investigation of how human capital impacts on business-level productivity has proceeded apace with the compilation of new datasets, initially across Northern Europe and in more recent times in the US and in the European Union. The need and use of these new datasets is implicitly based on the view that "the productivity of a country is ultimately set by the productivity of its companies" (Porter, 2005: 45). Furthermore to understand the impact of human capital development and the role of policy therein, firm-level research is required that facilitates focus on both individual firm and worker characteristics.

Such analyses is important for economies moving from an investment-led stage of economic growth towards an innovation-driven phase, such as Ireland, where the scope for economic growth generated from capital accumulation have largely been relatively exhausted (notwithstanding the remaining work required to bring transport infrastructures, in particular, up to international standards).

In the context of this research, databases of linked employer-employee data create the potential for comprehensive investigation of relationships between human capital and productivity at the level of firms. Specific questions that have been addressed based on the approach include (as highlighted by Abowd et al., 2002) the following:

1. How has the allocation and distribution of human capital changed in the economy? Are aggregate changes indicative of broad trends or are specific industries or specific firms within industries driving observed results?
2. How do changes occur? Do new firms with different levels of human capital replace old firms or do current firms adjust their workforce? Do high-tech firms increase employment and crowd out employment in low-tech firms?
3. What causes changes? Which changes in technology are associated with changes in human capital? How are skill intensity and skill dispersion affected by technological changes?

However, research on Ireland is limited by the absence of such data.

18.4.1 Some Evidence from Firm-Level Data

There are several additional benefits from using this type of firm-level data. The new datasets permit a better understanding of the role and degree of structural change on labour productivity (see Haltiwanger, 1998 for an example). This issue is often not explicitly addressed in the macroeconomic discussions of sources of productivity growth. Also, it has been shown that once researchers control for both individual and firm heterogeneity, approximately 90 per cent of wage rate variation can be explained. This is over twice what could be explained using alternative methods (see for example, Abowd et al., 2002).

Early firm-level studies provide evidence of a positive impact of computers/technology on productivity that macroeconomic studies were unable to identify, but the latter now also indicate the association between ICT usage, particularly, and macroeconomic growth.

The technology/productivity link is a crunch issue for Europe. Much is made of Europe's problem in converting ICT investment into productivity gains at macro level due to less effective ICT use, although Ireland rates relatively well here - along with Ireland, the US recorded the biggest increases in ICT contribution to labour productivity growth, from 1996 to 2002 (EIU, 2004).

Some of the key findings from the literature (Stiroh, 2001; Oliner and Sichel, 2000; O'Mahoney and Van Ark, 2003; Turcotte and Rennison, 2004; Black and Lynch 1995; 1996a; 1996b; Entorf and Kramarz, 1997; Abowd et al., 2002) are as follows:

- The most productive firms appear more likely to use advanced technology/ICT than the less productive.
- In the absence of longitudinal data, computer users possess unobserved skills that affect wages.
- Computer use, university education and computer skills development are associated with higher productivity, however, computer use is correlated with productivity benefits irrespective of whether workers have university degrees.
- The impact of education and technology on productivity is evident in both manufacturing and non-manufacturing sectors.
- Productivity improvements from employing a greater share of university graduates and using computers are larger for smaller firms (less than 20 employees).
- Businesses that upgraded their technology were also observed to upgrade their skills.
- In the US, firms in non-manufacturing industries that provided computer training to their workers had significantly higher productivity than competitors.

18.5 How Does Ireland's Human Capital Record Compare?

We have seen that there is compelling evidence in support of the view that increased human capital boosts growth, individual earnings, and firm level productivity. It is insightful therefore to examine Ireland's educational attainments in a comparative context.

Impressive gains in labour productivity have boosted economic growth since the early 1990s (OECD, 2006). However, they were underpinned by a steep rise in the educational attainment of the working-age population. As a result, educational outcomes, while broadly in line with the OECD average, are still below the results achieved by the best performers in the OECD. The most recent available data reveals the following:[18]

- **Attainment of Upper Secondary Level Qualification:** Of the population aged 25-64 in Ireland, 62 per cent have attained at least upper secondary education; this is below the OECD average of 66 per cent and well below the leader countries of Korea, Norway, Sweden, Canada, Finland and US, and Japan, for example. Even if we restrict the sample to the proportion of the population between 25-34 years, Ireland's performance (at 78 per cent) is still ranked below these leader countries, although slightly above the country mean of 75 per cent.

- **Attainment of Third Level Qualification:** At third level, Ireland's performance is somewhat better: approximately 26 per cent of the population aged 25-64 have attained some form of tertiary level qualification, compared to a country mean of 24 per cent and the figure is higher for the sample 25-34 and 35-44, at 37 per cent and 27 per cent respectively. Nevertheless, these figures are still below the average population attainment levels for Finland, Norway, Sweden, US and Canada, and also, the UK.
- **Graduation Rates – 2nd Level:** Rising skill demands in OECD countries have made qualifications at the upper secondary level of education the minimum credential for successful labour market entry. Upper secondary level education also serves at the foundation for advanced learning and training opportunities, as well as preparation for direct entry into the labour market. Hence, these graduation rates give one signal of the extent to which educational systems succeed in preparing students to meet the minimum requirements of the labour market. In terms of graduation rates, at second level, Ireland's performance at 91 per cent is at the top end of the ranking, along with Germany, Greece, Norway, Japan and Switzerland.
- **Graduation Rates – 3rd Level:** Tertiary graduation rates show the rate at which each country's education system produces advanced knowledge. Countries with high graduation rates at the tertiary level are also the ones most likely to be developing or maintaining a highly skilled labour force. For tertiary graduation rates of Type A, Ireland is ranked 8th out of 21 countries, and for tertiary graduation rates of Type B, Ireland is ranked second out of 18 countries.[19]
- **Advanced Research Degrees:** Ireland is well below the country mean for advanced research type of degrees. Out of 27 countries, Ireland is ranked 13.
- **Public Expenditure on Education:** In terms of public expenditure on education, total public expenditure on education, as a proportion of GDP fell from 5.1 per cent in 1995 to 4.4 per cent in 2002, which is lower than the OECD average of 5.4 per cent of GDP in 2002. This is in contrast to other countries, such as Denmark, Sweden and New Zealand, where there have been significant shifts in public funding in favour of education.
- **Skills Profiles of Recent Immigrants:** It is also interesting to examine the skills profiles of immigrants to Ireland. The ESRI (2005: 29) have shown that many recent immigrants have high educational attainment levels relative to the native population. They note "while 27.3 per cent of the native population have third level qualifications, the corresponding figure for immigrants is 54.2 per cent. At the other end of the educational distribution, while 32.9 per cent of the native population have only lower secondary qualifications or less, only 15.1 per cent of the immigrant population have this low level of attainment".

In summary, we can see that Ireland lags behind in several key areas and there is room for improvement.

18.6 Conclusions and Key Policy Issues for Ireland

18.6.1 Some Observations and Challenges Going Forward

A well educated and well-trained population is important for the social and economic well-being of countries and individuals. In addition to providing individuals with the knowledge, skills and competencies to participate actively in society, education also contributes to economic growth, and to the expansion of scientific and cultural knowledge. Since Ireland is a small open economy, it will continue to be strongly affected by globalisation. In this context, it is important to be able to respond rapidly to economic change. This requires workers to be flexible; as they will need to change occupations and industries as traditional sectors decline and new sectors (mainly services) emerge.

It is likely that labour productivity growth will be a key determinant of future economic performance since the extent to which employment can continue to grow is constrained by supply factors; there is probably limited scope to improve participation rates, there is a declining number of young people flowing into the workforce and any future requirements for expanding the labour supply, if required, must be met by immigration.

Labour productivity can be increased in several ways: by improving the quality of labour used in production; by increasing the use of capital per worker and improving its quality; or by attaining greater overall efficiency in how these factors or production are used together (which economists call Multifactor Productivity, MFP). MFP can therefore include many types of efficiency improvements such as improved managerial practices, organisational change, and innovations leading to more valuable output being produced with a given amount of capital and labour. However, the evidence indicates that the skills and competencies of the labour force play a critical role in raising labour productivity. Increases in the level of post-educational skills may be even more important in the future – this is particularly so given the greater emphasis on knowledge, innovation and Research and Development (R&D) in order to complete globally in the 21st century.

18.6.2 Key Policy Issues for Ireland

- **Financing of Education is Justified:** The evidence suggests that investing in the education of individuals raises their productivity in working life and thus contributes to productivity an output growth in the economy. This strengthening of the national economy justifies governmental involvement in the production and financing of education.
- **Education May Reduce Wage Inequality:** Evidence indicates that education contributes significantly to the wage differences observed in labour markets. Hence, improving the educational attainment level of the less educated is likely to reduce wage inequality.
- **Need to Improve Educational Attainment Levels:** It is widely acknowledged that the lack of educational attainment remains a critical factor in the risk and persistence of unemployment. This, together with an increasing demand for a higher skilled workforce, makes it imperative to improve upon educational attainment at all levels. Policymakers need to examine the factors relating to the low attainment of third level qualification (Type A). Also, there appears to be significant scope for improvement at the level of advanced

research. In order to raise the education attainments levels of the Irish population, it is likely that both structural reforms and the allocation of more resources to the education sector are required.

- **Up-skilling and Training is Vital:** It has been shown that training, especially up-skilling, increases workers' productivity, output growth, individual wages and employability. Research shows that training is unequally distributed with workers who are in a better position in the labour market having more opportunities and incentives to acquire news skills. FÁS have significantly increased its expenditure on training of employed workers since 2005, in particular, with the launch of the One-Step-Up Initiative that arose in response to the Enterprise Strategy Group recommendations. However, as noted by FÁS, it is imperative that the under-represented and least qualified are targeted in all such initiatives.
- **Need to Utilise More Effectively the Skills of Immigrants:** It appears recent Irish immigrants are in occupations that are not commensurate with their educational qualifications. As noted by the ESRI (2005), failure to employ immigrants in a way that fully captures their higher educational levels means Ireland is losing out. Policy should aim to improve this matching process so that better use is made of the skills and competencies of highly qualified immigrants.
- **Subsidising the Creation of New Ideas:** Evidence indicates that human capital is an important input in the creation of new ideas. This fact should further inform policy debate on, for example, the balance between direct support for R&D, and/or subsidisation of certain kinds of education, (perhaps those who could go on to work in R&D, such as PhD students and research masters students, etc.).

18.6.3 Further Research

There is still some uncertainty in the education-growth research. It is still unclear whether education (and increases in the stock of human capital implied by more education) increases the level or the growth rate of GDP.

Further research is required to inform other policy relevant questions such as: how is growth affected by investment in different states of education (from pre-school to advanced tertiary education and work-related training)? How is growth affected by investment in different types of education, such as engineering disciplines and the arts? How is growth affected by the quality of education? How, if at all, are growth effects from the expansion of one stage of education affected by the level of attainment achieved at an earlier stage?

The emergence of new firm level databases has created the potential for comprehensive investigation of relationships between human capital and productivity at the level of firms in the US and elsewhere. Research in Ireland of this kind is limited due to the absence of data. Such research would be extremely worthwhile.

Notes

1 See Murnane et al. (1995) and Cawley et al. (2000) for a discussion of the importance of greater cognitive skills on the earnings of workers.

2 South Korea, Spain, Taiwan and India are examples of countries that have invested significantly in human capital in recent times. See Bergheim (2005) for a discussion in particular, of the success stories of Spain and South Korea.

3 A fourth version, known as the social rate of return to education, builds on the second approach. It attempts to calculate the social internal return of educational investments, as the rate of return that balances individual and tax benefits with social costs, although in practice, it does not include all the costs and benefits to society. The aim is then to compare this social rate of return to other relevant rates (e.g. rate of other investments, interest paid on borrowed funds, social discount rates, etc.), to identify if the investment was worthwhile. Estimation of this rate of return is new to the literature and very little empirical evidence exists, given the difficulty with measurement. See OECD (2004) for evidence of the social rate of return for a sample of selected countries.

4 Solow's (1956) theory is also referred to as the neoclassical growth theory.

5 In empirical work, this approach is similar to the neoclassical approach. Lucas (1988) offered the influential contribution, which in turn related to previous work by Uzawa (1965).

6 This view emerges from the work of Romer (1986, 1990) and Redding (1996).

7 Sianesi and Van Reenan (2003) provide an excellent review of this literature. We draw on their research here.

8 Either augmented production functions (augmented with human capital) or cross-country growth regressions are standard methods of analysing human capital in the context of macro-economic growth. Most of the literature focuses on estimating cross-country macro growth regressions. Models based on the Solow growth theory typically use a measure of human capital in an augmented aggregate production function (for example, Mankiw et al., 1992, for the US) as follows: $Y = K^a H^b (AL)^{1-a-b}$. Here, H is the stock of human capital and A is labour-augmenting technical change.

9 Although Smith never used the term human capital, it is clear he was referring to the stock of knowledge, skills and experience of individuals.

10 A good discussion of the costs and benefits of human capital investment is offered by Elliott (1991).

11 It is worth noting that the screening/signalling approach offers a different view to human capital theory that has important policy implications. It suggests that education serves as a signal to employers who screen potential workers based on their educational record. In this view, education does not increase workers' productivity. Although it has proven difficult to disentangle the two approaches empirically, on balance, it appears that there is *more* support for the human capital approach. Hence, we conclude that education does increase workers' productivity and is not just a signalling device.

12 A general form of the model is: $\text{Log } W/P\ i = a_1 + a_2 I_i + a_3 X_i + e_i$. Here, W/P is the real wage, I the investment in education (usually measured by years of schooling), X is a vector of variables capturing a range of individual and workplace characteristics and e is the error term. Here, a_2 measures the proportionate effect of an extra year of schooling on earnings.

13 Education consistently emerges as the prime human capital investment for empirical analysis. Human capital is also perceived to contribute to health and nutrition (Schultz 1963, 1981), but education in the form of schooling is generally used in analysis because it can be measured in quantitative costs and years of tenure. Recent studies have also pointed to the importance of friends, ethnic affiliation, and neighbourhoods in the choice of human capital decisions of individuals, even after controlling for the effects of parental income or education (see for example, Charles and Luoh, 2003 and Gang and Zimmerman, 2000).

14 These results are based on research by Harmon et al. (2001) derived from Public Funding and Private Returns to Education (PURE), These rates of return are based on national surveys rather than a single source such as the ISSP. Earlier work for Ireland suggested the return to an extra year of schooling to be approximately eight per cent (see Callan and Harmon, 1999 and Callan and Wren, 1992). Research has indicated that it is important to distinguish between returns to males and females.

15 OECD (2003) argues that public policy may therefore have a role to play to improve individuals' and employers' incentives to invest in human capital. Also, fiscal incentives should be focused on those groups who are most at risk in the labour market and who are most in need of training, such as, part-time workers, older workers, low-skilled workers, etc.

16 The study examines the impact on earnings of the Vocational Preparation and Training Programme which can be taken following the Junior Certificate and Leaving Certificate. It therefore does not focus on work related training as such.

17 Similar positive effects have been found by Almeida and Carneiro (2005).

18 Latest available data is for 2002 from OECD (2005) *Education at a Glance*, OECD, Paris.

19 The OECD distinguishes between three different tertiary education levels: ISCED 5A, ISCED 5B and ISCED6. The former refers to a traditional university type qualification, type ISCEDB generally refers to shorter and often vocationally oriented courses, while ISCED 6 relates to advanced research qualifications at the doctorate level.

References

Abowd, J., Haltiwanger, J., Jarmin, R., Lane, J., Lengermann, P., McCue, K., McKinney, K., and Sandusky, K. (2002), *The Relation Among Human Capital, Productivity, and Market Value: Building Up from Micro Evidence*, Technical Paper no. TP-2002-14 US Census Bureau, LEHD Program.

Almeida, R. and Carneiro, P. (2005), "The Return to Firm Investment in Human Capital", *Institute for Fiscal Studies Working Paper* CWP21/05.

Barro, R. (1991), "Economic Growth in a Cross Section of Countries", *Quarterly Journal of Economics* 106, 407-443.

Barro, R. (1997), *Determinants of Economic Growth: A Cross-Country Empirical Study*, MIT Press, Cambridge, MA.

Barro, R. and Lee, J. (1994), "Sources of Economic Growth", *Carnegie-Rochester Conference Series on Public Policy*.

Bassanini, A. and Scarpetta, S. (2001), "Does Human Capital Matter for Growth in OECD Countries", *Economics Department Working Papers No. 282,* OECD, Paris.

Becker, G. (1962), "Investment in Human Capital: A Theoretical Analysis", *The Journal of Political Economy,* LXX 5, 2, 9-49.

Benhabib, J. and Spiegel, M.M. (1994), "The Role of Human Capital in Economic Development, Evidence from Aggregate Cross-Country Data", *Journal of Monetary Economics,* 34, 143-173.

Bergheim, S. (2005), "Human Capital is the Key to Growth: Success Stories and Polices for 2020", *Deutsche Bank Research, Current Issues,* August 1, 2005, Frankfurt am Main, Germany.

Bishop, J. (1990), "Job Performance, Turnover and Wage Growth", *Journal of Labour Economics,* 8, 363-86.

Black, S.E. and Lynch, L. M. (1995), "Beyond the Incidence of Training: Evidence from a National Employers Survey", *NBERW Working Paper,* No. 5231.

Black, S.E. and Lynch, L.M (1996a), "Human Capital Investments and Productivity", *American Economic Review Papers and Proceedings,* 86, (2), 263-67.

Black, S.E. and Lynch, L. M. (1996b), "How to Compete: The Impact of Workplace Practices and Information Technology on Productivity", Working Paper, *U.S. Department of Labor,* Office of the Chief Economist.

Blundell, R., Dearden, L. and Meighir, C. (1996), "The Determinants of Work-Related Training in Britain", *Institute of Fiscal Studies,* London.

Blundell, R., Dearden. L., Costas, M. and Sianesi, B. (1999), "Human Capital Investment: the Returns from Education and Training to the Individual, the Firm and the Economy", *Fiscal Studies,* 20, (1), 1-23.

Booth, A.L. (1991), "Job-Related Formal Training: Who Received It and What Is It Worth?" *Oxford Bulletin of Economics and Statistics,* 53, 284-94.

Bosworth, D.L. and Wilson, R.A. (1993), Qualified Scientists and Engineers and Economic Performance, in Swann, P. (ed.) *New Technologies and Firms: Innovation and Competition,* Routledge, London.

Callan, T. and Harmon, C. (1999), "The Economic Return to Schooling in Ireland", *Labour Economics,* 6, 543-550.

Callan, T. and Wren, A. (1992), "Male-Female Wage Differential Analysis and Policy Issues", the *Economic and Social Research Institute,* General Research Series Paper No. 166, Dublin.

Cameron, G., Proudman, J. and Redding, S. (1998), "Productivity Convergence and International Openness, in Proundman, J. and Redding, S. (eds.), *Openness and Growth,* Chapter 6, Bank of England, London.

Card, D. (1999), The Causal Effect of Education on Earnings, in *Handbook of Labour Economics*, Ashenfelter, O. and Card, D. (eds.), Elsevier, New York, 1802-1863.

Cawley, J., Heckman, J. and Vytlacil, E. (2000), "Understanding the Role of Cognitive Ability in Accounting for the Recent Rise in the Economic Return to Education", in Arrow, K., Bowles, S. and Durlauf, S. (eds.), *Meritocracy and Economic Inequality*, Princeton University Press, Princeton.

Chapman, B.J. and Tan, H.W. (1990), "An Analysis of Youth Training in Australia, 1985-1986: Technological Change and Wages", *Australian National University*, mimeo.

Charles, K.K. and Luoh, M.C. (2003), "Gender Differences in Completed Schooling", *Review of Economics and Statistics*, 85, 559-577.

De la Fuente, A. and Domenech, R. (2000), "Human Capital in Growth Regressions: How Much Difference does Data Quality Make?" *Economics Department Working Paper*, 262, OECD, Paris.

Dearden, L., Machin, S., Reed, H. and Wilkinson, D. (1997), "Labour Turnover and Work-Related Training", *Institute for Fiscal Studies*, London.

Dearden, L., Reed, H. and Van Reenan, J. (2000), "Who Gains when Workers Train?" *The Institute of Fiscal Studies*, Working Paper 00/04, UK.

Dearden, L., Reed, H. and Van Reenan, J. (2005), "The Impact of Training on Productivity and Wages: Evidence from British Panel Data", *The Institute of Fiscal Studies*, Working Paper 0516, UK.

Dee, T. (2004), "Are There Civic Returns to Education?" *Journal of Public Economics*, 88, 9, pp.1694-1720.

Denny, K. and Harmon, C. (2000), "The Impact of Education and Training on the Labour Market Experience of Young Adults", *IFS Working Paper*, 00/08.

Economic and Social Research Institute (2005), *Quarterly Economic Commentary*, Spring, Dublin

Economist Intelligence Unit (2004), "Reaping the Benefits of ICT: Europe's Productivity Challenge", *EIU*.

Elliott, R. (1991), *Labour Economics – A Comparative Text*, McGraw-Hill, London.

Englander, A.S. and Gurney, A. (1994), Medium Determinants of OECD Productivity, *OECD Economic Studies*, No. 22, 49-109.

Entorf, H. and Kramarz, F. (1997), "Does Unmeasured Ability Explain the Higher Wages of New Technology Workers", *European Economic Review*, 41, 1489-1509.

FÁS (2005), *Labour Market Review*, FÁS, Dublin.

Fuchs, V. (1979), "The Economics of Health in a Post-Industrial Society", *Public Interest,* Summer, 3-20

Gang, I.N. and Zimmerman, K.F. (2000), "Is Child Like Parent? Educational Attainment and Ethnic Origin", *Journal of Human Resources,* 35, 550-569.

Gemmell, N. (1996), "Evaluating the Impacts of Human Capital Stocks and Accumulation on Economic Growth: Some New Evidence", *Oxford Bulletin of Economics and Statistics,* 58, 9-28.

Green, F., Preston, J. and Sabates, R. (2003), *Education Equity and Social Cohesion: A Distributional Model,* Centre for Research on the Wider Benefits of Learning.

Greenlagh, C. A. and Stewart, M.B. (1987), "The Effects and Determinants of Training", *Oxford Bulletin of Economics and Statistics,* 55, 171-189.

Griffith, R., Redding, S. and Van Reenan, J. (2000), "Mapping the Two Faces of R&D: Productivity, R&D, Skills and Trade in an OECD Panel of Industries", *Institute of Fiscal Studies,* Mimeo.

Groot, W. (1995), "Type Specific Returns to Enterprise-Relating Training", *Economics of Education Review,* 14, 4, 323-333.

Hanushek, E. A. and Dongwook, K. (1995), "Schooling, Labour Force Quality and Economic Growth", NBER Working Paper, No. 5399.

Harmon, C., Oosterbeek, H. and Walker, I. (2003), "The Returns to Education: Microeconomics, *Journal of Economic Surveys,* 17, 115-155.

Harmon, C., Walker, I. and Westergaard-Nielsen, N. (2001), *Education and Earnings in Europe: A Cross Country Analysis of the Returns to Education,* Edward Elgar Publishing Ltd., Aldershot.

Johnson, G. (2004), "Healthy, Wealthy and Wise?" *New Zealand Treasury Working Paper.*

Leitch (2005), "Skills in the UK: The Long-Term Challenge", Interim Report, *HM Treasury,* London.

Levine, R. and Renelt, D. (1992), "A Sensitivity Analysis of Cross-country Growth Regressions", *American Economic Review,* 82, 942–63.

Lillard, L. A. and Tan, H.W. (1992), "Private Sector Training: Who Gets It and What Are Its Effects?" *Research in Labour Economics,* 13, 1-62.

Lucas, R. (1988), "On the Mechanics of Economic Development", *Journal of Monetary Economics,* 22, 3-42.

Lynch, L.M. (1991), "The Role of Off-the-Job Training vs On-the-Job Training for the Mobility of Women Workers", *American Economic Review, Papers and Proceedings,* 81, 151-156.

Mankiw, N.G, Romer, D. and Weil, D.N. (1992), "A Contribution to the Empirics of Economic Growth", *Quarterly Journal of Economics,* May, 407-437.

Mincer, J. (1958), "Investment in Human Capital and Personal Income Distribution", Journal of Political Economy, 66(4), 281-302.

Mincer, J. (1962), "On-the-Job Training: Costa, Returns and Some Implications", *Journal of Political Economy,* 70(5), S50-S79.

Mincer, J. (1974), *Schooling, Experience and Earnings.* New York: Columbia University Press.

Murnane, R. J., Willet, J.B. and Levy, F. (1995), "The Growing Importance of Cognitive Skills in Wage Determination", *Review of Economics and Statistics,* 77, 251-266.

Murphy, K., Schleifer, A. and Vishny, R. (1991), "The Allocation of Talent: Implications for Growth", *Quarterly Journal of Economics,* May, 503-530.

OECD (2001), *OECD Productivity Manual,* Paris.

OECD (2003), *Employment Outlook,* Paris.

OECD (2004), *The Sources of Economic Growth in OECD Countries,* Paris.

OECD (2005), *Education at a Glance,* OECD, Paris.

OECD (2006), *Economic Survey of Ireland,* OECD, Paris.

Oliner, S.D. and Sichel, D.E. (2000), "The Resurgence of Growth in the Late 1990s: Is Information Technology the Story", *Journal of Economic Perspectives,* 14, 3-22.

O'Mahony, M. and Van Ark, B. (2003), *EU Productivity and Competitiveness: An Industry Perspective. Can Europe Resume the Catching-Up Process?* Office for Official Publications of the European Communities, Luxembourg.

Porter, M. (2005), Building the Microeconomic Foundations of Prosperity, Chapter 1.2 in Lopez-Claros, A., Porter, M.E., Schwab, K. (2005), *The Global Competitiveness Report 2005-2006,* 43-78.

Redding, S. (1996), "Low-skill, Low-quality Trap: Strategic Complementarities Between Human Capital and R&D", *Economic Journal,* 106, 458–70.

Romer, P.M. (1986), "Increasing Returns and Long-Run Growth", *Journal of Political Economy,* 94, 1002-1037.

Romer, P.M. (1990), "Endogenous Technological Change", *Journal of Political Economy,* 89, 5, 71-102.

Romer, P.M. (1990b), "Human Capital and Growth: Theory and Evidence", *Carnegie-Rochester Conference Series in Public Policy: Unit Roots, Investment Measures and Other Essays,* 32, 251-285.

Rose, S. and Taubman, P. (1979), Changes in the Impact of Education and Income on Mortality in the US, *Statistical Uses of Administrative Records,* US Department of Health, Education and Welfare, Washington.

Schultz, T. W. (1961), "Investment in Human Capital", *American Economic Review,* 51, 1, 1-17.

Schultz, T.W. (1963), *The Economic Value of Education,* Columbia University Press, New York.

Sianesi, B. and Van Reenan J. (2003), "The Returns to Education: Macroeconomics", *Journal of Economic Surveys,* 17, 2, 157-200.

Skalli. A. (2001), "The Role of Schooling: Screening versus Human Capital", *Public Funds and Private Returns to Education.*

Smith, A. (1937), *The Wealth of Nations,* Modern Library, New York.

Smith, A. (2001), "Return on Investment in Education", *Australian Centre for Vocational and Educational Research.*

Solow, R.M. (1956), "A Contribution to the Theory of Economic Growth", *Quarterly Journal of Economics,* February, 65-94.

Stiroh, K.J. (2001), "Information Technology and the U.S. Productivity Revival: What do the Industry Data Say?", *Federal Reserve Bank of New York,* Staff Report 115.

Turcotte, J. and Whewell, R.L. (2004), "Productivity and Wages: Measuring the Effect of Human Capital and Technology Use from Linked Employer-Employee Data", *Department of Finance,* Canada, Working Paper 2004-01.

Uzawa, H. (1965), "Optimal Technical Change in an Aggregative Model of Economic Growth", *International Economic Review,* 6, 18-31.

CHAPTER 19

THE IMPACT OF R&D ON PRODUCTIVITY

DIRK CZARNITZKI AND NIALL O'BYRNES

ABSTRACT

Studies have shown that is not only firms' own internal Research and Development (R&D) that leads to positive productivity effects. Firms can also make use of knowledge which has been generated elsewhere if they maintain sufficient absorptive capacity to utilise such information. Further, more recent research suggests that the benefits from spillovers may be larger for firms or countries that are lying behind the 'technological frontier'. Such findings have important policy implications for the Irish economy. While Ireland has shown impressive growth rates and industry restructuring towards a modern knowledge economy, it still lags behind the European average when it comes to R&D investment.

19.1 Introduction

Ireland's economy has changed without recognition from the pre-boom year 1995 to the later years of the current boom. Gross Domestic Product (GDP) grew from $65 billion to $171 billion (current PPP), the labour force grew from 1.2 million to two million and unemployment dropped from 17 per cent to four per cent. While factors such as the 1970's population boom entering the workforce and the global environment (Information Technology boom) surely contributed to Ireland's transformation, it was its fiscal responsibility and openness to Foreign Direct Investment (FDI) that created the necessary conditions for such breakneck growth reaching 10.5 per cent per annum for ten years.

This inward investment boom, 23 per cent of GDP in 2002 (IMF, Balance of Payments Report 2005) was led by US multinationals in IT, financial services and remote customer services. The state supported its development through a massive infrastructure program and increased investment in education, particularly third level institutions. Its commitment to the Euro and successful wage pacts delivered a sound macro environment that allowed the productivity increases to deliver higher real wages. On the domestic front the indigenous sectors responded to competitive pressure, delivering international standards by adopting best international practices. As spare capacity in the economy was reduced (unemployment dropped from 16 per cent in 1993 to two per cent 2005), and real wages increased, the profile of Ireland's inwards investments began to change. Earlier low-skilled investments, for example the North West textile industry moved out to newly open foreign labour markets.

The economy in 2004-2005 has been characterised by continued growth but also a noted productivity growth change from 4.9 per cent to two per cent in 2004 (ESRI, 2005). Growth is now mostly due to demand for domestic services, from an increase in the working population through inward migration which is supported by sustained FDI. While these two factors will sustain the economy in the short term, it is not sustainable in long term growth projections. With higher inflation (3.7 per cent) and higher wage growth (five per cent) than the EU15 in 2005, Ireland must be careful that its higher wages are justified by increases in productivity (ESRI, 2005). Productivity is increased in various ways, but in an economy like Ireland's without significant natural resources or indigenous manufacturing industry, the 'knowledge stock' becomes very important. The accumulated R&D expenditures of a country or firm are often interpreted as its knowledge stock.

It can be seen from the simple correlation in Figure 19.1 that economies exhibit an increase in R&D with an increase in the size of the economy, because as 'knowledge stock' becomes more important to the economy, investments in R&D to generate new 'knowledge' becomes imperative. It has been shown that R&D indeed causes growth, to a certain extent, in many scholarly articles.

In this chapter, we first outline how scholars in economics have approached the relationship between productivity and R&D, and second we briefly summarise empirical studies on the impact of R&D on productivity. Furthermore, we stress the importance of spillovers, and discuss the 'technological frontier' of production. We close the discussion with an Irish perspective on the impact of R&D on productivity, where the fact that the Irish economy is largely dominated by foreign firms is a focus of the discussion. The final chapter closes with conclusions and policy recommendations.

Figure 19.1: Correlation of GDP and R&D

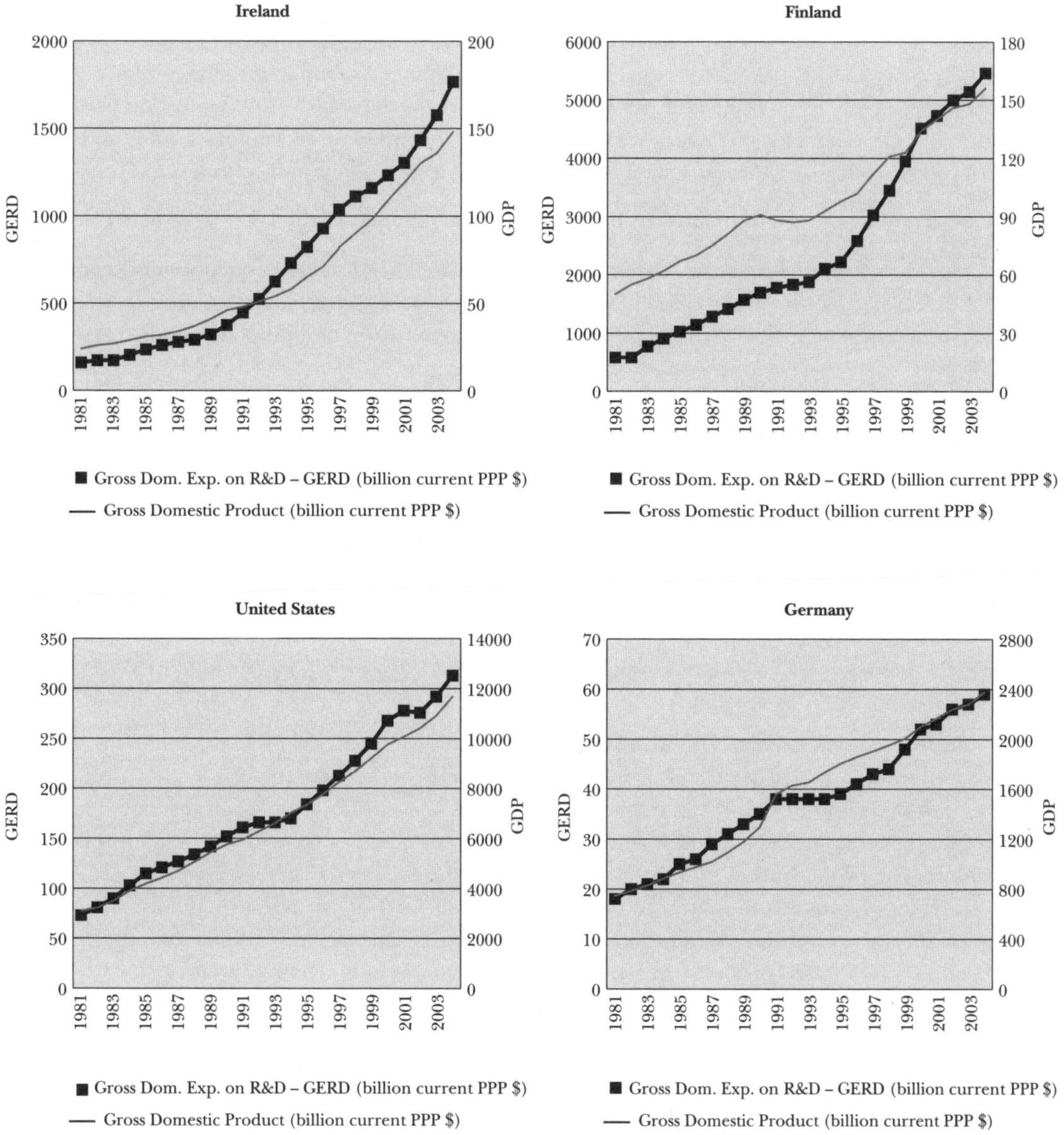

Source: OECD Main Science and Technology Indicators, 2006/1.

19.2 The Relationship between R&D and Productivity

19.2.1 The Production Function

When the contribution of R&D to productivity is considered, econometric studies typically start from a production function, that is, an equation describing how factor inputs such as capital and labour are combined to produce output. A common functional form is of Cobb-Douglas type:

$$Y_{it} = Ae^{\lambda t} K_{it}^{\alpha} L_{it}^{\beta} R_{it}^{\gamma} e^{\varepsilon_{it}} \qquad (1)$$

where Y = real output, A = total factor productivity, K = the stock of physical capital, L = labour, R = R&D and e is the error term, that is the difference between what is observed and what is predicted by the equation. The subscript I denotes firm (or sector or country) and t is time.[1] The R&D variable can be measured as the stock of R&D capital or the investment in a given year. The Total Factor Productivity (TFP) A denotes the output per unit of combined factor input, and is often estimated as a time trend or a constant in the regression model.

Eq. (1) can be rewritten in logs as

$$\log(Y_{it}) = log(A) + \lambda t = \alpha\, log(K_{it}) + \beta\, log(L_{it}) + \gamma\, log(R_{it}) + \varepsilon_{it} \qquad (2)$$

Scholars either estimate eq. (2) with (pooled) cross-sectional data of firms, (or industries or countries), so that it can be shown that firms with higher R&D realise higher output, or they make use of time-series methods for estimation such that changes in the right-hand side variables induce change in Y. In the latter case, one would estimate eq. (2) either in first differences, or in terms of growth rates. In all cases, the parameters α, β, and γ represent the elasticities of output with respect to capital, labour and R&D. If, for instance, the estimate of $\gamma = 0.15$, and is statistically significantly different from zero one would conclude that a ten per cent increase in R&D results in a 1.5 per cent increase in output (all else constant).[2]

Through the functional form of eq. (2), it is implicitly assumed that the elasticity of output with respect to R&D is constant over firms (and through time). Therefore, other researchers specified a different equation to be estimated as they preferred to estimate the rate of return of R&D rather than the elasticity. This can also be derived from eq. (2) (see Griliches, 1980, Griliches and Mairesse, 1984):

$$\frac{\Delta Y_{it}}{T_{i,t-1}} = \lambda + \alpha \frac{\Delta K_{it}}{K_{i,t-1}} + \beta \frac{\Delta L_{it}}{L_{i,t-1}} + p \frac{\Delta R_{it}}{Y_{i,t-1}} + \Delta\varepsilon_{it} \qquad (3)$$

where ΔR is the net investment in R&D capital, and p the rate of return to R&D.

Estimating the parameters of production functions is not a trivial task as many problems such as omitted variable bias, simultaneity and multicollinearity may bias the results. An omitted variable bias occurs if some firms are more productive than others due to reasons unrelated to R&D (and the other regressors in the estimation equation). For instance, firms could have better R&D management and are thus more successful in their R&D process which would lead to higher spending in R&D. Then there would be differences in productivity that are related to such unobserved factors which may be correlated with R&D. As a result, the estimated coefficient of R&D will be biased upwards. Nowadays, scholars control for such unobserved heterogeneity across firms by applying panel data econometric methods controlling for 'individual fixed effects', that is, one would include a firm specific parameter c_i in eq. (2). By estimating the equation in first differences over time, the individual firm effect is differenced out.

A simultaneity bias arises when one or more right-hand side variables are correlated with the error term. The variables are only uncorrelated with the error term if causality runs only from the factor inputs to productivity. If there is feedback, however, a simultaneity bias occurs. For instance, scholars mostly believe that R&D and productivity are mutually dependent, that is, growth of output is a function of R&D, but R&D investment is in turn a function of past output growth and expected future growth. Today's common practice is the use of instrumental variable techniques that allow consistent estimation of the production function's parameters even if output and factor inputs are simultaneously determined.

The common problem of multicollinearity refers to the fact that typically an almost linear relationship among independent variables, the factor inputs, exists. If the colinearity among regressors is high, researchers may not be able to calculate the separate effect of each regressor on the dependent variable. Colinearity results in imprecise estimates, that is, estimated coefficients exhibit large variance. Estimating in first differences usually reduces the problem of multicollinearity.

19.2.2 Private Returns to R&D

Table 19.1 shows an overview of studies that relate R&D to productivity at different levels of aggregation. The core of the empirical literature on R&D consists of studies on the private return to R&D. These studies are usually divided into two types, cross-sectional and combined cross-sectional time-series, i.e. panel data. The cross section studies look at either a number of firms or a number of countries and try to measure their productivity return due to R&D in a single point of time. The time-series studies try to measure the change in the productivity over time relative to inputs and so determine its effect. A listing of a number of these studies is detailed in Table 19.1. The relationship between productivity and R&D is usually stated as elasticity and is defined as a percentage increase in a variable in relation to a percentage change of the other. For example the Griliches (1980) study reports an elasticity of 0.07, so a ten per cent increase in R&D expenditure will be a 0.7 per cent increase in the output. This implies a rate of return on R&D of 27 per cent.

The cross-section studies report higher rates of return and with greater certainty than the time-series studies. The reason as stated by Mairesse and Sassenou (1991) attributes the difference to the treatment of the share of labour in the economy or its scale affects. The cross-sectional studies also consistently predict positive elasticities in the region of 0.10 and 0.20. Other studies examining time-series data show weaker and smaller (0.02 to 0.15) results but are still positive. The macroeconomic studies show a much wider band of predicted rates of return and are probably due to the specification of the model and production function used to estimate the data. Reconciling the results of the cross sectional data with time-series data and the macroeconomic evidence are an area of intense research, but nearly all studies show positive and significant rates of return to R&D.

Table 19.1: Empirical Studies on the Elasticity of Output with Respect to R&D

Selected Estimates of the Elasticity of Private R&D from Firm Level Data		
Study	**R&D Elasticity**	**Sample**
Griliches (1980a)	0.03 – 0.07	39 U.S. manufacturing industries; 1959 to 1977
Schankerman (1981)	0.10 – 0.16	110 U.S. firms (chemical and oil industries); 1963 cross-section
Griliches and Mairesse (1984)	0.19	77 U.S. firms (scientific sectors); 1966 to 1977
Griliches and Mairesse (1990)		
Sample 1	0.25 – 0.41	525 U.S. manufacturing firms; 1973 to 1980
Sample 2	0.20 – 0.56	406 Japanese manufacturing firms; 1973 to 1980
Hall and Mairesse (1995)	0.05 – 0.25	197 French firms; 1980 to 1987, cross-sectional estimation
	0.00 – 0.07	197 French firms; 1980 to 1987, time-series estimation
Minasian (1969)	0.08	17 U.S. firms; 1948 to 1957
Griliches and Mairesse (1984)	0.09	133 U.S. firms; 1966 to 1977
Hall and Mairesse (1995)		197 French firms; 1980 to 1987
Selected Estimates of the Elasticity of Private R&D from Studies Using Aggregate Data		
Study	**R&D Elasticity**	**Sample**
Patel and Soete (1988)	0.61	United States (TFP); 1967 to 1985
Lichtenberg (1992)	0.07	98 countries (per capita output); 1960 to 1985
Coe and Helpman (1995)	0.23	G7 countries (TFP);a 1971 to 1990
Australian Industry Commission (1995)		
Sub-sample 1	0.02	Australia (TFP); 1975 to 1991
Sub-sample 2	0.14	Australia (output); 1975 to 1991
Verspagen (1995)	(0.02) – 0.17	14 industries in 11 OECD countries; 1973 to 1988
Griliches and Lichtenberg (1984b)	-0.04	27 U.S. manufacturing industries; 1959 to 1976

Source: Based on Congressional Budget Office (2005), Mairesse and Sassenou (1991), Mohnen (1992), Griliches (1992), and Australian Industry Commission (1995).

19.2.3 Social Returns to R&D and Policy Implications

Besides the private return of R&D, scholars have emphasised that R&D is subject to positive externalities, that is, the returns of R&D are not only of private nature, but R&D also has social benefits. Unlike investments in tangible assets where firms can appropriate the returns of their investment more easily, the knowledge creating process of R&D investments is assumed to create high social returns as firms cannot capture all the returns of such investments. In a seminal paper, Arrow (1962: 615) stated that "no amount of legal protection can make a thoroughly appropriable commodity of something so intangible as information. The very use of the information in any productive way is bound to reveal it, at least in part. Mobility of personnel among firms provides a way of spreading information. Legally imposed property rights can provide only a partial barrier, since there are obviously enormous difficulties in defining in any sharp way an item of information and differentiating it from similar sounding items".

The imperfect appropriability of R&D gave rise to studies where scholars have estimated not only the private return to R&D, but also the social return to R&D. In a pioneer study, Mansfield et al. (1977) present results of case studies of four process and 13 product innovations. They find that the social return largely tends to exceed the private return. At the median, their estimates of social returns to R&D are more than twice as high as the private return.

Further quantitative studies that attempt to estimate the unintended benefits of pursuing some new research, the social return, also find consistently positive results and they are much larger than the private return. Table 19.2 summarises the social rate of return on various manufacturing firms. The first column presents the rate of return due to spillovers from the manufacturing sector while the second column gives the spillover return from other industries. Both added together give a combined rate of return of about 100 per cent.

Table 19.2: Estimates of the Social Rate of Return in the Manufacturing Industry

Study	Own R&D (Spillovers within Industry)	Used R&D (Spillovers from other industries)
Terleckyj (1980)	0.25	0.82
Sveikauskas (1981)	0.17	
Scherer (1982)	0.29	0.74
Griliches and Lichtenberg (1984a)	0.34	0.41
Griliches(1994)	0.30	

Source: Jones and Williams (1988). All studies are carried out on manufacturing industry except Scherer (1982) which includes some service sectors.

All these studies overwhelming show that R&D contributes significantly to productivity and that social rates of return are higher, and consequently spillovers are very important to growth. Griliches (1992) a pioneer in innovation economics summarised, "In spite of (many) difficulties, there have been a significant number of reasonable well-done studies all pointing in the same direction: R&D spillovers are present, their magnitude may be quite large and social rates of return remain significantly above private rates".

Griffith et al. (2004) extend the standard spill-over discussion to an analysis on countries leading in certain technologies, so-called frontier countries, and others lying "behind the frontier". They compute a TFP measure and rate those countries (or their firms) with the highest productivity as leaders, or "frontier" countries. The use of frontier is deliberate because of the idiom that knowledge created cannot be lost, though its value can change. Those countries on the frontier must be creating knowledge or using existing knowledge more effectively, but either way leads them to carry higher productivity rates. The other countries are termed as lying "behind the frontier".

They use industry-level data and show that some countries are more or less permanently on the frontier in some technologies, but "behind frontier" countries are typically catching up to the frontier over time. However, they also find evidence that single countries diverge in certain industries. The issue of convergence is intrinsically linked to the productivity growth rate, because those behind the frontier must exhibit higher growth rates, while the frontier countries may also be continually increasing. Griffith et al. (2004) also show some sectors that have experienced leap-frogging of the technological frontier. In the chemicals sector Japan and

Germany reciprocate the leadership. In 1971 Japan has higher productivity but by 1981 it has fallen into second place. Then again in 1990 Japan has regained the frontier position.[3]

In the study distance from the frontier is shown to exhibit greater potential for productivity growth as those countries capture spillovers from the frontier. However the authors also find "strong evidence that R&D has a second face, country industries lagging behind the productivity frontier catch up particularly fast if they invest heavily in R&D". Some knowledge is tacit, and difficult to imitate without direct investigation, so in order to fully benefit from new-knowledge they need to have some intellectual or technical experience already in that industry. This is usually called the 'absorptive capacity', and is assumed to be increased by increasing R&D within that technical field. Absorption can also be thought of as imitation costs, and Mansfield et al. (1986) present evidence of substantial costs of imitation: on average, 65 per cent of innovation costs. It is no use for non-frontier countries to hope to contribute or pick up the spillover effects to improve computing developed elsewhere if no-one in their country has ever heard of a qubit. Griffith et al. conclude that those countries behind the frontier, with higher spending on R&D display faster convergence. Another implication from this conclusion is firms behind the frontier will gain a higher return to their R&D because this is where most social return applies.

This raises the potential for governments to raise the absorptive capacity of the economy in order to capture higher social rates of return delivering higher overall productivity. While the results pointing to strong spill-over effects emphasise the importance of R&D for an economy, they, in turn, also highlight an economic dilemma: firms will only invest in innovation projects showing a positive expected private return. However, there may be many projects that promise a high social return, but those may not be privately profitable as firms cannot appropriate all returns as hypothesised by Arrow. The positive external effects of R&D lead to an underinvestment into R&D from a social point of view, which also gave rise for active innovation policies by the government. If the government subsidises such R&D projects that are privately not profitable but generate high positive social returns it is believed that the governmental intervention into the market for R&D would stimulate private R&D such that the gap between socially desirable R&D and actual private investment would close. Of course, for governmental agencies distributing subsidies, it may be difficult to detect such projects. Furthermore, as soon as subsidies are available in an economy, firms would always have an incentive to apply for subsidies even for privately profitable projects as public funding comes at zero marginal cost (if one abstracts from administrative cost for proposal submissions etc.) which may lead to crowding-out effects.

Whether or not the crowding-out effects of public R&D funding occur has been discussed at length in the economic literature. David et al. (2000) and Klette et al. (2000) review the literature on public R&D subsidies and find mixed evidence, but the majority of studies point to the conclusion that full crowding-out effects of policy measures can be rejected. They also highlighted several econometric problems that were not handled well in the literature; especially econometric results that were subject to sample selection bias. Aerts et al. (2006) review studies that have taken the comments on the econometric shortcomings into account, and find that there is vast support for the rejection of crowding-out effects in more recent literature. Hall and Van Reenen (2000) surveyed the literature on fiscal measures, that is, R&D tax credits, and also confirmed positive effects. They conclude that, on average, studies have found that $1 of R&D tax credit increases private R&D spending by about $1. Thus, the majority of policy studies indeed confirm that governments can overcome the gap between privately conducted and socially desirable levels of R&D by actively encouraging firms to invest.

19.3 Ireland's Potential from R&D and Spillovers

As the review of the literature shows, firms and, in turn, sectors and countries seem to exhibit higher productivity (growth) the more they engage in R&D activities. First, own internal R&D spurs productivity through new products being introduced in the market that increase firms' revenue or through the implementation of new processes in production that lower cost or increase quality. Second, firms may benefit from spillovers of knowledge that others generated. In order to absorb such spillover effects, scholars have pointed out that a certain level of own R&D is required for building the capacity to benefit from knowledge generated elsewhere. Without the necessary capability to understand such newly generated knowledge firms may not be able to utilise information for their own benefit.

The Irish policy towards a very open economy has been successful in the past not only for the creation of employment through the attraction of FDI, but also with respect to the acquisition of knowledge and technology from abroad. Until World War II, Ireland's economy largely relied on agriculture and depended on the United Kingdom as the destination of the vast majority of exports. From the 1950s onwards, restriction on ownership and trade were continuously removed which opened the opportunity to attract foreign investment and international trade other than to the UK. By the late 1960s Ireland had become an industrialised nation that no longer relied solely on agriculture. This success was due to certain policies such as relaxing foreign ownership restrictions, and tax breaks for export-orientated firms. FDI brought knowledge and technology into the country which, in turn, enabled an export diversification away from the UK to other European countries. Joining the European (Economic) Community in 1973 resulted in a further surge of inward investment and access to new markets. More recent industrial policy with focus on sectors such as chemicals, pharmaceuticals, financial services and electronics, along with privatisation efforts of former public business encouraging competition and in combination with a highly skilled labour force and moderate wage levels led to a further restructuring of Irish industry. The importance of high-technology industries has been on the rise steadily. In 2003, about one quarter of Ireland's total exports where pharmaceutical products and Ireland was a major exporter of computer software and emerging as an important centre for financial services.

Despite its tremendous success in attracting high-tech industries, Ireland lags behind in cutting-edge R&D. According to Gordon (2003), industry spending on R&D stood at about one per cent of GDP which was below the European average of 1.2 per cent and well below the United States (two per cent) and Japan (2.2 per cent). Figure 19.2 shows the development of total R&D expenditure (GERD) in relation to GDP for the past decades in comparison to selected other countries. While in 2004 the GERD to GDP ratio reaches about 2.5 per cent in Germany and 2.6 per cent in the US, Ireland is significantly below at about 1.2 per cent.

Figure 19.2: GERD as a Percentage of GDP for Ireland and Comparison Countries

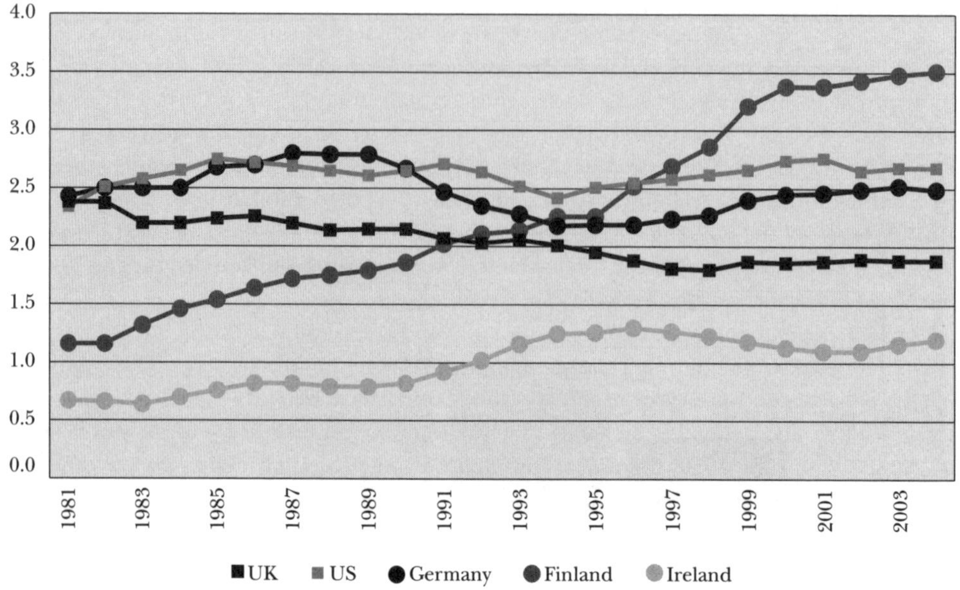

Source: OECD Main Science and Technology Indicators, 2006/1.

A remarkable difference with respect to R&D emerges between Ireland and Finland. Finland, also a small European economy on the rise, shows a much higher growth in R&D than Ireland. Finnish R&D to GDP started of at about 1.2 per cent in the early 1980s, and grew steadily to a value of about 3.5 per cent in 2004. While Finland almost tripled R&D relative to GDP, Ireland only doubled R&D from roughly 0.6 per cent to 1.2 per cent. This probably owes to the industry structure, the high extent of foreign ownership in Ireland. While FDI brought large multinational firms and, thus, employment to Ireland, R&D is still underdeveloped. While the country has a strong manufacturing base nowadays, the generation of ideas and knowledge may still be undertaken primarily in the parent companies' home bases. Figure 19.3 shows the share of R&D spend by foreign affiliates in Finland, Germany, the UK and Ireland. While Finland apparently managed to develop a strong R&D-intensive indigenous industry, Ireland heavily relies on R&D performed by foreign affiliates. This may have several implications for further productivity growth.

The currently low spend on total R&D may give room for additional innovation policy initiatives. However, this would have to be carefully evaluated beforehand. If the spillover arguments apply, the Irish situation should be a good starting point for a catching-up in cutting-edge research. The strong base in skilled labour force coupled with the recent developments in high-tech industry structure should constitute a necessary absorptive capacity allowing Ireland to utilise spillovers from local industries benefiting from the presence of large multi-national corporations.

Figure 19.3: R&D Expenditure of Foreign Affiliates as a Percentage of Total BERD in Ireland

Source: OECD Main Science and Technology Indicators, 2006/1.

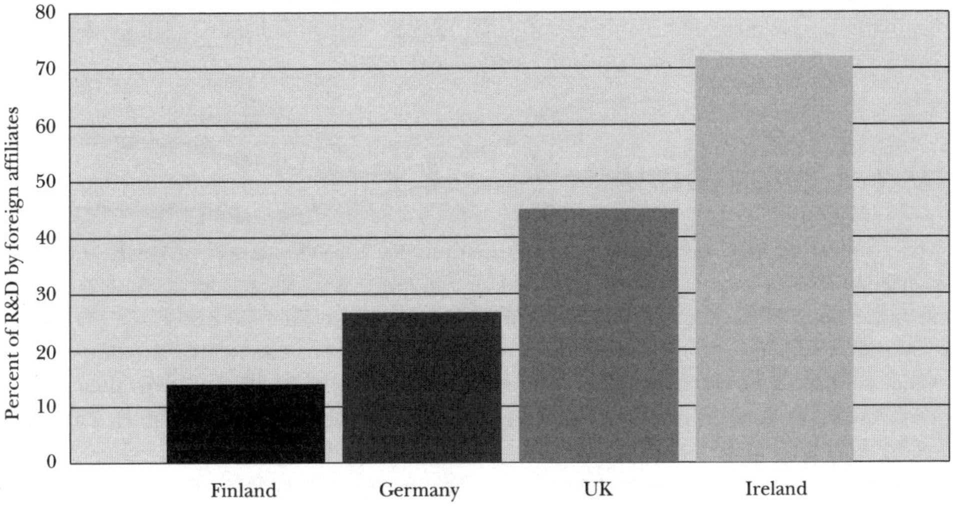

If one takes the Finnish case as a benchmark, fostering R&D collaborations among industry-industry or industry-science partnerships seems to be a possible initiative to stimulate the development of an Irish indigenous R&D-intensive industry. Recently, Czarnitzki et al. (2006) investigated the effects of innovation policies in Germany and Finland. They compare R&D projects conducted within consortia of firms and/or public research institutions with public R&D funding granted to individual firms. While they find that public innovation policies lead to more R&D in both countries, interesting differences are detected. The public funding of collaborative research seems to spur private R&D spending more than subsidies that go to single firms. However, they also conclude that Finland which exhibits a very high intensity of collaborative research already, may not gain from additional policies of this kind. In Germany, where joint research is less developed, possible effects of an extension of such policies seems to be more promising than in Finland. It should be noted, however, that it is not only the level of current policy intervention which is sufficient for the successful of implementation of such schemes. In addition, those strategies are subject to the risk that firms who collaborate in R&D also collude in product markets. In such a case, potential welfare benefits of additional R&D would be undermined by reduced consumer rents.

Fostering collaborative research among local firms and subsidiaries of multinationals may especially be promising if the productivity growth of local firms and foreign-owned firms is subject to divergence. Czarnitzki (2005) investigated productivity deficiencies in Eastern Germany by benchmarking Eastern German firms with comparable Western German firms. He found the alarming result that Eastern German firms not only exhibit a significant productivity gap when one controls for observable differences to Western German firms, it turned out that the productivity between Eastern German firms that are locally owned and those that are foreign-owned (or owned by Western German firms) is diverging since the German unification in 1990. Instead of a catching-up process of the local economy, it is found that the indigenous firms lose ground. This could be an interesting area to study for the Irish case and would possibly have important policy implications. Of course, it should be noted that Eastern German companies started basically from scratch in 1990. They thus lacked the necessary absorptive capacity for a fruitful catching-up process by making use of spillovers. The Irish situation may be different. Although the indigenous industry is lagging behind the high-tech multinational corporations, they may well maintain sufficient human capital and knowledge to show high growth rates as suggested in the study by Griffith et al. (2004).

19.4 Conclusions

The impact of R&D on productivity stems from the implementation of newly generated knowledge into new products or new production processes. Knowledge is interpreted as increasing the potential and capability of the economy to produce new products that better serve the needs of society or to produce existing goods more efficiently. Several empirical studies applying a production function framework have shown that R&D activity does indeed contribute to productivity resulting in improved competitiveness of firms or countries, and thus positive long-term growth and employment prospects in the economy.

The review of the productivity literature shows that R&D is an important input factor of production. Despite several econometric difficulties, studies have shown that not only firms own internal R&D leads to positive productivity effects, but those firms can also make use of knowledge which has been generated elsewhere if they maintain sufficient absorptive capacity to utilise such information. The benefits of spillovers may be significant so that complementaries among internal R&D and spill-over effects rise to an important factor when it comes to productivity growth and ensuring long term competitiveness.

More recent research suggests that there are important differences between firms or industries and countries producing on the 'technological frontier' and those that lag behind the frontier. Scholars suggested that the benefits from spillovers may be much larger for firms or countries behind the frontier than for those being currently on the frontier.

Such findings have important policy implications for the Irish economy. While Ireland has shown impressive growth rates and industry restructuring towards a modern knowledge economy, it still lags behind the European average when it comes to R&D. Thus, Ireland's situation with respect to cutting-edge research could be subject to future improvements, especially the industry structure which is characterised by a large share of foreign ownership in the high-tech sectors suggests that the local indigenous economy may have the tremendous opportunity to make use of spillovers if its R&D activity is spurred and reaches sufficient absorptive capacity. This may be beneficial for sustainable long-term development of the economy.

Notes

1 Henceforth we talk about 'firms' when we refer to the index *i*. It should be noted, however, that such analyses can also be conducted at the sectoral level or country level.

2 Sometimes, researchers did not use output on the left-hand side of the equation but TFP. In such case, one first has to estimate the production function (2) without R&D under the assumption of constant returns to scale ($\alpha + \beta = 1$). The estimates are used to calculate TFP, which is then related to R&D in a second regression.

3 The dynamics of technical leadership are complex and non-trivial but a discussion on leap frogging in a historical context can be found in Brezis et al. (1993).

References

Aerts, K., Czarnitzki, D. and Fier, A. (2006), *Econometric Evaluation of Public R&D Policies: Current State of the Art,* unpublished manuscript, Leuven.

Australian Industry Commission (1995), *Research and Development.* Report No. 44. Canberra: Government Publishing Service.

Brezis, E., Krugman, P. and Tsiddon, D. (1993), "Leapfrogging in International Competition: A Theory of Cycles in National Technological Leadership," *American Economic Review* 83, 1211–1219.

CBO (2005), "R&D and Productivity Growth", US Congressional Budget Office.

Coe, D. and Helpman, E. (1995), "International R&D Spillovers", *European Economic Review* 39(5), 859-887.

Czarnitzki, D. (2005), "Extent and Evolution of the Productivity Deficiency in Eastern Germany", *Journal of Productivity Analysis* 24(2), 209-229.

Czarnitzki, D., Ebersberger, B. and Fier, A. (2006), "The Relationship between R&D Collaboration, Subsidies and R&D Performance: Empirical Evidence from Finland and Germany", *Journal of Applied Econometrics,* forthcoming.

David, P.A., Hall, B.H. and Toole, A.A. (2000), "Is Public R&D a Complement or Substitute for Private R&D? A Review of the Econometric Evidence, *Research Policy* 29(4-5), 497-529.

ESRI (2005), "Quarterly Economic Commentary Spring 2005", *Economic and Social Research Institute,* Spring 2005.

Gordon, S. (2003), "Ireland Sets up Committee to Boost Industry R&D Spend", *EE Times UK,* Feb. 26, 2003.

Griffith, R., Redding, S. and Van Reenen, J. (2004), "Mapping the Two Faces of R&D: Productivity Growth in a Panel of OECD Industries", *The Review of Economics and Statistics* 86(4), 883–895.

Griliches, Z. (1980), "R&D and the Productivity Slowdown", *American Economic Review* 70, 343-348.

Griliches, Z. (1992), "The Search for R&D Spillovers", *The Scandinavian Journal of Economics* 94, 29–47.

Griliches, Z. (1994), "Productivity, R&D and the Data Constraint", *American Economic Review* 84(1), 1-23.

Griliches, Z. and Lichtenberg, F. (1984a), "Inter-industry Technology Flows and Productivity Growth: a Reexamination", *Review of Economics and Statistics* 66(2), 324-329.

Griliches, Z. and Lichtenberg, F. (1984b), "R&D and Productivity Growth at the Industry Level: Is There Still a Relationship?", in: Griliches, Z. (ed.), *R&D, Patents, and Productivity*, Chicago: University of Chicago Press.

Griliches, Z. and Mairesse, J. (1984), "Productivity and R&D at the Firm Level", in: Griliches, Z. (ed.), *R&D, Patents, and Productivity*. Chicago: University of Chicago Press.

Griliches, Z. and Mairesse, J. (1990), "R&D and Productivity Growth: Comparing Japanese and U.S. Manufacturing Firms", in: Hulten, C. (ed.), *Productivity Growth in Japan and the United States*, Chicago: University of Chicago Press.

Hall, B.H. and Mairesse, J. (1995), "Exploring the Relationship Between R&D and Productivity in French Manufacturing Firms", *Journal of Econometrics* 65, 263-293.

Hall, B.H. and Van Reenen, J. (2000), "How Effective are Fiscal Incentives for R&D? A Review of the Evidence", *Research Policy* 29(4-5), 449–469.

International Monetary Fund (2005), "Balance-of-Payments", CD-ROM, edition: March 05.

Jones, C. and Williams, J. (1998), "Measuring the Social Rate of Return to R&D", *Quarterly Journal of Economics* 113(4), 119–135.

Lichtenberg, F. (1992), *R&D Investment and International Productivity Differences*, NBER Working Paper no. 4161, Cambridge, MA.

Klette, T.J., Møen, J. and Griliches, Z. (2000), "Do Subsidies to Commercial R&D Reduce Market Failures? Microeconometric Evaluation Studies", *Research Policy* 29(4-5), 471-495.

Mairesse, J. and Sassenou, M. (1991), "R&D and Productivity: A Survey of Econometric Studies at the Firm Level", *OECD Science-Technology Review* 8, 9-44.

Mansfield, E.J., Rapoport, J., Romeo, A., Wagner, A. and Beardsley, G. (1977), "Social and Private Returns from Industrial Innovations", *Quarterly Journal of Economics* 91(2), 221-240.

Minasian, J.R. (1969), "Research and Development, Production Functions, and Rates of Return", *American Economic Review* 59(2), 80-85.

Mohnen, P. (1992), *The Relationship Between R&D and Productivity Growth in Canada and Other Major Industrialised Countries*, Ottawa: Economic Council of Canada.

Patel, P. and Soete, L. (1988), Measuring the Economic Effects of Technology, *OECD STI Review* 4, 121-166.

Schankerman, M. (1981), "The Effects of Double-Counting and Expensing on the Measured Returns to R&D", *Review of Economics and Statistics* 63(3), 454-458.

Scherer, F.M. (1982), "Inter-industry Technology Flows and Productivity Growth", *Review of Economics and Statistics* 64(4), 627-634.

Sveikauskas, L. (1981), "Technological Inputs and Multifactor Productivity Growth", *Review of Economics and Statistics*, LXIII, 275-282.

Terleckyj, N. (1980), "Direct and Indirect Effects of Industrial Research and Development on the Productivity Growth of Industries", in: J.W. Kendrick and B.N. Vaccara (eds.), *New Developments in Productivity Measurement and Analysis*, Chicago: University of Chicago Press.

Verspagen, B. (1995), "R&D and Productivity: A Broad Cross-Section Cross-Country Look", *Journal of Productivity Analysis* 6, 117-135.

CHAPTER 20

PUBLIC INVESTMENT IN R&D IN IRELAND

MAURICE DAGG[1]

ABSTRACT

The Government Strategy for Science Technology and Innovation 2006-2013, plans for a substantial increase in investment in Research and Development (R&D). This chapter examines recent evidence on the impact of such investment on productivity, human capital development and economic growth, and outlines the key characteristics of research expenditure in Ireland. Based on the evidence reviewed in this chapter, there is a strong case for suggesting that the Strategy will contribute to Ireland's long-term competitiveness, economic growth and improvements in the quality of life.

1 The views expressed are solely those of the authors and do not necessarily reflect the views of Forfás.

20.1 Introduction

Modern economies recognise the importance of a strong public science base to support improvements in welfare. The outputs we get from the science base, which include new knowledge, skilled people, new methodologies and new networks, have contributed to improvements in the things that matter to us, such as our wealth, education, health, environment, culture and public policy. This chapter examines recent evidence on the impact of such investment on productivity, human capital development and economic growth. The Irish experience of, and returns from, public investment in higher education and business research are also examined.

20.2 Returns to Public Investment in R&D

It is difficult to capture all the benefits science contributes to societal welfare, but a wide range of economic studies over a long period have recorded a range of direct benefits to the economy as a whole and to firms individually. Several studies have found academic research to be increasingly important for industrial innovation, accounting for 15 per cent of new products, 11 per cent of new processes and up to five percent of industry sales (Mansfield, 1991; Mansfield, 1998; Beise and Stahl, 1999). These figures capture only technological innovations based on academic research that has been carried out in the preceding 15 years. Patent data has also been used to identify the importance of public research for innovation (Narin et al., 1997). Evidence from Australia, for instance, found that 90 per cent of research papers cited in Australian-invented US patents were publicly funded. Studies of individual industries, in particular the pharmaceuticals industry, highlight the importance of public investment in science, with one study recording a 30 per cent return (Cockburn and Henderson, 2000; Toole, 2000).

Gurdgiev (2006) uses data from the EU Commission report 'Innovation Strengths and Weaknesses' (2005) to plot public sector innovation drivers against economic growth for EU countries. He concludes that "private spending on research outperforms public spending by a factor of at least 4:1, while public R&D spending has virtually nothing to do with economic growth". This is at variance with a recent OECD study, which includes Ireland and 15 other OECD countries, and which quantifies the long-term effects (over the period 1980-98) of various types of R&D on multifactor productivity growth. The study found that for any one country, the largest productivity effects are derived from R&D conducted by other countries, followed by the country's public R&D, and then it's Business Expenditure on R&D (BERD).[1] A one per cent increase in foreign R&D generates 0.46 per cent in productivity growth, a one per cent increase in public R&D generates 0.17 per cent in productivity growth and a one per cent increase in BERD generates 0.13 per cent in productivity growth. These effects are larger in countries which are intensive in BERD. The long-term impact of R&D may be higher when it is performed by the public sector rather than by the business sector, probably because the former concentrates more on basic research, which is known to generate a higher social return.[2]

The OECD also found that the effect of public R&D on productivity increases with the share of public science conducted in universities. Furthermore, the OECD found that the higher the share of business in the funding sources of university research, the lower is its impact on productivity, indicating the key role of universities in carrying out basic research, as opposed to more applied business funded research. Other studies confirm the positive contribution of academic research to economic growth (Bergman, 1990; Martin, 1998).

However, it is important to note that public and private research complement each other (Czarnitski et al., 2004). The productivity effect of public research will depend on firms' ability to absorb and exploit new technologies and, therefore, a substantial level of BERD is essential.[3]

While it could be argued that smaller countries may not benefit to the same extent as larger countries from funding R&D as much of the spillovers flow abroad, it is important to remember that R&D allows a country to (1) make new discoveries, or innovate, and (2) absorb knowledge generated abroad. This second component will be particularly important for countries behind the technological frontier. In order to assimilate R&D information that 'spills over' from other countries, an economy needs to be doing R&D itself (Griffith, Redding and Van Reenen, 1999). Absorptive capacity can be as important as innovation in contributing to the social rate of return from R&D.[4]

In much of the economic analysis, including that of Gurdgiev cited above, the view of basic research as a source merely of useful codified information is too simple and misleading. It neglects the many spillover benefits; in particular it omits the fact that by ensuring a supply of skilled graduates and trained researchers, public research underpins the capabilities of the private sector. Scott et al. (2000), outlined six channels of economic benefit from basic research: 1) increasing the stock of useful knowledge; 2) training skilled graduates; 3) creating new scientific instrumentation and methodologies; 4) forming networks and stimulating social interaction; 5) increasing the capacity for scientific and technological problem solving; and 6) creating new firms. The authors concluded; *"There is great heterogeneity in the relationship between basic research and innovation. Consequently, no simple model of the nature of the economic benefits is possible"*. The overall conclusions emerging from the surveys and case studies are that: (1) the economic benefits from basic research are both real and substantial; (2) they come in a variety of forms; and (3) the key issue is not so much whether the benefits are there but how best to organise the national research and innovation system to make the most effective use of them.

As to whether the state should fund more basic or applied research there are good arguments on both sides. For example, research by Rodriguez-Pose (1999) suggests that in an economy dominated by Small and Medium-Sized Firms (SMEs) with an intermediate technological and industrial base, the returns may be greater from more applied research which is more easily absorbed by local firms. Other commentators argue that the rationale for public funding of basic research needs to take account of the changing nature of research. The nature of knowledge production is shifting, with greater emphasis on collaboration and transdisciplinarity and with research being conducted 'in the context of application' (Gibbons et al., 1994). The distinction between what is public and what is private in knowledge production and therefore in science has become blurred, if not irrelevant.

20.3 Investment in the Public Research System in Ireland

Higher Education Expenditure on R&D (HERD) increased substantially in real terms in recent years, and Ireland has moved up the OECD league table (26 countries) from 19th place in 2002 to 16th in 2004 as a consequence. Over the same period the number of researchers in Higher Education Institutes (HEI) in Ireland increased from 2,695 in 2002 to 4,152 in 2004 (Forfás, 2004; ESRI, 2004).

In terms of the 2000-2006 NDP, the main direct supports for HERD in Ireland were:

- Science Foundation Ireland (SFI) which began work in 2001 with a focus on establishing world-class research capability in niche areas of ICT and biotechnology. Scientists from abroad may apply for SFI funding provided they conduct the resultant research in Ireland. SFI therefore serves as a powerful magnet to attract individuals and groups to add to our national research effort. As of 2006, SFI had established:
    - 204 research groups led by Principal Investigators, of whom 46 are new to Ireland. The groups employ 1,628 research staff - over a fifth of the entire research staff in Irish HEIs.
    - Six Centres for Science Engineering and Technology (CSETs) in core thematic areas. The CSETs bring together researchers from around the world in highly sophisticated, multi-faceted teams at Ireland's universities. These centres are now working with companies such as Bosch, GlaxoSmithKlien, Hewlett-Packard, IMB, Intel and Medtronic.
- The Programme for Research in Third Level Institutions (PRTLI), operated by the Higher Education Authority (HEA), was established in 1998, to develop high quality research infrastructure in third level institutions. Headline results reported by International Assessment Committee in 2004 included new capital, new research buildings along with 34 new academic appointments (14 professorial) as well as over 1,500 new postdoctoral or postgraduate research appointments. Other outputs include a range of new courses as well as extension of collaboration between Irish institutions and internationally.
- Two new research councils were also established in 2000/01: The Irish Research Council for Science, Engineering and Technology (IRCSET) and the Irish Research Council for Humanities and Social Sciences (IRCHSS). The research councils have annual budgets of around €24 million and €10 million respectively, and have funded hundreds of post-doctoral and postgraduate researchers over the last few years as well as providing substantial project based research funding.

Although it is early days to be making judgements about any of these initiatives, recent evaluations have been very positive about scheme outputs, and suggested the need for continuing funding in order to achieve sustained gains. An International Review Panel convened in 2005, for example, examined the work of SFI and concluded: "research excellence is being funded" and "impressive progress towards developing a world class research capability in biotechnology and ICT had been achieved in a short time...the existence of SFI funding is having a positive catalytic effect on the performance of research in its two fields". The review team recommended that "SFI investments are continued and made an established part of the innovation system" (Forfás, 2005). As regards PRTLI, an International Review Committee concluded that "investment in PRTLI is fully justified and should be continued...the important goals of PRTLI will only be achieved if funding on a significant scale is sustained over an extended period ... for at least another ten years" (HEA, 2004).

A key output of these initiatives has been the increase in postgraduate and postdoctoral research training in Irish HEIs. There is a growing recognition that high-level skills provide a key impetus for broad economic growth (Florida and Tingali, 2004). By ensuring a supply of skilled graduates public research underpins the capabilities of the private sector. Research-trained staff play a key role in increasing the absorptive capacity of firms and provide a strong inter-personal link between firms and universities. This type of personal linkage has repeatedly been shown to be an important element of knowledge transfer activity (Zucker et al., 1998).

Furthermore, the quality of R&D personnel is the most important factor determining the choice of location of R&D activities by multinational companies (OECD, 2006).

20.4 Investment in Business Enterprise Research

Despite a nominal growth in BERD of 19.4 per cent over the two year period 2001-2003, levels of BERD in Ireland remain below the EU average. Most SMEs in Ireland do not conduct R&D and large MNCs do most of their R&D abroad. For this reason the Government has invested significantly in BERD through the enterprise development agencies, Enterprise Ireland (EI) and Industrial Development Authority (IDA) Ireland.

BERD results in new goods and services, higher quality of output and new production processes. These are factors of productivity growth at the firm level and at the macroeconomic level. The effect of BERD on productivity has been investigated in many empirical studies, performed at all levels of aggregation – business units, firm, industry and country levels – and for many countries (especially the United States). All these studies reach the conclusion that R&D matters. The estimated output elasticity with respect to BERD varied from ten per cent to 30 per cent (Guellec and Van Pottelsberghe de la Potterie, 2001). For example, Coe and Helpman (1993) find that a one per cent increase in the stock of UK domestic R&D capital will lead to an increase in output of around 0.23 per cent. This large variation is mainly due to the fact that the studies differ in terms of the econometric model, data sources, number of economic units, measurement methods for R&D and economic performance, and periods under study.

There has been very few studies based on Irish data, however Gorg and Strobl (2005) investigated whether there is any link between R&D and plant level productivity for Irish firms. They find that own R&D activity of domestic exporters is positively linked to their total factor productivity. This is consistent with the international literature which finds a strong positive relationship between the stock of R&D and productivity at the firm level (Griliches, 1998). The authors did not find as strong a link in foreign firms but this is clouded by the fact that multinational companies carry out most of their R&D outside Ireland and there are difficulties in equating innovation inputs with enterprise performance metrics (sales, employment, etc) in the case of foreign owned companies in Ireland.

The social rate of return has been found in various studies to average about 50 per cent, which is considerably higher than the private return (Nadiri, 1993). The social rate of return is generally obtained by estimating the impact on growth in one firm of R&D done in other firms. These other firms could be within the same industry, the same country or in related industries (for example an upstream industry that supplies parts) or related countries (for example a trading partner). Care must be taken in interpreting estimates of the social rate of return to R&D. Estimates that are carried out at the firm level capture the social rate of return only to that firm. Those at the industry-level capture the social rate of return to that industry, but not spillovers to other industries. Similarly estimates conducted at the national level capture within country spillovers, but not those between countries. In addition, an important part of innovative output is the introduction of new goods and there are considerable difficulties that arise in measuring the value and benefit of these new goods. Estimates for the social rate of return at the industry level from R&D conducted by firms within the same industry range from 17 per cent to 30 per cent (Jones and Williams, 1998). Estimates of the social rate of return attributable to R&D conducted in one country but used in another are significantly higher. Adding these two together implies a social rate of return of around 100 per cent. These estimates are largely based on data for the manufacturing sector (Griffith, 2002).

The social return on R&D is likely to be underestimated in many studies, because spillovers are often estimated only for a limited number of firms and industries. Another way in which these models will underestimate the social rate of return to R&D is that they assume that imitation is costless. However, knowledge is 'tacit' in nature: it takes time and effort to explain and imitate new ideas. Imitation itself can be costly.[5] BERD enhances firms' ability to absorb external science and technology developments. BERD can particularly help firms to digest the knowledge generated in universities.[6] This is because business research develops technologies that in many cases have first been explored by public research.

20.5 Crowding out Versus Additionality

Much of the literature on R&D is concerned with the question of whether public funding stimulates private R&D expenditure or whether it simply acts as a substitute for private financing. There are three mechanisms by which public funding can crowd out private investment. First, it is likely that the labour supply of scientists is quite inelastic, so that when the government provides a subsidy to R&D this may be spent on increased wages rather than new R&D, at least in the short run (Goolsbee, 1998). There may still be positive benefits from these subsidies from encouraging people to become scientists, or by increasing their effort at work by paying them higher salaries. Second, public funding could also simply replace private funding if business substituted public funding for their own funds. Third, public funding could distort resource allocation favouring areas with lower opportunities.

Despite the fact that most developed countries employ some form or other of government R&D subsidy, the empirical evidence regarding their success is generally scarce and mixed. For instance, a substantial literature review on the subject carried out in 1999 found that "the econometric results obtained from careful studies at both the micro and macro levels tend to be running in favour of findings of complementarity between public and private R&D investments. However, that reading is simply an un-weighted summary based upon some 30 diverse studies; it is not a conclusion derived from a formal statistical 'meta-analysis,' and in no sense is it offered here as a judgement that would pretend to settle the issue definitively" (David, Hall and Toole, 2000).

Public support for BERD can encourage private sector investments by addressing market failures associated with incomplete information, inappropriability of the benefits of privately funded research or lack of suitable finance for innovation. An OECD study (Guellec and Van Pottelsberghe, 2004) attempted to quantify the aggregate net effect of government funding on BERD in 17 OECD countries over the previous two decades. The study found:

- Direct government funding of R&D performed by firms (either grants or procurement) has a positive effect on BERD (one dollar given to firms results in 1.70 dollars of research on average);
- The stimulating effect of government funding increases up to a certain threshold (about 13 per cent of BERD) and then decreases beyond;
- Tax incentives have a positive effect on BERD;

- The impact of direct government funding on BERD can be more long-lived than that of tax incentives, reflecting the fact that government programmes target research projects with a longer time horizon than those on the agenda of business;
- These two policy instruments are more effective when they are stable over time;
- Targeted government programmes help firms to digest knowledge generated by universities; and
- Defence research performed in public laboratories and universities crowds out private R&D.

In Ireland, Evaltec's review of the IDA's R&D Capability Grants Scheme 2003 found:

- Public money committed to the Scheme by way of grant approvals over the period 2001-2003, namely €38.2 million, leveraged an R&D spend totalling €147.7 million, over two years. This is a very substantial amount, as the total expenditure on R&D performed by multinational companies in Ireland in 2001 was €598 million;
- The companies themselves funded some three-quarters of the project implementation costs, thereby providing substantial tax revenues;
- The Scheme has had a substantial positive influence on corporate planners' decision to locate in Ireland; and
- The companies increased their R&D staffing levels, resulting in more jobs and higher added value employment.

Evaluations of the Research and Technological Development and Innovation (RTDI) Scheme and the R&D Capability Scheme, both operated by EI, found similar benefits for the Irish economy (Evaltec, 2004). Under both Schemes, most companies described their project as business critical or core business. Some evidence of deadweight was found in 85 per cent of RTDI projects and in 72 per cent of the Capability Scheme projects. However, only 23 per cent RTDI projects and 17 per cent Capability Scheme projects exhibited full deadweight (i.e. the project would have proceeded in an identical manner even if no grant had been received). In many of these cases of full deadweight the companies commented that the funding had allowed them to work on other R&D projects that they would have otherwise postponed or not undertaken at all. Most of the projects supported under the Schemes involved the employment of additional R&D staff, who were subsequently retained, thereby contributing to enhanced R&D expenditure, capability and sustainability within firms. The R&D Capability Scheme funding has allowed companies to take on an average of four additional researchers. Furthermore, allocation of funding enhanced companies' ability to obtain further investment from private sector sources.

These evaluations made a number of recommendations that have guided the design of R&D grant assistance packages currently offered by the agencies:

- The agencies should actively promote inter-firm co-operation on R&D, particularly between indigenous and foreign owned firms;
- The agencies should provide greater financial incentives for firms to undertake longer-term and more risky research. EU state aid rules allow such research to attract higher grant rates than are currently given by the agencies;
- More emphasis should be placed on process research and development;
- The requirements for companies to receive repeat support should be clarified, namely that they have achieved a significant enhancement of their R&D activities; and

- Other recommendations include simplifying the project approval process and optimising operational procedures generally to enhance efficiency and effectiveness, and thereby eventual impacts.

The R&D Tax Credit, introduced in 2004, marked a further step forward in Government support for company R&D.[7] The tax credit scheme should complement EI and IDA direct funding programmes and applies to the full spectrum of R&D, from basic to applied research through to experimental development, and will play an important part in FDI strategy aimed at attracting more research intensive activity to Ireland. In contrast, direct funding programmes will target applied research in strategically important technologies.

The success of any R&D tax credit scheme will depend on a number of factors. It is estimated that the US tax credit, introduced in 1981, stimulated additional R&D spending in the short-run of about $2 billion (1982 dollar value) per year, while the foregone tax revenue was about $1 billion per year (Hall, 1998). In other countries, for example Spain, tax credits have had less of an impact. This suggests that the effectiveness of any tax credit scheme will depend not only on its design, but also on other factors such as the availability of skills, the degree of local competition and cultural openness to new technologies, products and services.

20.6 A Systems Approach

The relationship between R&D and innovation is not a linear one. The outputs from science and technology activities depend not only on the amount of R&D input, but also on the efficiency of the entire innovation system (OECD, 1999a). In order to optimise the efficiency of this system it is vital that effective linkages are developed between its different components, which would facilitate the transfer of scientific knowledge. The Government has a key role to play in this area (OECD, 1999b).

The most important support for Higher Education-industry collaboration under the NDP 2000-2006 was the RTDI for Collaboration Programme. The principal schemes supported under the programme were:

- Innovation Partnerships, which aimed to build R&D partnerships between industry and the Third Level Institutions;
- The Commercialisation Fund, which financed 'technology push' projects within academia - testing and developing their commercial and technical potential; and
- The Programmes in Advanced Technology, which focused on commercialisation of academic research and some research and innovation support services to industry.

Other initiatives include the Centres for Science, Engineering and Technology (CSETs), established by SFI in 2001 and the IRCSET 'Enterprise Partnership Scheme' which facilitated the movement of researchers between academia and enterprise.

Given the concentration of scientific and technological resources in the major cities, companies in regional locations can find it more difficult to access support for innovation. The Institutes of Technology represent an important resource in this context. Their multi-regional location and openness to working with industry will allow them to develop into effective technology resources, focused on collaboration with local industry on the basis of applied research.

A key action outlined in the Strategy for Science Technology and Innovation, 2006-2013, is that all HEIs would encompass Intellectual Property management and commercialisation as a central part of their mission, equal to teaching and research. This has the potential to increase the value added derived from public funding of higher education research activity and to help to embed mobile firms in Ireland by increasing the strength of their relationship to local knowledge providers (ESRI, 2006).

20.7 Conclusion

There are mixed messages in the economic literature as to the extent of the returns from publicly funded research. However, the weight of evidence suggests that publicly funded research does make a substantial positive contribution to productivity, human capital development and economic growth. The challenge is to organise the national research and innovation system in such a way as to maximise return on investment. The benefits that spill over from public and private research are becoming increasingly important, as knowledge, high-level skills and innovative capacity are key sources of competitive advantage going forward. Independent evaluations of publicly funded research programmes have concluded that progress to date has been impressive and that funding must be continued in order to achieve sustained gains. The Government's Strategy for Science Technology and Innovation, 2006-2013, outlines a comprehensive programme, which will build on recent progress. The initiatives outlined in the Strategy are designed to enhance Ireland's research capability, improve the quantity and quality of BERD and ensure coherence within our National System of Innovation. Based on the evidence reviewed in this chapter, there is a strong case for suggesting that the Strategy will contribute to Ireland's long-term competitiveness, economic growth and improvements in the quality of life.

Notes

1 Guellec and Van Pottelsberghe de la Potterie (2001), R&D and Productivity Growth : Panel Data Analysis of 16 OECD countries, OECD Economic Studies No. 33, 200/11.

2 The OECD Frascatti Manual defines 'basic research' as "experimental or theoretical work undertaken primarily to acquire new knowledge of the underlying foundation of phenomena and observable facts, without any particular application or use in view".

3 See Swan (2002), Guellec and Van Pottlesberghe (2001), Cohen and Levinthal (1989), Schmidt (2005), and Coe and Helpman (1995).

4 Ibid.

5 Mansfield et al. (1986) present evidence of substantial costs of imitation (on average 65 per cent of innovation costs).

6 See Swan (2002), Guellec and Van Pottlesberghe (2001), Cohen and Levinthal (1989), Schmidt (2005), Coe and Helpman (1995).

7 The Scheme currently provides for a 20 per cent tax credit available to companies for qualifying incremental expenditure on R&D.

References

Beise, M. and Stahl, H. (1999), "Public Research and Industrial Innovations in Germany", *Research Policy,* 28(4): 397-422.

Bergman, E.M. (1990), "The Impact of Industry Funded University R&D", *Research Policy,* 19: 340–355.

Cockburn, I. and Henderson, R. (2000), "Publicly Funded Science and the Productivity of the Pharmaceutical Industry," in *Innovation Policy and the Economy,* Vol. 1, A. B. Jaffe, J. Lerner and S. Stern, eds., Cambridge, MA: MIT Press, 2001: 1-34.

Coe, D. and Helpman. E. (1995), "International R&D Spillovers," *National Bureau of Economic Research Working Papers,* 4444.

Cohen, W. and Levinthal, D. (1989), "Innovation and Learning: The Two Faces of R&D", *The Economic Journal,* 99: 569-596.

Czarnitzki, D. (2004), *European Competitiveness Report,* EU Commission, Brussels.

David, P., Hall, B. and Toole, A. (2000), "Is Public R&D a Complement or Substitute for Private R&D? A Review of the Econometric Evidence", *Research Policy,* 29: 497-529.

ESRI (2004), *Survey of Research and Development in the Higher Education Sector,* Economic and Social Research institute, Dublin.

ESRI (2006), *Ex-ante Evaluation of the Investment Priorities for the National Development Plan (2007-2013),* Economic and Social Research Institute, Dublin.

EU Commission (2005), '*Innovation Strengths and Weaknesses*', December 5, 2005.
Evaltec (2004), *Evaluation of Agency Supports for R&D Performed in the Business Sector,* Forfás, Dublin.

Florida, R. (2002), *The Rise of the Creative Class,* Basic Books, New York.

Forfás (2004), *Survey of Research and Development in the Higher Education Sector,* Forfás, Dublin.

Forfás (2005), *Report of an International Evaluation Panel, SFI, The First Years 2001-2005,* Forfás, Dublin.

Gibbons, M. (1994), *The New Production of Knowledge: The Dynamics of Science and Research in Contemporary Societies,* Sage, London.

Goolsbee, A. (1998), "Does Government R&D Policy Mainly Benefit Scientists and Engineers?", *American Economic Review,* American Economic Association, Vol. 88(2), 298-302, May.

Gorg, H. and Strobl, E. (2005), "The Effect of R&D Subsidies on Private R&D", *GEP Research Papers,* 2005/38.

Griffith R., Redding S. and Van Reenen, J. (1999), "Mapping the Two Faces of R&D; Productivity Growth in a Panel of OECD Industries", *Centre for Economic Policy Research,* Discussion Paper.

Griffith, R. (2002), "How Important is Business R&D for Economic Growth and Should the Government Subsidise it?", *Institute for Fiscal Studies Briefing Note,* 12.

Griliches, Z. (1998), "R&D and Productivity", *National Bureau of Economic Research Working Paper,* 1778.

Guellec, D. and Van Pottelsberghe de la Potterie, B. (2001), "R&D and Productivity Growth", *OECD Science, Technology and Industry Working Papers,* 2001/3.

Guellec, D. and Van Pottelsberghe, B. (2004), "The Impact of Public R&D Expenditure on Business R&D", *OECD Science, Technology and Industry Working Papers,* 2000/4.

Gurdgiev, C. (2006), "MNCs: Mothers of Invention", *Business and Finance Magazine,* July 2006.

Hall, B. (1992), "R&D Tax Policy During the Eighties", *National Bureau of Economic Research Working Paper,* 4240.

Hall, B. and Mairesse, J. (1995), "How Effective are Fiscal Measures to Support R&D? A Review of the Evidence", *Research Policy,* 29: 449-469.

HEA (2004), *Report by the International Assessment Committee, PRTLI – Impact Assessment,* Higher Education Authority, Dublin.

Jones, C. and Williams, J. (1998), "Measuring the Social Rate of Return to R&D", *Quarterly Journal of Economics,* 113(4): 1119-1135.

Mansfield, E. (1991), "Academic Research and Industrial Innovation", *Research Policy,* 20(1).

Mansfield, E. (1986), "Patents and Innovation: An Empirical Study", *Management Science* 32: 173-181.

Mansfield, E. (1998), "Academic Research and Industrial Innovation: An Update of Empirical Findings", *Research Policy* 26: 773-776.

Martin, W. (1998), "The Economic Impact of Canadian University R&D", *Research Policy,* 27(7): 677-687.

Nadiri, M. (1993), "Innovations and Technological Spillovers", *National Bureau of Economic Research Working Paper,* 4423.

Narin, M. (1997), "The Linkages between US Technology and Public Science", *Research Policy,* 26: 317-330.

OECD (1999a), *Managing National Innovation Systems*, OECD, Paris.

OECD (1999b), *Science, Technology and Industry Scoreboard, Benchmarking KBEs*, OECD, Paris.

OECD (2006), *Recent Trends in the Internationalisation of R&D in the Enterprise Sector*, OECD, Paris.

Rodríguez-Pose, A. (1999), Innovation Prone and Innovation Averse Societies: Economic Performance in Europe, Growth and Change, 30, 1, 75-105.

Schmidt, T. (2005), "Absorptive Capacity – One size fits all? A Firm Level Analysis of Absorptive Capacity for Different Kinds of Knowledge", Centre for European Economic Research, *ZEW Discussion Paper*, 05-72.

Scott, A. (2000), "The Economic Returns to Basic Research and the Benefits of University-Industry Relationships", *Research Policy*, 30: 509–532.

Swan, J. (2002), *Innovative Business and the Science and Technology Base: An Analysis Using CIS 3 Data*, Report for UK Department of Trade and Industry.

Toole, A. (2000), "The Impact of Public Research on Industrial Innovation: Evidence From the Pharmaceutical Industry", *SIEPR Discussion Paper*.

Zucker, L. (1998), "Intellectual Human Capital and the Birth of US Biotechnology Enterprises", *American Economic Review*, 88: 209-306.

CHAPTER 21

ICT AND COMPETITIVENESS: WHAT PROSPECTS FOR THE LISBON STRATEGY?

SUSANNE MUNDSCHENK[1]

ABSTRACT

At the Lisbon Summit in March 2000, Europe's heads of state declared their ambition to make the European Union "the most competitive and dynamic knowledge-based economy in the world by 2010". The underlying assumption of the Lisbon Agenda is that an increased role for ICT will improve the overall economic performance in terms of competitiveness - measured by the level of productivity - and employment. This chapter argues that this assumption is flawed on a number of grounds, both on theoretical and practical grounds.

1 Susanne Mundschenk is a director of Eurointelligence Advisors, an internet-based economic commentary and analysis company.

21.1 Introduction

At the Lisbon Summit in March 2000, Europe's heads of state declared their ambition to make the European Union "the most competitive and dynamic knowledge-based economy in the world by 2010, capable of sustainable economic growth, with more and better jobs and greater social cohesion".[1] This broad objective includes an increase in the employment rate from an average of 63 per cent in the EU25 to an average of 70 per cent by 2010, which will require an EU average annual real growth rate of three per cent, considerably higher than the average of 2.1 per cent over the past ten years. To achieve it, the heads of state adopted the *Lisbon Strategy*, a far-reaching agenda combining short-term political initiatives and medium and long-term economic reforms. The Lisbon objective is that EU member states should implement policies that increase the standard of living of their citizens in order to enable the EU to reach and even surpass US levels (Ilzkovitz and Dierx, 2006).

Information and Communication Technology (ICT) is one of the key mechanisms for implementing the Lisbon strategy. Many EU member states have established National Information Society Action Plans. Accession countries developed their own action plans to increase internet access, backed by the EU Commission with the e-Europe Plus initiative. While these strategies often have goals other than promoting economic activity – such as the need to strengthen social cohesion – a key policy question is what impact the adoption of ICT has on the economy and in particular on productivity and employment.

The underlying assumption is that an increased role for ICT will improve the overall economic performance in terms of competitiveness - measured by the level of productivity - and employment. This assessment draws from the experience in the US, especially since 1995, where economic growth was accompanied by high sectoral productivity gains that have been interpreted as being largely a result of the successful adoption of ICT. Compared with the US, productivity growth in the EU started to fall behind the US for the first time since the mid-nineties. Van Ark et al. (2003) argued that this is particularly due to a substantial acceleration in the ICT-using sectors in the US unmatched by the EU. Thus, the productivity slowdown in the EU could be reversed or at least put to a halt if national governments target the ICT deficiency in the relevant sectors.

There are three categories of ICT policies under the Lisbon Strategy: (1) policies that focus on the production of ICT technologies with the declared objective of increasing ICT research spending to match the US; (2) policies that aim to improve and broaden access to ICT and (3) policies that focus on the use of ICT with the intention of increasing efficiency and product innovation.

Can ICT help to achieve the Lisbon targets? How does Europe compare to the United States and how does Ireland compare to other EU member states? These are the questions we will address in this study. We find that there is no clear relationship between the role of ICT and productivity performance that is valid for all EU countries. For the European Union as a whole the analysis presented raises significant doubts that ICT can become an instrument to achieve the Lisbon Agenda, whether we look at ICT capital spending or the share of ICT-intensive sectors in the economy.

21.2 Comparison within Member States

At the level of the member states, a more diverse picture emerges. Comparing the labour productivity performance over the past two decades shows that Luxembourg and Ireland had the most remarkable productivity performance. Together with France, the Netherlands, Belgium and Austria – these countries were more competitive than the US for most of the time.

What is notable is that if we look at four ICT indicators defined by the Lisbon Strategy (namely ICT expenditure, communication expenditure, broadband penetration and ecommerce via internet) we find that success in productivity terms does not seem to be strongly linked to meeting the four ICT indicators as identified by the EU. Ireland has the highest percentage of turnover created through e-commerce but spends much less on ICT or communication measured as percentage of GDP than ten other EU-15 countries. The United Kingdom seems to be the most consistent country in the sense that though it is part of the leading countries in all categories where data is available, it is not a leading country in terms of overall productivity performance. The ten new member countries invest heavily in communication and will certainly benefit from a new vintage of infrastructure investments, but whether all of these new entrants will also succeed in translating higher spending into higher competitive performance against other states is less clear. Other factors, such as Research and Development (R&D) and human capital as well as market institutions will be important factors in this process.

21.3 The Linkage between ICT Expenditure and Productivity Growth

The assumption that investment in ICT can raise the overall economic performance of a region draws from the experience of the US, especially since 1995 where strong economic growth was accompanied by high sectoral productivity gains. When it comes to growth in productivity and employment, the majority of EU member states performed better with respect to the latter. In 2003, six countries had already achieved the Lisbon target of a 70 per cent employment rate. Measuring competitiveness in terms of productivity per hour, eight EU countries had similar or higher levels of productivity than the US but the EU itself is only at 93.4 per cent of US level. Assuming that the US will continue to grow by an average productivity rate of 1.5 per cent per annum, the EU would need an average annual productivity growth rate of more than 2.5 per cent if the EU were to reach the Lisbon objective by 2010. Six years after the launch of the Lisbon strategy, it seems unlikely that the EU will achieve its goal.

Figure 21.1: Productivity per Hour: Laggards and Leaders

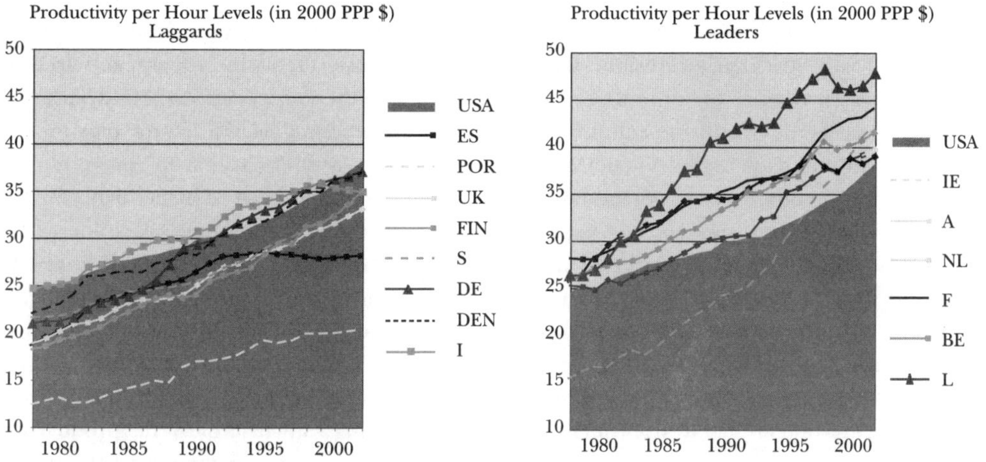

Source: Groningen Growth and Development Centre and OECD.

Are there reasons why we might not find a positive relationship between ICT and higher productivity growth? There are three possible explanations for the absence of a link between the two.

The first explanation is specifically related to the effectiveness of higher ICT research spending. Commissioner Viviane Reding proposed to increase public and private research spending in ICT by 80 per cent in order to match the US.[2] However, if the better productivity performance of the US is due to its comparative advantage in the production of high technology (Roeger, 2001), then there is no point in trying to replicate the US if other countries can benefit from technological spillovers. It would then be wiser to spend more R&D in the technologically leading country (the US), and to increase the absorption capacity of those countries that are lagging behind. This would suggest that parts of the money spend on the implementation of the ICT action plans of the Lisbon Strategy would be better spent in Silicon Valley or at IT centres in India and to focus on comparative advantages in the EU instead. The policy task for the EU is then reduced to whether Europe uses ICT efficiently enough to benefit from dissemination of ICT.

The second explanation occurs if ICT is not the cause but a symptom of the innovation process. This is the case when other innovation input factors such as R&D and human capital are crucial for the success of ICT. It would then be worth reflecting on whether the Euro spend on ICT would not be better spent on education or R&D in sectors that promises a higher comparative advantage and a higher return in terms of economic growth. Private economic actors would then add any ICT they needed to complement these other inputs.

The third explanation is that the absence of any measured impact of ICT on productivity is purely a failing of data, where measurement errors especially in the service sector can misestimate the impact of ICT on productivity. Robert Solow was famously quoted saying that “there are computers everywhere, except in the statistics”. But the direction of the bias is not clear, nor is it clear whether there are significant differences between the US and the EU that explain the different performance of the two economies.

21.4 Decomposing the EU – US Productivity Gap

The US has outperformed the EU in terms of aggregate economy-wide economic growth from 1996 to 2002. Figure 21.2 shows the average growth rates of real productivity per employee for ICT intensive sectors in the EU15 and the US over the period 1996-2002.[3] The sectors are categorised as ICT-producing and ICT-using industries and within each of these two categories a breakdown is made between manufacturing and services. As can be seen from the graph, the reason for the difference in performance between the two regions can be explained primarily by two economic sectors – ICT-producing manufacturing and ICT-using services.

In the 1996-2002 period aggregate productivity in the EU15 had been falling despite strong productivity gains in the ICT-producing sector. At the same time the upsurge in US aggregate labour productivity was reflected in high productivity gains especially in the ICT-producing manufacturing and ICT-using service sectors.

ICT-producing manufacturing productivity growth has always been stronger in the US than in Europe, while growth in ICT-using services increased markedly in the US since 1996 while stagnating in the EU15. This is the period when the US started to outperform the EU in terms of productivity growth. ICT-using services are financial intermediation; wholesale trade; retail trade; machinery renting; R&D; legal, technical and advertising services. They are showing outstanding productivity growth, especially in the first three service industries. They are the second most important sector in the US with 26 per cent (EU 23 per cent) of total value added and 23 per cent (EU 21 per cent) of total employment.

Figure 21.2: Productivity Growth: Europe and US, 1996-2002

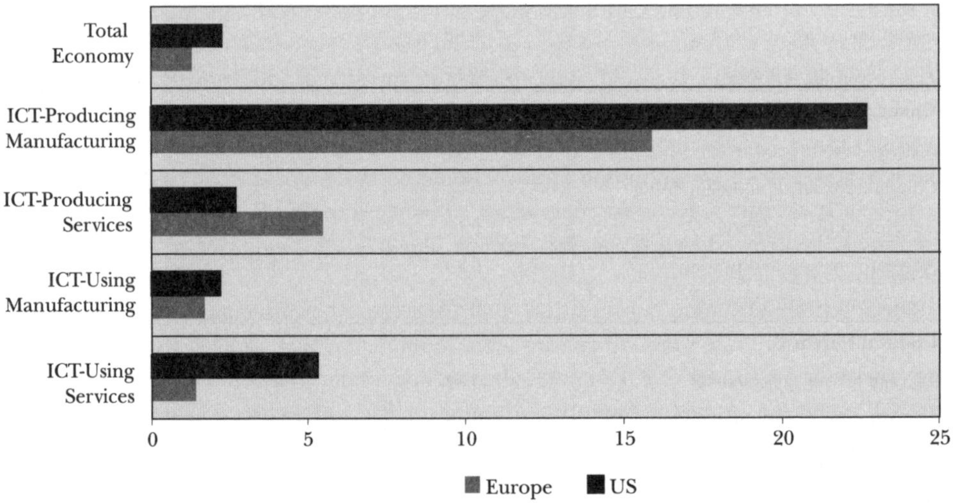

Source: Groningen Growth and Development Centre.

Total Factor Productivity (TFP) in sectors that use ICT intensively has also risen in the second half of the 1990s for the US and it has been argued that this is a sign of a more productive use of ICT. Also, as a general purpose technology, ICT is expected to spill over towards other sectors. Thus, the contribution of the ICT-producing sector to the TFP of the whole economy should be positive.

Another way of examining differential productivity performance at the aggregate level is by means of growth accounting exercises. Rather than examining the influence of ICT by comparing industries based on their ICT production/usage patterns, it tries to compare the level of ICT expenditures and their likely impact on economic performance. This methodology returns a similar result. Investment in ICT capital makes a significant contribution towards TFP growth in sectors that use ICT intensively. TFP growth is what the European Union needs in order to fulfill the Lisbon Agenda. Increases in TFP are productivity improvement without job losses. Thus, growth in TFP is consistent with both objectives of the Lisbon Strategy, namely higher growth and employment.

Table 21.1 reports the value added per hour worked for the European Union and the US and its contributions. For the EU4 (Germany, France, Netherlands and the UK) the growth rate of value-added per man hour declined continuously to 1.37 per cent for 1995-2001, which is nearly one percentage point lower than for the 1980-1990 period. It shows that since 1980, ICT investment has always been stronger in the US than in Europe. The positive productivity growth gap in 1995-2001 is more than 50 per cent due to higher contributions by IT capital deepening. The second half of the 1990s also shows a sharp rise in TFP for the US and a sharp decline for the EU.

Table 21.1: Growth Accounting for the European Union and the US

European Union (EU4)	**1980-1989**	**1990-1995**	**1996-2001**
Average labour productivity	2.28	2.43	1.37
Contribution of capital deepening	1.16	1.30	0.90
Information technology	0.34	0.29	0.42
Non-information technology	0.82	1.01	0.48
Total factor productivity	1.12	1.14	0.46
United States			
Average labour productivity	1.46	1.19	1.85
Contribution of capital deepening	0.71	0.58	1.05
Information technology	0.52	0.40	0.72
Non-information technology	0.19	0.19	0.32
Total factor productivity	0.75	0.61	0.80
US-EU difference			
Average labour productivity	-0.82	-1.24	0.48
Contribution of capital deepening	-0.45	-0.71	0.14
Information technology	0.18	0.11	0.30
Non-information technology	-0.63	-0.82	-0.16
Total factor productivity	-0.37	-0.53	0.34

Source: Van Ark, Timmer and Ypma (2003). EU4 consists of France, Germany, the Netherlands and the UK.

Why has ICT benefited the US and not the EU? The first point to note is that the ICT producing manufacturing sector and ICT using services sector are entirely separate sectors with weak links between them. The success of the US ICT-using services industries reflects a greater absorptive capacity on their part than their European partners, and certainly did not require as a pre-requisite that the US be a leader in ICT producing goods. As such, while the US may have a comparative advantage in ICT production, this does not translate automatically into a comparative advantage in the ICT using sector. In wholesale and retail trade, the two sectors with the highest productivity growth, higher economies of scale and higher competition benefited the US compared to the still fragmented and highly regulated service sector in Europe. Employment protection as well as product market regulations significantly reduce the effectiveness of ICT investment in the EU.

Another explanation is that the adoption of general purpose technologies such as ICT requires a lengthy learning period with temporarily lower productivity before the boom. The US has undergone this process in the 1980s and early 1990s while many European countries are still in the process. There is however no convincing reason for this assumption given that ICT is considered as a global good with international externalities. There may be delays in adaptation but it is hard to imagine that ICT investment benefits should show up after more than 15 years, even in the EU.

Another factor mentioned above as to why Europe and US performance may have diverged relates to other input factors such as R&D and human capital, which are crucial for the success of ICT. What is notable from an analysis of the data, however, is that the three ICT service sectors that were found to explain the latest acceleration in the US - financial intermediation, wholesale and retail trade - do not have substantial spending on R&D, or are not typified by an intensity of highly skilled workers, although financial intermediation might be the exception to this.

Finally, there is a possibility that while ICT has had a significant impact on the economy, the statistical measures do not account for them. Business services are likely to provide indirect productivity effects that are not accounted for in the service sector. Innovation and diffusion of knowledge passes through their client relationship and creates positive productivity gains even if the service sector itself is stagnant. ICT investment requires complementary investment in organisational change and retraining. Since those expenditures are classified as intermediate consumption under conventional national accounting systems, they get netted out of the final GDP although it is in fact investment and should be included in GDP. As long as the Lisbon Agenda ultimate goal is to increase the GDP per capita from current 70 per cent of US level, we might not see ICT to be part of this strategy.

21.5 Conclusions

At the Lisbon Summit in March 2000, Europe's heads of state declared their ambition to make the European Union "the most competitive and dynamic knowledge-based economy in the world by 2010, capable of sustainable economic growth, with more and better jobs and greater social cohesion". The underlying assumption of the Lisbon Agenda is that an increased role for ICT will improve the overall economic performance in terms of competitiveness - measured by the level of productivity - and employment. This chapter has argued that this assumption is flawed on a number of grounds, both on theoretical and practical grounds.

In theoretic terms, increasing ICT expenditure will not necessarily result in improved productivity. If the better productivity performance of the US is due to its comparative advantage in the production of high technology then trying to replicate the US is sub-optimal as long as other countries can benefit from technological spillovers of inventions discovered by US research. Further, if ICT is not the cause but a symptom of innovation process, then EU governments should be investing more in complementary inputs such as education and R&D.

In practical terms, the four ICT indicators as identified by the EU in the Lisbon Strategy (namely ICT expenditure, communication expenditure, broadband penetration and ecommerce via internet) do not seem to be strongly linked to success in productivity terms. Furthermore, the success of the US ICT-using services industries reflects a greater absorptive capacity on their part than their European partners. Employment protection and product market regulations in the EU significantly reduce the effectiveness of ICT investment.

Notes

1 The full text (Presidency Conclusions, Lisbon European Council, 23 and 24 March 2000) can be downloaded from: www.europa.eu.int/comm/off/index/_en.htm.

2 Viviane Reding, Member of the European Commission responsible for Information Society and Media. Press release on the occasion of the launch of the initiative European Information Society 2010, Brussels, 1 June 2005.

3 The data is derived from the 60-Industry Database from the Groningen Growth and Development Centre.

References

Van Ark, B. and O'Mahony, M. (2003), "EU Productivity and Competitiveness: An Industry Perspective, Can Europe Resume the Catching up Process?" DG Enterprise, Luxembourg, European Commission.

Van Ark, B., Trimmer, M. and Ypma, G. (2003), "IT in the European Union: Driving Productivity Convergence?", *CGDC Research Memorandum*, University of Groningen, Netherlands.

Ilzkovitz, F. and Dierx, A. (2006), "Economic Growth in Europe: Pursuing the Lisbon Strategy" in: Mundschenk, S., Traistaru, I., Stierle, M. and Stierle-von Schütz, U. (eds.): *Competitiveness and Growth in Europe, Lessons and Policy Implications for the Lisbon Strategy*, Edward Elgar.

Roeger, W. (2001), "The Contribution of Information and Communication Technologies to Growth in Europe and the US: A Macroeconomic Analysis"; *Economic Papers*, No. 147, January 2001, European Commission, Brussels.

CHAPTER 22

INFORMATION TECHNOLOGY PERFORMANCE AND PROCESS: FOUR CASE STUDIES

DANIEL MADDOX AND GERRY BOYLE

ABSTRACT

The payoffs from investment in Information and Technology (IT) and the organisational, managerial and technological requirements necessary to bring about successful performance have proved difficult to find since the advent of the IT era. In this chapter, we investigate the levels of IT investment undertaken, and the subsequent performance benefits found in a number of Irish organisations. The chapter also focuses on the processes that contribute to successful performance and with the difficulties of attempting to measure results. Our results indicate that organisations that have a clear strategic focus that embraces IT investment achieve greater benefits. We also find that the management component is the most critical issue in terms of assuring successful performance outcomes. Finally, the chapter presents a model for optimising the benefits from IT investment.

22.1 Introduction

A question that has puzzled economists and IT managers and practitioners for the best part of the last 20 years has been whether IT investment leads to greater productivity growth at the level of the individual firm. In addressing this question there has been a long-standing debate as to whether the revolution in IT was paying off in the form of higher productivity (Strassmann, 1990; Brynjolfsson and Hitt 1995; 1996; 1998). The results of early studies were mixed, with service firms in particular, showing weak or non-existent links between IT and productivity (Strassmann, 1990), with some manufacturing firms showing positive results on IT investment (Barua et al., 1995). Later and more rigorous studies found that IT investments contributed to firm productivity, and that over time firms were learning to apply IT capital more productively (Bresnahan 1999; Brynjolfsson and Hitt, 1995; 1996; 1998).

The empirical research to date indicates a number of factors that have been found to affect IT performance. Key amongst these are the need for strategic alignment (Henderson and Venkatraman, 1993), alignment between business and IT strategies (Croteau and Bergeron, 1999), close IT and business strategy alignment (Tallon, Kraemer and Gurbuxani, 2000), executive support for IT and joint IT and business strategy development (Luftman, Papp And Brier, 1999), and bi-directional strategic leadership involving IT and business functions (Rockart et al., 2000). An additional key research finding has been that value from IT emerges only through its use by an organisation, both strategically and operationally, incorporating its interactions with customers, suppliers and perhaps even regulatory authorities (Tiernan and Peppard, 2004), and that IT productivity and firm performance is affected by the levels of capital deepening and diffusion.

The research linking IT investment to benefits and performance in Ireland is limited (Remanyi and Brown, 2001). This paper attempts to partially remedy this deficit. It will examine the principal managerial and other practices that impact on IT performance, as well as the impacts and benefits that arise from IT investment. Four case studies from different sectors are examined.

22.2 Research Questions

This chapter addresses three fundamental questions:

1. How does IT affect organisational performance?
2. How significant is strategic alignment to the optimisation of organisational performance?
3. What other significant factors contribute to the impact of IT on organisational performance?

22.3 Case Organisations and Methodology

The research questions were explored in four diverse Irish organisations. The organisations are referred to as case firms from here on and are shown in the following Figure 22.1.

Figure 22.1: The Case Organisations

Case Study A Large traditional manufacturer. Long established firm. Large employer. IT Manager not on TMT (Top Management Team). Wide product range. Intensely competitive industry sector. Considerable change underway in organisation. Major investment in IT. Declining profitability.	**Case Study B** Medium-sized bank. Long established firm. Also operates outside of Ireland in three distinct market areas. Employs 500. IT Manager on TMT. Bespoke banking products. Niche operator. Competitive industry. Maintaining IT investment levels.
Case Study C Large local authority. Long established. Employs 500 and increasing. New IT Manager not on TMT and IT function new. Long established firm. Monopoly provider. Limited change underway in administrative processes. Annual budgetary allocation for IT investment.	**Case Study D** High-tech manufacturer of computer printer products. Subsidiary status. In operation just three years. Employs 200 and growing. Tight management team. IT Manager on TMT. Massive IT investment. Fiercely competitive industry.

Two of the organisations are manufacturing firms, a high-tech multinational manufacturer and the other a traditional indigenous manufacturing firm. The third is a medium-sized bank with bespoke products and the final organisation is a municipal authority. The organisations will be referred to respectively as the High-Tech Manufacturer, the Traditional Manufacturer, the Bank and the Authority.

The case studies differed substantially from each other and so exhibited the extreme situations and polar types suggested by Pettigrew (1990) as being an important feature of case study research design. Yin (2003) describes the scope of a case study as an "empirical enquiry that investigates a contemporary phenomenon within its real-life context, when the boundaries between phenomenon and context are not clearly evident, and in which multiple sources of evidence are used". He also indicates that the case approach is preferable when 'how' or 'why' questions are being asked, when the investigator has little control over events, and where the focus is on contemporary phenomena. For these reasons the case approach has been adopted.

22.4 Findings

22.4.1 Strategic Alignment

All of the case organisations professed to having either formal written or unwritten strategic plans, with three of these conceding that there was a weak relationship between these overall strategies and their IT strategies. The Authority indicated that the concept of strategic planning was new to the organisation, having only recently been introduced. Decisions about IT activities for municipal authorities in Ireland are centralised. This has resulted in the Authority depending on national directives to progress its IT development. In addition the Authority was subject to a national rollout of its IT plans (Strategic Management Initiative, 2006). This had led to its strategic plans being compiled at short notice, and mainly because of the bureaucratic process involved, a weak sense of ownership of the plan by individual departments and managers. As a result, the role of IT was viewed as peripheral to the work of the Authority, being viewed mainly as a service provider to its activities.

The Traditional Manufacturer had a five-year strategic plan but there was no apparent or serious attempt to integrate the IT function into the plan. As a result, IT was perceived as fulfilling the role of a service provider to the main production and administrative departments. In the two previous years the Traditional Manufacturer had largely introduced a new Enterprise Resource Planning (ERP) system using SAP (Systems, Applications and Products) software to which the IT function, as a service provider, had released some of its staff. This system had been implemented with the strategic aim of introducing a computerised 'customer-pull' system, linking sales orders from its various markets to activate production requirements and delivery. The firm had failed to realise this key strategic aim; no progress being made up to this case enquiry stage, and almost three years after the overall programme had been instigated. Aside from this, there was no strategic connection between the IT function and the top management team and the IT Manager was not a member of this team.

In the Bank's case the role of IT was accepted by its senior managers as serving a purely transactional purpose with high selling skills at the customer interface viewed as being more critical to business success. This successful bank nevertheless had a clear strategic intent and rationale and this focused approach was perceived as being largely responsible for driving the business forward. Resulting from its transactional focus the IT function played a reactionary role in responding to the service and operational demands placed on it. On a more strategic basis, there was no evident or coherent approach to overall IT planning visible, and as a result piecemeal approaches were adopted for the development of IT systems within the Bank.

On the issue of strategic alignment the High-Tech Manufacturer showed itself to be clearly superior to the other case firms. This firm was a new multinational subsidiary in Ireland, and followed a clear corporate strategic plan. The High-Tech Manufacturer also represented the clearest case of integration of the IT function with an overall corporate and subsidiary strategy. Essentially, the aim of this strategy involved being the lowest-cost producer within the industry and within worldwide markets for its products. Internally, the firm also displayed a high and effective integration of IT within its operational and administrative departments. Its relative newness as an organisation was in contrast to the other case firms each of which had been in operation for at least forty years. IT processes in this case firm used the most up-to-date hardware and software. It also had a fully integrated and automated production system, managed through an effective ERP system, coupled with an administrative and office-based software system. The latter system incorporated its HR and payroll systems. It was very evident that this case firm utilised IT to considerable strategic advantage. This was a prime reason for it becoming the second most competitive producer throughout all worldwide group subsidiaries, a considerable achievement in competitive terms. These results were attributed by the management team to the clear linkage achieved between overall and IT strategy at corporate and subsidiary level, and between the strategic and operational components of the business. Success was also attributed to how IT had been instrumental in integrating its production processes, mainly through a computer-controlled statistical process system at shop-floor level, and its successfully computerised integration of its production and administrative systems.

This organisation had virtually succeeded in achieving real-time communication with its parent company in the United States through the use of an Electronic Data Interchange system, which converted data and information from the manufacturer, for corporate use. As a result of the effective use of IT, the organisation's management claimed a half-day turnaround performance from receipt of product material to customer dispatch, and have become the second best performer in cost and delivery performance terms within the group's twenty-eight group subsidiaries. By any yardstick, these achievements are quite exceptional. For these reasons, this organisation clearly distinguished itself from the other case organisations studied. Its key distinguishing and advantageous features lay in its relative newness, its focus on strategy at different operational levels, the visible integration of its strategic and operational activities and its centralising of the IT function.

22.4.2 Strategic and Operational Integration

In three of the four studies there was an acceptance that the IT function was not being valued as a strategic resource. Only in the case of the High-Tech Manufacturer was there a clear indication that the IT function had been viewed, and used, as a strategic resource. In this sense, it was central to bringing about low-cost production, acknowledged superior cost and quality performance, and extremely short customer delivery times. It achieved these key strategic targets by the use of IT systems, through its strategic and operational alignment and coherence, and also through the management of its operational and administrative processes and controls. The final component in its success lay in its ability to communicate effectively, through the medium of IT, with its parent organisation. This linkage was critical to success for the High-Tech subsidiary since the parent company dealt directly with all suppliers in the interests of subsidiary organisations. It was clear that there was a strong interplay between the successful functioning of IT and the quality of its management, both strategically and operationally, and that this led to successful outcomes. The successful harmonisation of the organisation's general and IT technology, with its functional and office departments, further contributed to this success. The quality of management in this situation would have been assisted by the tightly knit nature, and limited size, of the top management team as well as by its strong parent company direction. It was apparent that IT, together with management quality, served a critical role in furthering the organisation's competitive advantage.

None of the other organisations succeeded in matching the performance levels of the High-Tech Manufacturer. It was not possible to get details of tangible benefits from investment in, and use of IT. In the case of the Traditional Manufacturer the newly introduced ERP system, despite its considerable investment, had failed to realise many of its targeted aims and benefits. At the conclusion of this case research several key areas of the organisation's operations had not been integrated into the system and the organisation had not attempted, partly for funding and cost reasons, to achieve integration of the system with other group companies, suppliers, or customers. This failure mainly came about because different companies and suppliers with which the case firm did its business used different version ERP systems, leading to an inability to 'talk' successfully to each other. ERP systems, unlike older IT systems are fully integrated, enterprise-wide, real-time information systems. ERP system products, such as SAP, JDEdwards, Oracle and Peoplesoft, are offered mainly by German and American proprietors. A further reason for failure in this area was that its key overseas trading company was reluctant to changeover to a SAP system so that the necessary integration between both organisations could be achieved. In addition to its new ERP system, the Traditional Manufacturer also used Peoplesoft software, for all its HR activities, together with separate software systems for its payroll and ordering systems.

Neither the Bank nor the Authority had an enterprise-based IT system, with IT operations being focused on a number of separate software systems. Also, none of the organisations had as yet attempted direct on-line electronic interchange with external organisations, their suppliers or their customers. Management style in these organisations varied from traditional/ bureaucratic to very reactive styles. These styles are not conducive to planned management processes, or to emphasising the need for strategic, as well as managerial planning and control. There was no evidence of an alignment of overall strategic approaches with any obvious IT strategy, or of any overall alignment of IT technology with the organisational infrastructure concerned.

The realisation of the full benefits of an ERP system is extremely challenging for any organisation. This includes the possibilities for gaining external advantages. Electronic Data Interchange (EDI) and ERP systems attempt to mix and match various hardware and software systems, internally and externally, to an organisation's advantage. Achieving this successfully can lead to the realisation of synergies, economies and cost improvements. The inability to realise these benefits occurs because of the difficulties created in attempting to get various software systems to 'talk' to each other. This is aside from any incompatibilities of hardware systems that may also exist. The case involving the incompatibility of the ERP systems used by the Traditional Manufacturer's main trading company, already cited, is a clear example of IT systems failing to 'talk' to each other, with the loss of probable benefits. In the working of ERP systems, an organisation is not likely to admit that the ERP system that it uses is less than satisfactory, or does not achieve all that is claimed for it, in case this confers by such an admission, advantage to a competitor. Systems such as SAP, JD Edwards, Oracle and Peoplesoft may not work in particular situations but for the reason stated there may be an unwillingness to admit this. Furthermore, the companies that distribute the various ERP systems have shown a reluctance to date in collaborating on the use of common ERP software since this would remove what they perceive to be their own distinctive competitive advantage. These issues are compounded further by the whole question of ensuring that these IT systems are secure, particularly when they work outside of the firm's internal environment. The need for security may therefore further inhibit management willingness to participate in EDI and ERP systems that operate outside of these boundaries. Arising from the above challenges it can be very difficult, very costly, and very time-consuming for organisations to achieve electronic data interchange between various IT systems. Only in the case of the High-Tech Manufacturer was there satisfactory evidence that a relevant and worthwhile level of interchange and integration had taken place.

22.4.3 Inclusion of the IT Manager on the Top Management Team (TMT)

Although cited by some of the literature as essential to the successful functioning of IT in an organisation, only two IT Managers in the case studies were included in the top management team and only one in a top management team that considered IT strategy as part of a wider overall business strategy. The most successful case was that of the High-Tech Manufacturer where the IT Manager also had a dual role as Engineering Manager and sat on the top team. In this joint capacity he had responsibility for the installation of all plant, machinery and IT systems. His actions were entirely governed by the need for performance achievement, within strategic aims and goals, and within a philosophy of continuous improvement in output, cost, quality and safety. Since its inception the firm had succeeded in achieving a 20 per cent annual improvement in these performance indicators and at the time of the case enquiry had been asked for a further improvement of the same magnitude for the following year.

In the case of the Bank, the IT Manager was a member of the top management team but this membership arose entirely because of his position as a head of function. The IT manager reported directly to the Bank's Chief Executive. Because the Bank didn't have a formal IT strategy, top management tended to concentrate on operational issues to the detriment of more strategic IT issues. The focus of attention therefore tended to be on the maintenance of the status quo in IT matters rather than on any radical or revolutionary review, or action, aimed at assisting IT as a function to support the future success of the Bank. During the term of this case enquiry, it was revealed that Bank's management had taken the first step in exploring the possibility of outsourcing its IT services. The pursuit of the outsourcing option reinforced the bank's IT operational focus and the wisdom of this possible move was not fully understood by, or agreed with, some of the management team.

In the remaining cases of the Traditional Manufacturer and the Authority, the respective IT Managers were not members of their top management teams and both position-holders reported to the senior financial executive of each organisation. In each case the separate IT managers had a bias towards the technical aspects of their roles and were limited in their overall business exposure and to the business of their top management teams. Under these circumstances, IT decisions within both organisations were made by members of the respective top management team, most of which had little, or no, appreciation of IT systems or for the technological and business opportunities that they presented.

22.4.4 Hybrid Managers and the Rotation of Roles

Of the four case studies undertaken, the highest level of hybrid skills amongst managers was evident in the case of the High-Tech Manufacturer. Hybrid skills refer to the possession of dual business and IT skills. A hybrid manager therefore is one that displays equal competencies and ease when faced with either operational or IT issues. In this case firm it was also evident that the entire workforce had a high level of IT skills that fully supported operations. There was a strong consensus within management, which indicated that these high-skill levels came from the substantial training provided by the organisation to its general workforce. Formal training in IT for all shop-floor employees varied from six to eight working weeks during the first year of their employment, although this decreased in the second and subsequent years as the levels of IT mastery increased. Managerial and office-based personnel were expected to have at least a working knowledge of most IT applications prior to joining the organisation. These knowledge and skill levels were further built on by relevant booster-training programmes, which were specially designed to improve user skills when working with organisational IT systems.

None of the other organisations succeeded in matching this level of hybrid skills amongst its managers or workforce. In the case of the Traditional Manufacturer, a minority of managers displayed high-level business as well as IT skills. This was however mainly confined to professional incumbents, including financial executives. Most managers displayed a basic level of IT ability, although some were very poor in this area, possessing little or no ability. Hybrid skills amongst IT staff were low; skill levels being heavily biased towards their technical and user IT strengths. It was evident that the greatest levels of IT and business-related skills rested with the trainers who were concerned with the training of personnel for the newly installed SAP system. Essentially, these personnel were very familiar with shop-floor processes and had progressed to becoming IT trainers. In these roles, the personnel involved had managed to successfully integrate their shop-floor skills with a high mastery of related IT skills. In the cases of the Bank and the Authority the levels of hybrid skills were variable. However, the clearest example of an IT manager having very strong hybrid skills was found in the case of the Bank. This manager exhibited superior IT and technical skills together with very strong business and project management skills. He clearly understood the necessity for a strategic approach to IT and to business development but his view did not prevail within the top management team. Otherwise, with some exceptions, mainly confined to the executives heading up, or engaged with specific executive functions, the levels of hybrid skills in both case firms were extremely limited. In both organisations, and outside of the functions just referred to, the highest levels of IT proficiency rested with specialist administrative or professional staff, such as accountants, engineers, statisticians and office-based staff. Personnel in these situations displayed high IT ability related to their own immediate work responsibilities, but their overall business awareness tended to be confined to these responsibilities.

In the case of the Authority, a localisation of skills arose because of the natural division of the Authority's work between inside and outside operations, with computerisation being largely confined to in-house staff and some departments such as planning and engineering services. Because of the unsuitability of most outdoor services for computerisation, it was considered unlikely that the substantial bulk of outdoor staff engaged in cleaning, maintenance and other similar activities would ever have to use IT in their everyday work.

With the Bank, IT personnel were hired as IT specialists. They were not perceived to be bankers, so it was difficult for them to acquire, or to be perceived as having, hybrid business and IT skills. In the case of the Traditional Manufacturer, some personnel were rotated between IT and business roles, but this was a one-dimensional approach confined to a limited number of IT personnel being seconded to support training for the installation of the new SAP system. Reciprocation of business personnel to IT positions didn't occur. In sum therefore, outside of the exemplary practices exhibited by the High-Tech Manufacturer on the issue of hybrid skills, the other organisations displayed, with some exceptions only, variable and limited hybrid skills amongst their personnel.

22.4.5 IT Capital Deepening and Diffusion

Capital deepening concerns the per capita allocation of IT equipment and resources to employees. A comparison of the four case studies revealed varying levels of capital deepening across the four organisations. The heaviest capital deepening occurred in the case of the High-Tech Manufacturer where everyone in the organisation either had a computer or instant access to one. IT capital deepening was therefore extremely high. This level of deepening and accessibility afforded numerous benefits including the key achievement that operatives managed and controlled the operational process, mainly through a system of Statistical Process Control (SPC). The basis of control in this computerised system lay in the information it produced regarding output, quality and defect levels. This organisation also displayed the highest levels of capital diffusion amongst the four studied organisations. Capital diffusion refers to the breadth of operations covered by IT coverage; high diffusion exists when the technology spills over to cover areas not previously covered and full diffusion exists where IT technology has diffused or spread to all operational and support areas covered by an organisation. The High–Tech Manufacturer had reached a state of full diffusion since computerisation had spread to all organisational processes and departments. This included IT communication, through data interchange facilities with its corporate organisation, full computerisation of its materials receiving procedures, all manufacturing and shipping processes and all administrative and office-based systems.

The level of capital deepening experienced by the Traditional Manufacturer had increased with the introduction of its SAP based ERP system. However, the progress of this new IT investment was being seriously impeded because of restrictions imposed on funding of the SAP system. In addition, major difficulties were encountered in achieving data interchange between its SAP system and the different version ERP system operated by its most major trading company located in its key overseas market. Change of management and people difficulties lay at the core of this problem and as a result the firm failed to achieve computer integration, between both trading entities. In this case study, it was confirmed that despite the considerable investment that had been expended on the SAP system, renewal investment in computers and related software had actually declined due to limitations on overall investment funding. In capital diffusion terms, although most of the organisation's operations were covered by IT technology, large gaps still existed in the computerisation of the organisation's production and stock control functions.

In the case of the Authority, although there was evidence of IT capital deepening in some office, engineering and planning processes, there still remained large parts of the organisation where capital deepening had not occurred. Capital deepening in the office environment had been recently prompted by the introduction of a newly computerised financial system. This system was a commercially available software financial package titled Agresso. Despite its introduction it is probable that many of the remaining work areas of the Authority will continue to be unsuitable for computerisation, including many of the outdoor activities covered by its remit, including roads, sewerage and water services. Some capital diffusion of IT had taken place, just prior to the case enquiry, with the computerisation of motor taxation services through an internet-based system. It was also intended that some rent collection processes would be partly computerised with the introduction of hand-held computer devices.

In the Bank's situation there was little evidence of IT capital deepening or diffusion with the ratio of staff to computers being about three staff to each computer. Specialist and executive staff however, had access to their own computers. Most of the Bank's stock of computers was at least three years old. Coincidental with this case enquiry, the Bank had taken its first steps towards outsourcing its IT requirements. In this case a 'piecemeal' approach to the development of IT systems appears to have been adopted over the years. Piecemeal systems contrast with strategic approaches and tend to emphasise short-term and reactive solutions rather than business-centered, longer-term solutions. It is possible that the Bank's short-term approach originated from the lack of strategic importance placed on IT within the Bank's operations and the higher strategic importance attached to pure banking processes.

22.4.6 Use of Complementary Organisational Capital

Bynjolfsson and Hitt (1999) claim that IT capital is disproportionately associated with other complementary assets and support this claim by the assertion that for every dollar of IT capital spent, a typical firm accumulates between four times and 19 times that amount on complementary costs. These complementary costs include the cost of developing new software, populating a database, implementing a new business process, acquiring a more highly skilled staff, or undergoing a major organisational transformation; all of which go unaccounted on a firm's balance sheet. An explanation of this is that firms must incur substantial adjustment costs before IT becomes effective. Based on best manager estimates within the case organisations, combined hardware and software costs were running at between two per cent and four per cent of each case organisation's revenue. If Brynjolfsson's assertion is accurate, then it is apparent that, relative to IT investment, complementary organisational investment is very substantial. However, on the issue of IT measurement, none of the four case firms concerned could provide any detailed or accurate information on the annual levels of hardware, software or complementary organisational expenditure experienced by them. This problem is partly caused by the accounting treatment of software systems as being revenue rather than a capital expenditure item in Britain and Ireland, and by the absence of detailed management accounting information.

Aside from cost considerations, all the case study firms viewed complementary organisational investment as being essential to success. The two manufacturing case firms invested the most heavily in this regard, although the High-Tech Manufacturer followed a clearer strategic direction. Both had invested heavily in ERP systems, with associated hardware and software systems, and had followed clear implementation, change management and quality management programmes. Additionally, both organisations had employed either vendor or consultancy support, and had carried out substantial training and re-training of all employees in new IT systems and procedures. They had also introduced IT steering committees, and project teams to guide their separate organisations, to steer and support development and to measure results. All four case firms had failed in their efforts to measure results in any tangible sense, although senior management with the High-Tech Manufacturer were forceful in claiming major benefits in competitive position, cost reduction, quality improvement, high labour skill levels and high productivity as a result of the firm's investment in, and use, of IT. The system set up for measuring IT benefits in the case of the Traditional Manufacturer had failed to do so while the Bank only attempted to measure likely benefits at the pre-investment planning stage. The Authority made no attempt to measure benefits. Despite its failure to formally measure results, the High-Tech Manufacturer had been the most effective in surmounting the many human and organisational challenges experienced when new IT technology had been introduced and used. The fact that it was a relatively new organisation may have been helpful in this, since this was accompanied by a facilitating learning culture, where negative attitudes and resistance to change had not yet been encountered. The other case firms had been in operation for between 35 and 80 years where distinct cultures and practices had grown apace with the growth of the organisations.

In the cases of the Bank and the Authority, each had employed complementary organisational capital, but the level of this investment was in no way as substantial as that of the manufacturing organisations. Both, however, displayed some of the complementary investment features of the manufacturing organisations, such as IT steering committees, IT training for new employees, and training for work applications. In the case of the Authority this extended to training for office staff in its newly computerised financial system. Both organisations were also actively supported by IT functions that strongly emphasised IT operational efficiency. In the absence of more strategic or integrated IT investment, the role of complementary organisational capital was not as readily apparent. Also, in both organisational cases, the levels of complementary organisational investment were limited, either by a system of budgetary funding which emphasised annual rather than strategic investment, or by a management system that almost exclusively emphasised the operational and transactional aspects of IT investment.

22.5 Conclusions

This study has examined four contrasting case studies with a view to establishing the impacts that IT had on organisational and IT performance. The results of the separate case studies indicate that IT significantly impacts on performance, both positively and negatively. It does this mainly through the ways that IT investment is managed and used, and through the levels of IT effectiveness and IT efficiency that are achieved. This research has indicated that IT investment and use affected one of the case firms in a most significant and positive way. This high-technology case firm was also the newest of the four case firms studied, being in operation for a period of just three years. In terms of claimed and perceived benefits, including competitive performance, this was the most successful of the four cases examined. The causes of this success included the possession of a defined and acted upon overall business strategy, integrated with an overall business vision and with a subsidiary IT strategy, coupled with executive support for effective IT investment and use. Effective IT investment and use embraced a commitment to the training and utilisation of hybrid managers and the deployment of bi-directional leadership, as well as to satisfactory levels of IT capital deepening and diffusion and the successful integration of the strategic and operational business components. The final factor in its success lay in its exploitation of an ERP system, which permitted seamless electronic integration inside, and outside, of its internal operating environment. The managing of these issues largely determines how IT affects organisational performance. Although the other case firms exhibited use of some, or a number, of these practices the perceived results were either limited, or non-existent.

None of the other case firms could claim to be as successful in terms of achieving cost reduction and other competitiveness benefits, including flexible and responsive production, effective quality improvement and high productivity, or in meeting the requirements identified for success. The main obstacles to more successful performance in the other firms stemmed from either weak strategy articulation or action, from lack of executive commitment to the effective management of change or to constraints imposed by cultural, capital or operating expenditure limitations.

A model encapsulating the major and minor issues revealed by the case enquiries is presented in the proposed model for 'The Enhancement of IT Performance' shown in Figure 22.2 below.

Figure 22.2: The Enhancement of IT Performance

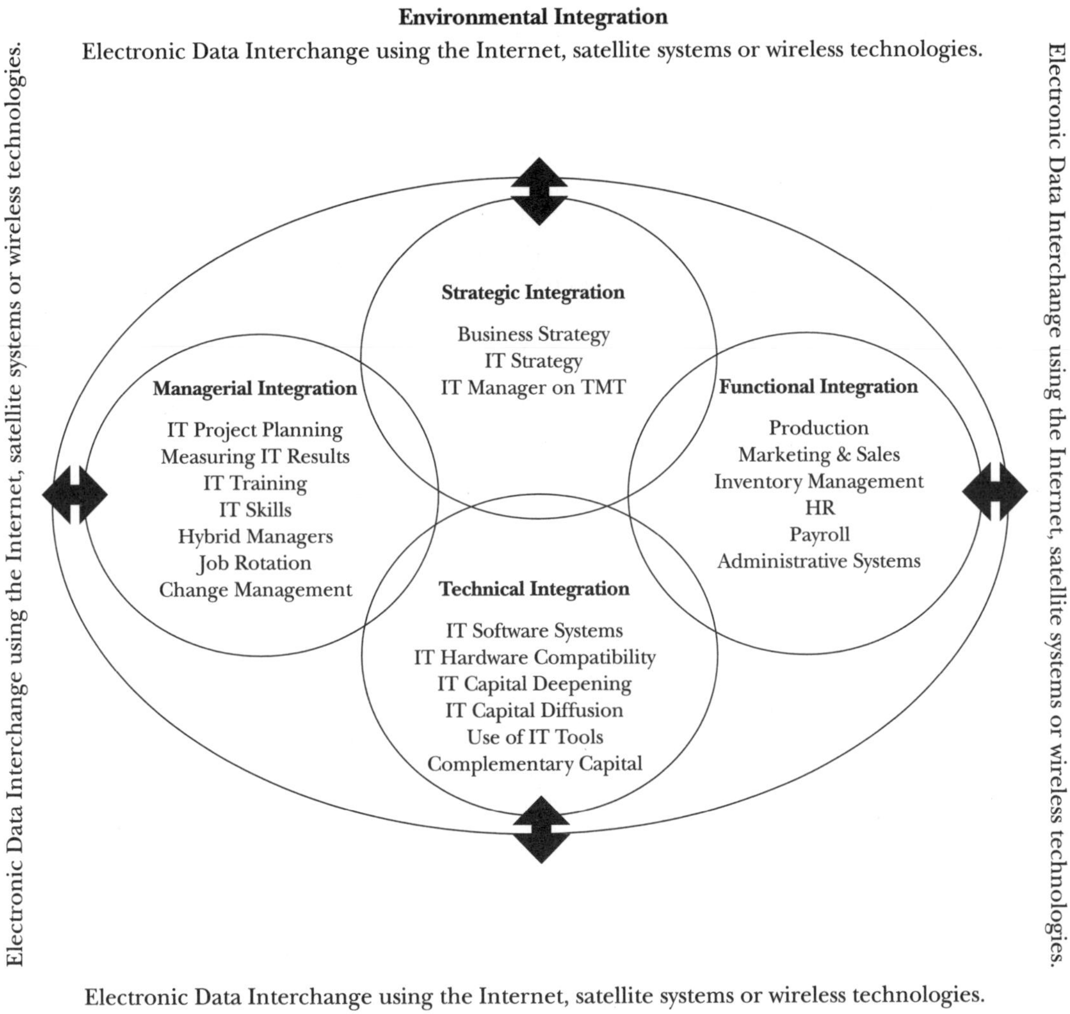

This model emphasises that organisations must successfully cope with two environments when investing in and using IT systems; the internal organisational environment, and the external environment. Successful IT performance will come from the degree to which these environments are integrated and harmonised with the strategic, managerial, technical and functional components within the business shown by the Model.

The proposed model accords with much of the relevant literature and reinforces the view that a business strategy which incorporates an IT strategy component is intrinsic to successful IT and overall business performance. The results also add to the existing literature by indicating that optimum performance cannot be achieved unless all of the factors highlighted by the model are aligned and integrated within a clear strategic perspective, including the need to integrate IT systems and their management across an organisation's internal and external environments.

It is concluded that IT affects performance depending on how it is deployed and managed in a firm, that strategic alignment is a necessary prerequisite to the optimisation of organisational performance, and that five main factors, together with many associated subsidiary factors, contribute to the impact that IT has on organisational performance.

References

Barua, A., Kriebel, C.H. and Mukhopadhyay, T. (1995), "Information Technologies and Business Value: An Analytic and Empirical Investigation", *Information Systems Research,* 6: 1, 3-23.

Bresnahan, T.F. (1999), "Computerisation and Wage Dispersion: An Analytical Reinterpretation", *Journal of Royal Economic Society,* 109. 456, F390-415.

Brynjolfsson, E. and Hitt, L. M. (1995), "Information Technology as a Factor of Production: The Role of Differences Among Firms", *Economics of Innovation and New Technology,* 3: 3, 183-199.

Brynjolfsson, E. and Hitt, L. M. (1996), "Paradox Lost? Firm-level Evidence on the Returns to Information Systems Spending", *Management Science,* 42: 4, 541-558.

Brynjolfsson, E. and Hitt, L. M. (1998), "Beyond the Productivity Paradox: Computers are the Catalyst for Bigger Changes", *Communications of the ACM,* 41: 8 (Aug), 49-55.

Brynjolfsson, E. and Hitt, L. M. (2000), "Beyond Computation: Information Technology, Organisational Transformation and Business Performance". *Journal of Economic Perspectives,* 14, 4, 1-48.

Cassidy, M. (2004), "Productivity in Ireland: Trends and Issues". *Central Bank of Ireland, Quarterly Bulletin* (Spring), 84-93.

Croteau, A.M. and Bergeron, F. (1999), La Trilogie de L'harmonisation Technologique: Strategie D'enterprise, Deploiement des Technologies de L'information et Performance Organisationnelle. *Proceedings of the Administrative Sciences Association of Canada Conference,* St-John, New Brunswick, 57-67.

Department of Finance (2006), *The Strategic Management Initiative,* Dublin, Ireland.

Henderson, J.C. and Venkatraman, N. (1993), "Strategic Alignment: Leveraging Information Technology for Transforming Organisations", *IBM Systems Journal,* 4-16.

Henderson, J.C. and Venkatraman, N. (1999), "Strategic Alignment: Leveraging Information Technology for Transforming Organisations", *IBM Systems Journal 38*, 472-484.

Luftman, J., Papp, R. and Brier, T. (1999), "Enablers and Inhibitors of Business-IT Alignment", *Communications of the Association for Information Systems,* 1, Article 11, 4-23.

Pettigrew, A.M. (1990), "Longitudinal Field Research on Change: Theory and Practice", *Organisation Science,* 1, 267-271.

Remanyi, D. and Brown, A. (2001), Proceedings of the 8th European Conference on Information Technology Evaluation, 263.

Rockart, J.F., Earl, M.J. and Ross, J.W. (2000), "Eight Imperatives for the New IT Organisation", *Sloan Management Review 38,* 43-55.

Slevin, G. (2002), "Is There a New Economy in Ireland?" *Central Bank of Ireland. Technical Paper 3/RT/02,* 2-7.

Strassmann, P. A. (1990), *The Business Value of Computers: An Executive's Guide,* Information Economics Press, New Canaan, CT.

Tallon, P.P., Kraemer, K.L. and Gurbaxani, V. (2000), "Executives Perceptions of the Business Value of Information Technology: A Process-Oriented Approach", *Journal of Management Information Systems,* 16, 145-173.

Tiernan, C. and Peppard, J. (2004), "Information Technology: of Value or a Vulture", *European Management Journal,* 22, 609-623.

Yin, R.K. (2003), "Case Study Research Design and Methods", 3rd Ed., U.K: *Sage Publications.*

PART VI

PRODUCTIVITY AND FIRM BEHAVIOUR

INTRODUCTION

An important area of study for economists is determining which firm characteristics are associated with higher productivity, and whether these characteristics actually cause the higher productivity or are just associated with it. One relationship that economists have been particularly interested in is the extent to which the decision to export or invest abroad impacts on firms productivity. In Chapter 23, Kneller shows that the superior productivity growth of exporting firms generally occurs before rather than after the decision was made to export, suggesting that self selection by firms is important, and that the policy of encouraging non-exporters to export may be of limited value. Chapter 24 focuses on outward investment from Ireland, the pace and scale of which is likely to emerge as one of the most important features of Irish economic development over the next decade. The evidence shows that investment is associated with higher productivity, though the evidence is mixed regarding which firms/activities benefit most. Chapter 25 by Haller shows that at the root of productivity dynamics at the aggregate level are large differences in productivity between plants in even narrowly defined sectors. This paper decomposes the changes in labour productivity in Irish manufacturing industries from 1995 to 2003.

CHAPTER 23

EXPORTS AND PRODUCTIVITY

RICHARD KNELLER

ABSTRACT

This chapter investigates whether the best firms become exporters or whether a firm becomes better as a result of being an exporter. The evidence reviewed suggests that productivity growth in exporting firms generally occurs before rather than after the firm starts to export. It concludes that policy intervention to encourage exports is often useful, in particular where firms don't recognise the benefits of exporting, cannot find customers or when there are barriers to exporting. However the economic evidence presented in this chapter underpins a case for general rather than targeted intervention.

23.1 Introduction

Over the last decade there has been a dramatic increase in the amount of empirical research on the manner through which firms engage with global markets, either as exporters or through the establishment of production and sales facilities abroad. The fundamental insight of this literature has been that multinationals, exporting and non-exporting firms all co-exist in the same industry, but are marked by clear defining characteristics. Multinationals are more productive, larger, more innovative, more capital intensive, more skill intensive, and pay higher wages than exporters, who in turn, are on average 'better' than non-exporters.

A key question that follows from this positive association between the level of engagement in global markets and improved firm performance is the direction of causality. Does exporting or becoming a multinational help to raise productivity or not? Here we concentrate on the relationship between exports and productivity.

First, what constitutes the most important parts of aggregate productivity growth? Is it individual firms becoming more productive or the best firms getting bigger? In a similar manner, we establish some stylised facts about exporting. From this we then order the review of the empirical evidence to concentrate on the dominant forces of productivity growth. This process is helpful for indicating where policy might be best focused and what the value of that policy might be. Finally, we discuss a complication to the strong positive correlation between exports and productivity found at the aggregate level: the role that multinationals play in exports.

23.2 An Introduction to Productivity

Aggregate productivity is simple to describe: it is the sum of the individual productivity of all firms within the economy, where the contribution of any one firm is weighted by its relative size. Productivity growth is more complicated and depends not only on how productivity changes over time within the firm (within-firm changes), but also on how firms relative weight changes within and across industries in the overall index (between-firm changes) as well as the dynamic process of firms entering and leaving the industry (net-entry). It follows that to understand the impact of exporting on aggregate productivity we need to investigate its effect on the productivity of individual firms and the size of firms.

The process of aggregate productivity growth is summarised in Figure 23.1 below. Within-firm productivity changes combine with the changing relative size of firms (between firm effects) and the entry and exit of firms to give the rate of productivity growth within an industry. Within-firm productivity growth depends on improvements in efficiency and intensity with which inputs are used by firms, and depending on whether it is being measured as labour productivity (rather than total factor productivity), the contribution of physical capital investment.[1] Shifts in market shares (the between effect) and net entry will reflect resource reallocation and aggregate productivity trends and therefore competitive pressures within the market (both from domestic and from overseas firms) as well as technological progress in the industry. This same process occurs in other industries and in addition, there is reallocation of resources across industries (some industries grow while others decline) to give an economy-wide rate of productivity growth.

Figure 23.1: Aggregate Productivity and its Components

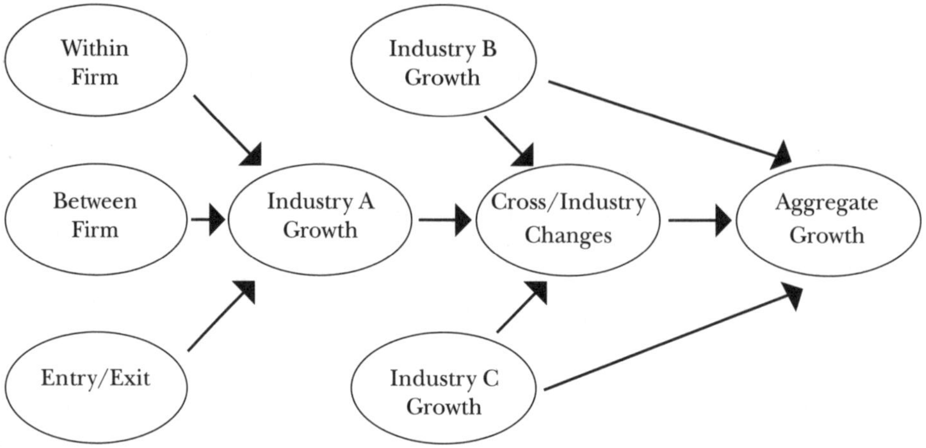

A sensible place to begin our understanding of the relationship between exports and productivity is to focus on the channels in Figure 23.1 that make up the major part of overall productivity growth. While there are many studies that might be useful here, Scarpetta et al. (2002) provides a set of cross-country comparisons measured on a consistent basis. We summarise the evidence for the manufacturing sector for various countries and time periods drawn from the paper in Table 23.1 below.

According to their estimates the within, between and net-entry components are all important. As can be seen in Table 23.1 the rate of productivity growth varies considerably across countries, from 1.6 per cent per annum in the US (1987-92) to 5.3 per cent in Portugal (1987-92). The relative contribution of the within, between and net-entry components differs across countries and time. The within effect accounts for some 50 to 85 per cent of the total, net entry for between 20 and 40 per cent and the between component for -20 to 18 per cent.[2]

Scarpetta et al. (2002) also describe the patterns in the components of aggregate productivity across time. As one might expect they find the net-entry component becomes relatively more important in industries undergoing rapid technical change (i.e. ICT industries).

Table 23.1: Productivity Growth across Countries and Time

Country	Time Period	Productivity Growth (per cent annual growth)	Within component per cent	Between component per cent	Net Entry component per cent
Finland	1987-92	5.0	52	18	30
	1989-94	5.2	58	17	25
France	1987-92	2.3	87	0	9
Italy	1987-92	3.9	51	13	36
	1992-97	4.3	58	12	30
Netherlands	1987-92	2.3	78	4	17
	1992-97	4.1	68	-7	37
Portugal	1987-92	5.3	75	-9	34
	1992-97	4.7	79	-6	40
UK	1987-92	2.5	60	12	32
	1992-97	3.1	77	-6	29
US	1987-92	1.6	88	-6	19
	1992-97	3.0	100	-20	20

Source: Scarpetta et al., (2002).

The central message to draw from Table 23.1 is that particular attention should be focused on the evidence of the sources of within-firm productivity growth as they relate to exporting and less to the reallocation effects from the between effects and net entry. Perhaps not by coincidence, the literature has chosen to distribute its research effort in a similar manner.

With possible policy conclusions in mind, it is helpful to add two other pieces of information about productivity. As Figure 23.1 suggests, what is important for aggregate productivity within an industry is the relative productivity of the best and worst firms and the relative size of these firms. Small and large firms co-exist within the same industry, with differences in employment that can be measured in thousands. Similar differences exist for productivity. Bartelsman and Doms (2000) estimate that in the US, the best firms have productivity two to four times that of the worst firms, while the DTI (2004) estimate that in some UK industries the productivity differences are as large as 800 per cent. It follows that large and productive firms account for the dominant part of overall industry productivity.

Where then do exporters fit into the productivity distribution? The general consensus would suggest that they lie in the middle, between non-exporters and multinationals (see Figure 23.7). In almost all countries studied, exporters are found to be more productive and bigger than non-exporters, but less productive than multinational firms (see Greenaway and Kneller, 2006).

23.3 The Stylised Facts about Exporters and Exporting

It is helpful to have some stylised facts about the pattern of exports across firms. This literature is limited to a small sub-set of countries, namely France, Sweden and the US. However, the patterns derived look very similar across these countries which suggests that they are generally quite consistent.

Most firms do not of course export, and where they do, they tend to export to a limited number of markets. Figure 23.2 uses information taken from Eaton, Kortum and Kramarz (2006) to highlight this. On the left hand axis is the number of firms and on the horizontal scale the number of export markets (with a maximum of 113 countries).

The first point on the far left hand side of the diagram represents selling within France, the second to France and to one other country. As can be seen, the line declines very smoothly and relatively quickly. Around 35 per cent of all firms export to one overseas country, close to 20 per cent export to ten or more countries and only 1.5 per cent to more than 50 countries. Few firms export to all countries.

Figure 23.2: The Number of Export Markets Served in France

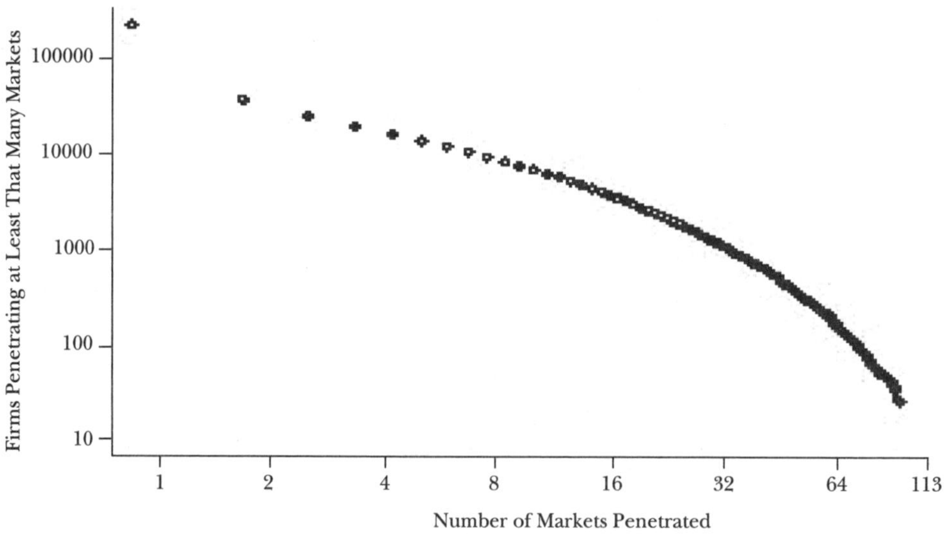

Source: Eaton, Kortum and Kramarz, (2005).

The number of overseas markets the firm exports to is strongly correlated with its size and productivity. In Figure 23.3 the number of markets served is plotted against the size of the firm (measured by its sales in the domestic market). This figure shows that big firms sell to more markets.

Figure 23.3: The Number of Export Markets Served and Firm Size

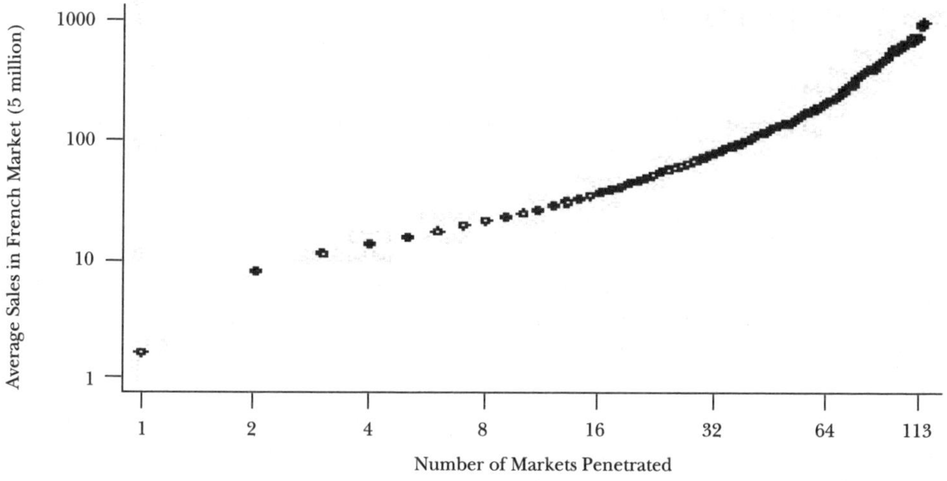

Source: Eaton, Kortum and Kramarz, (2005).

A final pattern of note is that of the firms that do export, the distribution of sales to those markets is strongly skewed. For the US, Bernard, Jensen and Schott, (2006) show that when ranked by the distribution of export sales the top one per cent of firms account for 80 per cent of total trade, the top ten per cent account for 96 per cent and the top 25 per cent for 99 per cent of all trade. A similar pattern can be seen in Figure 23.4 below (Eaton et al., 2006). The figure describes the sales across different market sizes according to their percentile in French sales to that market. According to the Figure firms in the 99th percentile sell more than 10,000 times those in the first percentile.

Figure 23.4: The Distribution of Export Sales and Firm Size

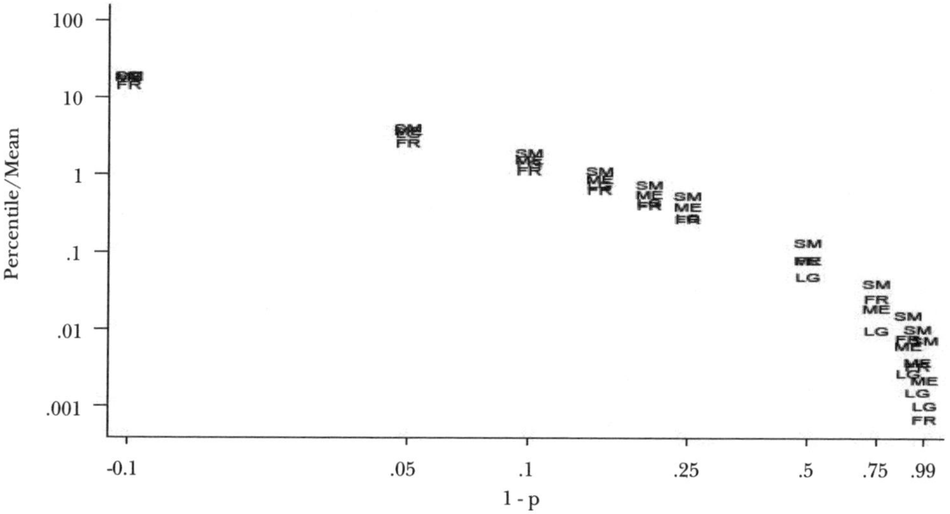

Source: Eaton, Kortum and Kramarz, (2005).

To summarise the message that we might draw from these patterns, like productivity, exporting is highly concentrated in the largest and most productive firms. These firms export to the most markets and export larger volumes to any given market.

23.4 The Evidence – Within Firm Effects

As described in the introduction, all but a few of the studies within this literature show that exporters have higher productivity than non-exporters (see Lopez, 2005, or Greenaway and Kneller, 2005, for a review). It has been more difficult to demonstrate the direction of causality between exporting and productivity. This has become known as the self-selection versus learning debate. Do the best firms become exporters or do they somehow benefit as a result of being an exporter?

Given that the majority of aggregate productivity growth is driven by within firm improvements to productivity we start our review of the evidence on the relationship between exporting and productivity here.

We begin by briefly reflecting on the concepts of learning and self-selection. The umbrella label 'learning' in fact describes four separate effects on the firm. First, observation or interaction with foreign competitors and customers provides the firm with information about best-practice production processes and product requirements encouraging the firm to invest and improve itself, reducing costs and raising quality. Second, exporting allows firms to increase the scale of production.[3] Third, increased competition in foreign markets forces firms to become more efficient and stimulates innovation, and fourth, along similar lines, firms invest in new equipment or products in order to start exporting. The common theme amongst these is that the productivity of the firm is within its control, it is endogenous, and is affected by decision made as a result of starting to export.

Self-selection in this context is often taken to mean that high productivity firms 'select' themselves by becoming exporters: the firm is productive and therefore becomes an exporter. The fact that the firm serves foreign markets does not influence the decisions that managers make, nor does it affect its productivity performance.

In the earliest literature the hypothesis being examined was a simple test of self-selection versus learning. It was a debate that was won by those advocating self-selection. The argument is made up of several parts and was most powerfully put by Bernard and Jensen (1999; 2004b). In their study of US plants they found first, that the productivity growth of exporters was not significantly different from that of non-exporters. This implies that the productivity distribution of firms in any given industry does not widen continuously over time. Or put differently, to the extent that learning effects exist, the growth effects are not permanent (though they will have a permanent effect on the *level* of productivity).

The second part of the argument relates to new exporters. They showed that out of the pool of non-export firms, firms that went on to become exporters were already amongst the best. They also found that for new exporters, any productivity improvement pre-dated the point in time in which export sales began and did not last long after it. Future entrants had many of the right characteristics that make them likely to export and were improving relative to non-exporters before they entered export markets. Then, after a short period, they become indistinguishable from other exporters. The improvement in productivity appeared poorly timed with the firms' first exposure to export markets and therefore the type of mechanisms discussed by the proponents of the 'learning by exporting' school of thought.

This evidence has been replicated almost without fail across numerous countries. Based on data from Bernard and Jensen (2004b), Figure 23.5 displays the productivity level of firms that always export, firms that never export, those that start and those that stop relative to the industry mean for the time periods leading up to, and following the commencement of exporting. Firms that never exported have productivity close to the industry mean. Firms that always exported have productivity levels that are around ten per cent higher, while new exporters and firms that stop exporting lie somewhere in between. Over time, firms that start exporting catch-up with established exporters, while firms that stop exporting regress towards firms that never exported.

Figure 23.5: Productivity Levels of Exporters and Non-Exporters

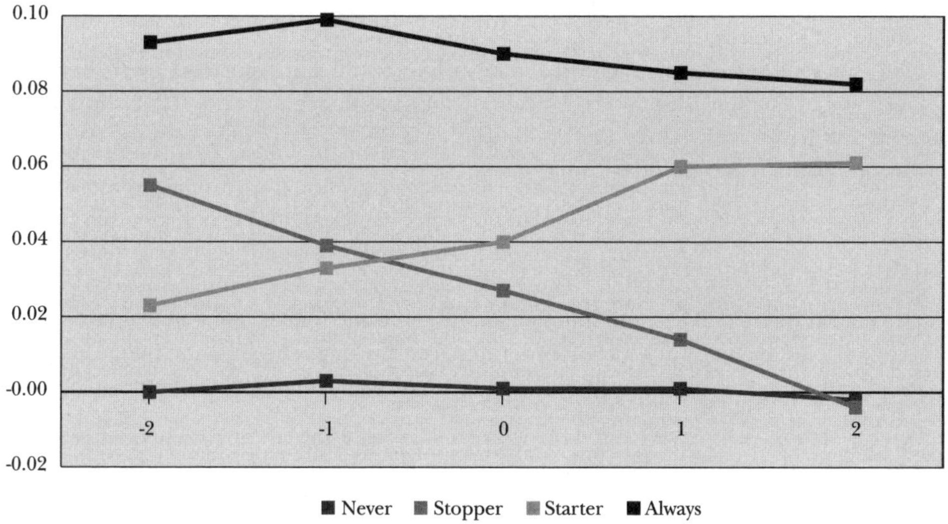

Source: Bernard and Jensen, (2004).

The strong conclusions reached by Bernard and Jensen (1999) in favour of self-selection led quickly to an adaptation of the hypothesis being tested. Recognising that new exporters appeared to already have many of the right characteristics to become exporters, the test then became whether the surge in productivity associated with entry was explained by the decision to become an exporter, or whether the productivity surge led to the export decision. This is suggestive of a kind of learning conditional on self-selection. As argued in Van Biesebroeck (2005), not controlling for self-selection will overstate evidence of learning for new exporters in the data.

The evidence from this literature would appear to be more mixed than earlier evidence. The best support for the idea that firms benefit from exposure to export markets is that the effect is confined to a sub-set of firms. Firms that are young (Delgado et al., 2002; Fernandes and Isgut, 2005), or those highly exposed to export markets (Kraay, 1999; Castellani, 2002; Girma et al., 2004; Damijan et al., 2004) appear most likely to benefit. Others have found that post-entry changes depend on existing industry characteristics. Productivity changes are lower in industries in which current exposure to foreign firms is high (Greenaway and Kneller, 2003).

An alternative explanation put forward by Lopez (2004) and Alvarez and Lopez (2005) muddies the water still further by arguing that the surge in productivity found amongst new exporters in the period leading up to the start of export sales is in fact explained by firms investments in new products or capital in order to successfully serve the foreign market.

A more direct approach to testing evidence of learning through exporting has come from literature studying investments in new technologies that firms make in order to, or as a result of, entering export markets. These studies have tried to see inside the black-box of learning by exporting and generally find more supportive evidence. Exporting affects firm decisions that then impact on productivity.

Good examples of this can be found in those studies that have considered whether exporters invest in Research and Development (R&D) to a greater extent than before they started exporting, and a second strand that considers how exporters undertake their R&D activities, specifically whether they now use foreign information or skills. In the first strand exporting acts as an incentive to undertake R&D, while the second strand explores differences in the production of knowledge between exporters and non-exporters.

Of the studies based on firm data sets, a number have found that exporters have higher levels of R&D, see for example Bleaney and Wakelin (2002) and Roper and Love (2002) for the UK, Bernard and Jensen (2004a) for the US, Barrios et al. (2001) for Spain, Aw et al. (2005) for Taiwan and Baldwin and Gu (2004) for Canada.

Of these, only Baldwin and Gu (2004), Solomon and Shaver (2005) and Aw et al. (2005) provide evidence that causation flows from exporting to R&D investment or outputs. Baldwin and Gu (2004) find that there is no statistical difference between the R&D intensity of exporters and non-exporters prior to their internationalisation (but there is following it), while for Spanish firms, Solomon and Shaver (2005) find that exporting affects patent applications only with a two to three year lag. Along similar lines Criscuolo et al. (2005) report that globally engaged firms, including exporters, are more innovative.

Aw et al. (2005) take a very different approach, recognising the interdependence of the export and R&D decisions. They find that for a panel of Taiwanese firms in the electronics industry, those that do not invest in R&D have lower productivity growth than those that just export which in turn is lower than those firms that invest in both. They argue that these findings are consistent with the interpretation that R&D investments are necessary for firms to benefit from their exposure to international markets.

Evidence on differences in the inputs used to produce new knowledge by exporters and non-exporters is generally offered through case studies and survey work. This choice reflects difficulties in collating the detailed information necessary to study the R&D production function for large numbers of firms or time periods. The general hypothesis tested here is that external knowledge is an important input into the innovation process of firms and that some of this comes from abroad. In this literature, a number of studies report case study evidence that domestic firms receive technical information from overseas customers or suppliers which improves product quality (Lopez 2004; Alvarez and Lopez, 2005; Van Biesebroeck, 2005; and Blalock and Gertler, 2004).

The alternative approach has been to focus on a single input into the production process. Criscuolo et al. (2005) reports on the extent of the use of foreign information used in innovation. They concern themselves with the type of information - whether it is internal to the firm, or whether it is free from a university. They report that on average, multinationals use information from more sources than exporters who in turn make more use of information external to the firms than non-exporters.

A novel approach adopted by Baldwin and Gu (2004) is to combine the firm data typically used with detailed survey data on a smaller number of firms. The authors test whether Canadian exporters are more likely to collaborate with foreign buyers than non-exporters in their R&D, and find strong evidence to support the idea that they do.

To summarise the evidence from this section: on balance the weight of evidence would point to a relationship between exporting and productivity that is two-way causal. But, importantly, it is skewed towards self-selection. Firm productivity would appear largely independent of the firm's export decision. There is evidence that firms benefit from their exposure to export markets, but it is confined to a sub-set of new exporters.

While the within firm component is very important in the overall rate of productivity growth, because new exporters are small in number and the productivity improvements are relatively small and temporary, the contribution of exporting to overall productivity growth is likely to be small.

23.5 The Evidence – Between Firm Effects

Only a limited number of studies have considered the role of exporting in explaining the between firm effect. For this reason, we refer to economic theory to explain the dynamics of how exporting is expected to impact on productivity and refer to the empirics to provide the detail and magnitudes.

The pioneering paper here is Melitz (2003). He builds on the empirical facts described above to derive a dynamic industry model (there is entry and exit for firms and reallocation of market shares) with heterogeneous firms (some firms have higher productivity than others). Fundamental to the outcome is the interaction of these firm differences with the up-front fixed costs that firms are required to pay to enter export markets. The outcome is that only the best firms can pay the up-front cost of export market entry and still make a profit. This is consistent with the idea that exporters are more productive than non-exporters.

This sorting of firms is outlined in Figure 23.6. Firms with productivity greater than some critical level (black), serve the domestic market and export, while those with productivity less than that serve just the domestic market.

Figure 23.6: Productivity and the Decision to Export

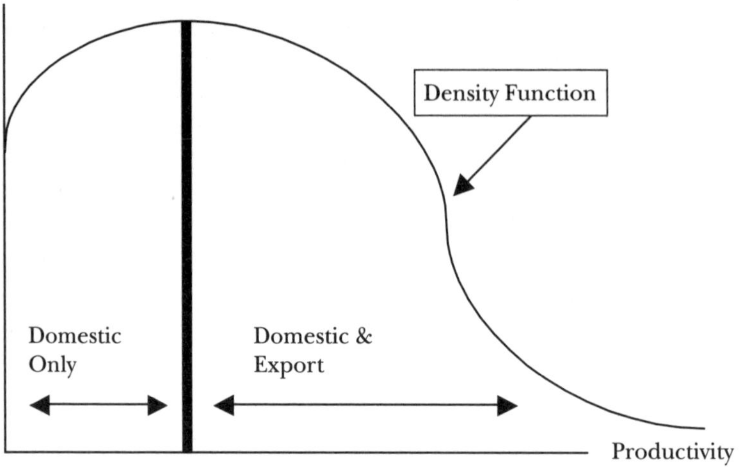

In the model however, exporting raises *industry* productivity. First, there is a rationalisation effect. Exporting increases profits for firms, which induces the entry of new firms to the market, driving out the least efficient firms in a Schumpterian wave of 'creative destruction'. Clearly this raises average industry productivity. Second, exporting allows the most productive firms to expand and causes less productive firms to contract. This between-firm reallocation effect again acts to raise average industry productivity.

Empirically Bernard and Jensen (2004a) for the US and Hansson and Lundin (2004) for Sweden estimate that the contribution of exporters to the between component as 60 per cent in the US (they estimate a lower bound at 8 per cent) and 62 per cent in Sweden. Also for Sweden, Falvey et al. (2004) follow up the prediction that increased export opportunities attract new entrants to the market and force low productivity firms to quit. They estimate that the effect occurs primarily through the first channel.[4]

To summarise: while between effects account for a smaller proportion of overall productivity growth in the economy there is perhaps clearer evidence that exporting contributes positively to this process.

23.6 The Evidence – Exporting and Multinationality

So far we have discussed the relationship between exporting and productivity without the complication that some firms have production facilities abroad, i.e., that they are multinational. At the simplest level this is reasonable; exports and FDI are substitute channels for firms wishing to globalise. The conditions for foreign production become more favourable relative to exporting as the size of the foreign market increases and costs of exporting increase. They become less favourable as the costs of setting up a foreign production facility grow. This is the proximity - concentration trade-off as explained by Brainard (1993).

In practice the stylised facts for exports suggest a more complicated relationship. First, we find that most multinationals still export to some countries. The numbers of non-exporting multinational firms are relatively small in number. Second, multinational firms dominate total export flows between countries and third, part of these exports are trades back to firms within the same group (intra-firm trade).

Figure 23.7, using data taken from Bernard et al. (2005), displays the share of US exports (and imports) accounted for by firms that undertake arms length exports only and by multinationals, where the latter is broken into that within the firm (intra firm) and that to non-related parties. According to the evidence in Figure 23.7, multinationals account for the lion's share of total US exports, around 95 per cent by 2000. Around 60 per cent of all exports (about two-thirds of total exports by multinationals) is to non-related parties and between 30-35 per cent represents intra-firm trade.

Figure 23.7: Exports and Imports by Multinationals

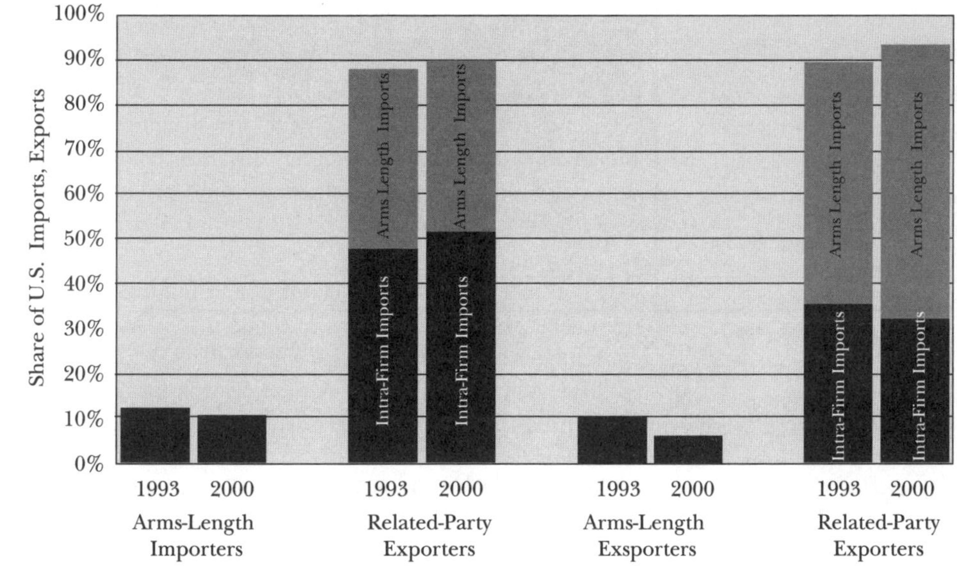

Source: Bernard, Jensen and Schott, (2005).

Detailed information on other countries is not available, so it is not possible to establish how representative the data for the US are. However, according to the United Nations World Development Report, one third of world trade is within firm exports (exports from one part of a multinational to another), similar to the US figure.

Some of this greater export performance would be expected of course. A well-established result is the superior performance of foreign firms over domestic companies with respect to employment, wages and productivity, all of which have been found to be good predictors of firm exports. Kneller and Pisu (2004) show however, that even controlling for these advantages, foreign multinationals located in the UK are still more likely to export than indigenous ones, and when they do export they do so more intensively.

So what explains export decisions of multinationals and what is the relationship with productivity? The answer would appear to be that it is complicated. Using the fact that exports and multinationals are substitute methods of serving foreign markets, Helpman, Melitz and Yeaple (2004) extend Meltiz (2003) to allow firms to become multinational. Now when firms become sufficiently productive they swap exports for overseas production, as shown in Figure 23.8 below, and the correlation between productivity and exports becomes negative.

Figure 23.8: Productivity and the Decision to Export or Become Multinational

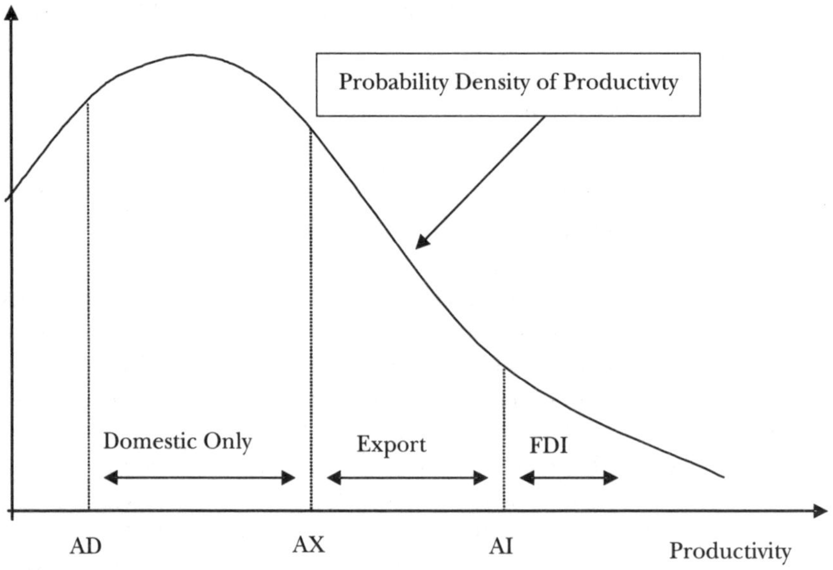

Source: Helpman, Melitz and Yeaple, (2004).

Head and Ries (2003a) extend the Melitz (2003) model to allow firms to break up the production chain and locate some of this abroad to take advantage of low labour costs. They show that for a certain range of the parameter of the model, it is the least productive firms that locate abroad whereas more productive ones produce at home. Again the relationship between exporting and productivity is reversed.

Others have considered the motivation for multinationals to locate production within one member of a Free Trade Area (FTA), such as the EU, and then export to other members (see Motta and Norman, 1996, or Ekholm et al., 2003). The relationship between productivity and exports then depends on the method through which the multinational locates production within the FTA, whether it establishes new production facilities or acquires a domestic firm, and in the case of the latter whether that domestic firm already exported. For example, for the UK Girma et al. (2005b) finds foreign multinationals tend to acquire domestic firms that export – i.e., they cherry-pick the best firms – such that the productivity impact is uncertain. They also find differences in the post-acquisition export trajectories of the acquired firm according to whether the foreign firm is from inside or outside the EU. When the acquiring firm is from outside the EU, the export intensity of the acquired firm rises, whereas it falls for firms inside the EU. The net export impact is again ambiguous.

Grossman, Helpman and Szeidl (2003), developing a model of 'complex FDI' to show that firm characteristics may also be important. If firms within the same industry are heterogeneous in their productivity levels they may make different choices, even though costs of exporting and FDI are the same. Their analysis allows for the coexistence in the same sector of a rich array of profitable FDI strategies. In brief, the general lesson is that least productive firms will not undertake FDI, whereas more productive firms choose complex strategies that involve a mix of FDI and exports.

To summarise: up until this section the evidence was that exports and productivity were positively correlated, even if establishing the direction of causation between the two was difficult. Adding multinationals complicates this, with the exporting-productivity relationship varying across the different motives for becoming multinational. Exports by multinationals are the dominant part of international trade flows, and their size and productivity are important in overall productivity. At the moment the empirical literature is not developed enough to answer what the net effect between exports and productivity will be.

23.7 Policy Dimension

Intervention to promote exports is very widespread - every WTO Trade Policy Review contains a chapter on 'Measures Directly Affecting Exports' and there are always numerous measures to report.[5] These range from intervention to improve market intelligence (for example public support for trade missions), to sector specific fiscal intervention (for example, tax concessions or duty drawbacks), to export processing zones (i.e. free zones).

Does the microeconometric evidence we have reviewed reinforce or undermine a case for active export promotion of this type? Lopez (2005) concludes that the microeconometric evidence reinforces the rationale for intervention. He argues that even if self-selection is the key driver of export market entry and therefore exporting has a reduced impact on the within component of productivity, it may nevertheless be 'conscious self-selection'. What he means is that firms consciously improve their productivity with the international market in mind, rather than the best firms just starting to export. Policy intervention could then stimulate more conscious self-selection and deliver a productivity boost. Clearly if other types of learning by exporting occur, as the evidence suggests, productivity gains are boosted further.

Lopez (2005) himself stresses the importance of reducing (overseas) barriers to exports. If sunk costs to export market entry are important, intervention to improve aspects of infrastructure, reducing regulatory burdens, promoting clustering and so on may be beneficial.

Of the barriers to exporting, networks may be important to improve information flows between customers and suppliers. Eaton estimates that the self-selection model is capable of explaining about 60 per cent of firm export behaviour, suggesting such network effects may be important for the residual - there are some firms that could export but do not because they do not fully recognise the benefits or cannot find customers. Providing introductions and networks is a common form of support used by export promotion agencies in developed countries.

Altogether this is a plausible argument in support of state intervention, though it underpins a case for general rather than targeted intervention. As the stylised facts about exporting suggest (Section 23.3), new exporters make up a very small faction of overall exports and therefore policy should not be biased away from firms that are well established in export markets to help new entrants. Policy will have a larger impact on overall exports if it is used to encourage exporters to expand sales in existing markets and to enter new ones.

However the stylised facts about productivity and exports, combined with the evidence from the relationship between exports and within-firm productivity growth, suggest that such interventions are likely to have only a small positive impact on overall productivity growth through the within firm effect. Exports and productivity is highly skewed towards the largest firms and to the extent that learning effects exist they are for a sub-set of new exporters only.

Perhaps a stronger motivation for policy intervention comes from the literature studying the effect of exporting on the between component of overall productivity growth (Section 23.5). Although the between component is relatively less important, there is much clearer evidence that exports is a driving factor behind it and that its contribution might be large (some 60 per cent of the total). Exporting allows good firms to get bigger and has some impact on making them perform better. The relative contribution of these effects is not yet known, and ignores the importance of large and productive multinational firms on exporting.

All this said, a final point of caution: existing evidence has found limited impact from export promotion policies. Bernard and Jensen (2004a), Alvarez (2004) and Görg et al. (2005) all find weak or no significant effect from export promotion schemes.

Notes

1 We abstract from a discussion of whether labour or total factor is the appropriate measure of productivity and of their measurement.

2 Negative growth suggests that for some periods there was a reallocation of market share towards the least productive firms.

3 Evidence from Tybout and Westbrook (1995) suggests that this may be an unimportant source of efficiency change.

4 There is a related industry which has looked at the productivity impact of trade liberalisation - Roberts and Tybout (1991) and Pavcnik (2002).

5 The WTO's Trade Policy Review Mechanism ensures that the trade policies of Members are audited on a regular basis. For the 'big three' (US, EU and Japan) this means every two years; for the smallest Members, it takes place every seven years.

References

Alvarez, R. (2004), "Sources of Export Success in Small and Medium-Sized Enterprises: The Impact of Public Programs", *International Business Review*, Vol.13, 383 -400.

Alvarez, R. and López, R.A. (2005), "Exporting and Firm Performance: Evidence from Chilean Plants", *Canadian Journal of Economics*, Vol. 38, 1384-1400.

Aw, B. Y., Roberts, M.J. and Winston, T. (2005), "The Complementary Role of Exports and R&D Investments as Sources of Productivity Growth", *The World Economy*.

Baldwin, J.R. and Gu, W. (2004), "Trade Liberalisation: Export-Market Participation, Productivity Growth and Innovation", *Oxford Review of Economic Policy*, Vol. 20, 372-392.

Barrios, S., Görg, H. and Strobl, E. (2003), "Explaining Firms' Export Behaviour: R&D, Spillovers and the Destination Market", *Oxford Bulletin of Economics and Statistics*, Vol. 65, 475-496.

Bartelsman, E.J. and Doms, M. (2000), "Understanding Productivity: Lessons from Longitudinal Micro Datasets", *Journal of Economic Literature*, Vol. 38.

Bernard, A. and Jensen, J.B. (1999), "Exceptional Exporters Performance: Cause, Effect or Both?", *Journal of International Economics*, Vol. 47, 1-25.

Bernard, A. and Jensen, J. (2004a), "Why Some Firms Export", *Review of Economics and Statistics*, Vol. 86, 561-569.

Bernard, A. and Jensen, J. (2004b), "Exporting and Productivity in the USA", *Oxford Review of Economic Policy*, Vol. 20.

Bernard, A. Jensen, J. and Schott, P. (2006), "Importers, Exporters and Multinationals: A Portrait of Firms in the U.S. that Trade Goods", Tuck School of Business, mimeo.

Blalock, G. and Gertler, P.J. (2004), "Learning From Exporting Revisited in Less Developed Setting", *Journal of Development Economics*, Vol. 75, 397-416.

Bleaney, M. F. and Wakelin, K. (2002), "Efficiency, Innovation and Exports", *Oxford Bulletin of Economics and Statistics*, Vol. 64, 3-15.

Brainard, S.L. (1993), "A Simple Theory of Multinational Corporations and Trade with a Trade-off between Proximity and Concentration". *NBER Working Paper*, No. 4269.

Castellani, D. (2002), "Export Behaviour and Productivity Growth: Evidence from Italian Manufacturing Firms", *Weltwirtschaftliches Archiv*, Vol. 138, 605-628.

Coe, D. and Helpman, E. (1995), "International R&D Spillovers", *European Economic Review*, 39, 859-887.

Coe, D., Helpman, E. and Hoffmeister, A. (1997), "North-South Spillovers", *Economic Journal*, 107, 134-149.

Criscuolo, C. Haskel, J. and Slaughter, M. (2004), "Why are Some Firms More Innovative? Knowledge Inputs, Knowledge Stocks and the Role of Global Engagement" Queen Mary University, mimeo.

Damijan, J., Polanec S. and Prašnikar J. (2006), "Self-selection, Export Market Heterogeneity and Productivity Improvements: Firm Level Evidence from Slovenia", *The World Economy*, Vol. 29, (forthcoming).

Delgado, M., Fariñas, J. and Ruano, S. (2002), "Firm Productivity and Export Markets: A Non-Parametric Approach", *Journal of International Economics*, Vol. 57, 397-422.

DTI (2004), "Raising UK Productivity – Developing the Evidence Base for Policy", *DTI Economics Paper No. 8.*

Eaton, J. and Kortum, S. (1999), "International Patenting and Technology Diffusion: Theory and Evidence", *International Economic Review*, 40, 537-570.

Eaton, J. Kortum, S. and Kramarz, F. (2005), "An Anatomy of International Trade: Evidence from French Firms" New York University, mimeo.

Ekholm, K., Forslid, R. and Markusen, J. R. (2003), "Export-Platform Foreign Direct Investment", NBER Working Paper No. 9517.

Falvey, R., Greenaway, D., Gullstrand, J. and Yu, Z. (2004), "Exports, Restructuring and Industry Productivity Growth", *GEP Research Paper 04/40*, Leverhulme Centre for Research on Globalisation and Economic Policy, University of Nottingham.

Fernandes, A. M. and Isgut, A. (2005), "Learning-by-Doing, Learning-by-Exporting, and Productivity: Evidence from Colombia" World Bank Policy Research Working Paper No. 3544.

Girma, S., Greenaway, D. and Kneller, R. (2004), "Does Exporting Increase Productivity? A Microeconometric Analysis of Matched Firms", *Review of International Economics*, Vol. 12, 855-866.

Girma, S., Kneller, R. and Pisu, M. (2005b), "Trade Creation, Destruction and Replacement in Regional Trade Agreements: Micro Level Evidence for the UK", mimeo, GEP University of Nottingham.

Görg, H., Henry, M. and Strobl, E. (2005), *Grant Support and Exporting Activity: Evidence from Irish Manufacturing*, mimeo, Aston University Business School.

Greenaway, D. and Kneller, R. (2003), "Exporting, Productivity and Agglomeration: A Matched Difference in Difference Analysis of Matched Firms", *GEP Research Paper 03/45*, Leverhulme Centre for Research on Globalisation and Economic Policy, University of Nottingham.

Greenaway, D. and Kneller, R. (2006), "Firm Heterogeneity, Exporting and Foreign Direct Investment", *The Economic Journal*, (forthcoming).

Grossman, G. M., Helpman E. and Szeidl, A. (2003), "Optimal Integration Strategies for the Multinational Firm", NBER Working Paper No. 10189.

Hall, R.E., and Jones, C.I. (1999), "Why Do Some Countries Produce So Much More Output per Worker than Others", *Quarterly Journal of Economics*, 114, 83-116.

Hansson, P. and Lundin, N. (2004), "Exports as Indicator on or a Promoter of Successful Swedish Manufacturing Firms in the 1990's", *Review of World Economics / Weltwirtschaftliches Archive*, Vol. 140, 415-445.

Head, K. and Ries, J. (2003), "Heterogeneity and the Foreign Direct Investment versus Exports Decision of Japanese Manufacturers". *Journal of the Japanese and International Economies* Vol. 17, 448-467.

Helpman, E., Melitz, M. and Yeaple, S. (2004), "Export Versus FDI", *American Economic Review*, Vol. 94, 300-316.

Keller, W. (2000), "Do Trade Patterns and Technology Flows Affect Productivity Growth?", *World Bank Economic Review*, 14, 17-47.

Keller, W. (2004), "International Technology Diffusion", *Journal of Economic Literature*, 42, 752-782.

Kneller, R. and Pisu, M. (2004), "Export-Oriented FDI in the UK", *Oxford Review of Economic Policy*, Vol. 20, 424-439.

Kraay, A. (1999), "Exports and Economic Performance: Evidence from a Panel of Chinese Enterprises", *Revue d'Economie du Developpement.*

Lichtenberg, F.R. and Van Pottelsberghe de la Potterie, B. (1998), "International R&D Spillovers: A Comment", *European Economic Review*, 42, 1483-91.

López, R. A. (2004), "Self-selection into the Export Markets: A Conscious Decision?", mimeo, *Department of Economics, Indiana University.*

López, R. A. (2005), "Trade and Growth: Reconciling the Macroeconomic and Microeconomic Evidence", *Journal of Economic Surveys*, Vol. 19, 623-648.

McGrattan, E.R. and Schmitz, J.A. (1999), *Explaining Cross-Country Income Differences*, in Taylor, J.B. and Woodford, M. eds. Handbook of Macroeconomics Volume 1A, North Holland Amsterdam, 669-737.

Melitz, M. (2003), "The Impact of Trade on Intra-Industry Reallocations and Aggregate Industry Productivity", *Econometrica*, Vol. 71, 1695-1725.

Motta, M. and Norman, G. (1996), "Does Economic Integration Cause Foreign Direct Investment?", *International Economic Review*, Vol. 37:4, 757-783.

Pavcnik, N. (2002), "Trade Liberalization, Exit, and Productivity Improvements: Evidence from Chilean Plants", *Review of Economic Studies*, Vol. 69, 245-76.

Prescott, E. (1998), "Needed: A Theory of Total Factor Productivity", *International Economic Review*, 39, 525-551.

Roberts, M.J. and Tybout, J. (1991), "Size Rationalization and Trade Exposure in Developing Countries" in Baldwin, R. (ed.), *Empirical Studies of Commercial Policy*, Chicago Press, Chicago.

Roper, S. and Love, J.H. (2002), "Innovation and Export Performance: Evidence from the UK and German Manufacturing Plants", *Research Policy*, Vol. 31, 1087-1102.

Scarpetta, S., Hemmings, P., Tressel, T. and Woo, J. (2002), "The Role of Policy and Institutions for Productivity and Firm Dynamics: Evidence from Micro and Industry Data", *OECD Working Paper No. 329.*

Solomon, R.M. and Shaver, J. M. (2005), "Learning by Exporting: New Insights from Examining firm Innovation", *Journal of Economics and Management Strategy*, Vol. 14, 431-460.

Van Biesebroeck, J. (2005), "Exporting Raises Productivity in Sub-Saharan Manufacturing Plants", *Journal of International Economics*, Vol. 67, No. 2, 373-391.

CHAPTER 24

OUTWARD DIRECT INVESTMENT AND PRODUCTIVITY

RONNIE O'TOOLE[1]

ABSTRACT

The pace and scale of direct investment flows from Ireland is likely to emerge as one of the most important features of Irish economic development over the next decade. The evidence presented in this chapter shows that much of the outward investment over the last number of years has been motivated by market access, as well as the need to access lower cost inputs. The econometric evidence shows that outward direct investment has generally had a positive effect on productivity, though the evidence is mixed regarding which firms/activities benefit most.

1 The views expressed are solely those of the author and do not necessarily reflect the views of Forfás

24.1 Introduction

The pace and scale of direct investment flows is reshaping the international division of labour and the structures of developing and developed economies alike. To date, Ireland has benefited significantly from flows of foreign capital into our economy. As a result, Ireland is one of the most open economies in the world in terms of our trade and investment performance. This chapter gives an overview of evidence of the likely productivity impact of Outward Direct Investment (ODI) by Irish firms.

Section 24.2 of this chapter reviews some of the salient global trends in terms of investment flows. The productivity impact of ODI can be gleaned from two principal sources. Survey data can help to develop an understanding of the type of firm that is investing abroad, their motivation for so-doing, and the impact that this investment is having on their domestic operations. Survey and other data relating to Irish firms reviewing these questions are covered in Section 24.3. Furthermore, there is a growing body of research at the firm level estimating the impact that foreign investment has on the 'home' plant. This evidence is reviewed in Section 24.4, while Section 24.5 concludes.

24.2 Global Trends in Investment Flows

The role of multinational companies in the world economy has expanded rapidly over the last decade. According to the World Investment Report 2006 by the UN Conference on Trade and Development, the sum of world ODI stocks, calculated as a percentage of the world's GDP, rose from ten per cent in 1980 to 23 per cent in 2005. The importance of ODI as a phenomenon can also be seen when compared with trade flows. While trade flows have increased strongly in the period 1970 – 2004, they have been surpassed by the increase in ODI flows which, as expressed as a percentage of goods trade, rose from 18 per cent in 1970-1974 to 57 per cent in the period 2000-2004.

More recently, while there was a slowdown in global ODI flows following the economic downturn after the turn of the millennium, data from the UNCTAD 2006 World Investment Report indicates that ODI from OECD countries continued recovering strongly in 2005 on the back of an improved economic climate. Global FDI flows increased by 29 per cent to €916 billion in 2005, which was on the back of an increase of 27 per cent in 2004.

24.2.1 Forms of ODI Investment

As in the late 1990s, the growth in ODI witnessed from 2004 to 2005 was driven by increases in cross border Mergers and Acquisitions (M&As). This form of ODI differs from Greenfield investment in that M&A ODI does not add directly to the productive capacity (or employment) of the host country, ceteris paribus. It merely results in a change in ownership. Greenfield investment does, however, involve an immediate augmentation of the capital stock of the host country.

There are a number of similarities and differences in these two forms of ODI. Cross-border M&As and Greenfield investments both attract subsequent investment flows. Evidence from developing countries suggests that new (sequential) investments can be sizeable. Further, ODI usually involves a lot more than just the transfer of capital. For example, a host country is likely to benefit from flows of technology, organisational and managerial practices through ODI. These are more associated with Greenfield investment, though M&As often involve substantial efforts to improve efficiency. In many situations, M&As may be the most appropriate form of investment. Cases where M&As may be more suitable than Greenfield investment include privatisations, where there are high barriers to entry, where the target firm has valuable firm specific assets or where the industry already suffers from excess capacity.

Figure 24.1: Changes in World Trade and ODI Flows, 1970 - 2004

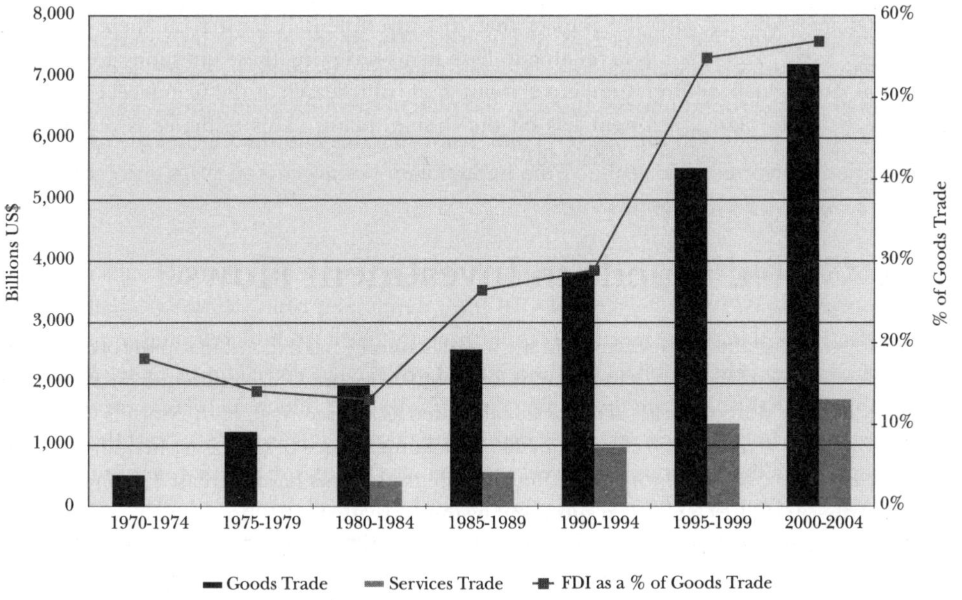

Source: Authors calculation, based on UNCTAD data.

24.2.2 Regional Patterns in ODI

The regional pattern of ODI has undergone some major shifts over the last few decades (UNCTAD, 2006):

1. There has been a significant change in the structure of ODI within the triad of developed regions (i.e. EU, US and Japan) In particular, there has been a significant increase in the importance of the EU at the expense of the US. In 1980, there was slightly more ODI from the US (37.7 per cent of global ODI) than from all EU member states combined (37.2 per cent of global ODI). By 2005 this had changed significantly. EU members states now account for over half of all outflows, compared to less than one-fifth for the US. While the level of ODI from Japan rose sharply over the course of the 1980s, the subsequent prolonged Japanese recession has reduced this stock, which by 2005 was little higher than the level witnessed in 1980.

The UK, Germany, France and the Netherlands make up a large share of EU ODI activity and account for almost 70 per cent of EU outward stocks. Mutual investment between principal member countries plays an important role in continental European investment. While the EU's principal trade relationship is with the US, internal EU investment significantly exceeded both EU investment to the US and US investment to the EU. It is a notable feature of EU FDI that the mutual investment between the principal continental European countries has increased (Sasaki, 2004). However for the UK, like Ireland, the US is relatively more important.

2. While developed countries dominate both direct investment inflows and outflows, the importance of developing countries is growing, driven in particular by China. From 2003 to 2005, an average of 35 per cent of all FDI was invested in developing countries, with China accounting for almost half of this total. The share of total inflows destined for African countries fell gradually from one-tenth of total developing country inflows in the early 1980s, to around one-twentieth by the turn of the millennium, but it has recovered some of this ground in the last few years. Latin America and the Caribbean region have experienced a noticeable decline from its dominant position of the 1970s and early 1980s, and have yet to recover to this level.

3. There is growing evidence of increased activity by developing countries as a source of investment flows. While the flow of ODI from developing countries was negligible up to the late 1980s, it has since increased significantly. By 2005 ODI by developing countries had reached 15 per cent of global ODI flows, half of which is accounted for by China. While the cumulative ODI stock from developing countries was $72 billion in 1980, it breached the trillion mark in 2005. This growth in developing country ODI reflects in part the growing importance of these economies in world commerce. Developing countries account for over half of global output at purchasing power parity in 2005, 40 per cent of world exports and two-thirds of global foreign exchange reserves. In 1986 there was only one developing country in the World Economic Forum's ranking of the top twenty most competitive economies (Turkey), while this had increased to five by 2005 (Taiwan, Singapore, South Korea, UAE and Qatar).

4. Ex-communist European countries have experienced significant growth in both inward and outward FDI, though their share in inward and outward stocks remain small. The figure for this grouping of countries is dominated by activities related to the Russian Federation.

24.2.3 Sectoral Composition of ODI

Services are also becoming increasingly important in terms of global ODI flows. As can be seen from Figure 24.2, services now account for 67 per cent of the stock of ODI globally. This is for two primary reasons. Improvements in ICT and cheaper communications are making the outsourcing of many services activities possible. These technological developments, combined with improving educational standards and the adoption of English in developing countries, are facilitating firms to outsource many activities that can be reproduced/conducted in digital form. These include IT support, back office functions (payroll administration and accounting), call-centres, software programming and some R&D functions (UNCTAD, 2004a).

Figure 24.2: Sectoral Distribution of World ODI Stock, 1990 and 2002

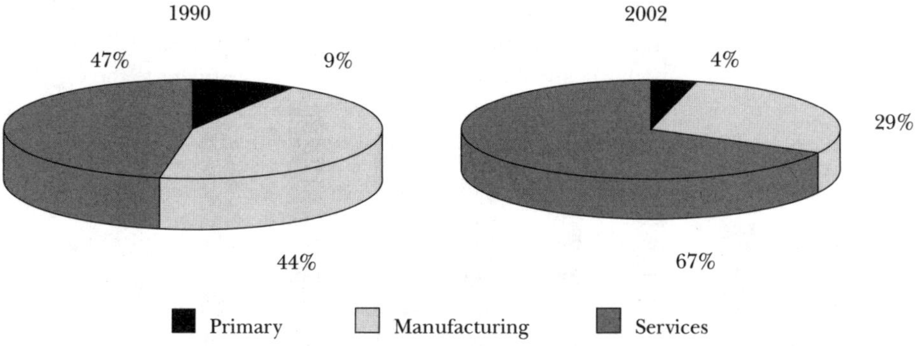

Source: UNCTAD World Investment Report (2004).

Secondly, ODI in services industries is often motivated by firms wishing to gain market access in new markets, rather than offshoring the production of services for existing markets. A growing number of the world's largest MNCs are in services industries, while even among manufacturing MNCs, services activities are accounting for a rising portion of value added. In addition, the privatisation of many services industries (telecommunications, energy, banking, etc.) in recent years has boosted services ODI flows further. Ireland is an important location for ODI from other countries in sectors such as computer software, international financial services and other business process activities such as call centres and shared services (Barry and Van Welsum, 2005).

24.2.4 R&D and ODI

There has been a global increase in ODI related to Research and Development (R&D) activities. While traditionally it was assumed that core economic activities such as R&D would remain tied to a MNCs home country, R&D activities are increasingly highly mobile. Figure 24.3 shows that R&D expenditure by foreign affiliates, measured in both nominal dollar amounts and as a percentage of the host economy's total business R&D, has been growing steadily since 1993.

MNCs are both outsourcing to and investing in overseas R&D units for a number of reasons. Key advantages include the ability to utilise the labour skills of other countries, to achieve costs savings and to tailor products and services for the local market. Local presence can be important in understanding local preferences, trends and regulations. The US is the source for much of this outward R&D investment, accounting for over 42 per cent of the 700 largest R&D spending firms (UNCTAD, 2005). Japan is the second most important home economy (22 per cent), while Germany is the most important EU country with less than eight per cent.

Figure 24.3: R&D Investment by Foreign Affiliates

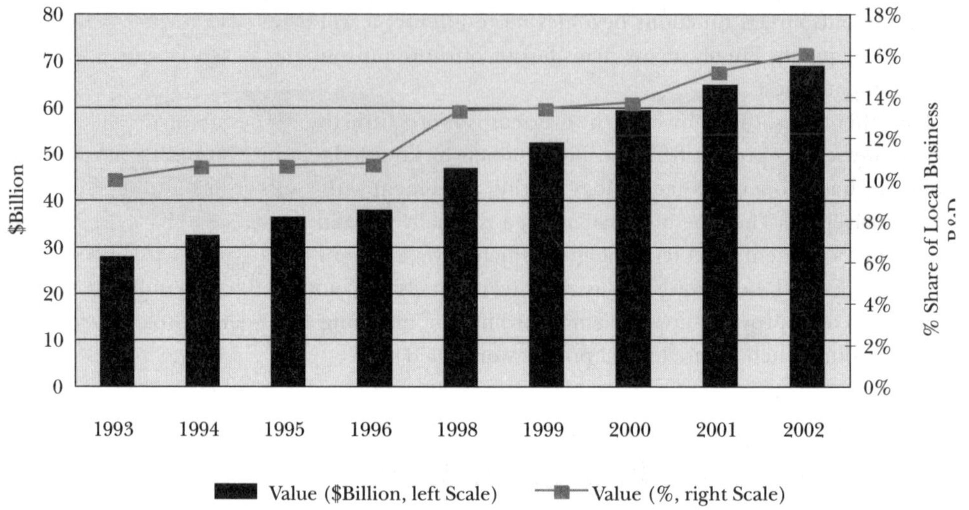

Source: UNCTAD (2005).

The importance of developing countries as investment centres for global R&D is also increasing. Developing Asian countries have tripled their share of overseas investment in R&D by MNCs from the US from 3.4 per cent to ten per cent from 1994 to 2002. China has become the second largest R&D performer behind the US, largely due to the rapid growth in researcher salaries that have encouraged talented Chinese scientists and engineers to remain in China (OECD, 2006). For example, China and Taiwan are developing world class expertise in wireless chips and wireless software (McKinsey, 2004).

24.2.5 Trade and ODI

More firms outsource activities to firms in other countries rather than provide the same good/service internally through direct investment in facilities overseas. A measure of the importance of each can be gauged by assessing the extent of inter-company trade in unfinished products that takes place across borders (a measure of offshore outsourcing) vis-à-vis intra-company trade in unfinished products that takes place across borders (captive offshoring). According to research by the International Labour Organization (ILO), around two thirds of US international trade in unfinished products takes place between different firms, while around one third takes place between cross border subsidiaries of the same MNC (Milberg, 2004).

The decision as whether to engage in offshore outsourcing or whether to favour captive offshoring by investing overseas depends on a wide range of factors, and differs greatly from industry to industry. Some company's favour offshore outsourcing, as the ownership and management of an overseas facility entails significant costs, both in terms of higher set-up costs and ongoing management costs. Further, offshore outsourcing offers greater flexibility, in particular by allowing a firm to change sub-suppliers in response to a change in market conditions, product design, wage levels, exchange rates or government policy. For many firms, competition amongst sub-contractors is also of critical importance. In fact, some economists argue that the higher levels of sub-contracting will result in a snow-ball effect, as competition for these outsourced functions becomes more intense, it will drive costs further down while improving quality. Finally, many firms favour offshore outsourcing so as to retain a focus on core competencies.

For other firms, direct investment overseas is more attractive. Generally, firms will typically invest overseas to protect firm specific products or knowledge, which would be at risk if the company was to operate a technology sharing agreement with a sub-supplier, while remaining based in Ireland. The type of firms involved is usually R&D intensive firms that have built up a portfolio of patents and technologies, which have sufficient market power to both develop and profit from these 'knowledge assets'. Firms can also be motivated to invest directly abroad as a means of improving supply chain co-ordination, imposing a company ethos or accessing a scarce resource such as intellectual property or skilled staff.

24.3 Irish Firms Engaged in ODI

Irish firms are investing more abroad than ever before. Data from CSO (2006) shows that Ireland was a net investor abroad in 2004 for the first time. Once seen as a relatively low cost manufacturing base, Ireland has become a higher cost economy. This places a greater emphasis on value added activities such as high-skill manufacturing and internationally traded services as the key to Irish economic growth. Ireland's experience is consistent with the investment development path theory, which predicts that ODI from successful economies will increase as their firms increasingly seek overseas markets (Barry, Gorg and McDowell, 2003). This section assesses the profile of Irish firms investing abroad, their motivation for doing so and the impact that this investment is having on their Irish operations.[1]

24.3.1 Profile of Firms Investing Abroad

LOCO monitor has tracked 212 Irish firms that have invested in Greenfield facilities overseas since 2002. Table 24.1 below subdivides the firms that engaged in ODI by broad economic sector. As can be seen, the practice of engaging in ODI seems to be very broadly based across a number of industries. Of the services firms engaged in ODI, over half were providers of business and financial services, while over one third were classed as property, tourism and leisure activities. This table only gives information about the number of projects established by Irish firms, and does not give information about the size of these deals.

Table 24.1: Firms Investing Abroad by Sector, 2002 - 2006

	2002		2003		2004		2005		2006 (Jan-Feb)		2002-2006	
Sector	**No**	**%**	**No**	**%**	**No**	**%**	**No**	**%**	**No**	**%**	**No**	**%**
Business & Financial Services	9	17.6	8	17.4	8	17.4	17	28.8	2	20.0	44	20.8
Chemicals, Plastics & Rubber	-	-	1	2.2	3	6.5	8	13.6	-	-	12	5.7
Consumer Products	-	-	1	2.2	-	-	1	1.7	-	-	2	0.9
Electronics	-	-	1	2.2	1	2.2	-	-	-	-	2	0.9
Food/Bev/Tobacco	6	11.8	4	8.7	1	2.2	3	5.1	-	-	14	6.6
Heavy Industry	6	11.8	13	28.3	7	15.2	10	16.9	2	20.0	38	17.9
ICT	11	21.6	5	10.9	4	8.7	5	8.5	2	20.0	27	12.7
Life Sciences	2	3.9	1	2.2	2	4.3	3	5.1	1	10.0	9	4.2
Light Industry	-	-	6	13.0	5	10.9	1	1.7	1	10.0	13	6.1
Logistics & Distribution	-	-	-	-	2	4.3	-	-	-	-	2	0.9
Property, Tourism & Leisure	12	23.5	4	8.7	6	13.0	8	13.6	1	10.0	31	14.6
Transport Equipment	5	9.8	2	4.3	7	15.2	3	5.1	1	10.0	18	8.5
Total	**51**	**100**	**46**	**100**	**46**	**100**	**59**	**100**	**10**	**100**	**212**	**100**

Source: LOCOmonitor (2006).

24.3.2 Destination of Irish ODI

What is striking about the Irish ODI experience is that the most important destinations are geographically close to Ireland. Of the 212 Irish firms tracked by LOCOmonitor, Western Europe (58 per cent), Eastern Europe (15 per cent) and North America (11 per cent) form the three most important locations respectively. Within Western Europe, ODI to the United Kingdom is by far the most important destination, accounting for two-thirds of Irish ODI to Europe.

Conversely, the number of ODI projects destined for developing countries is relatively small, but growing. In particular, the number of ODI projects undertaken by Irish firms in developing Eastern European economies has been rising. In the earlier 2002-2003 period, developing European economies only attracted seven per cent of Irish ODI projects, though this subsequently tripled to 21 per cent from 2004 to 2006. This indicates the increased attractiveness of this region to Irish firms due both to continued economic reforms in many Eastern European countries, alongside the accession to the EU of many of them in 2005. It is also notable that Asia, including both developed countries such as Japan and developing countries such as China, attracted less than ten per cent of Irish ODI projects in the period 2002-2006.

Table 24.2: Regional Location of Irish ODI, 2002 - 2006

	2002		2003		2004		2005		2006 (Jan-Feb)		2002-2006	
Region	**No**	**%**	**No**	**%**	**No**	**%**	**No**	**%**	**No**	**%**	**No**	**%**
Africa	1	2.0	2	4.3	2	4.3	1	1.7	-	-	6	3
Developed Asia Pacific	2	3.9	-	-	2	4.3	2	3.4	-	-	6	3
Western Europe	34	66.7	25	54.3	21	45.7	36	61.0	7	70.0	123	58
Developing Asia Pacific	2	3.9	5	10.9	2	4.3	4	6.8	-	-	13	6
Eastern Europe	4	7.8	3	6.5	13	28.3	10	16.9	1	10.0	31	15
Latin America & Caribbean	1	2.0	2	4.3	2	4.3	2	3.4	-	-	7	3
Middle East	-	-	2	4.3	1	2.2	-	-	-	-	3	1
North America	7	13.7	7	15.2	3	6.5	4	6.8	2	20.0	23	11
Total	**51**	**100**	**46**	**100**	**46**	**100**	**59**	**100**	**10**	**100**	**212**	**100**

Source: LOCOmonitor (2006).

24.3.3 Employment in Ireland and Overseas

Turning to employment levels, PACEC (2004) found that the average Irish firm with investments abroad employed 97 workers in their Irish operations, with employment in subsidiaries outside of Ireland averaging 147. Virtually all sectors employed more workers in their overseas subsidiaries than they did in Ireland.

Supporting the LOCOmonitor data, PACEC data also indicates that the UK is the primary destination of ODI from Ireland in terms of the number of people employed by Irish firms that have invested overseas. The data also suggests that Irish investors have their largest overseas investments in the UK, presumably because they have had more time to grow their operations. While employment in Irish owned affiliates in the UK shows large size distribution ranges, investments in other countries tend to be relatively small in terms of employment.

Figure 24.4: Average Number of Direct Employees in Irish Affiliates Abroad by Country/ Region, 2004

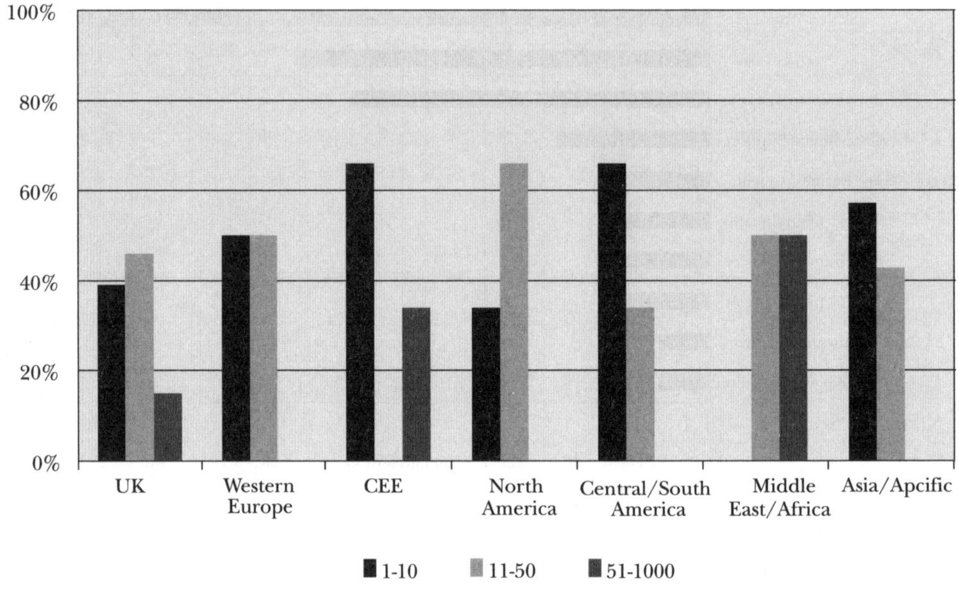

Source: PACEC (2004).

24.3.4 Motivations for Irish ODI

The key motivations cited for ODI are typically easier access to overseas markets and managing costs. Most of the ODI from Ireland is motivated by gaining access to overseas markets. This can be seen in Figure 24.5, with proximity to market and foreign market growth being two of the four most important reasons given for investing overseas. This is also supported by earlier evidence which highlights that most Irish investment overseas is targeted at developed, high cost markets in Western Europe and North America. It should be noted that market access is not necessarily restricted to the market of the host country, but often for the region as whole. Empirical evidence shows that MNC affiliates located inside free-trade areas display significant levels of sales to other free-trade member countries as well as to the host market (Ekholm, Forslid, and Markusen, 2004).

The ability to mange cost competitiveness is another primary motivation for ODI. This can be seen in the fact that two of the primary motivations for ODI were lower costs and the availability of a skilled workforce. Numerous reports suggest that firms can make savings of between 20 to 50 per cent when they offshore in regions such as Asia (See McKinsey, 2004 and Agrawel, and Farrell, 2003). Labour costs make up a significant proportion of these savings, with large wage differentials between developed and developing countries at almost all skill levels (See Boston Consulting Group, 2005 and McKinsey, 2004). However, cost saving on this scale is rarely achieved in practise. For example, some of these savings are lost when increased management overheads, start-up and communication costs are factored in (Deloitte, 2004). This is particularly true when a facility is directly owned and managed from great distance, such as an Irish firm managing a Chinese production facility.

Figure 24.5: Motivation for Irish Enterprises Investing Abroad, 2002-2006

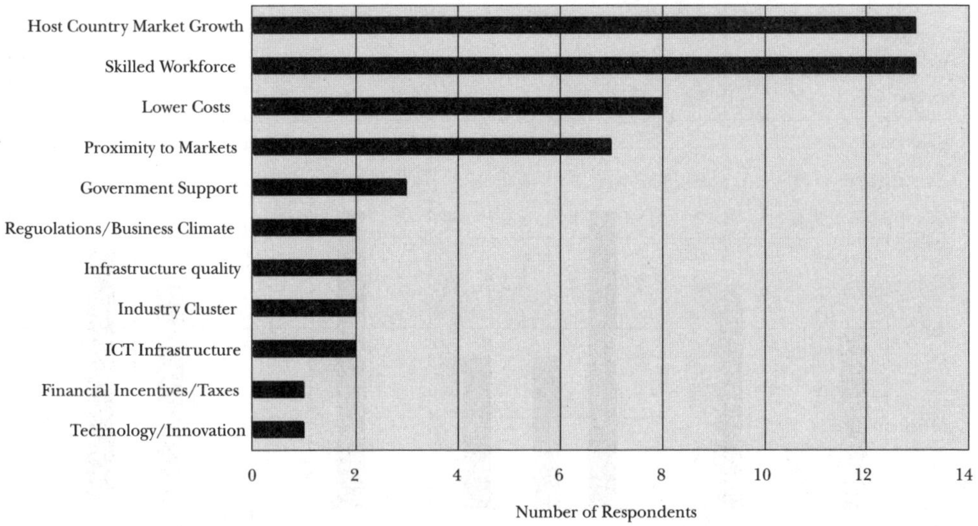

Source LOCOmonitor (2006).

24.3.5 Activities Undertaken by Foreign Affiliates of Irish Firms

Table 24.3 shows that the establishment of manufacturing facilities overseas accounted for more than a quarter of all investments in the period 2002-2006. This is followed in importance by business services (21.2 per cent) and construction (12.3 per cent). Other services functions such as sales and marketing (eight per cent), logistics (7.5 percent) and R&D (2.8 percent) account for a relatively small proportion of activities overseas.

Table 24.3: Activities Undertaken by Foreign Affiliates of Irish Firms

	2002		2003		2004		2005		2006 (Jan-Feb)		2002-2006	
Sector	**No**	**%**	**No**	**%**	**No**	**%**	**No**	**%**	**No**	**%**	**No**	**%**
Business Services	13	25.5	7	15.2	8	17.4	15	25.4	2	20.0	45	21.2
Construction	10	19.6	3	6.5	5	10.9	7	11.9	1	10.0	26	12.3
Customer Support Centre	2	3.9	1	2.2	-	-	-	-	-	-	3	1.4
Electricity	1	2.0	2	4.3	2	4.3	1	1.7	2	20.0	8	3.8
Extraction	2	3.9	7	15.2	3	6.5	4	6.8	-	-	16	7.5
HQ	2	3.9	-	-	2	4.3	3	5.1	2	20.0	9	4.2
Internet/ICT Infrastructure	1	2.0	-	-	-	-	-	-	-	-	1	0.5
Logistics	3	5.9	2	4.3	8	17.4	2	3.4	1	10.0	16	7.5
Maintenance/Service	1	2.0	1	2.2	-	-	-	-	-	-	2	0.9
Manufacturing	9	17.6	17	37.0	12	26.1	16	27.1	-	-	54	25.5
R&D	1	2.0	-	-	2	4.3	3	5.1	-	-	6	2.8
Retail	3	5.9	2	4.3	-	-	1	1.7	-	-	6	2.8
Sales & Marketing	2	3.9	4	8.7	3	6.5	6	10.2	2	20.0	17	8.0
Shared Service Centre	-	-	-	-	1	2.2	1	1.7	-	-	2	0.9
Testing /Training	1	2.0	-	-	-	-	-	-	-	-	1	0.5
Total	**51**	**100**	**46**	**100**	**46**	**100**	**59**	**100**	**10**	**100**	**212**	**100**

Source: LOCOmonitor (2006).

24.3.6 Implications for the Irish Operations

Over 70 per cent of firms who have engaged in ODI believe that it has produced positive effects on their strategic management and marketing and sales capabilities in Ireland. There is a common perception that international management skills have also improved, as have R&D and design capabilities. Forty three per cent remarked that there had been a reciprocal effect of technology upgrading by technology transfer from affiliates abroad.

Table 24.4: Implications for the Irish Operations

Business Process	%
Enhanced Strategic Management	71
Enhanced Marketing & Sales	71
Enhanced International Management Skills	57
Enhanced R&D	57
Enhanced Design	57
Increased Specialisation of Irish Activities	43
Enhancement of Business Processes	29
Enhanced Ability to Raise Processes	14

Source: PACEC (2004).

24.4 Econometric Estimates of Effect of ODI on Productivity

As Ireland is now characterised by full employment, rises in future economic welfare will depend primarily on increases in productivity. ODI can enhance the productivity of the Irish economy, by allowing Irish firms to focus on areas where they have a comparative advantage, by creating new market opportunities for a firm's existing products and by promoting the creation of new dynamic firms, and the destruction of old inefficient ones.

Given the ways by which ODI can affect productivity, this section reviews the available evidence at both the economy level and the industry/plant level. The section then concludes with a discussion on the evidence regarding changes in total output as opposed to productivity.

24.4.1 Economy Level Productivity Effects

The small numbers of studies that examine the productivity effects of offshoring production at an aggregate economy wide level suggest that it has a positive impact in the long run, particularly for small countries like Ireland. A study on the effect of offshoring production on the European Union found a positive long run impact, while a study which focused solely on the offshoring of the production of materials inputs in the US also found a small but positive productivity effect.[2]

Research on the Austrian economy, a smaller economy, showed that offshoring production had a much larger productivity impact (Egger et al., 2001a). A possible explanation for this difference is that large economic regions such as the EU or the US tend to be less open in terms of trade flows, and as such any benefit from ODI might be more difficult to detect statistically. For example, some of the offshoring from Austria was to other EU countries, such as Germany. In the study of the EU as a whole, this is not classed as ODI, as it takes place entirely within the EU.

24.4.2 Firm Level Effects

The results of the firm level research is consistent with the economy level evidence discussed above, namely that offshoring production is associated with higher productivity. Research conducted at the firm level, however, allows researchers to probe this result further, and identify the specific conditions under which ODI is most likely to be conducive to higher productivity. In particular, the research has examined three characteristics which are thought to affect the productivity impact of ODI:

- Whether the firm is offshoring production to overseas operations that produce material inputs (such as hard drives) or services inputs (such as software).
- Whether the Irish based plant is domestically or foreign owned.
- Whether the Irish based plant trades locally or is export focused.

Research results to date by different researchers on different data sets have often come up with mixed conclusions as to when offshoring production is most likely to result in higher productivity.

In recent years, firms seem to have made the most gains from offshoring the production of services rather than material inputs. For example, the offshoring of services production by the Irish electronics manufacturing industry was found to have a positive impact on productivity, though no benefit was detected from goods offshoring (Görg and Hanley, 2003). One possible explanation for this finding is that as material outsourcing has a much longer history than services outsourcing, the productivity gains have already have been achieved. The data coverage in these studies might not stretch back far enough to capture the phenomenon's original productivity enhancing effects. Other studies from the UK and US show more mixed results.[3]

Offshoring by Irish firms can potentially be just as important in terms of enhancing productivity as offshoring by foreign MNCs based in Ireland. The productivity effects of goods offshoring are of a similar positive magnitude regardless of whether the plant is foreign or domestically owned (Görg et al., 2004). Evidence based on research in the UK is more mixed. A study of UK manufacturing found that foreign ownership re-enforces the positive effects of outsourcing on productivity (Girma and Görg, 2004). Conversely, a second study found that a positive productivity effect is only significant for domestically owned firms (Criscuolo and Leaver, 2005).

24.4.3 Level of Output

While offshoring some element of production is associated with higher productivity, it does not necessarily follow that it is associated with higher aggregate output. The cumulative transfer of elements of manufacturing to overseas locations over the last number of decades is often identified as the principle cause of deindustrialisation, the term used for the observed decline in the importance of manufacturing in rich, developed countries.[4]

However, a recent study showed that net trade with low wage countries is associated with only one-fifth of the deindustrialisation observed in a range of OECD countries between 1970 and 2002 (Boulhol and Fontagne, 2005). As such, while internationalisation had a noticeable effect on the reduction in the share of manufacturing, much of the observed deindustrialisation happened because of relatively high productivity growth in manufacturing.

Even if offshoring of production is contributing to the decline in the importance of manufacturing, they seem to support a higher level of economic output in aggregate. Survey evidence suggests that ODI by Irish firms – including both manufacturing and services firms - has generally had a positive impact on exports (PACEC, 2004). Of the firms interviewed, 57 per cent reported that the ODI had resulted in an increase in exports from their operations in Ireland, while only 14 per cent reported that the ODI had resulted in a decrease in exports from Ireland.

24.5 Conclusion

The pace and scale of direct investment flows from Ireland is likely to be one of the most important features of Irish economic development over the next decade. The evidence presented in this chapter shows that much of the outward investment over the last number of years has been motivated by market access, rather than by accessing lower cost inputs. This can be interpreted as *prima facie* evidence that the impact on the Irish operations of much ODI has been positive, in that it entails moving to higher value added functions such as management. Firms also report that this in fact has been the case, with over 70 percent of firms who have engaged in ODI reporting a positive effect on their strategic management and marketing and sales capabilities in Ireland. Finally, the econometric evidence shows that offshoring (whether involving ODI or not) has a generally positive effect on productivity, though the evidence is mixed regarding which firms/activities benefit most.

Notes

1 The section is based on two primary data sources on Irish firms. The first is a study by PACEC consulting commissioned by Forfás. This is a quantitative and qualitative survey into ODI from Ireland which was undertaken on behalf of Forfás in 2004 with 20 Irish-owned firms active in international trade. Specifically, those interviewed were in senior positions – directors, managing directors and financial director/managers. The second source is LOCOmonitor, a global database that tracks Greenfield ODI projects internationally. Of the 35,800 ODI projects worldwide tracked by LOCOmonitor since 2002, 212 originated from Ireland.

2 The EU study was conducted by Egger and Egger (2001b), and the US study by Amiti and Wei (2004).

3 The US study was conducted by Amity and Wei (2004b), and the UK study of services establishments was conducted by Criscuolo and Leaver (2005).

4 The transfer of elements of manufacturing from developed to developing countries involves more than offshoring. Offshore outsourcing or offshoring through ODI includes the transfer elements of manufacturing out of developed countries such as Ireland while retaining some production in Ireland. However, a company can transfer its entire manufacturing operations abroad, or can go into liquidation. Deindustrialisation because of net trade with developing countries captures both of these ways that manufacturing can leave Ireland.

References

Agrawal, V. and Farrell, D. (2003), "Who Wins in Offshoring", *The McKinsey Quarterly*, Special Edition: Global Directions.

Amiti, M. and Wei, S. (2004), "Services Outsourcing, Production and Employment: Evidence from the US", *IMF Working Paper.*

Barry. F. and Van Welsum, D. (2005), "Services FDI and Offshoring into Ireland". Paper prepared for the *OECD Directorate for Science, Technology and Industry Panel Session on Offshoring*, June 9-10, 2005.

Barry, F., Gorg, H. and McDowell, A. (2003), "Outward FDI and the Investment Development Path of a Late-industrializing Economy: Evidence from Ireland", *Regional Studies,* Vol. 37, No. 4.

Boston Consulting Group (2005), "Navigating the Five Currents of Globalisation: How Leading Companies Are Capturing Global Advantage".

Boulhol, H. and Fontagne, L. (2005), "Deindustrialisation and the Fear of Relocations in Industry", Paper Prepared for *OECD Work Shop on Globalisation,* Paris, November 2005.

Criscuolo, C. and Leaver, M. (2005), "Offshore Outsourcing and Productivity", OECD and Office of National Statistics.

CSO (2006), "Balance of Payments", Quarter 4 and Year 2005, CSO, Dublin.

Deloitte (2004), "Deloitte Management Briefing: Offshoring – Lets have a look before you Leap".

Egger, H. and Egger, P. (2001a), "Cross-Border Sourcing and Outward Processing in EU Manufacturing", *The North American Journal of Economics and Finance.*

Egger, H. and Egger, P. (2001b), "International Outsourcing and the Productivity of Low-skilled Labour in the EU", *Economic Inquiry,* Vol. 44, Issue 1, 2006.

Ekholm, K., Forslid, R. and Markusen, J. (2004), "Export-Platform Foreign Direct Investment", *IIIS Discussion Papers,* Number 50.

Girma, S. and Görg, H. (2004), "Outsourcing, Foreign Ownership, and Productivity: Evidence from UK Establishment-level Data", *Review of International Economics,* Vol. 12, Issue 15.

Görg, H. and Hanley, A. (2003), "International Outsourcing and Productivity: Evidence from Plant Level Data", Research Paper 2003/20, University of Nottingham.

Görg, H., Hanley, A. and Strobl, E. (2004), "Outsourcing, Foreign Ownership, Exporting and Productivity: An Empirical Investigation with Plant Level Data", Research Paper 08, University of Nottingham.

LOCOmonitor (2006), "Trends in Irish Outward Direct Investment", unpublished report for Forfás.

McKinsey (2004), McKinsey Quarterly, 2004, Quarter 2.

Milberg, W. (2004), "The Changing Structure of International Trade Linked to Global Production Systems: What are the Policy Implications?", *International Labour Organization, Working Paper,* Number 33.

OCO Consulting (2004), "Eastwards: The Relocation of Manufacturing and Services";

OECD (2005a), "Helping Workers to Navigate in Globalised Labour Markets", Policy Brief.

OECD (2005b), "Offshoring and Job Losses in French Industry", Paper Prepared for *Special Session on Globalisation and Workshop on the Globalisation of Production,* November 2005, OECD Paris.

OECD (2006), *Science Technology and Industry Outlook 2006,* OECD, Paris.

PACEC (2004), "Outward Direct Investment from Ireland: Update Report", Unpublished report, Forfás.

Sasaki, N. (2004), "The Recent Trend in EU Foreign Direct Investment and Intra-EU Investment", Fukuoka University, Japan.

UNCTAD (2004a), "Service Offshoring Takes Off in Europe – In Search of Improved Competitiveness". Available online: www.unctad.org/sections/press/docs/SurveyOffshoring_en.pdf, accessed on 12 December 2006.

UNCTAD (2004b), *World Investment Report 2004: The Shift Towards Services,* New York and Geneva: United Nations.

UNCTAD (2005), *World Investment Report 2005: Transnational Corporations and the Internationalization of R&D,* New York and Geneva: United Nations.

UNCTAD (2006), *World Investment Report 2006: FDI from Developing and Transition Economies: Implications for Development,* New York and Geneva: United Nations.

CHAPTER 25

THE DISTRIBUTION OF PRODUCTIVITY IN IRISH MANUFACTURING, 1995-2003

STEFANIE HALLER

ABSTRACT

At the root of productivity dynamics at the aggregate level are huge differences in productivity between plants in even narrowly defined sectors. This chapter provides a synthesis of the results of a study using relative distribution methods and transition matrices to describe the changes in labour productivity in Irish manufacturing industries from 1995 to 2003. While labour productivity may be a poor measure to compare performance across plants, at the industry level comparisons over time should still produce reasonably reliable results.

25.1 Introduction

At the root of productivity dynamics at the aggregate level are huge differences in productivity between plants in even narrowly defined sectors. The increasing availability of plant-level data sets has directed attention to this productivity 'spread', i.e., the difference between the best and the worst performing firms in an industry as well as to its causes and implications (e.g. Bartelsman and Doms (2000), Ahn (2001), Haskel and Martin (2002), Martin (2004)).

There are different perceptions as to whether one should be concerned about the productivity spread (Martin, 2004). First, the productivity spread is an expression of the co-existence of more and less successful firms in the competitive selection process in a market economy. Second, the presence of 'a long tail of underperforming firms' could indicate that the selection process is hampered and, therefore, resources are bound in an unproductive way in firms that do not exit. And third, any observed differences in productivity might be attributed to measurement problems. The last point applies in particular to labour productivity as a measure of productivity. That is, a plant that substitutes few higher skilled employees for more lower skilled employees will have higher measured labour productivity, but their contributions to welfare need not be any different.

For Ireland two studies have looked at productivity: Girma, Görg and Strobl (2004) compare the performance of purely domestic plants, domestic exporters and domestic multinationals using a non-parametric approach based on the principle of first order stochastic dominance. They find that the distributions for multinationals dominate those of domestic exporters and non-exporters. They do not find clear differences in plant performance between domestic exporters and non-exporters. Ruane and Ugur (2004) decompose labour productivity into the components attributable to surviving, entering and exiting domestic and foreign-owned plants. Their analysis shows that foreign-owned plants in Ireland contributed a substantial share to overall productivity growth between 1991 and 1999. Most of the productivity growth is generated within surviving plants. The process of entry and exit is also productivity enhancing except in some of the low-tech industries where substantial restructuring is evident.

This chapter provides a synthesis of the results of a study using relative distribution methods (Handcock and Morris, 1999) and transition matrices to describe the changes in labour productivity in Irish manufacturing industries from 1995 to 2003. While labour productivity may be a poor measure to compare performance across plants, at the industry level comparisons over time should still produce reasonably reliable results. The analysis is based on the data set of local units, which is collected as part of the annual Census of Industrial Production.[1]

25.2 Discussion of Results

As labour productivity is defined as the natural log of turnover per employee, Table 25.1 provides summary statistics of turnover per employee in ten broadly defined manufacturing sectors for 1995 and 2003. In 1993, plants in the food and tobacco, chemical, rubber, mineral and electrical and optical equipment sectors had on average higher levels of turnover per employee than the manufacturing sector as a whole. At the other end, textiles and clothing and leather stand out with a median level of turnover per employee well below average. There are large differences within and between sectors among the best and the worst performing plants. Turnover per employee of an average plant in manufacturing at the 90th percentile of the distribution is 8.2 times higher than that of an average plant at the 10th percentile of the distribution. In food and tobacco this spread is twice as large, and also the chemical, mineral, electrical and optical equipment sectors plants at the 90th percentile have about ten times as much turnover per employee as plants at the 10th percentile.

By 2003 the median of turnover per employee has increased in all sectors. Those industries with a substantially higher median than the all manufacturing average are food and tobacco, chemicals and electrical and optical equipment. At the lower end are textiles, clothing and leather together with other manufacturing. On average productivity spreads have decreased between 1995 and 2003, although in a number of industries they have increased.[2] Obviously in Table 25.1 the presence of highly productive foreign-owned plants alleviates the differences between and within sectors. Both the median of turnover per employee as well as the productivity spreads are lower when only domestic plants are considered, but the ranking of sectors according to these criteria remains roughly the same.

Table 25.1: Turnover (€1,000) per Employee in Constant Prices (2000) Across Industries and Over Time

CSO Nace Code	Industry	Median	1995 p90/p10	Median	2003 p90/p10
15,16	Food & Tobacco	118.6	16.9	128.0	11.9
17-19	Textiles, Clothing & Leather	43.6	4.6	73.4	6.2
20	Wood	57.2	4.5	89.0	5.8
21-22	Paper, Printing & Publishing	60.3	4.9	87.0	3.9
24	Chemical	150.2	10.0	190.6	10.3
25	Rubber	78.2	5.0	98.4	4.1
26	Mineral	74.0	9.6	84.3	6.7
27,28	Basic Metal & Metal Products	58.8	4.2	80.5	4.9
29	Machinery	67.6	4.2	85.6	4.1
30-33	Electrical & Optical Equipment	73.1	9.7	119.0	9.6
34,35	Transport	66.2	4.8	86.8	5.8
36,37	Other Manufacturing	50.8	4.2	73.7	4.1
	All Manufacturing	**65.9**	**8.2**	**90.2**	**6.5**

When looking at the sectoral distributions of labour productivity in more detail another interesting observation emerges. In most sectors in Irish manufacturing the range of values labour productivity takes above the median is larger than below. That is, if anything, we observe a long thin tail of overperforming plants. However, it has to be borne in mind that this is relative to other plants in Ireland only.

The long thin tail of very productive plants is a particularly salient feature of the chemical and the optical and electrical equipment sectors. Both of them have a large share of foreign-owned plants. Yet even when the foreign-owned plants are excluded from the analysis, there is still a high incidence of very productive plants in these sectors albeit to a somewhat smaller extent. This suggests that the presence of foreign-owned firms in these sectors has strengthened the indigenous plants as well. The question to what extent this has been through technology or productivity spillovers or through increased competition has yet to be resolved (for a survey of the evidence on spillovers in Ireland see Görg, 2006).

In the textile, clothing and leather sectors substantial restructuring is visible. This is not surprising, given that the Multi Fibre Agreement that restricted market access for developing country producers of textiles and clothing to developed countries was finally phased out on 1st January 2005. A prominent Irish example that fell victim to this process was the 'Fruit of the Loom' plant in Donegal. By 2003, the ongoing restructuring had left the sector with on average higher labour productivity than in 1995, but also with a large share of poorly performing plants. That is, this is the one industry where one can in fact speak of a long tail of underperforming plants. Given that the implications of the end of the Multi Fibre Agreement did not hit seriously until 2005 when imports from developing countries soared, it is more than likely that continued restructuring, including the exit of inefficient plants has brought about further changes in the distribution of productivity in this sector.

The only sector that has seen hardly any changes at all from 1995 to 2003 is food and tobacco. In this sector, the plants at the lower end of the productivity distribution have increased their labour productivity marginally, whereas the high-productivity plants witnessed a decline in their levels of labour productivity. This may be attributable to the still fairly regulated and supported environment a lot these plants operate in which shields them from the common forces of competition.

Overall the increase in labour productivity over time together with the observed dynamics of plants within the productivity distribution indicates that the competitive selection process ensures a rather efficient reallocation of resources. When examining how plants move within the productivity distribution, it emerges that the increase in productivity over time must be largely due to a positive external environment together with relatively more entry of efficient plants and relatively more exit among the inefficient plants.

Evidence from transition matrices suggests that, after three years 30-50 per cent of plants are still in the same quintile, i.e., in the same position of the productivity distribution. Taking the full nine-year period, almost half of those plants that have not gone out of business by 2003 are still in the same quintile of the productivity distribution as they were in 1995. This holds in particular for plants at the very top of the distribution and even more so for plants at the lower end. This large degree of persistence suggests that a lot of plants manage to improve their productivity by just about enough to keep up with their competitors, but very few plants manage to strengthen their performance enough to move upwards in the productivity distribution. This raises questions about the effectiveness of grants to improve firm performance.

There is an additional caveat to the observed increase in productivity from 1995 to 2003. Comparing the productivity distributions in the two years under the assumption that the median shift had not happened reveals that there would have been a smaller share of plants at the very top of the distribution in 2003 than there was in 1995. This is true when looking at manufacturing as a whole as well as for several of the individual sectors, but not for those sectors that host a large share of foreign-owned plants. This is somewhat discomforting, as it suggests that the plants in industrial production in Ireland in 2003 are not working as hard to achieve a productivity performance in the top range as they did nine years earlier. As the sectors with a large share of foreign-owned plants together with textiles are also the ones where also the indigenous plants are most export-oriented (Lane and Ruane, 2006: 36), one might even take this as an indication that the focus on the Irish market of plants in the remaining sectors has sheltered them from increasing international competition.

Notes

1 The possibility for controlled access to this anonymised micro data set on the premises of the CSO is provided for in the Statistics Act 1993. Assistance with the data by George Hussey, CSO is most gratefully acknowledged. The chapter has been screened by the CSO to ensure that no confidential information is revealed.

2 Haskel and Martin (2002) document a small increase in the UK between 1980 and 2000.

References

Ahn, S. (2001), "Firm Dynamics and Productivity Growth: A Review of Micro Evidence from OECD Countries", *OECD Economics Department Working Paper,* No. 297, June.

Bartelsman, E. and Doms, M. (2000), "Understanding Productivity: Lessons from Longitudinal Microdata", *Journal of Economic Literature,* 38: 569-594.

Girma, S., Görg, H. and Strobl, E. (2004), "Exports, International Investment, and Plant Performance: Evidence from a Non-parametric Test", *Economics Letters,* 83(3): 317-24.

Görg, H. (2006), "Productivity Spillovers from Multinational Companies", Chapter 14 in this volume.

Handcock, M.S. and Morris, M. (1999), *Relative Distribution Methods in the Social Sciences,* New York: Springer.

Haskel, J. and Martin, R. (2002), "The UK Manufacturing Productivity Spread", CeRiBA Discussion Paper, London.

Lane, P.R. and Ruane, F. (2006), "Globalisation and the Irish Economy", IIIS Occasional Paper No. 1, *Institute for International Integration Studies,* Trinity College Dublin.

Martin, R. (2005), "Computing the True Spread", CEP Discussion Paper No. 692, Centre for Economic Performance, London School of Economics.

Ruane, F. and Ugur, A. (2004), "Labour Productivity and Foreign Direct Investment in Irish Manufacturing Industry: A Decomposition Analysis", *IIIS Discussion paper,* No. 27, Trinity College, Dublin

SUBJECT INDEX

E

F

G

H